# Springs, Arkansas

## Surrounding Countryside

## (Volume 1)

Charles Henry Ford II

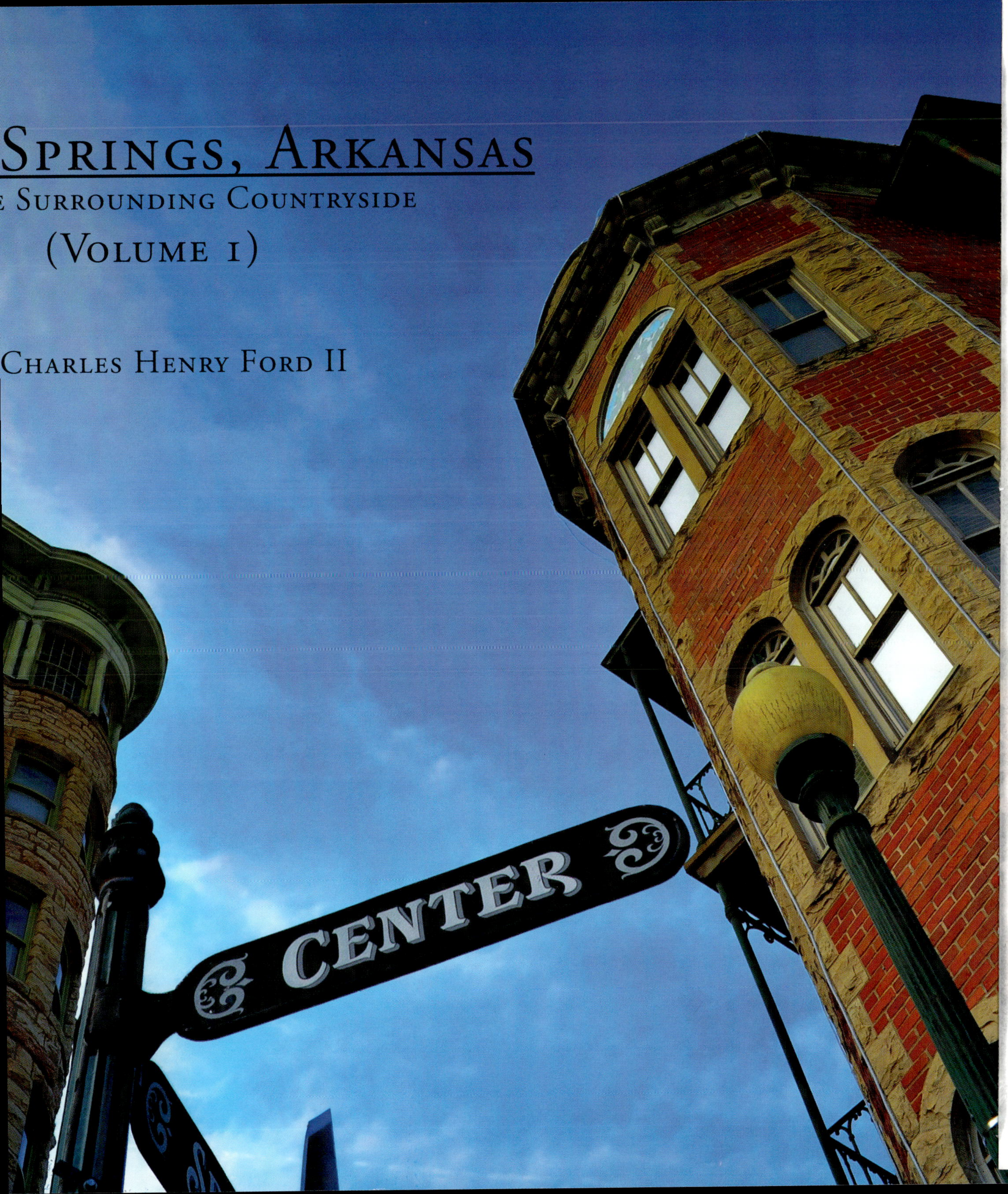

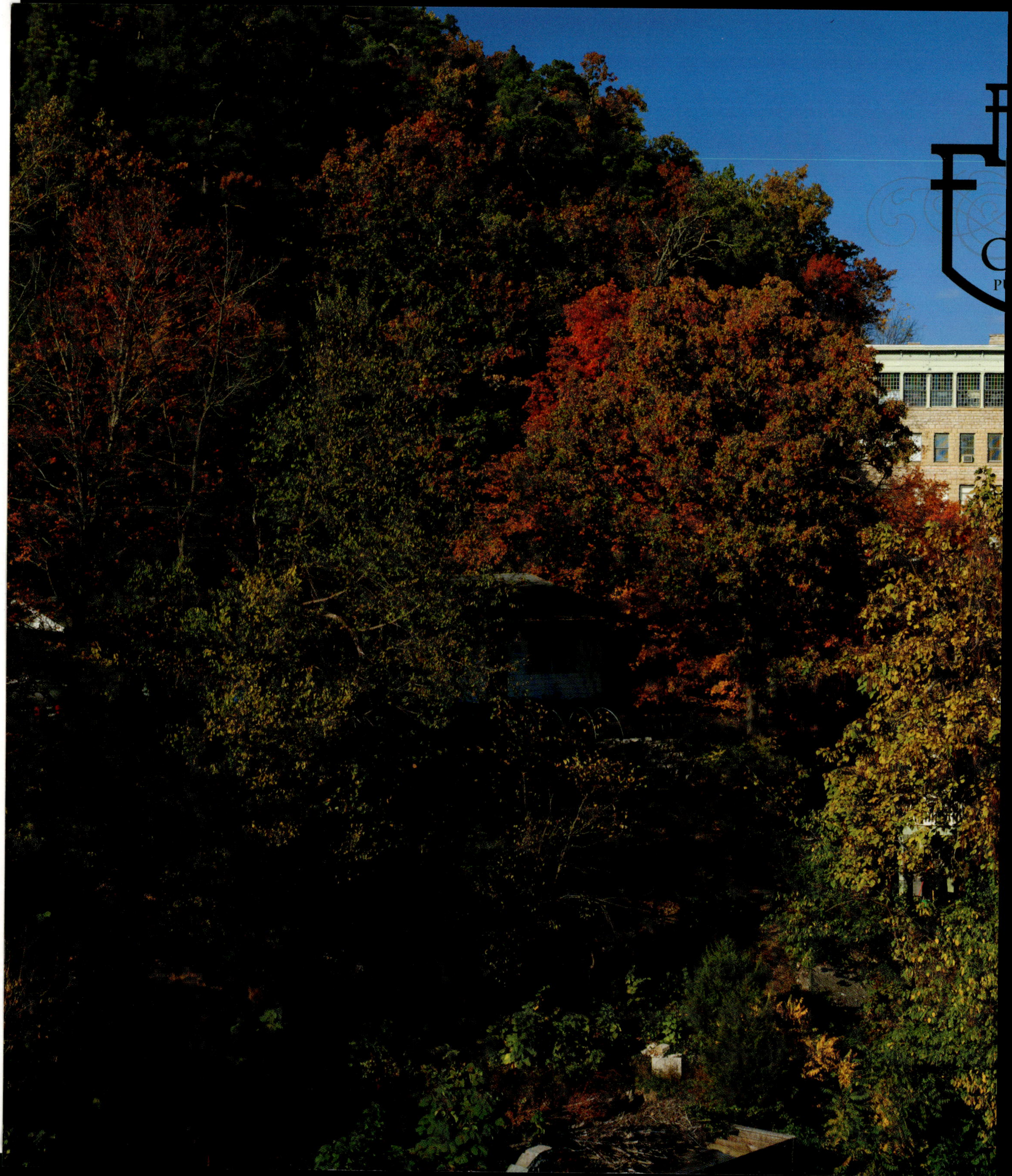

ISBN 978-0-9850127-0-0

1st Edition – 1st Print Run – Spring 2012

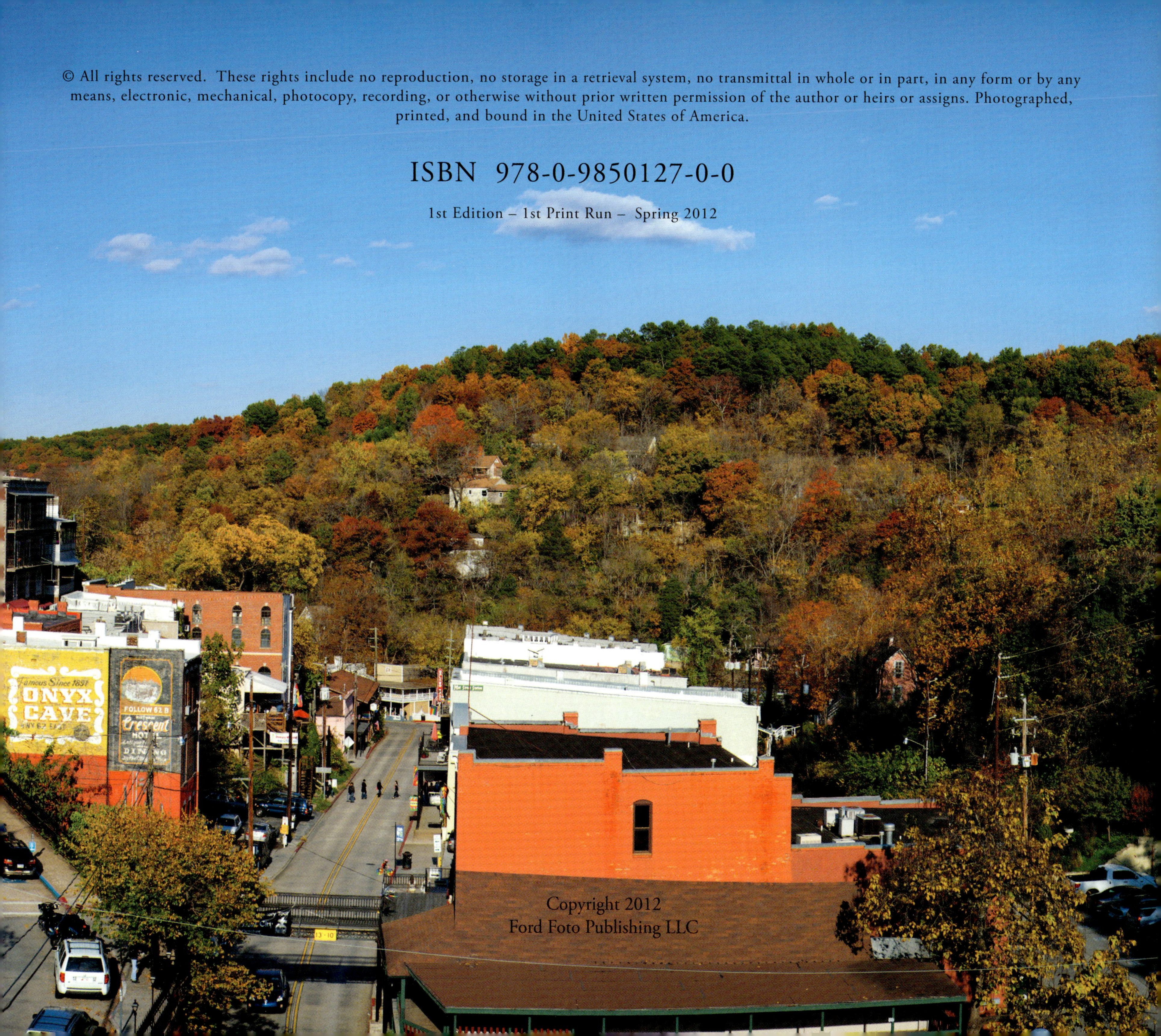

This book is dedicated to the citizens of Carroll County, specifically Vernon Tucker. Without whom, this book would not exist.

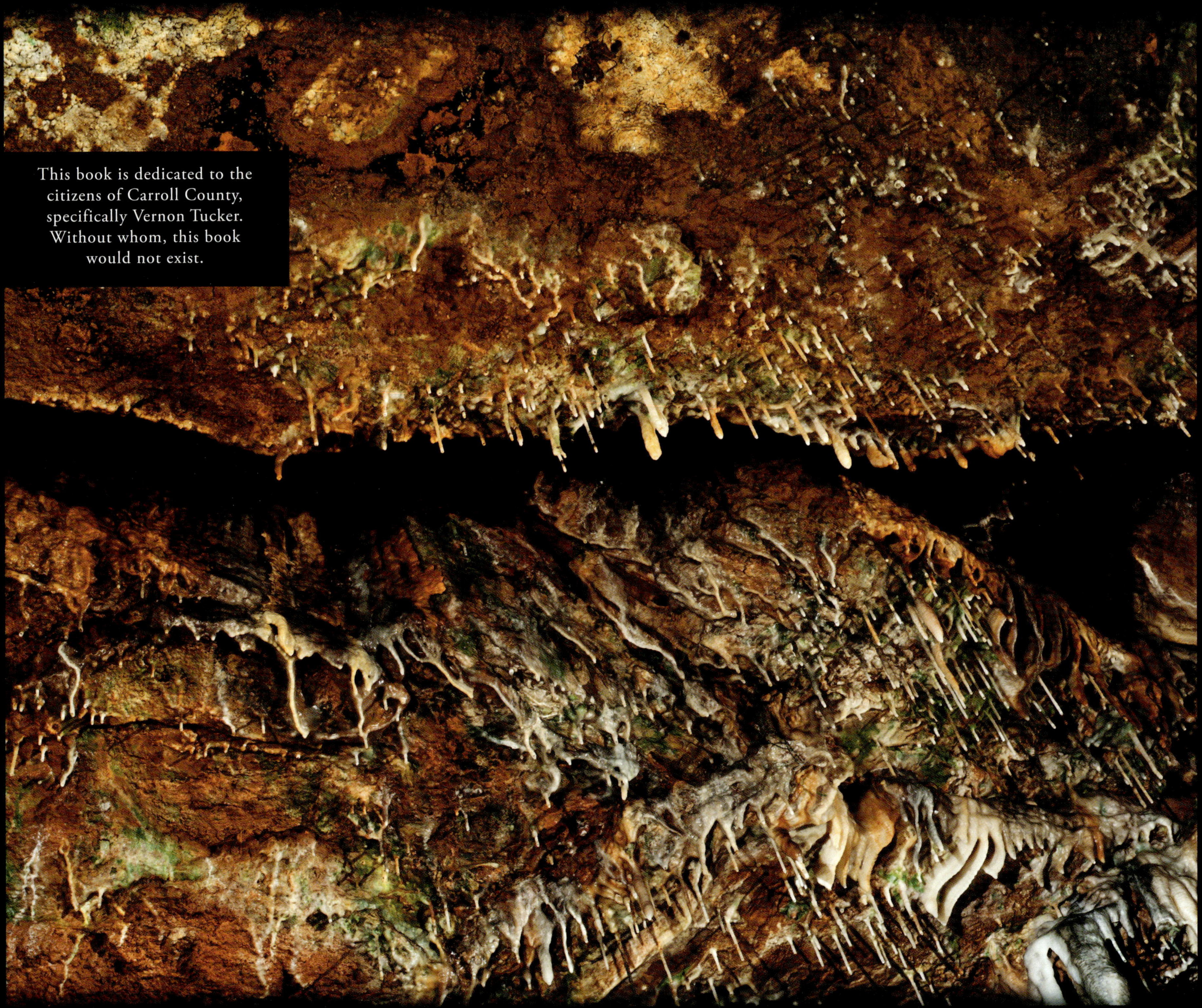

# To the viewer,

I invite you to embark upon a visual journey into this wonderful part of Arkansas we call home. Chip Ford has captured the essence of what makes us tick and your memories stick. Each photograph tells a story of its own that would surely fail if spoken instead. Enjoy the culmination of fun, fact, and fiction that Chip has gathered for your viewing pleasure. Remember, this book offers just a sample taste of Eureka Springs and our surrounding areas... you will have to come visit us for the real thing!

Morris R. Pate
Mayor
City of Eureka Springs, Arkansas

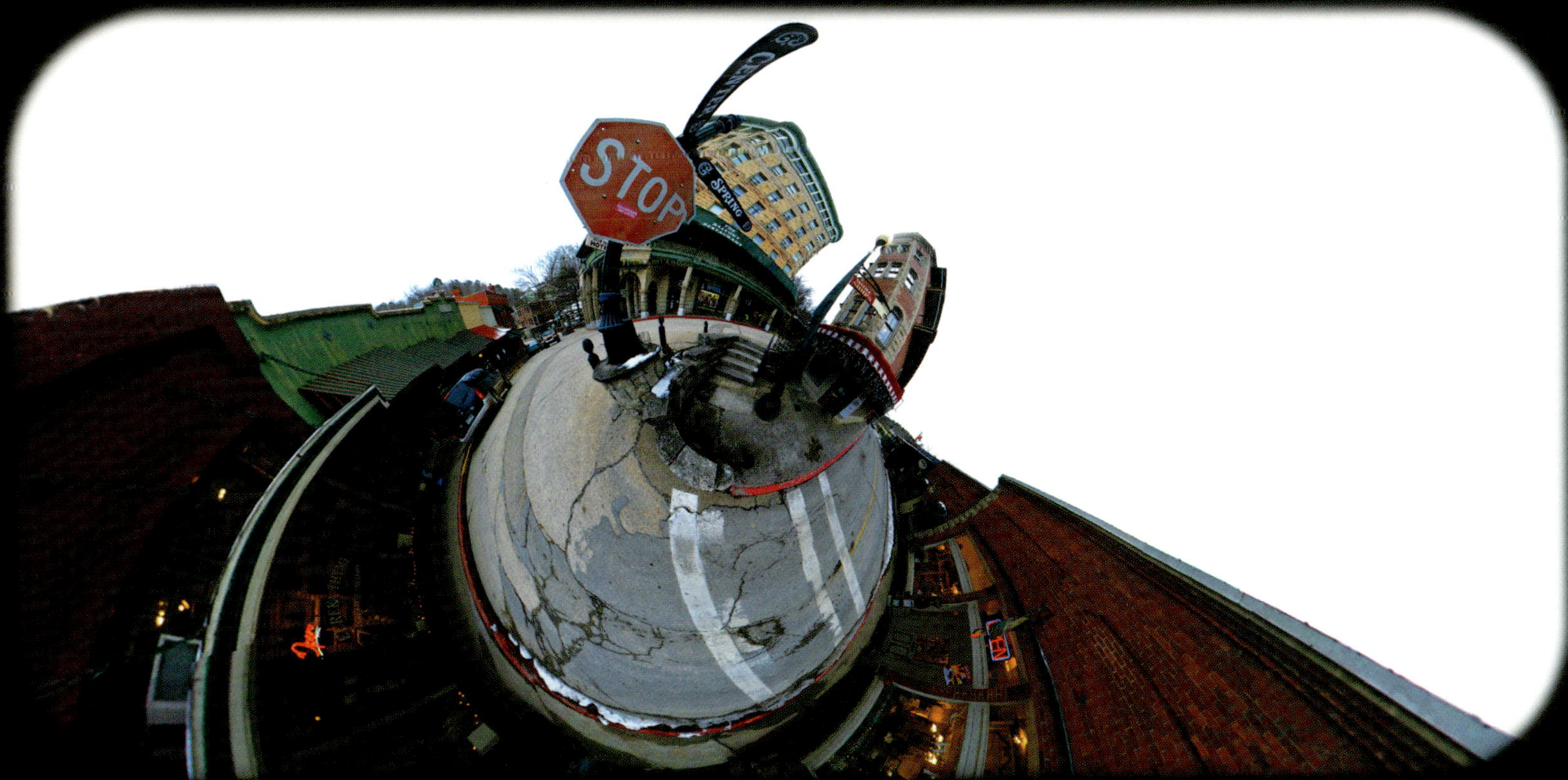

I thank you – my family and friends;
Rachel F., Rylee F., Becky F., Chuck F., Virginia F., Henry F., Veralice M., Dee M., Hope F., Holly F., Debbie R., Rock R., Barry F., Debbie F., Cheri W., Perlinda O., Vernon T., MPB, Phil H., Chris F., ECR3, Jeremy M. M., Susan S., Larry P., Ben R., Amber H., Dorthey G., Angelo Y., Margo P., Valerie D., Elise R., Marty R., Gwen E., June W., Catharine O., Lata L., Steve L., Bob M., Eric M., Melody P., Jean F., Iris F., Rick F., Bill O., Jack M., Mikey H., Logan H., Colton H., Lisa H., Eric M., Becky P., Lisa H., Francie S., Thomas T., Ginni M., Sondra T., Keith S., Rachal H., Earl H., Rhys W., Christian F., Thomas A., Brian Y., Brian J., Marsha H., Don L., Butch B., Lynn B., John C., Enid S., Alvin B., Amanda P., Ashley H., Billy B., Chad O., Will A., Courtney L., Tyler M., Ryan D., Ben H., Shelby F., Travis G., Wes A., Sean H., Sean C., Shaman H., Reillot W., Bill K., John R., Billy M., Blayne T., Bobby S., Brad B., Anna M., Bob M., Jerry D., Linda C., Bian B., Lydia B., Brian W., Caleb L., Carma L., Carol P., Carol S., Chuck D., Clare L., Cody R., Cosmo M., Curtis E., Justin B., Jimmy K., Brandon B., Britt E., Connie E., Bobbie F., John C., Joe M., Randy W., Sam R., Raven D., Mike B., Mike M., Jim S., Matthew W., Willie C., Andy G., Earl H., Rachal H., and many others.

All the information within this book can easily be accessed with a trip to the Eureka Springs Historic Museum, the Eureka Springs Carnegie Public Library or to any of the historic sites with plaques positioned throughout town.

Most images list GPS coordinates and GPS elevation readings. The coordinates will take you, in most instances, to the exact position where I captured the photograph. Some readings were excluded due to privacy issues or because I was on private and/or city property to which the public would not have access.

Many of the events, festivals, and parades pictured are consistent year to year, however actual published dates and times can be found on the following web sites:

- EurekaSprings.org
- LovelyCitizen.com
- EurekaSpringsChamber.com

Thank you
Without these sponsors and underwriters this book would have never seen the light of day.

- The Queen Anne Mansion
- The Eureka Springs City Advertising and Promotion Commision
- The Greater Eureka Springs Chamber of Commerce
- The 1886 Crescent Hotel & Spa
- 1905 Basin Park Hotel
- Local Flavor Cafe
- Mud Street Cafe
- The Great Passion Play
- The Citizen and Carroll County Newspapers
- Flatiron Flats
- Blue Springs Heritage Center
- Best Western Inn of the Ozarks
- Practial Magic Art Supply

# Table of Contents



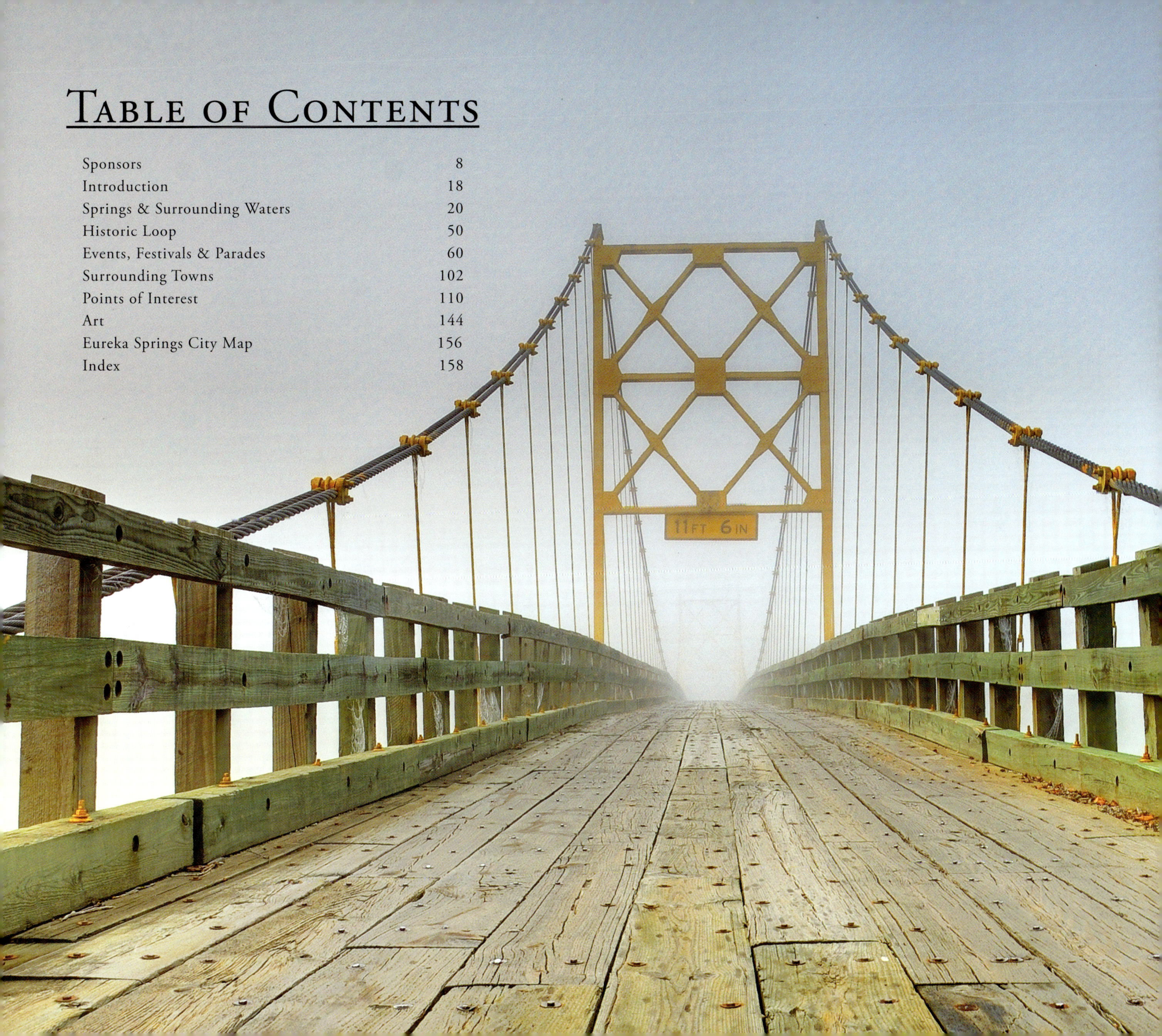

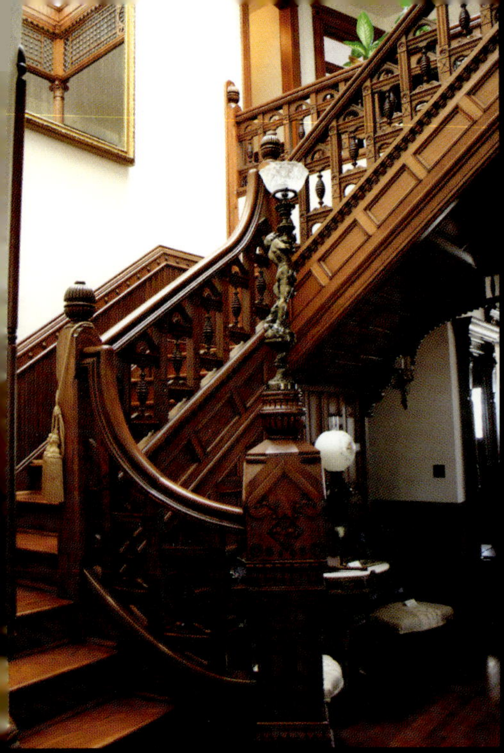

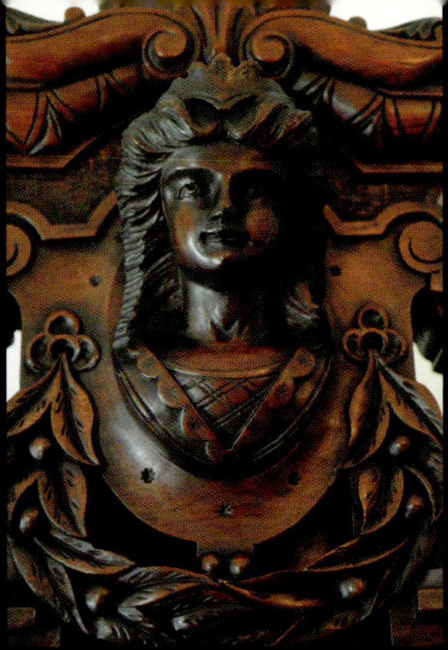

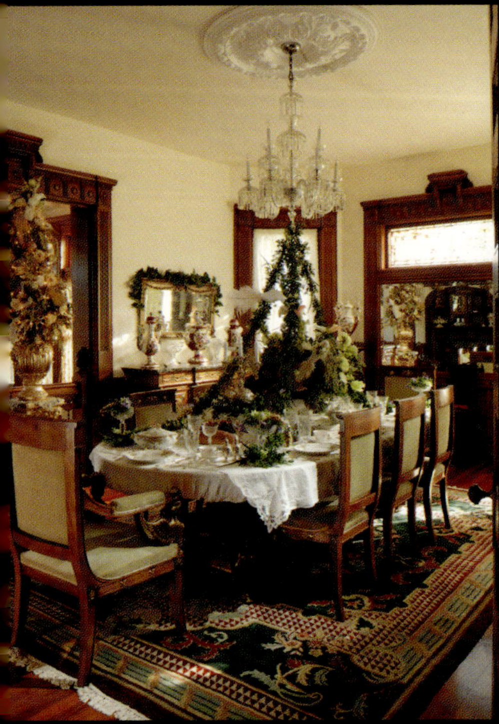

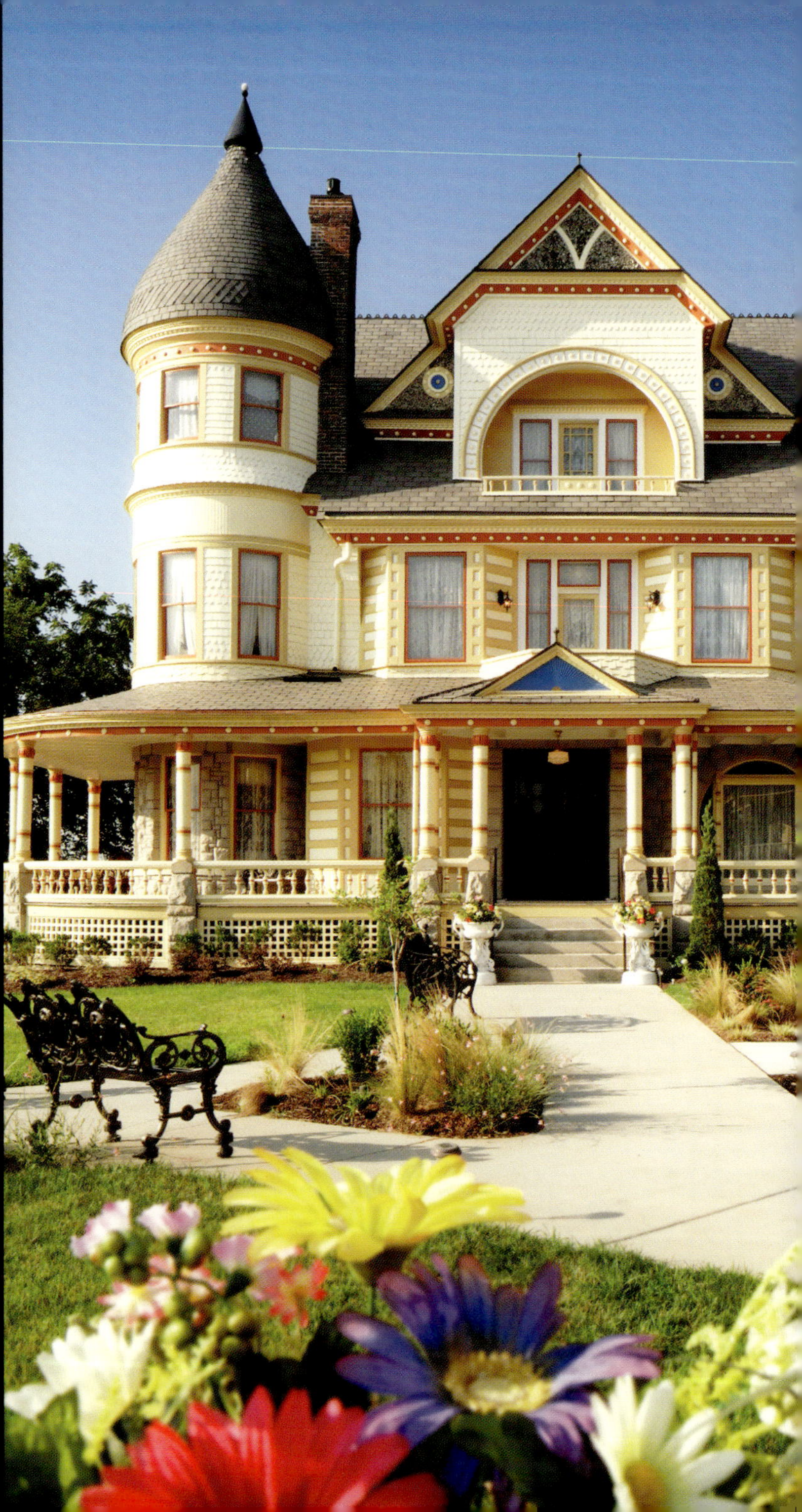

At the entrance to Eureka Springs' historical district resides, in striking fashion, The Queen Anne Mansion. A superb example of the whimsical American architectural style popularized by wealthy industrialists in the late 1800s, the mansion has been lovingly restored to its 19th Century grandeur down to the smallest and most exquisite detail. The mansion's landmarked exterior plays off a plethora of geometric shapes with its turreted wing, elongated windows, spindled porch rail and countless decorative touches. A walk around the home reveals secrets and surprises including asymmetrical stained glass windows and a sunken garden with marble fountain. Inside, the mansion holds a unique and priceless collection of museum quality antiques, artifacts and decoration from some of the finest artists, craftsmen and cabinet makers of the period. The entrance foyer offers rich-in-detail, floor-to-ceiling woodwork, including hand-tooled balustrades and massive cherry and oak pocket doors, showcasing the work of owner Curtis Wright's furniture factory artisans.

Photography by: Jeremy Mason McGraw (www.EurekaPostcards.com)

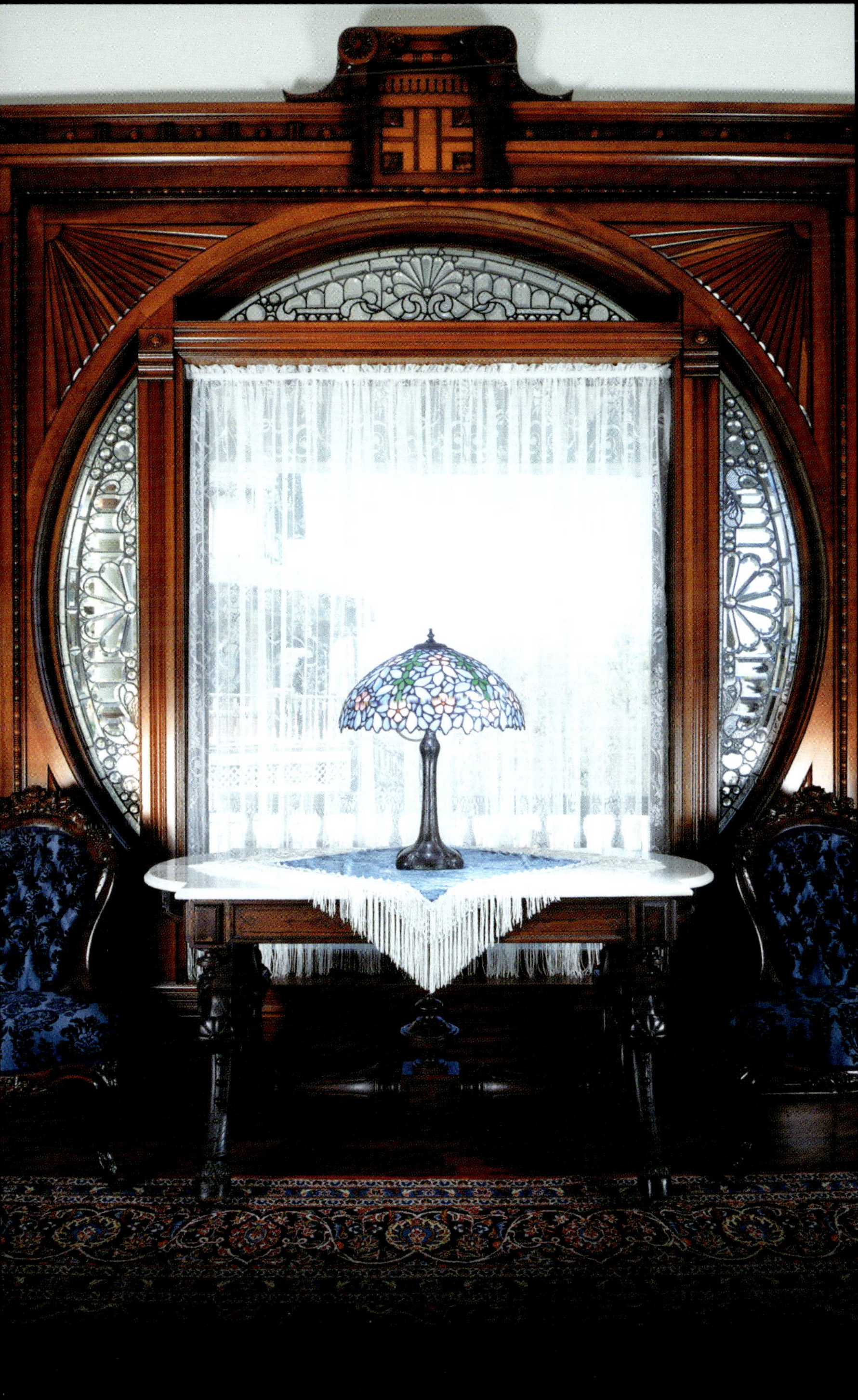

Throughout The Queen Anne Mansion are many fine examples of period styles, including Federal, Rococo, Empire and Renaissance. Dominating every room is an important piece of furniture or cabinetry. In every corner and nook is a treasure from the houses of Waterford, Limoges, Dresden, Flow Blue Willow and many others. Details – like the collection of delicate moustache cups and a leather-bound volume of bible stories written exclusively for a wealthy German family – provide an unforgettable glimpse into the lives of the well-to-do at the turn of the century.
A treasure, indeed.

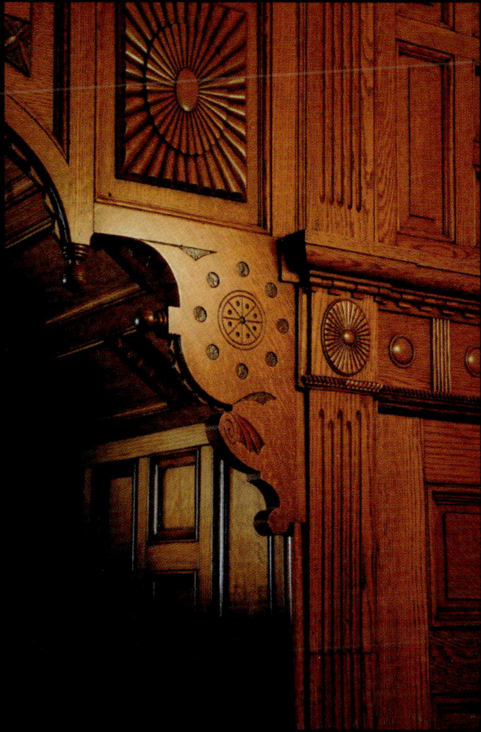

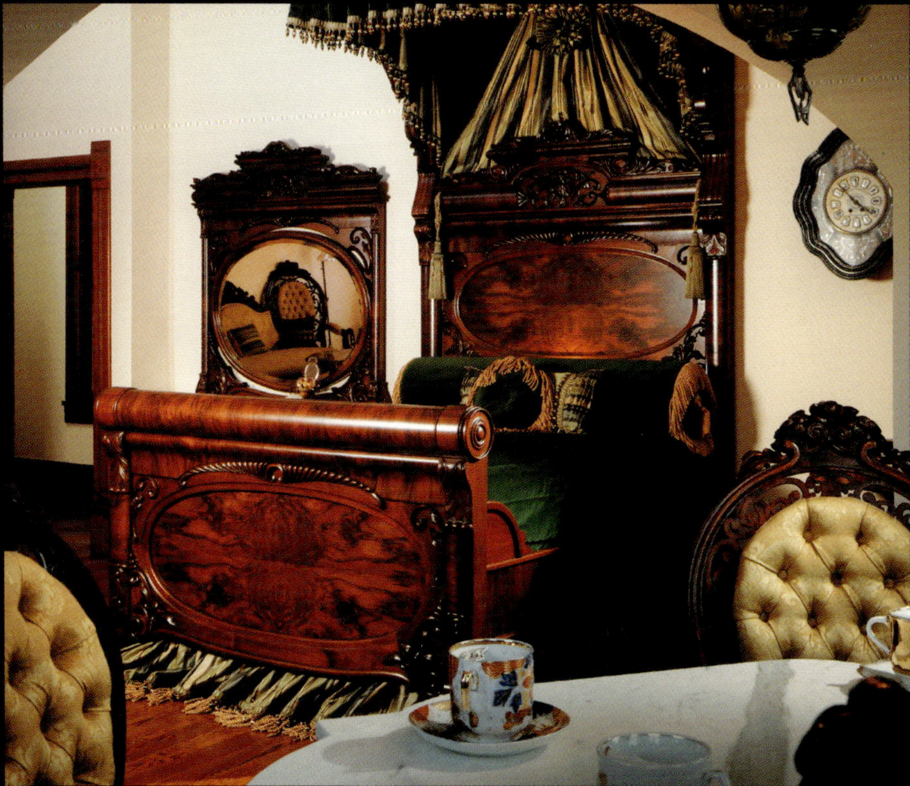

*Eureka Springs City Advertising and Promotion Commission is proud to be an underwriter of this book.*

*Thank you, Chip, for this valuable and handsome volume of photos that illustrates our town.*

www.EurekaSprings.org

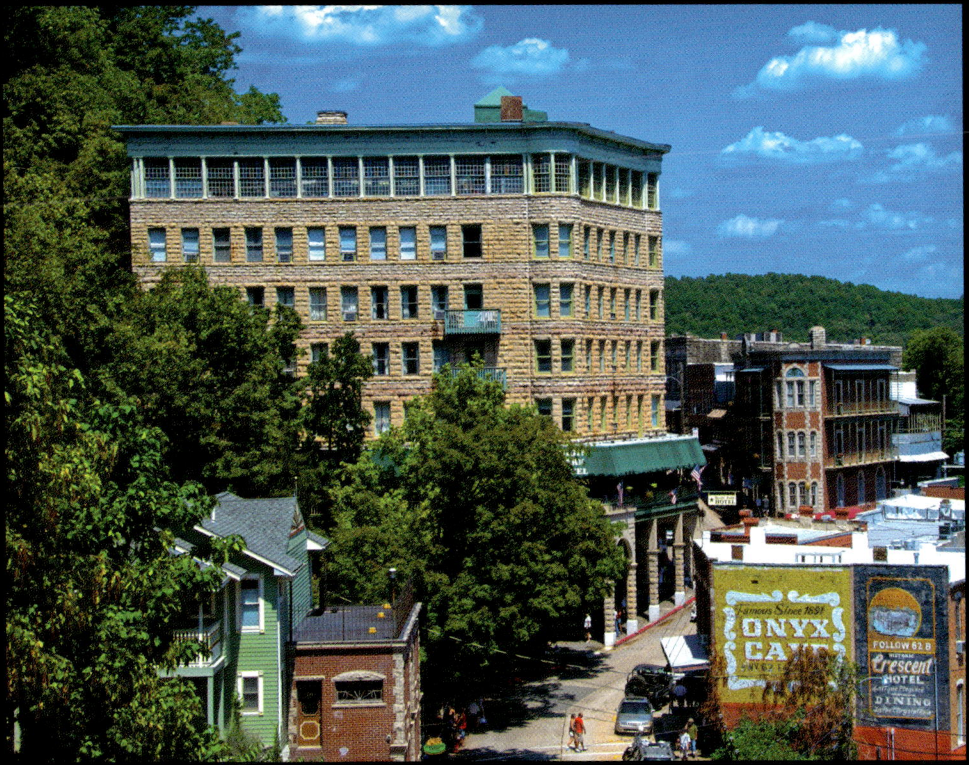


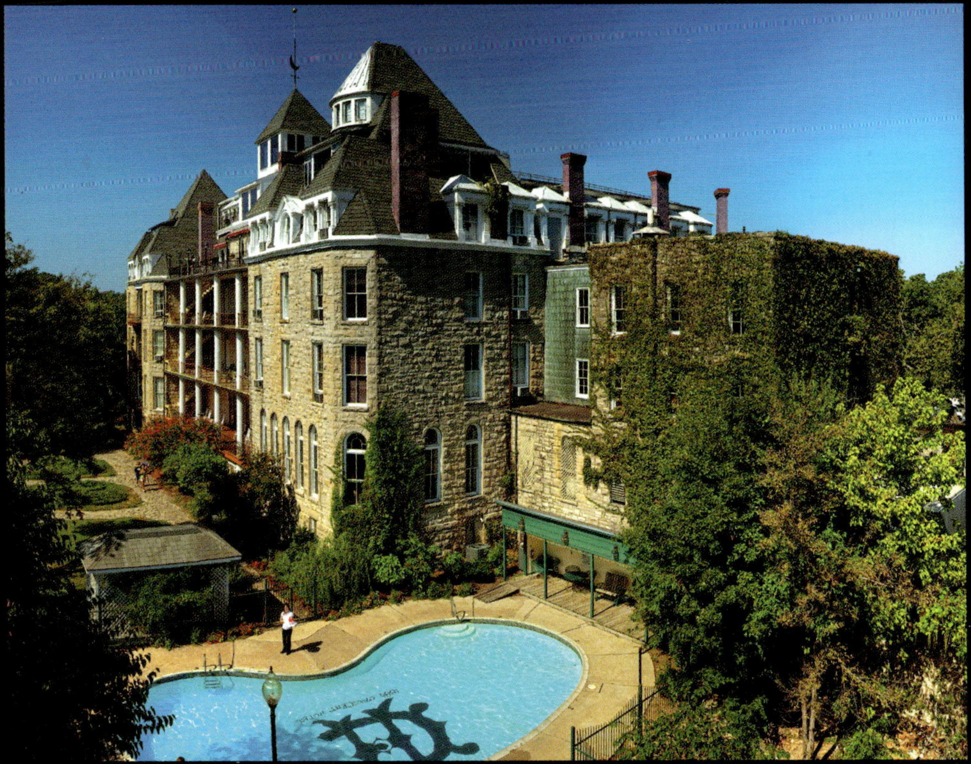

Eureka Springs' two historic landmark hotels have seen an exciting and intriguing past but it wasn't until 1997 that both properties saw a truly sustainably bright future. That is when two devoted preservationists, Martin and Elise Roenigk from the Midwest via East Hampton, Connecticut, purchased both the 1905 Basin Park Hotel and the 1886 Crescent Hotel & Spa. Both hotels have seen a miraculous renaissance under the Roenigk proprietorship.

The 1905 Basin Park Hotel sits on the footprint made by the Perry House, a property that burned during the Great Fire of 1890. The Basin Park Hotel from day one was the epicenter of fun and celebration in downtown. This towering hotel constructed of limestone and pink dolomite held the distinction by "Ripley's Believe It Or Not" to be the only eight-story hotel with all floors being "ground floors". Inside this wonder sat a very popular "locals'" restaurant and on the top floor, surrounded by its iconic stained glass windows, was the ballroom, sight of many orchestra-led gala balls. One such event was in 1948. A popular radio quiz show, "Truth or Consequences" hosted by Ralph Edwards, had a couple from Santa Ana, California, win a two-week stay at The Basin Park but the consequence was they had to stay barefooted during those 14 days. The town of Eureka Springs, wanting to show their appreciation for these two celebrity visitors, held a Barefoot Ball in the hotel ballroom in their honor and everyone who attended had to be barefooted as well. History shows that through the decades the Basin Park Hotel has been where the most fun is in downtown Eureka Springs. That tradition continues today.

The 1886 Crescent Hotel & Spa was constructed by the Eureka Springs Improvement Company, a group of well-to-do businessmen who, because of their railroad ties, wanted to sell more train tickets so they constructed an exclusive and palatial resort atop Crescent Mountain. On May 20, 1886, The Crescent Hotel opened its doors to the "carriage set" during a spectacular opening with the kind of pageantry that has never been duplicated in this Ozark community. This proud member of Historic Hotels of America has not always been a hotel however. During the early 20th century the hotel doubled as a girls college during the off-seasons and, during three infamous years in the late 1930s, a charlatan from Muscatine, Iowa purchased and operated the hotel as a cancer curing hospital. Through its more than 125 year history, it is said that The Crescent has had quite a few guests who "checked out but never left". Today, although the hotel is primarily a resort family destination, an escape for romantic couples, and the premiere wedding choice here in the "Wedding Capital of The South", the Crescent has also been tagged with the moniker "America's Most Haunted Hotel" featuring nightly ghost tours. Regardless of the reason for the visit, generations upon generations have been returning to this mountaintop spa resort for yet another scrapbook full of lifetime memories.

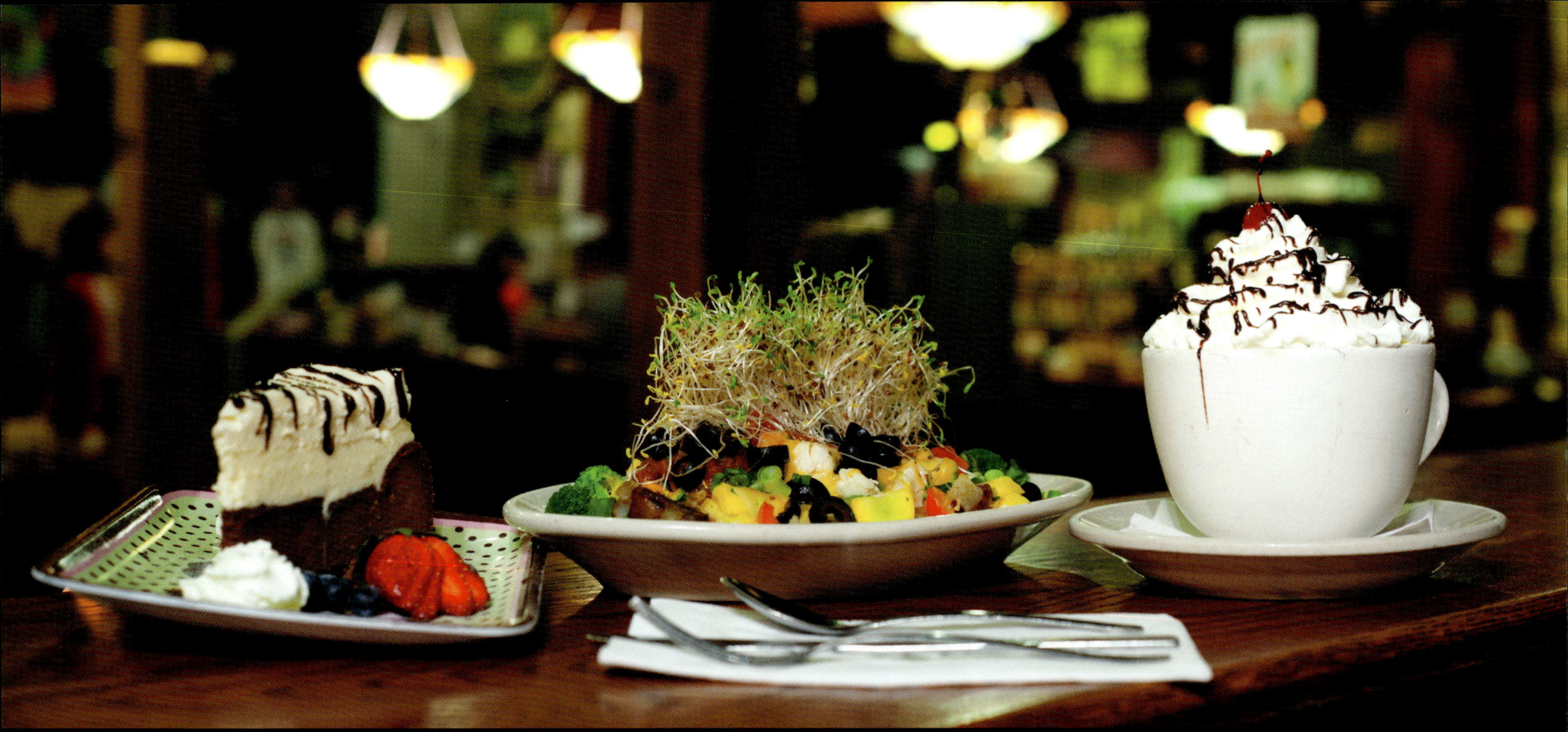

Nestled in the basement of an 1888 structure in what locals call "Underground Eureka" sits Mud Street Cafe' a true Dining Experience. In the 1800's Mud Street Cafe' would have been street level and you would have entered the building and peered through the windows where three beautiful stained glass pieces are now situated on the wall. The street kept flooding due to a spring that runs underneath, thus the name "Mud Street". The Owner, Bobbie Foster, likes to imagine what it would have been like to wander the streets back then. A native Eurekan whose family not only dates back five generations, but this same family left an undeniable legacy for Foster to live up to. "I am proud of my heritage and proud to call Eureka home". "I was born and raised in this community and cut my teeth in the restaurant business. My father was leasing The Basin Park Cafe' (once located in the bottom level of the Basin Park Hotel) from my great grandfather who owned the Hotel at that time and offered me a position the summer I turned 11". "Some of my fondest childhood memories revolve around that Cafe'. As a child I would have breakfast there every Sunday morning and then skip up the street to the Penn Memorial Baptist Church to meet my grandmother and great grandfather for the service. Afterwards it was always back down to the Cafe' for lunch where I would order the fruit plate because it had a big scoop of orange sherbet in the middle"! "I never dreamed that my first job would someday lead to owning and operating Mud Street Cafe' but I now realize that during the years I worked at the Basin Park Cafe' I was learning everything I needed to know to run my own Restaurant: "Work hard, offer delicious food, and treat people the way you would want to be treated". She and her staff implement this same strategy today to maintain their award winning status throughout the State of Arkansas. Some of the freshest food and friendliest service can be found within the original limestone walls. The street that kept flooding has now been built up, putting Mud Street Cafe' down a flight of stairs. The centerpiece of the dining room is a turn of the century oak bar with beveled mirrors and the Cafe' has wonderful local art on the walls, large wooden beams, an eclectic blend of oak tables and chairs, Victorian carpet and cozy sitting areas to relax and enjoy the atmosphere. Today the only thing that floods this space is the aroma of the award winning coffee, desserts and delectable food. There is a charm and warmth that envelops you every time you visit and if you want to taste the magic of Eureka Springs you need to visit Mud Street Cafe'.

www.mudstreetcafe.com 479-253-6732

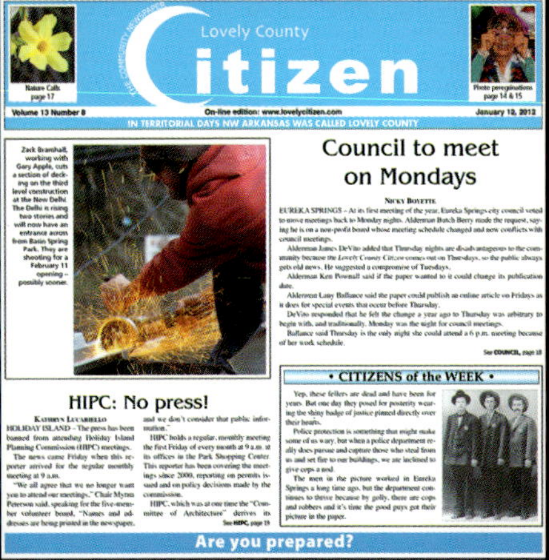


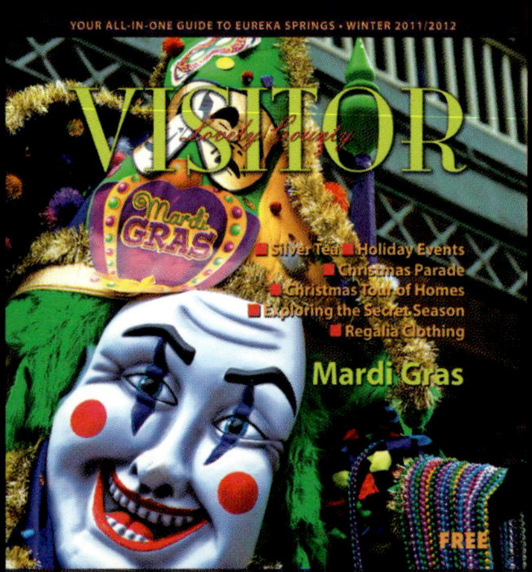


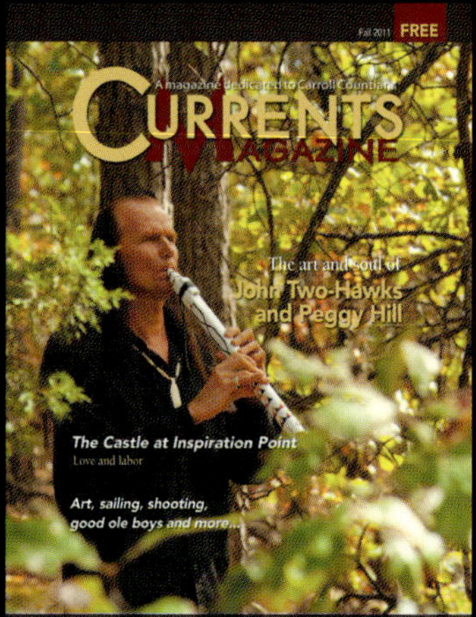


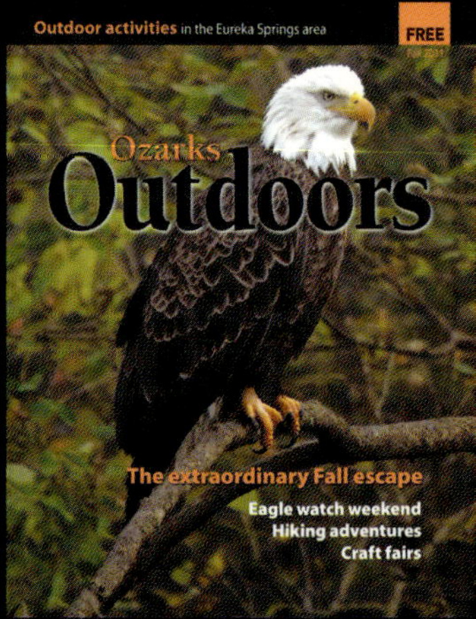


*A lineage that dates back to the 1880s*

*the Lovely County Citizen and Carroll County Newspaper.*

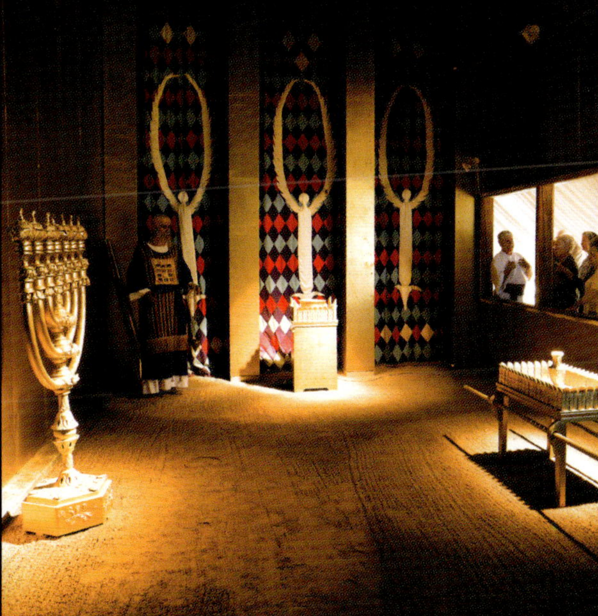

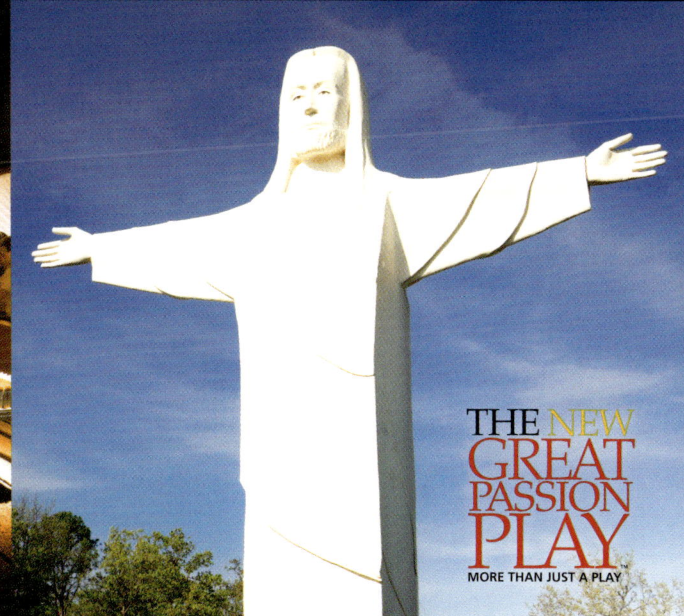
THE NEW
GREAT
PASSION
PLAY
MORE THAN JUST A PLAY



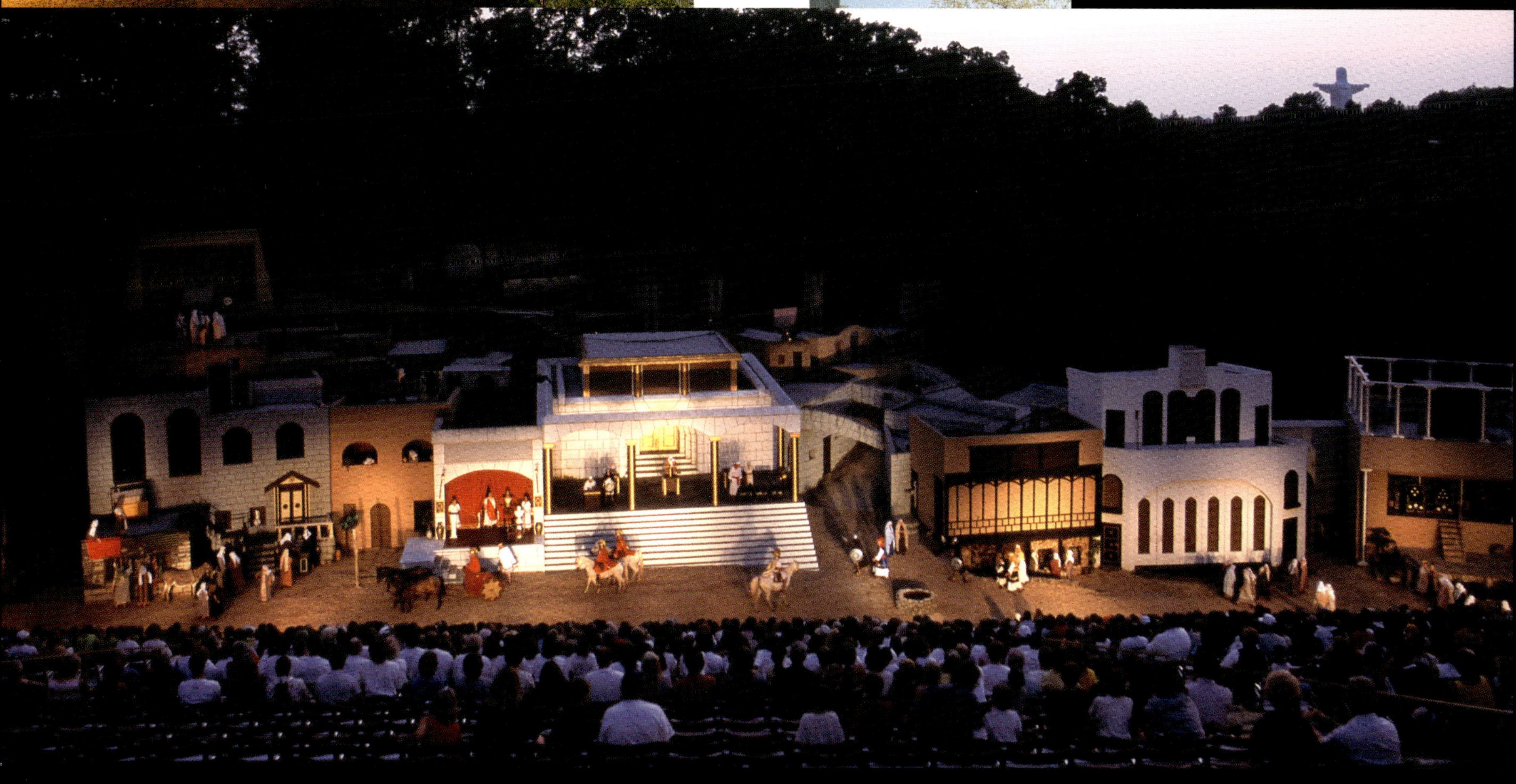

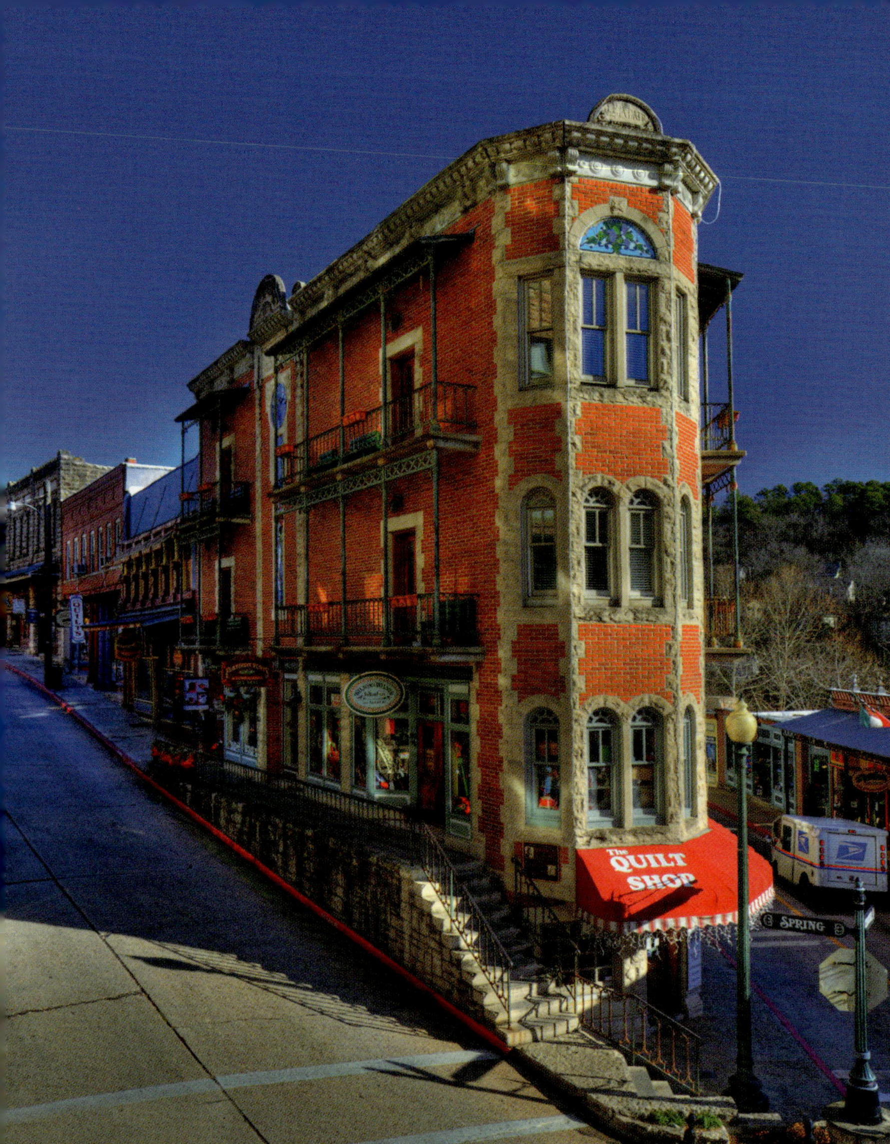


Positioned in the heart of the historic district's downtown corridor is the Flatiron Flats – with shopping, fine dining, spa relaxation and night life all at your doorstep. Upon arriving to one of our suites, our guests are greeted with a gracious wine, fruit and cheese basket to help you settle in and enjoy the comforts only a Victorian village can offer. Well appointed suites with grand king beds, comfy towels, biscotti for your morning coffee, are all waiting for you to enjoy during your next stay in the unique pampering of Eureka Springs.

1-800-421-9615 www.FlatironFlats.com



# The Greater Eureka Springs Chamber of Commerce

The Greater Eureka Springs Chamber of Commerce congratulates Mr. Ford on a beautiful collection of photographs, capturing the varied and awesome spirit of our city.

When planning a trip to Eureka Springs or for information during your visit feel free to contact our Visitor Center.

1-800 6EUREKA or www.EurekaSpringsChamber.com

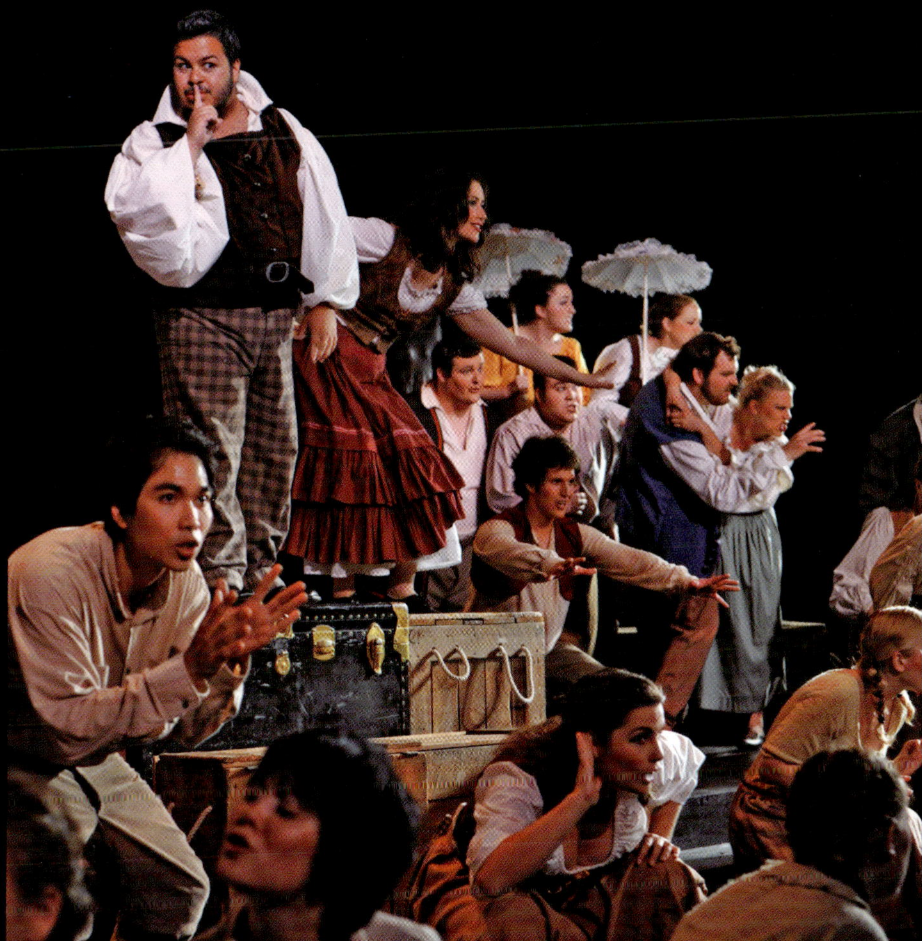

Is there "Magic" on the mountain? Yes! Over 60 successful years of incredible productions have energized the arts in the lives of those who have come to Rock Candy Mountain, 5 miles west of Eureka Springs and underscores the importance of music in our culture. This unique program nurtures the young artists who will continue the tradition of our famous alumni who grace the stages of opera throughout the world. Each season provides visitors to the beautiful Ozark Mountains the opportunity to see a different opera each evening and enjoy a live production in an intimate setting. We make a real difference in the lives of our alumni. Quote from William Johns, Metropolitan Opera, Musica Bayreuth, La Scala, Covent Garden "Without Inspiration Point, my life would have taken an entirely different course. A challenging, wonderful opportunity for young performers. Opera in the Ozarks instills certain values and an outlook essential to the professional singer." Northwest Arkansas is certainly a destination for the arts lover and a rich experience in the visual and performing arts. Visit Soon!

opera.org 479-253-8595

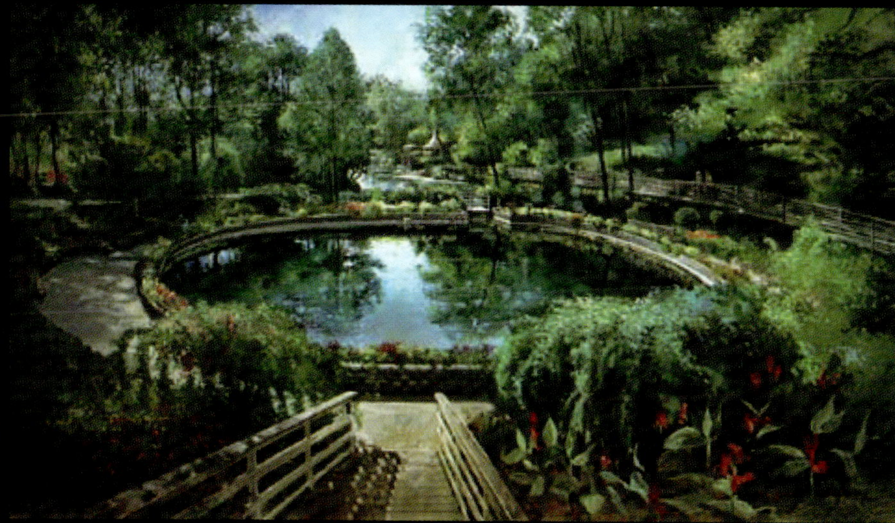

Visit the historic bluff shelter, now on the National Register of Historic Places. Walk on ground that nurtured the Cherokee people during the Trail of Tears. Connect with the natural beauty of our many native gardens. See the power and wonder of Blue Spring, pouring 38 million gallons of cold, clear water each day into its trout-filled lagoon.

www.eurekagardens.com 479-253-9244

BEST WESTERN
INN OF THE OZARKS

www.innoftheozarks.com 479-253-9768

PRACTICAL MAGIC
ART SUPPLY

www.practicalmagicartsupply.com 479-363-6395

# Introduction

Exactly who stumbled upon the area in Northwestern Arkansas known as Eureka Springs is highly debatable.

Known throughout the Tribal Nations for its 'Great Healing Springs', Eureka Springs has a rich historical and cultural background. Native Americans used the lands around Carroll County for everything they needed day-to-day, including the natural springs which they believed held mystical healing powers. One of the more elaborate versions of the founding of Eureka Springs' core, Basin Spring Park, explains it thus: Somewhere around the 1780's an Indian chief known as "Black Dog" stumbled upon the spring and was impressed enough to start spreading word of the areas natural resource. A Sioux chief took his blind daughter to the spring to bathe under moonlight, and her vision was restored. Word traveled among the tribes. The Osage hunted these lands until ceding their rights to Northwest Arkansas in an 1808 treaty. In 1847, word of the epic saga of springs in Northwestern Arkansas and their 'healing' powers reached J. M. Richardson. Word continued to spread among the western-bound, and by the time it reached European-American, Dr. Alvah Jackson, the springs were considered downright 'magical.' Jackson quickly traveled to The Healing City in the 1850's, and soon after claimed the pristine waters of Basin Spring cured his son's ailing eye. Jackson then set up a makeshift hospital in a nearby cave and used Basin Spring water to treat patients from both North and South during the American Civil War. Jackson also sold the waters as 'Dr. Jackson's Eye Water'.

Over the course of one year, the village population bloomed to 10,000 – officially a boomtown. Visitors converged on "the Healing City" to explore the benefits of the healing springs. In 1879, Jackson's son, Thomas, erected the Basin Bath House; which suffered two fires and one relocation before becoming the structure that stands. The city took the name Eureka Springs on July 4, 1879; and on February 14, 1880, Eureka Springs became an official city with a population of 3,984. Wooden shanties and tents sprouted up along the hillsides, and in 1881, Eureka became the fourth largest city in Arkansas. The Eureka Springs Improvement Company members worked vigorously on improving the infrastructure what was then referred to as 'Little Switzerland.' On January 24, 1883, the Frisco Railroad and Eureka Springs Railroad Company of Arkansas connected via the town's first depot, a plan in the works for around three years. The town exploded in popularity, and as many as six passenger railcars were visiting Eureka Springs every day. The Crescent Hotel, atop one of a sprawling series of hills was completed in 1886. In the same year, The Grand Central Hotel spanned Leatherwood Creek, now underground at that site, which emerged as one of the busiest parts of town.

In 1883, 1888 and 1890 fires destroyed the majority of the city's earliest buildings. The 1883 five-acre fire claimed around 75 homes as it swept from the around foot of Mountain Street to Eureka Street. The 1888 fire covered the area from Sweet Spring to south of the Perry House, which is now the Basin Park Hotel. By 1889, the city had grown to the state's second largest city. The influx in population eventually forced the widening of Mud (now Main) and Spring Streets. In the 1890's, Spring Street barely allowed two wagons to pass. The project to widen Main and Spring Streets by building limestone retaining walls and filling in the street raised some streets above the current storefront level, resulting in ground floor doors and windows now looking out onto the retaining walls and forcing owners to move up a story. Reportedly, in 1899, as many as 30 hotels sprouted forth from seemingly nowhere.

During the transition from the 1890s into the 1900's, limestone became the choice construction material for many projects. It is estimated the limestone walls within the city stretch from 44 to 74 miles at the present, but constantly changes due to the crumbling of existing walls, new discoveries of existing walls, and new walls being constructed on a regular basis. Most of the limestone brought into Eureka came from neighboring Beaver, 6 miles away. The Basin Park Hotel, completed by 1905, sported 100 guest rooms. The Ozarka Water Company, formed in 1905, bottled their from The Roundhouse, formerly the Eureka Springs Improvement Company's gas works. In 1907, using the waters from Magnetic and Bays Springs, the company was moving an estimated four freight cars every seven days out of town. In 1908, a Eureka local, W.O. Perkins, designed and had completed the Italianate-style District Courthouse building. The courthouse serves as one of two in the county, the other residing east of the Kings River in nearby Berryville. The year of 1915 rang in the year of the Basin Spring Park bandshell and hosted local brass and Ozark musicians, giving free daily or weekly concerts – as they still do today.

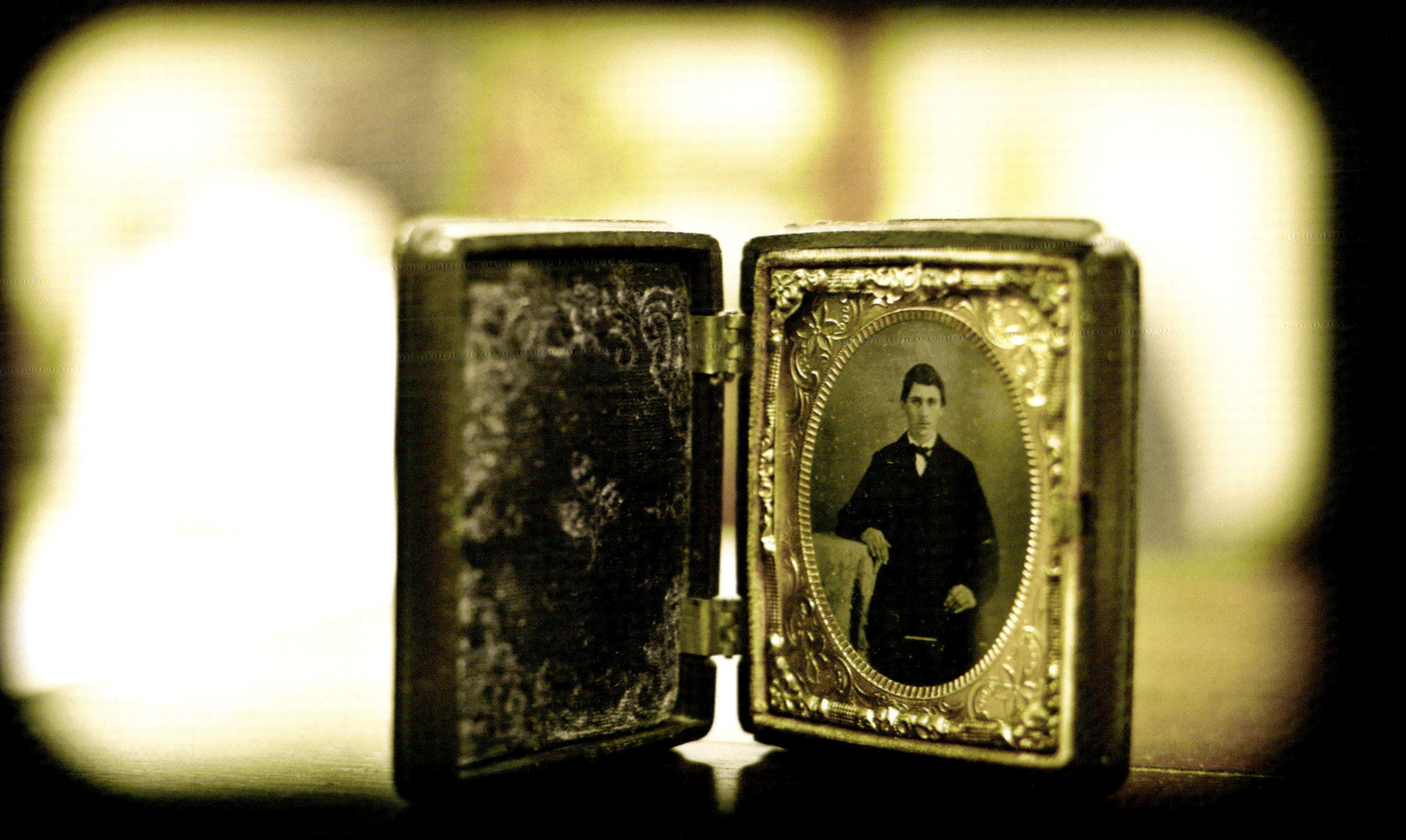

# The Springs & Surrounding Waters

On November 1, 1883, Carroll became an official county. The population had grown to 27,446 and in an area covering 638.81 square miles, of which 8.54 square miles is under water. Horses, mules, asses, oxen, cattle, sheep, swine, butter, corn, wheat, rye, oats, potatoes, grapes, plumbs, apples, peaches, cotton, hay, wool, and tobacco have all been raised in the county over the centuries with the help of the area's mineral rich waters. The first townships in the area were Carrollton, Prairie, and Osage.

N 36°23.954'
W 093°44.115'
Elevation 1178'



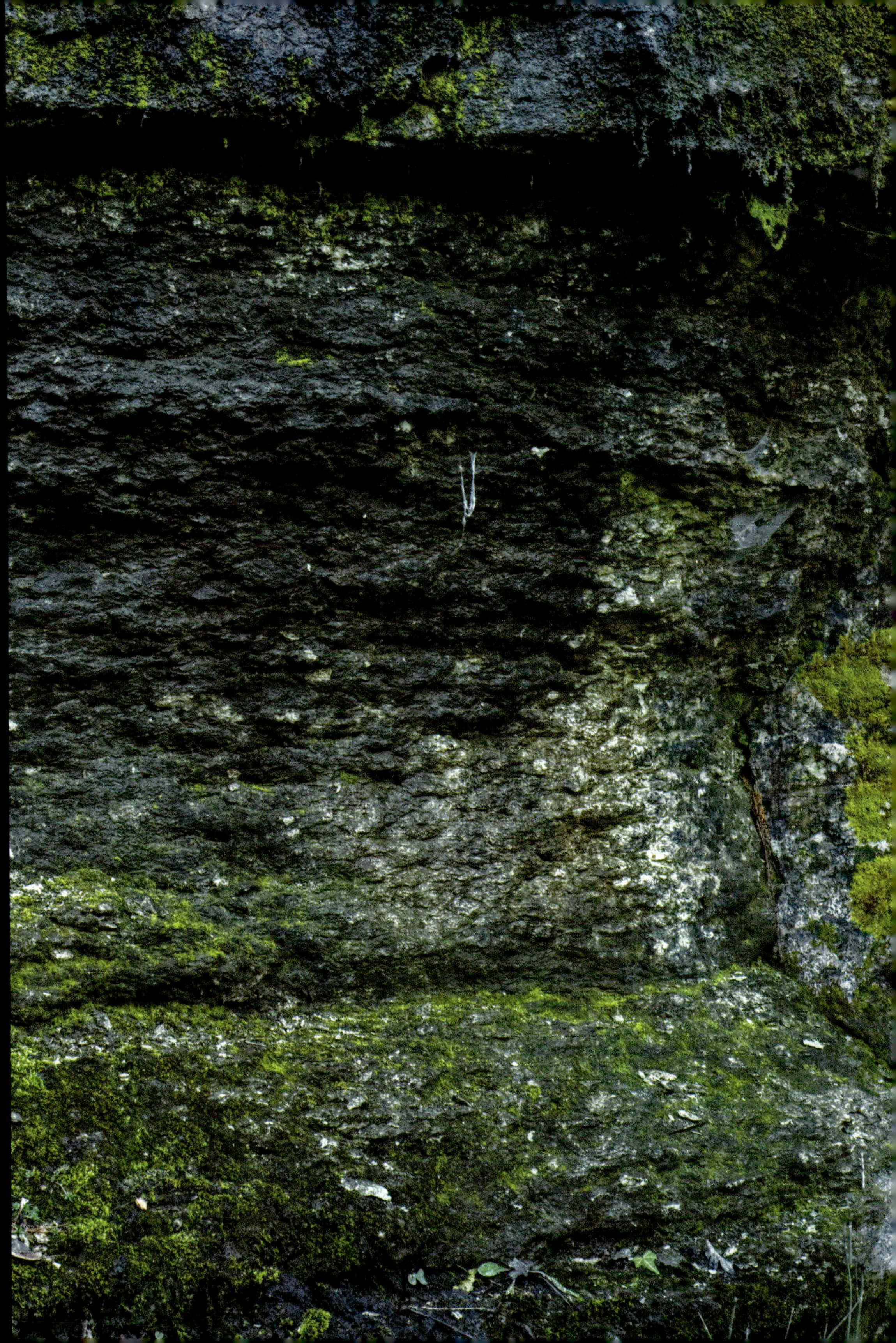

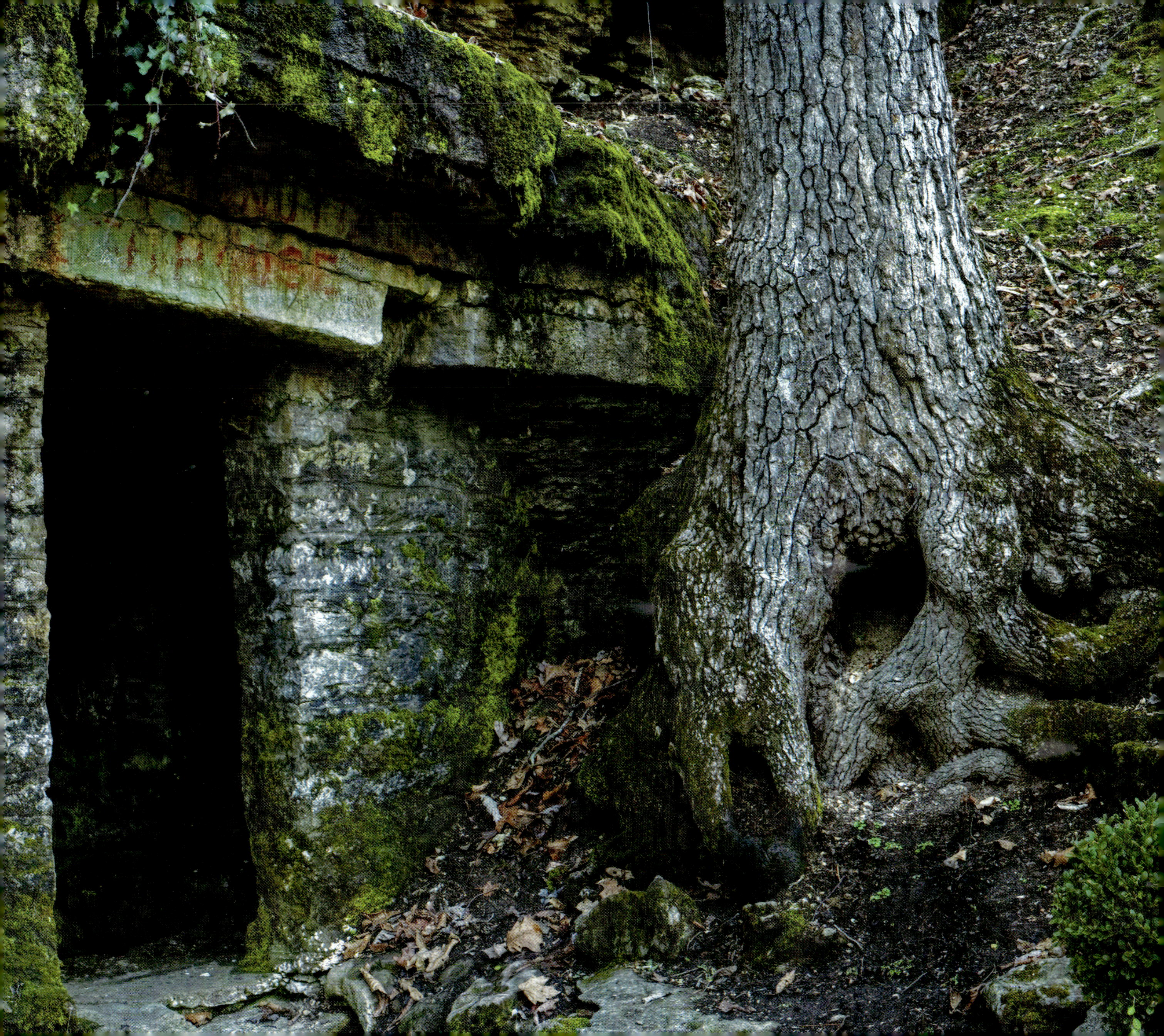

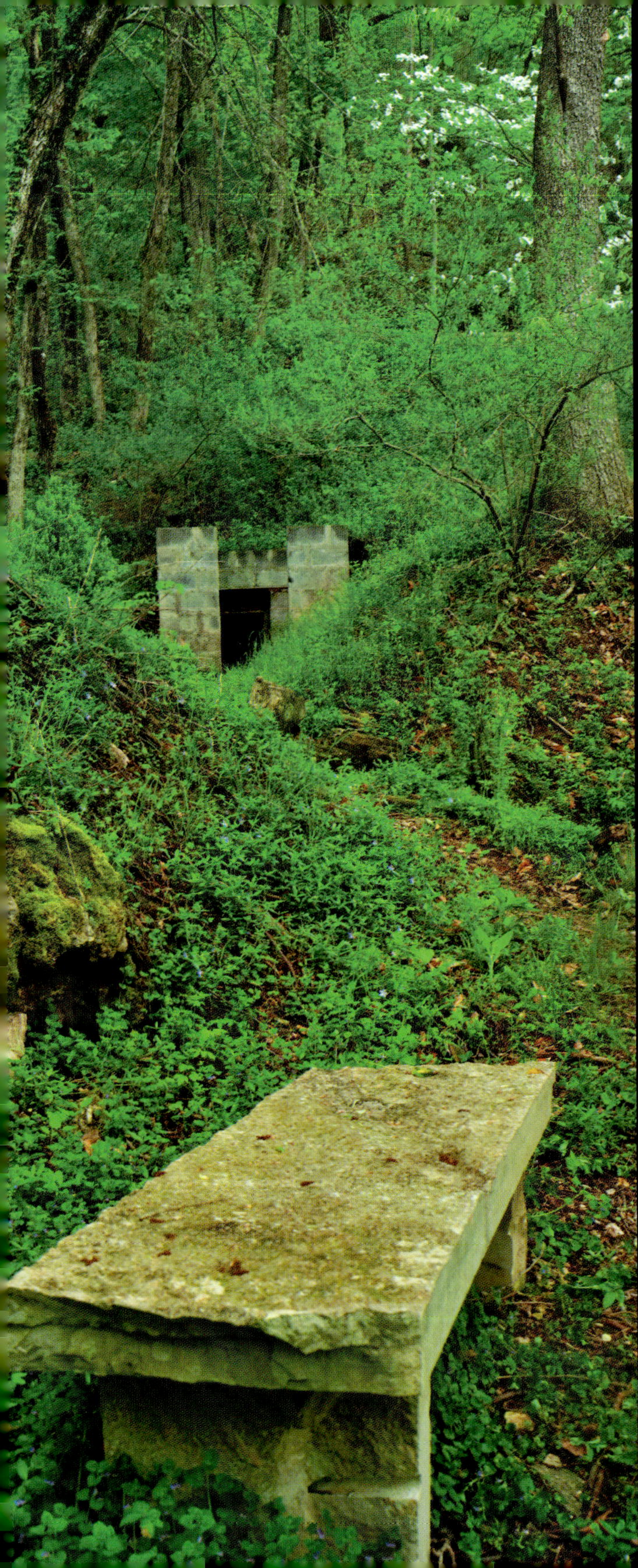

Nestled along a narrow paved road marked as a dead-end, even though it is not, is Cold Spring. The spring never really gained the notoriety, except with the deer herds, that the other springs did and had relocated at least once. A rusted and overturned bathtub sits as a faded memory from the days when many washed their clothes at Cold Spring, known to earlier residents as Site Spring.

N 36°24.263'
W 093°43.916'
Elevation 1066'

N 36°24.270'
W 093°44.299'
Elevation 1266'

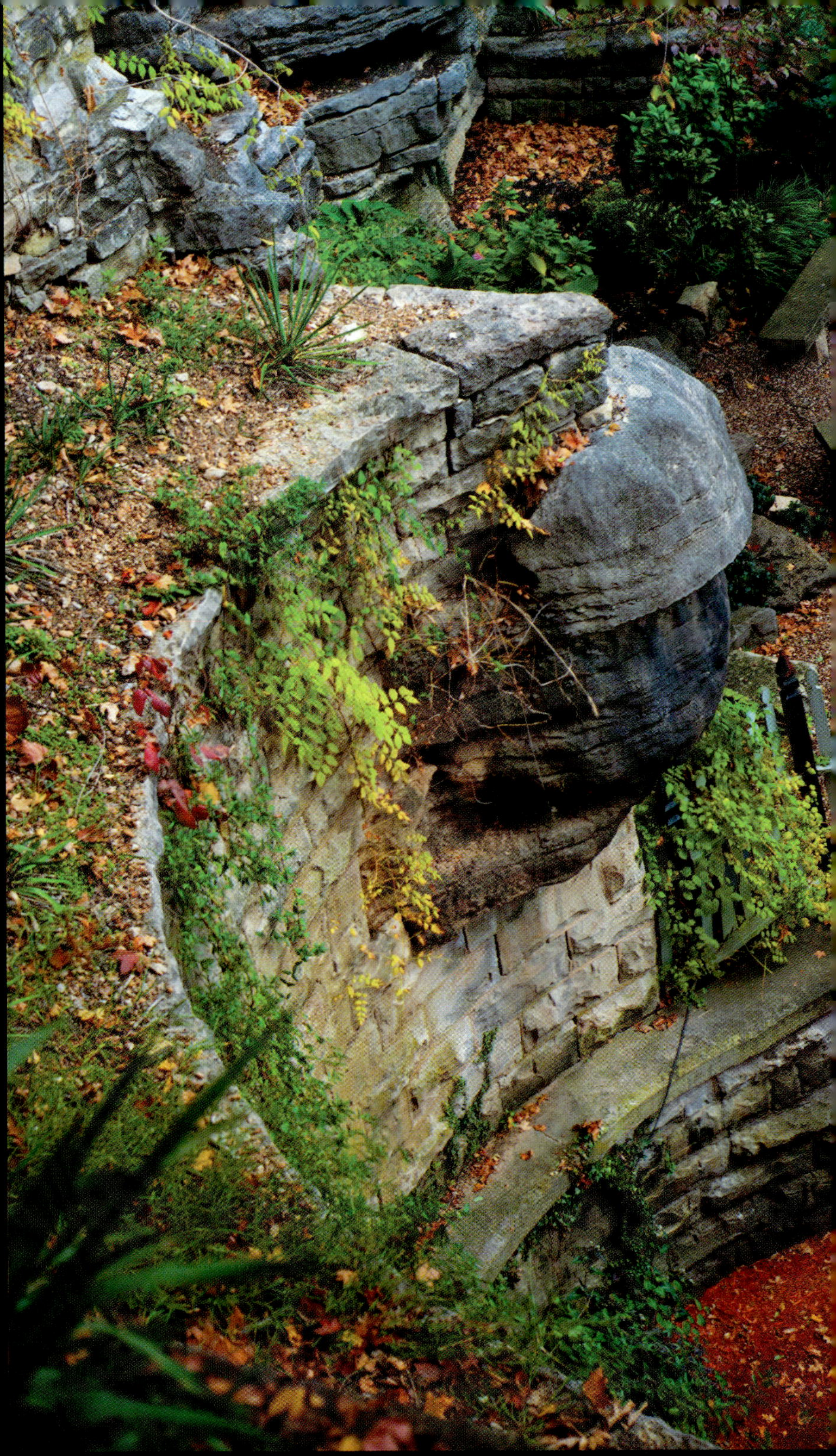

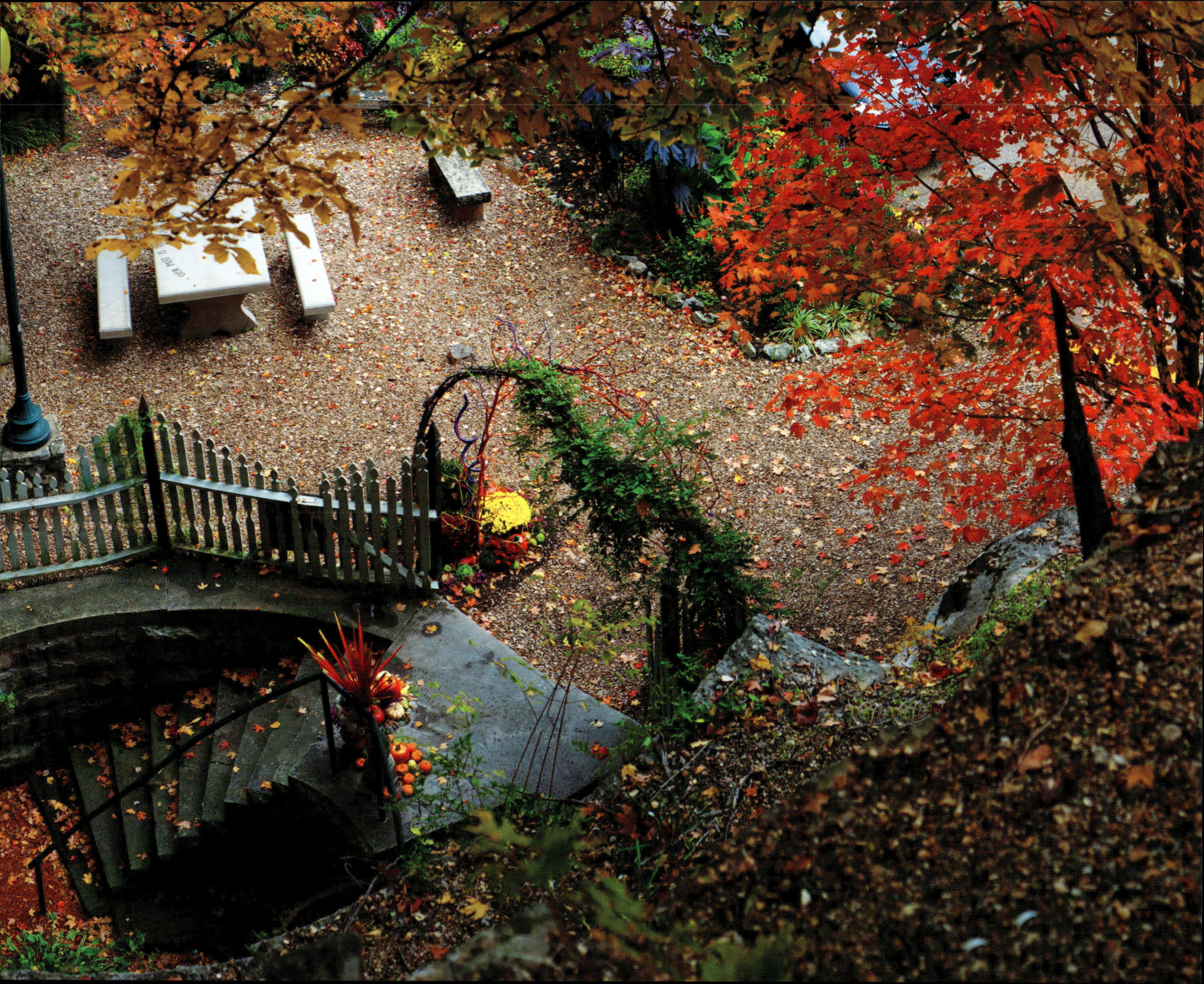

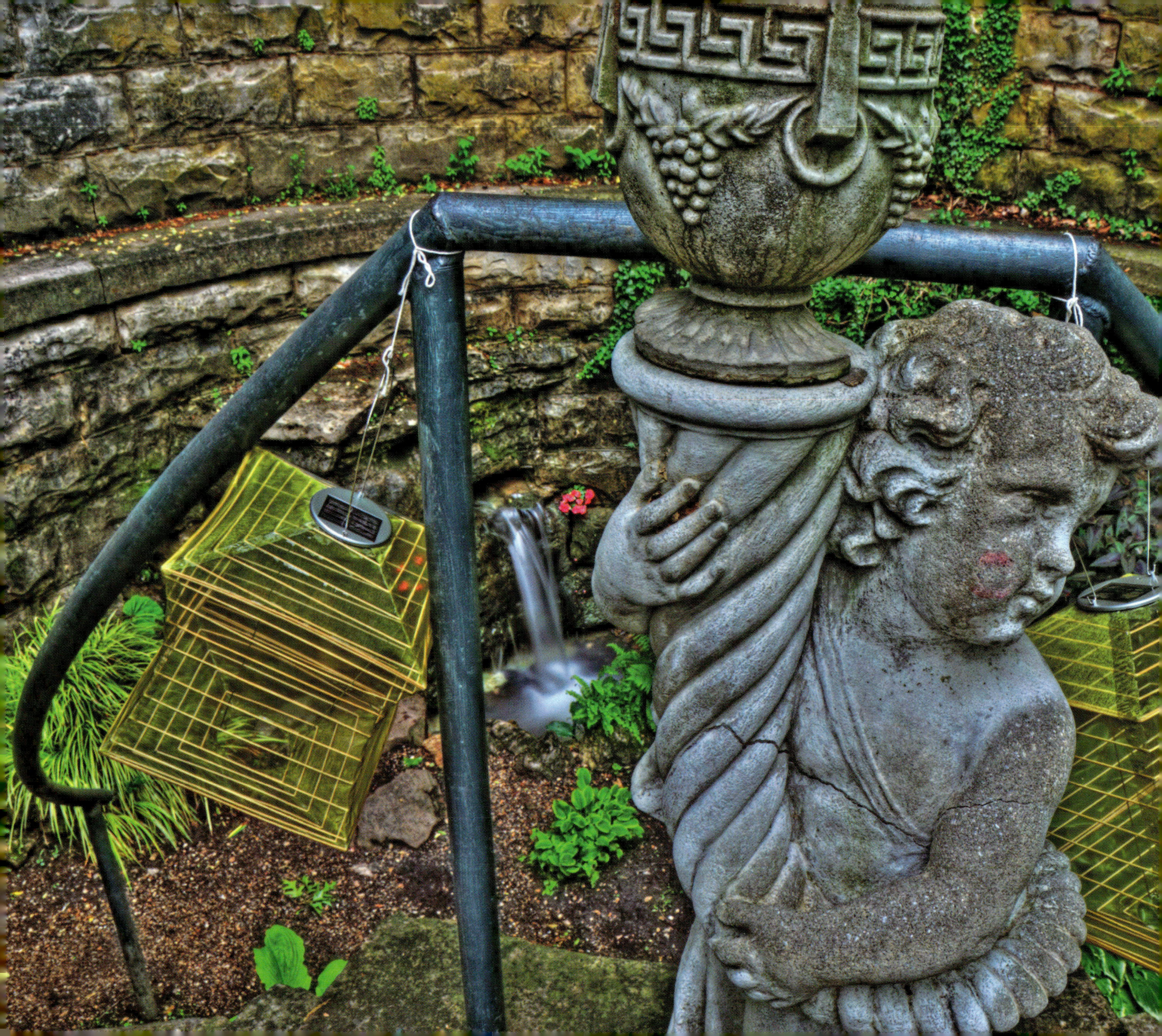

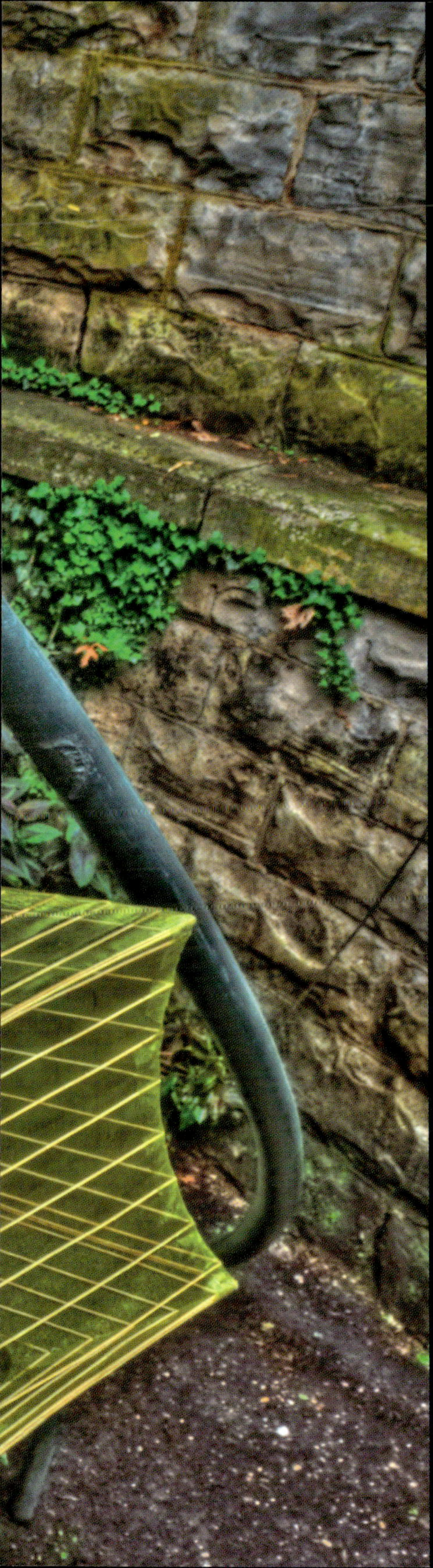

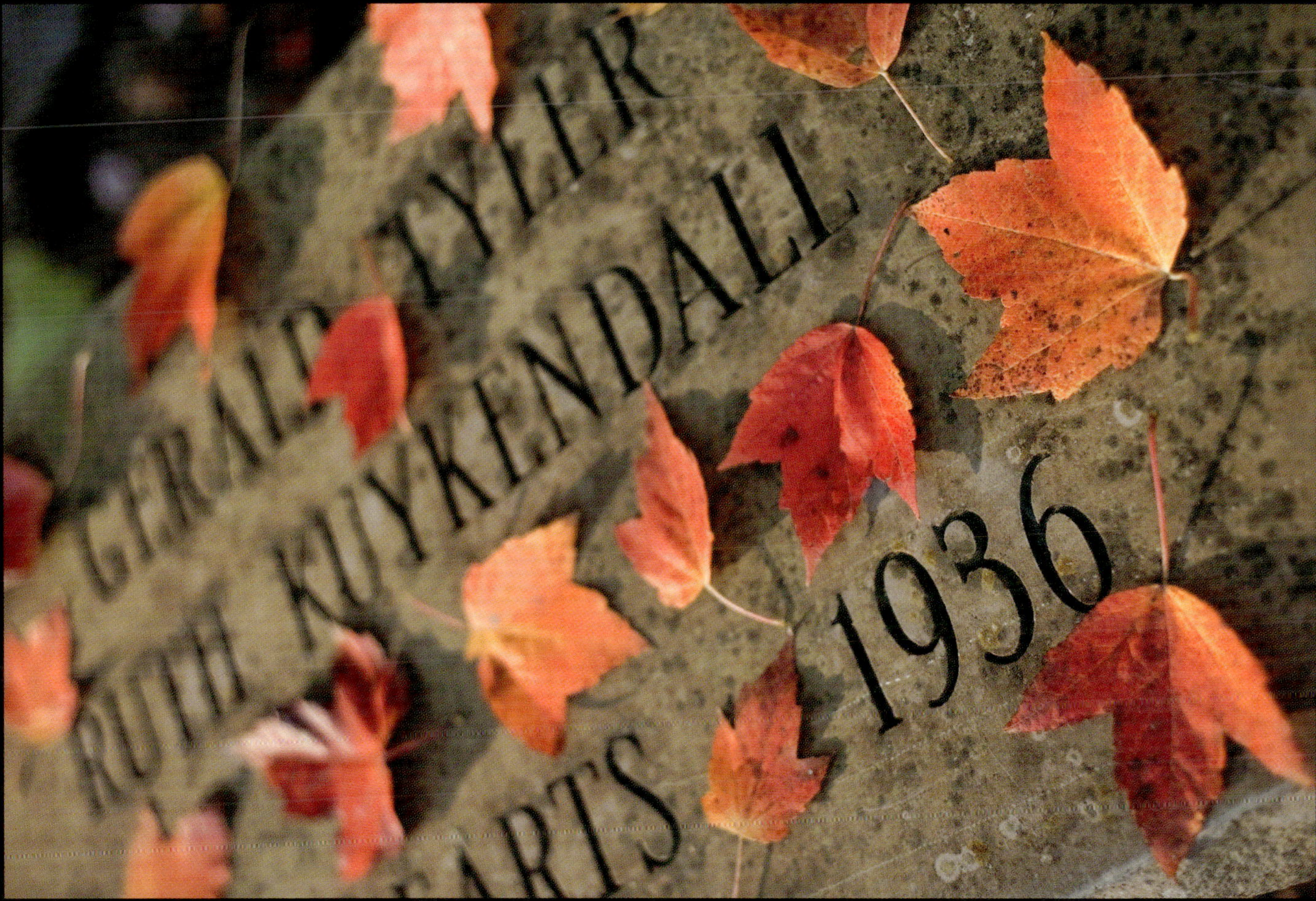


N 36°24.272’
W 093°44.291’
Elevation 1247’

N 36°24.273’
W 093°44.288’
Elevation 1248’

*(Previous right and current pages)* Sweet Spring apparently got its name from the taste of its waters. Previously known as Spout Springs, it was originally located in the valley below where it sits today. Local laborers dug and searched for the waters above the hillside before finding the more assessable location seen today. William James and John Waldrip constructed the semi-circular limestone enclosure *(pictured at left)* that still stands today. The spring incorporated officially on February 15, 1886, with Ordinance #77. *(Pictured above)* Gracing the park are benches etched with names of donors, previous lovers of the spring park.

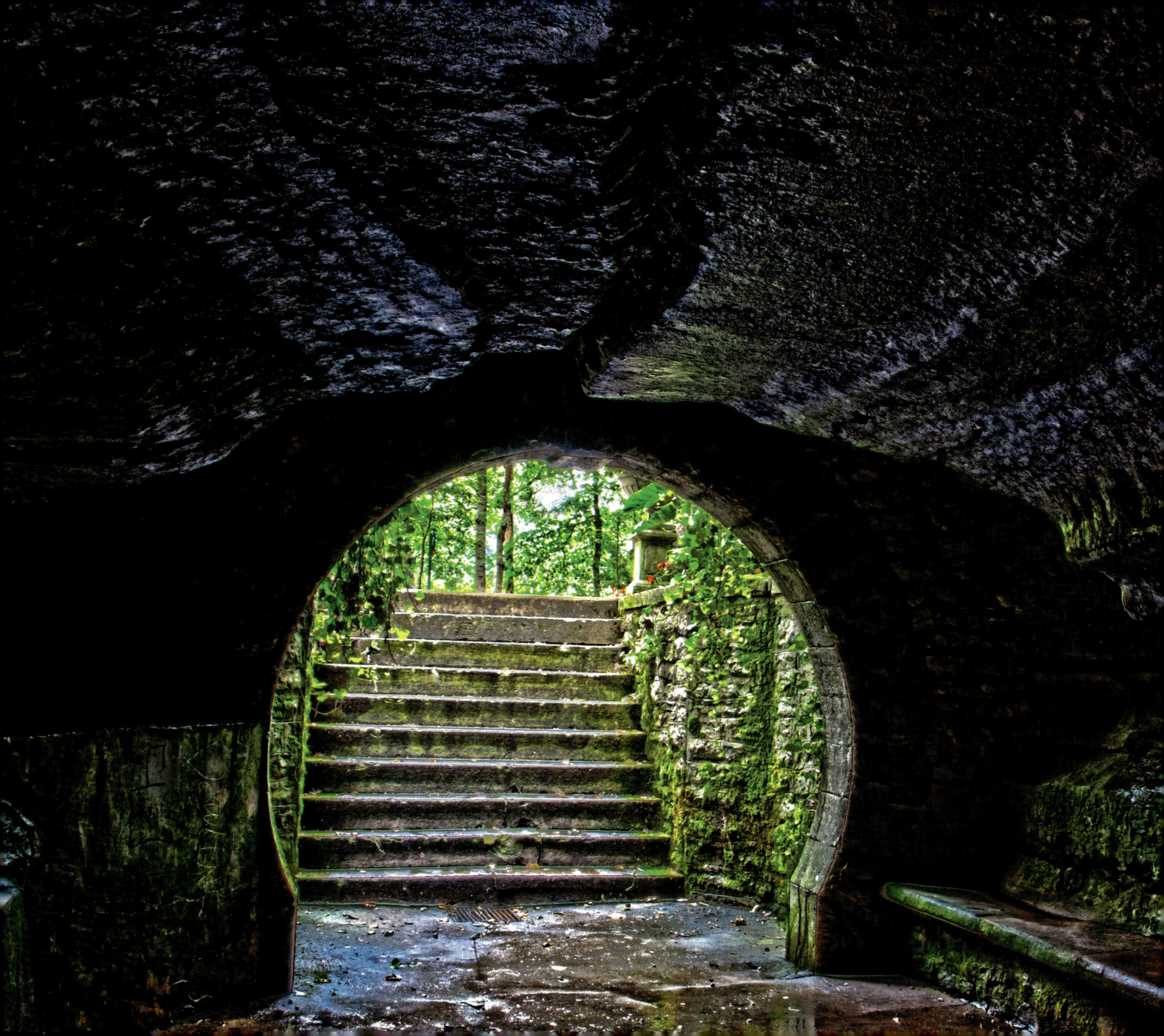

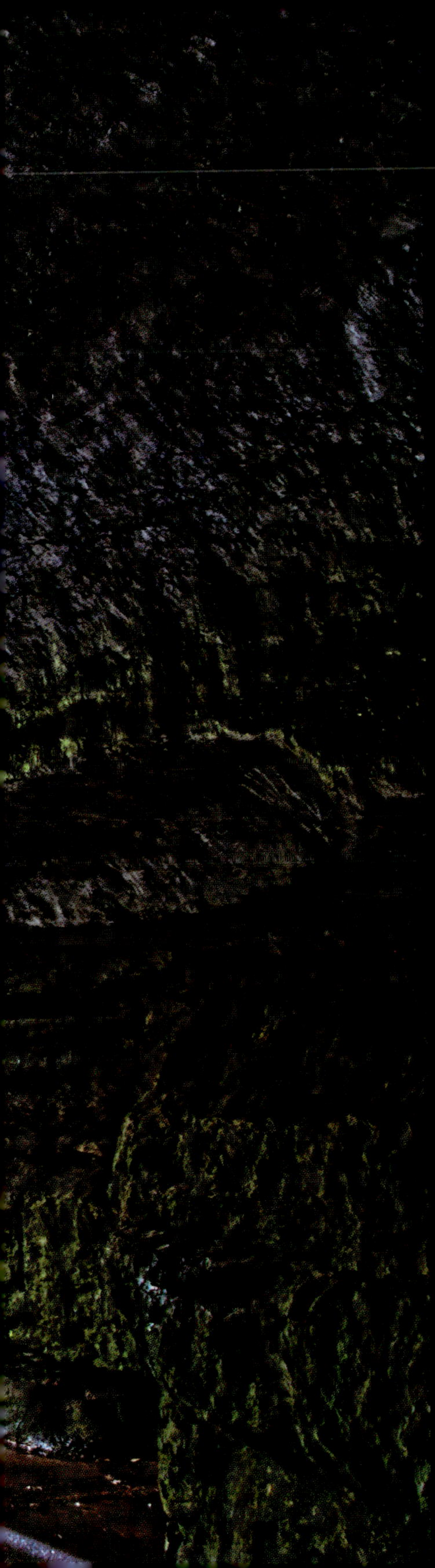

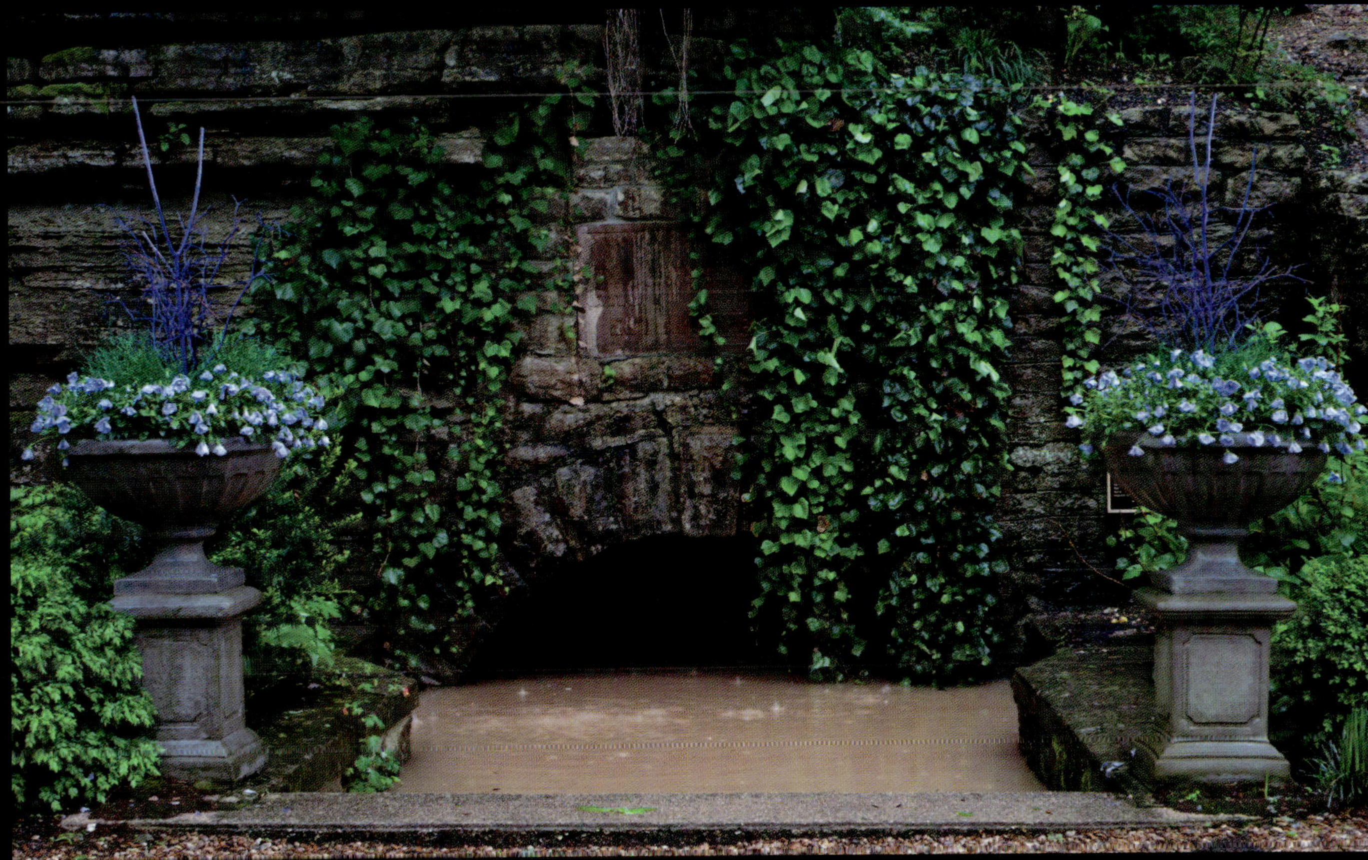

The last words of theologian and mathematician Paolo Sarpi found emblazoned upon the entrance to Grotto Spring are "Esto Perpetua" or let it be perpetual. Once the early townspeople found the spring nestled under an overhanging rock ledge just above Dairy Hollow, they constructed the ornate limestone enclosure to showcase this spring, which still stands today, believing it would flow forever. *(Pictured at left)* This is a view from inside the limestone enclosure looking out onto Spring Street, previously known as The Boulevard. *(Pictured above)* The view from outside as the spring engulfs the enclosure due to heavy rains in 2011. The rains almost washed a section of Spring Street down the hillside. The area is such a perfect humid climate for mushrooms during the spring that morels have sprouted up around the stairs leading into the Grotto. Inside the limestone enclosure, one can often find makeshift honor shrines like a solitary burning candle with hand-written notes to fallen loved ones strewn at its base.

N 36°24.671'
W 093°44.309'
Elevation 1270'

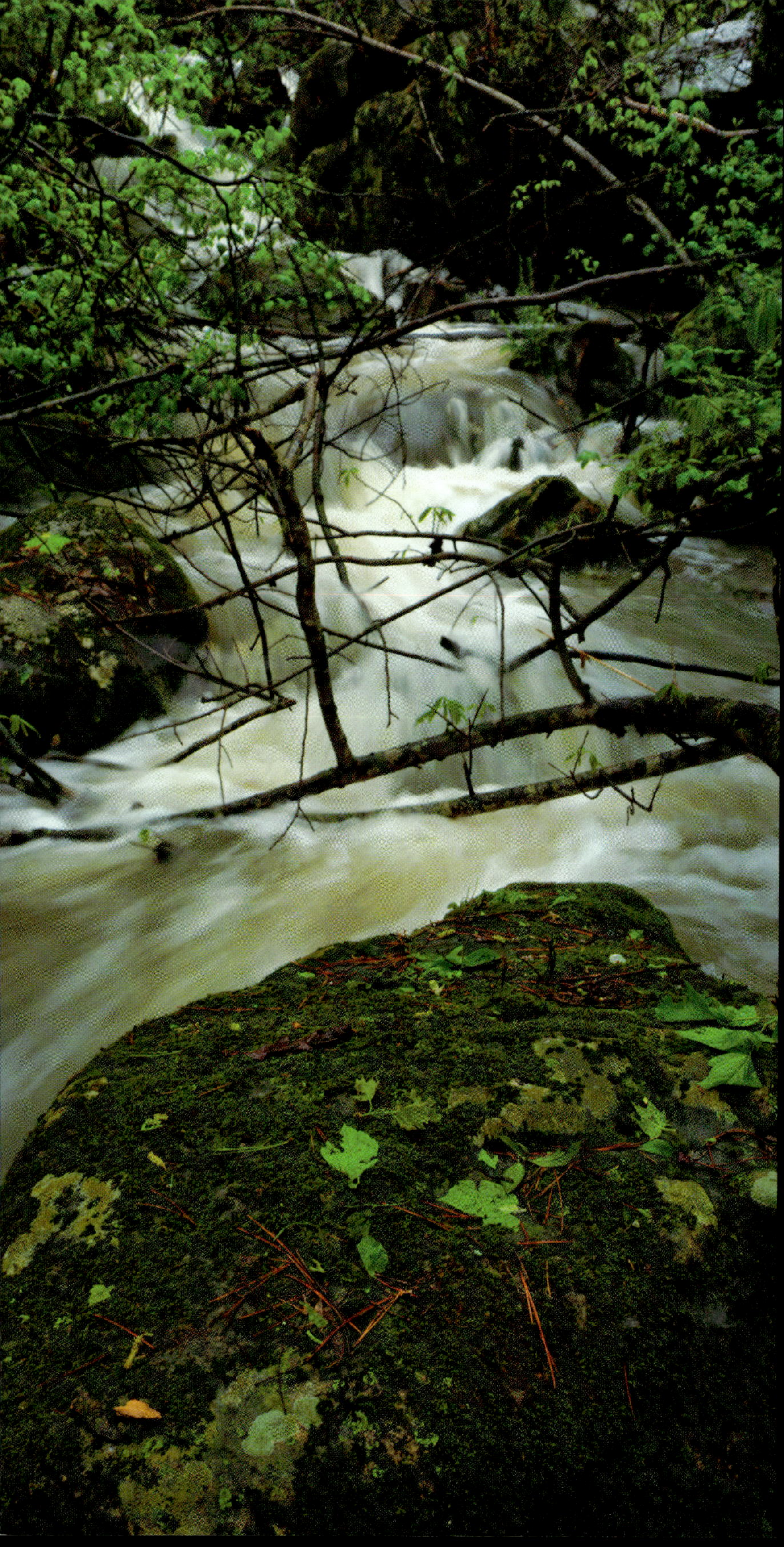

Though Magnetic spring never did magnetize the metal objects placed within its waters as first thought, it did draw locals and tourists to the free-flowing spring from the 1890s to the present. General Powell Clayton turned over ownership of the spring to the City of Eureka Springs in 1911. Workers hand excavated an area of 38' to open the main 'head' of one of Eureka's bigger springs. Restoration of the gardens and the spring shelter area took place in the 1980s. Today the park offers a covered picnic pavilion, seasonally decorated gardens, a wet-weather waterfall, moss-covered rock outcroppings, and of course, the historic spring.

N 36°24.605'
W 093°43.827'
Elevation 1114'

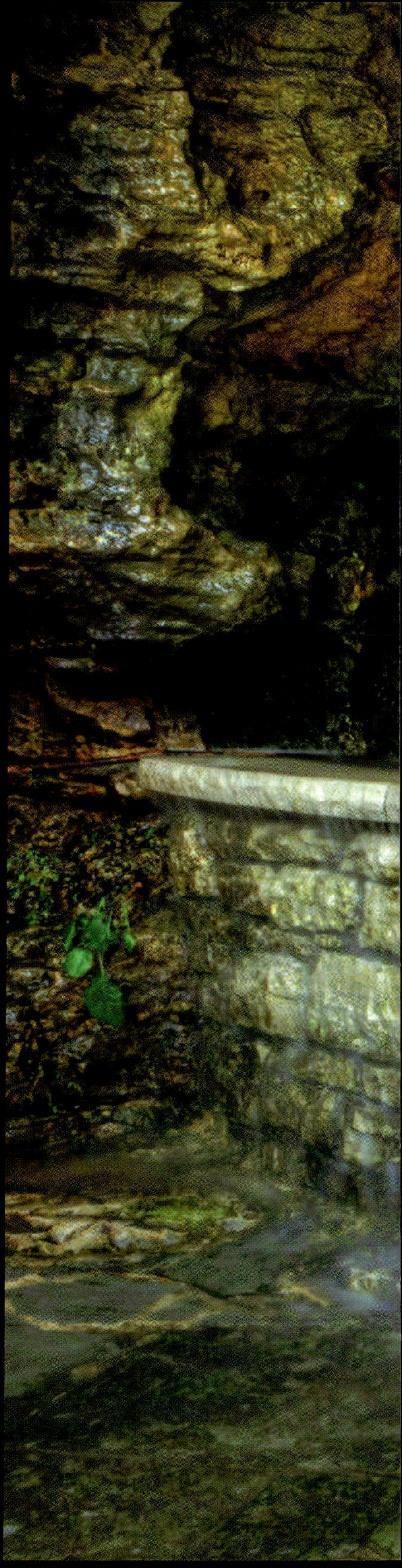

Individuals flocked to the area to seek out healing waters during the turn of the century – damming up springs and creeks into makeshift ponds and swimming holes. Many have crumbled with time, but others have stood the test of time and are still standing today. At left is a damned-up pond alongside Lake Lucerne Road as springtime rain showers send water over the petite dam face and into the valley.

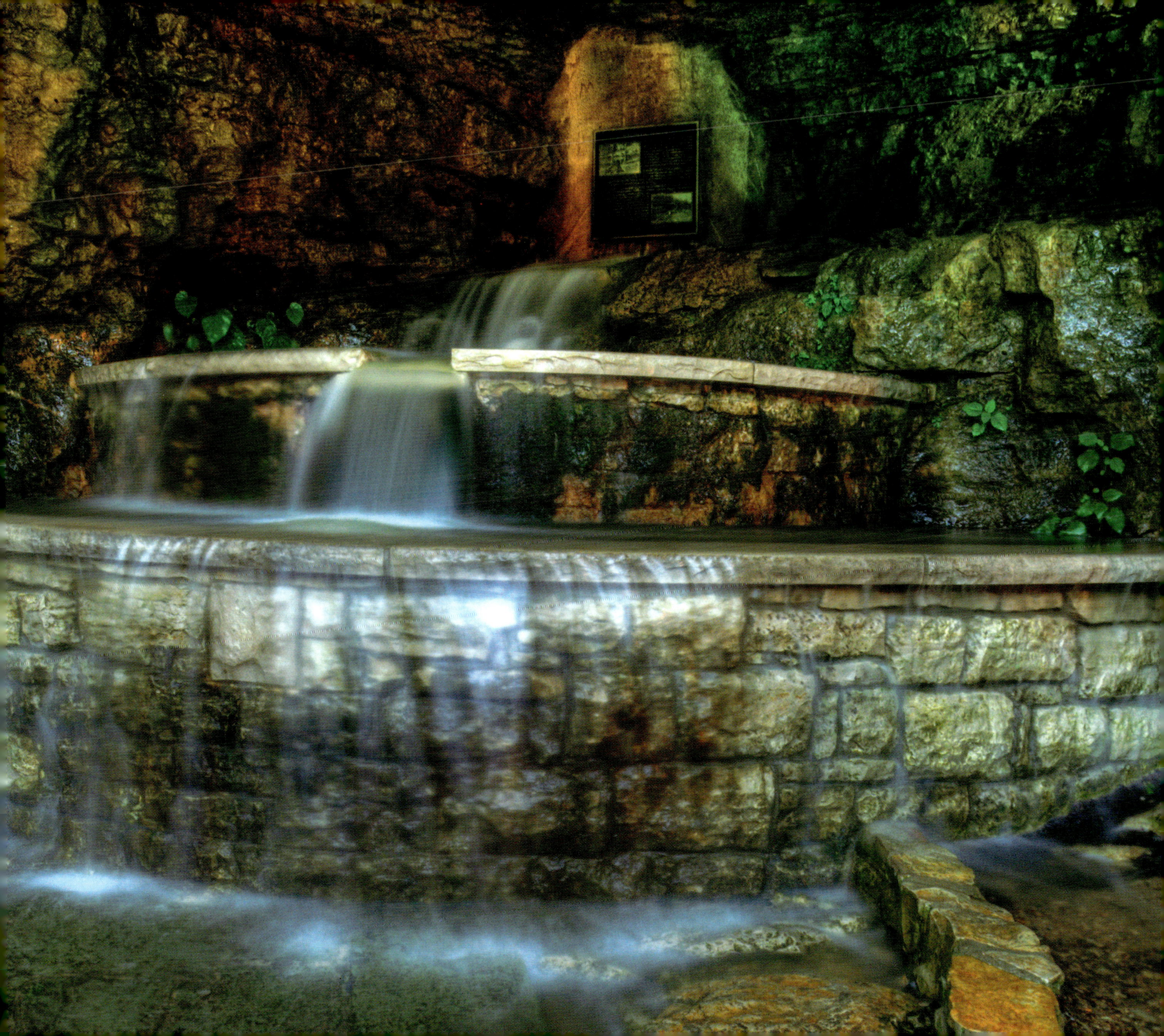

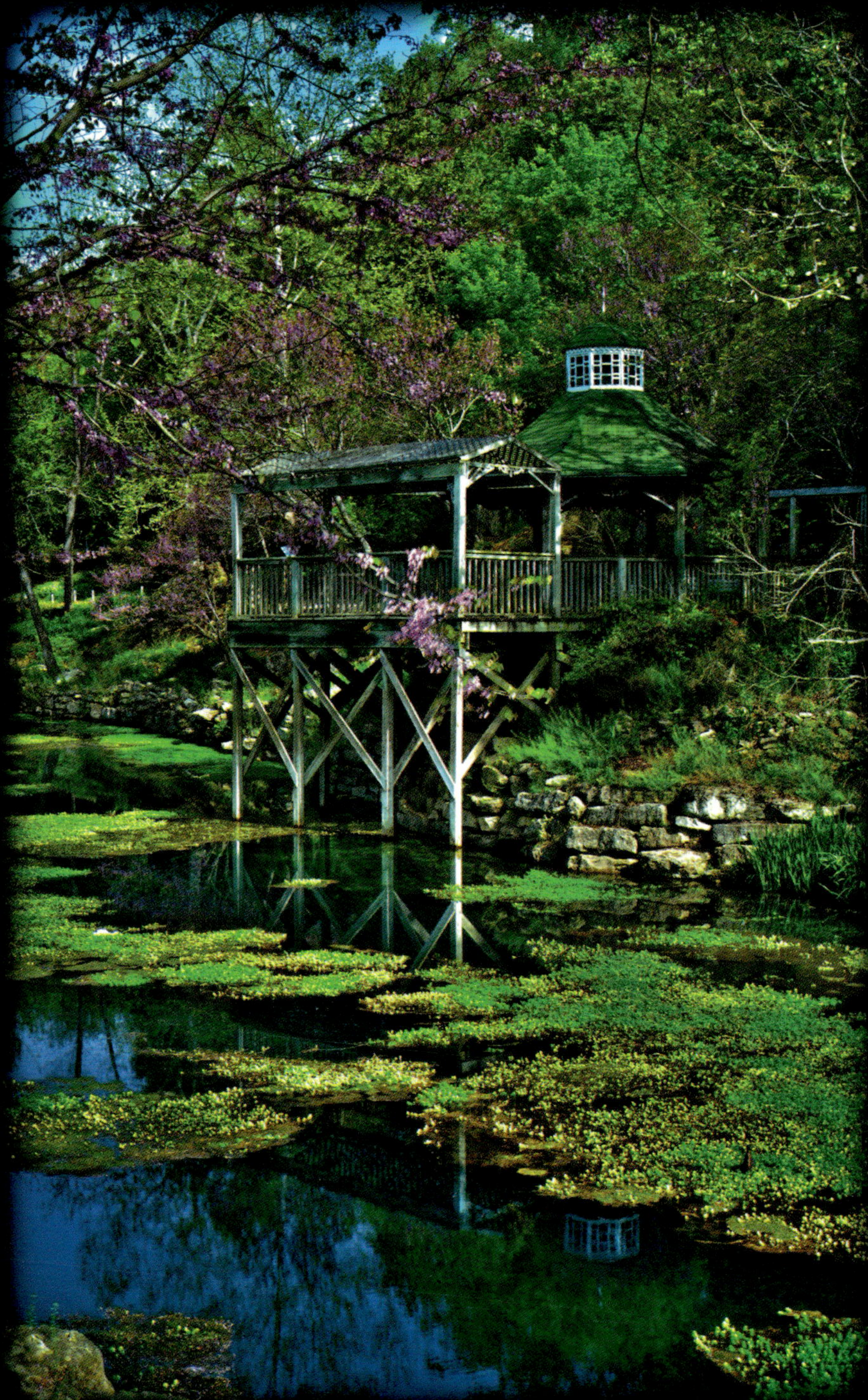

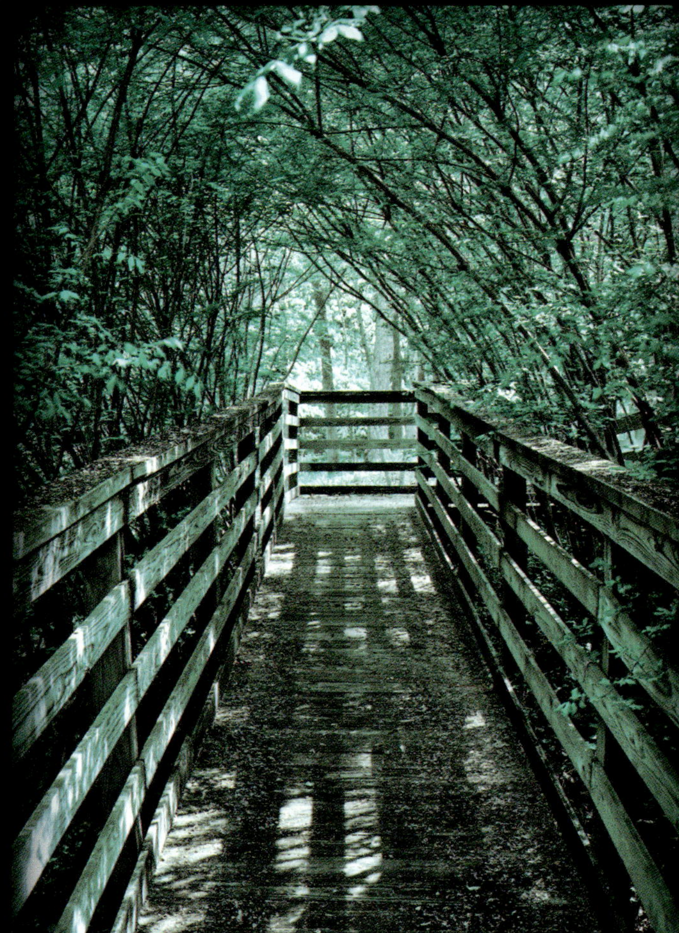

*(Opposite page)* Blue Springs Heritage Center sits on 33 acres adjacent to the White River. The spring sits along the Trail of Tears, emptying an astounding 38 million gallons of pure potable water daily into a blue-hued lagoon stocked with trout. Indians were the first to stumble upon the site and considered it sacred ground. The Osage Indians set a trading post in the area. The Cherokee, bound for Echoto, Georgia, in an involuntary march, stopped at the spring for healing and hope while on the Trail of Tears. The flowing Blue Spring waters powered a corn-grinding mill erected in the 1840's. From 1948 to 1993, the spring served as a tourist attraction with only the mill's turbine remaining.

N 36°27.857'
W 093°48.745'
Elevation 908'

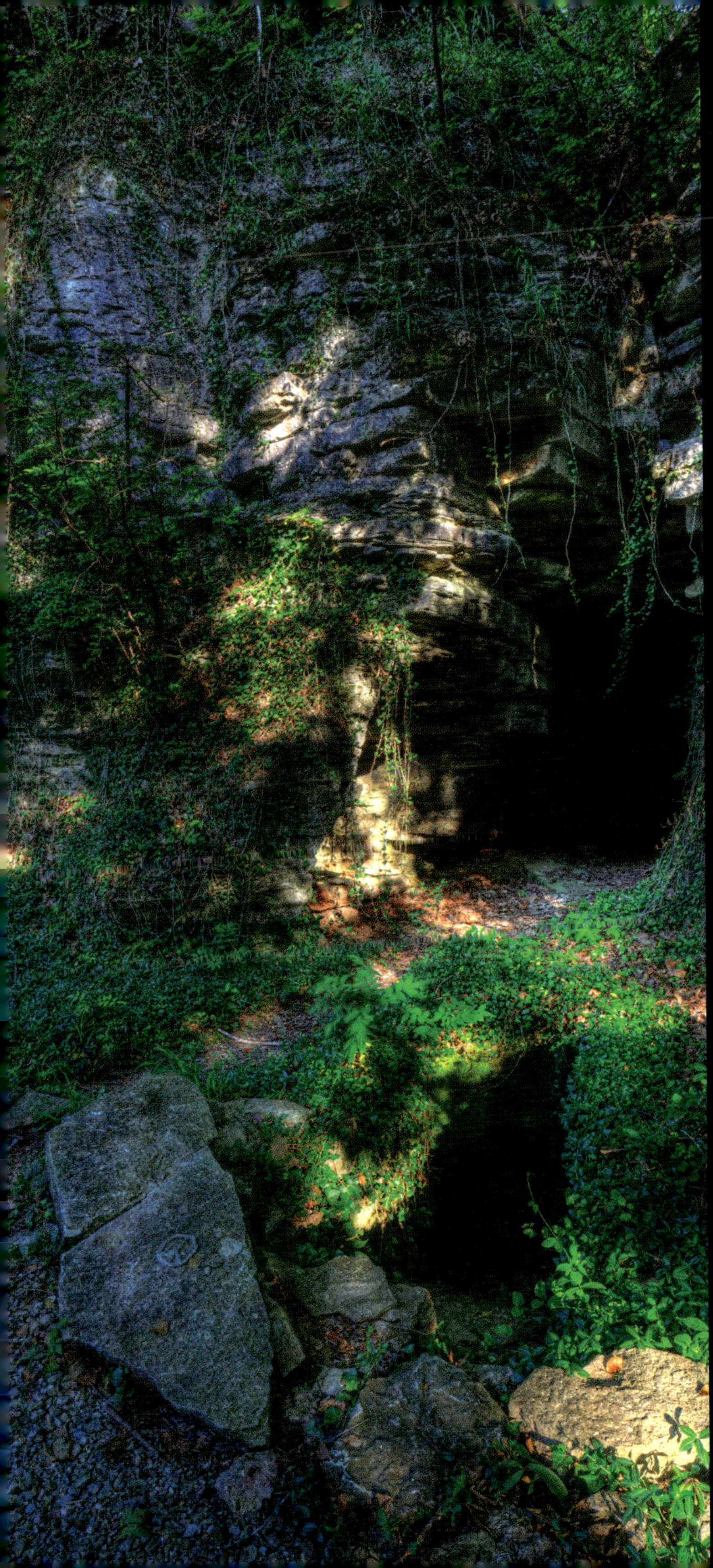

Old Solider Spring sits alongside a one-lane dirt road off East Mountain. The spring flows forth from a small cave where water collects as it drips from a pipe into a small pot sitting inside a dugout area in the cave.

N 36°24.296'
W 093°44.047'
Elevation 1252'

Alongside Oil Spring Road, previously Johnson Spring Road, sits Oil Spring. Black Bass Lake, once the source of Eureka Springs' drinking water, sits at the bottom of an area called Oil Spring Gulch. There is evidence of Native American trails weaving through the hillsides and even a small logging operation from a lost era.

N 36°23.937'
W 093°44.001'
Elevation 1393'

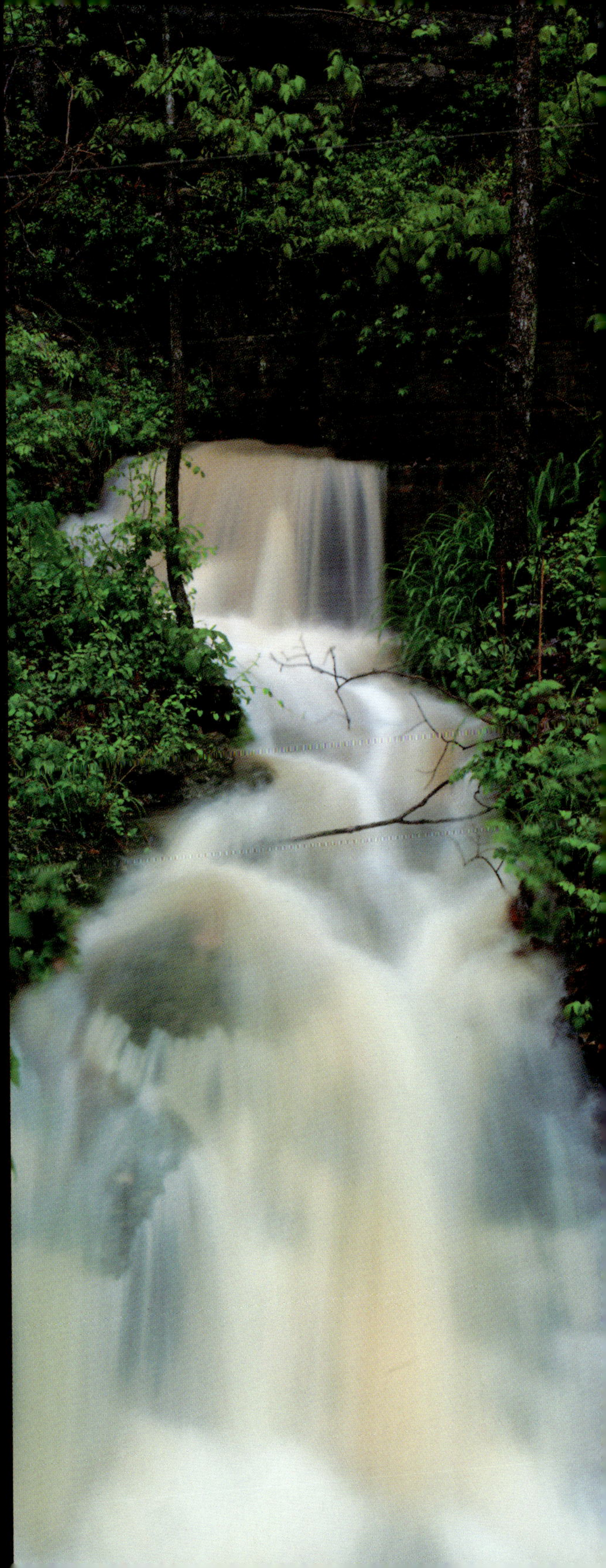

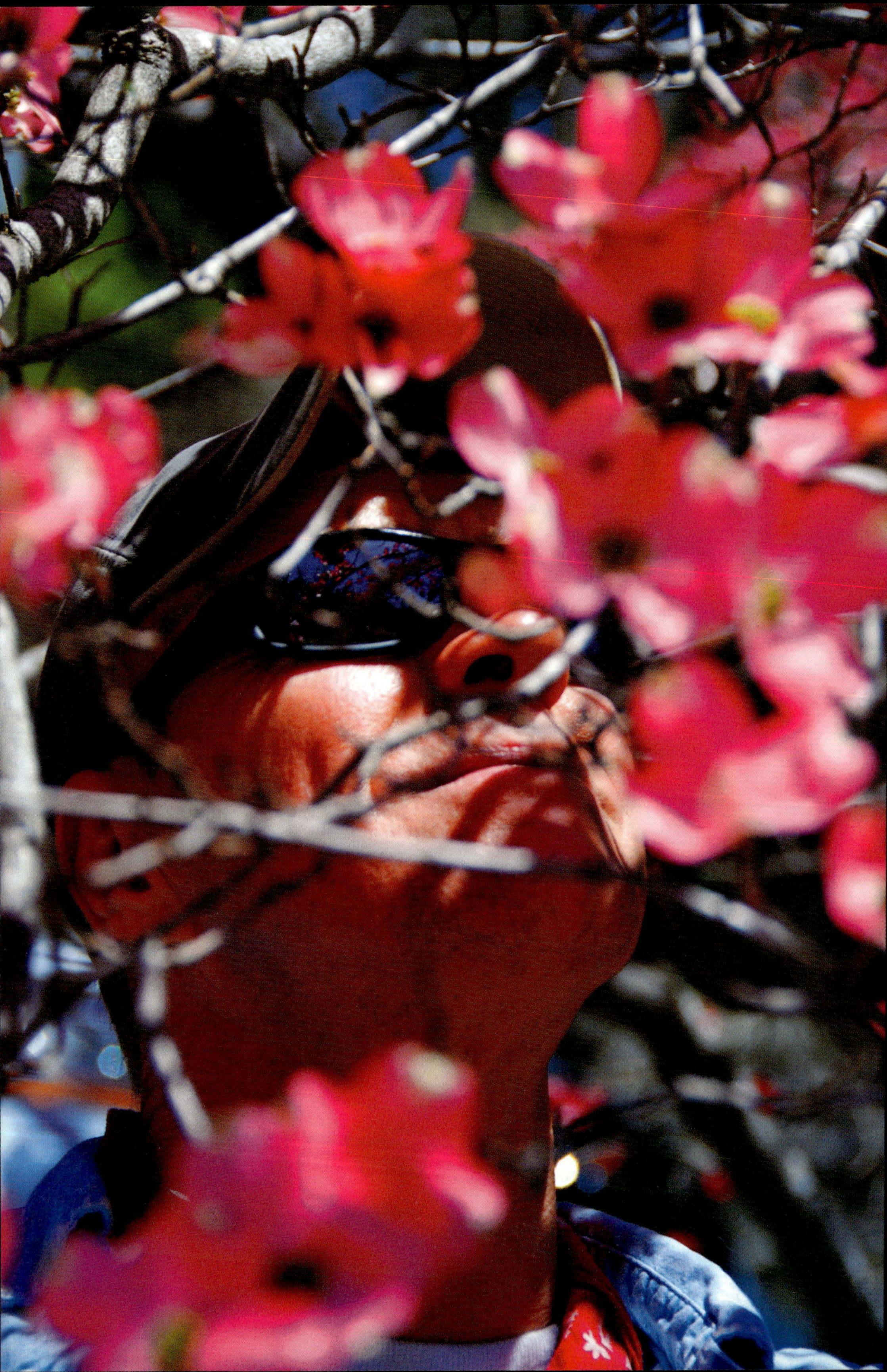

Harding Spring has always been one of Eureka Springs' most treasured springs. Originally, folklore led to the belief that the spring held the cure for blindness, garnered mostly from the story of the youthful Jennie Cowan whose eyesight returned after using the waters. Namesake of the spring, photographer Emmett Harding, enjoyed photographing locals and tourists as they passed through the spring area. Harding fell so much in love with the spring that in 1879 he constructed a petite dwelling near the spring to spend more time in there. On February 16, 1886, Harding Spring incorporated into Eureka Springs under ordinance No. 80, making it one of the first spring reservations. A wooden set of stairs leads to a boardwalk for those wanting the view from the top of the massive rock face for which the spring is known. A precarious rock within the park has etched on its face the words, "God's little miracles are all around us - Loving memories of Dave Whyte." Eastview Cottage, built before 1880 and one of the oldest original structures within the Historic District, is adjacent to the park.

N 36°24.334'
W 093°44.235'
Elevation 1214'

Upon first seeing one of the city parks, it is obvious something is different. Art meets landscaping in an eclectic mix that only one resident can effectively meld – DonE Allen. Thanks to much of DonE's work, each park is elaborately designed and laid out to match the current season, and no two are ever alike.

N 36°24.275'
W 093°44.307'
Elevation 1388'

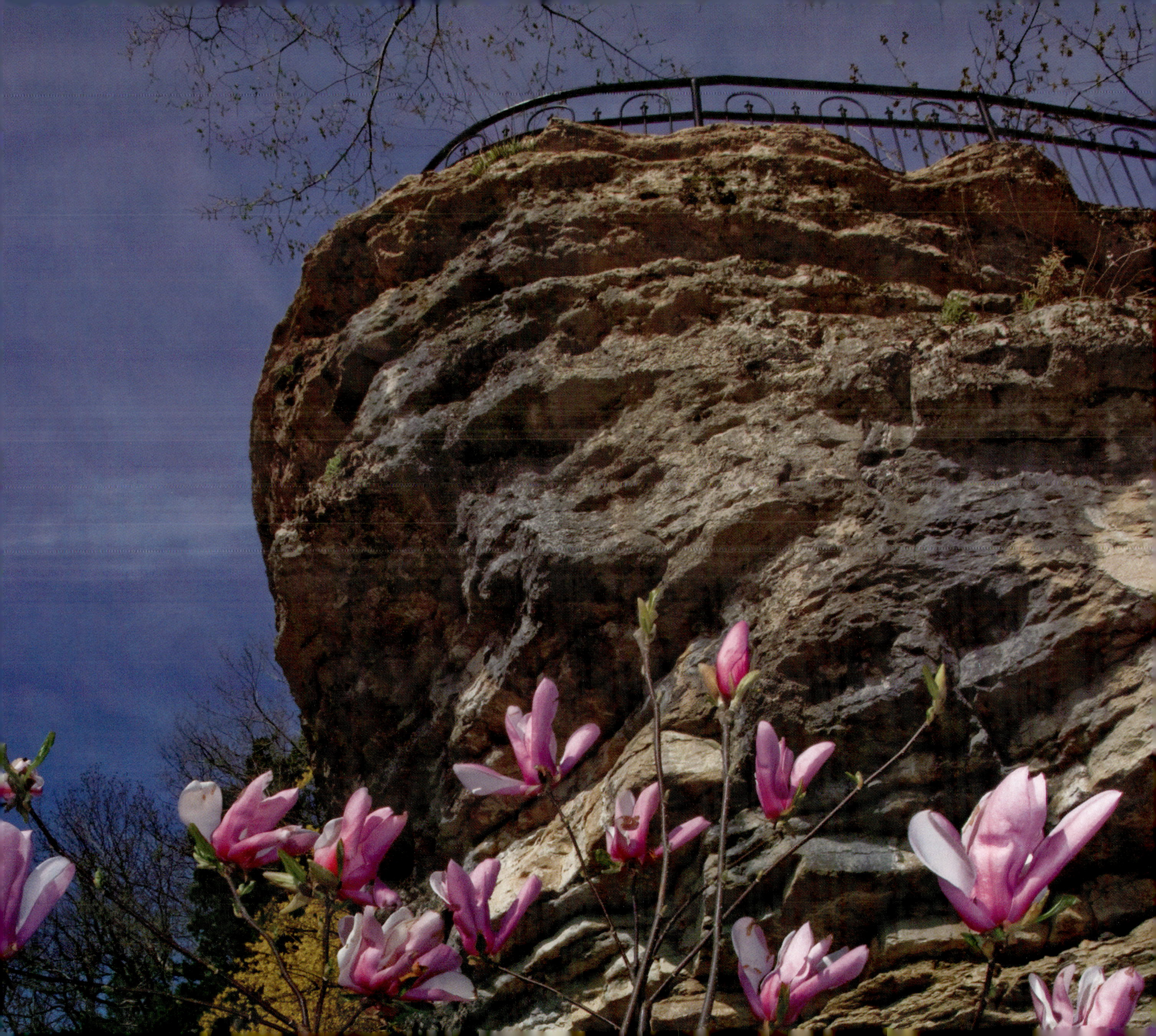

Massive flooding in the 1920s and 1930s resulted in the U.S. Army Corps of Engineers approaching Congress with a plan to cull future flooding disasters. The town of Beaver was to be a dam construction area until later surveying concluded the area's geography and geology were too rough. Though it was later built outside of Beaver, the dam continued to be called Beaver Dam, named after Beaver's founder, Wilson Beaver. The U. S. Army Corps of Engineers created this lake by impeding the White River and flooding the valley, including the town of Monte Ne. Beaver Dam was under construction from 1960 until1966, with May 1965 marking the start of power generation. The Beaver Lake construction project amounted to around $43 million (some say closer to $60 million). First erected to control flooding and for power generation, after completion it was utilized for commercial and municipal water supply. Beaver Lake stretches 31,700 acres in Benton, Carroll, Madison, and Washington counties including caves, a large variety of flora, and massive limestone bluffs lining the 487 miles of shoreline. The lake is known nationally for its crystal clear waters, fishing, and sailing.

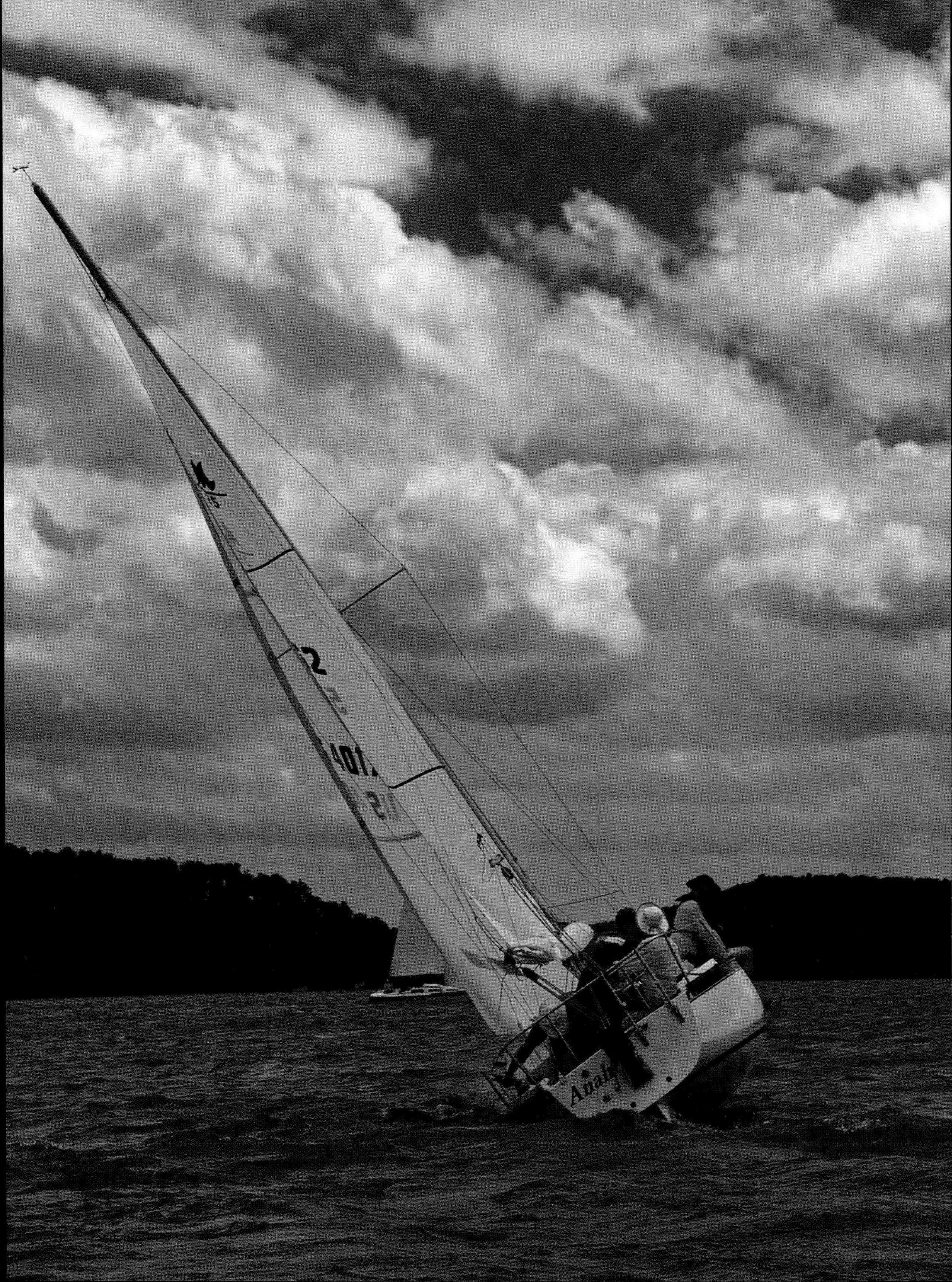

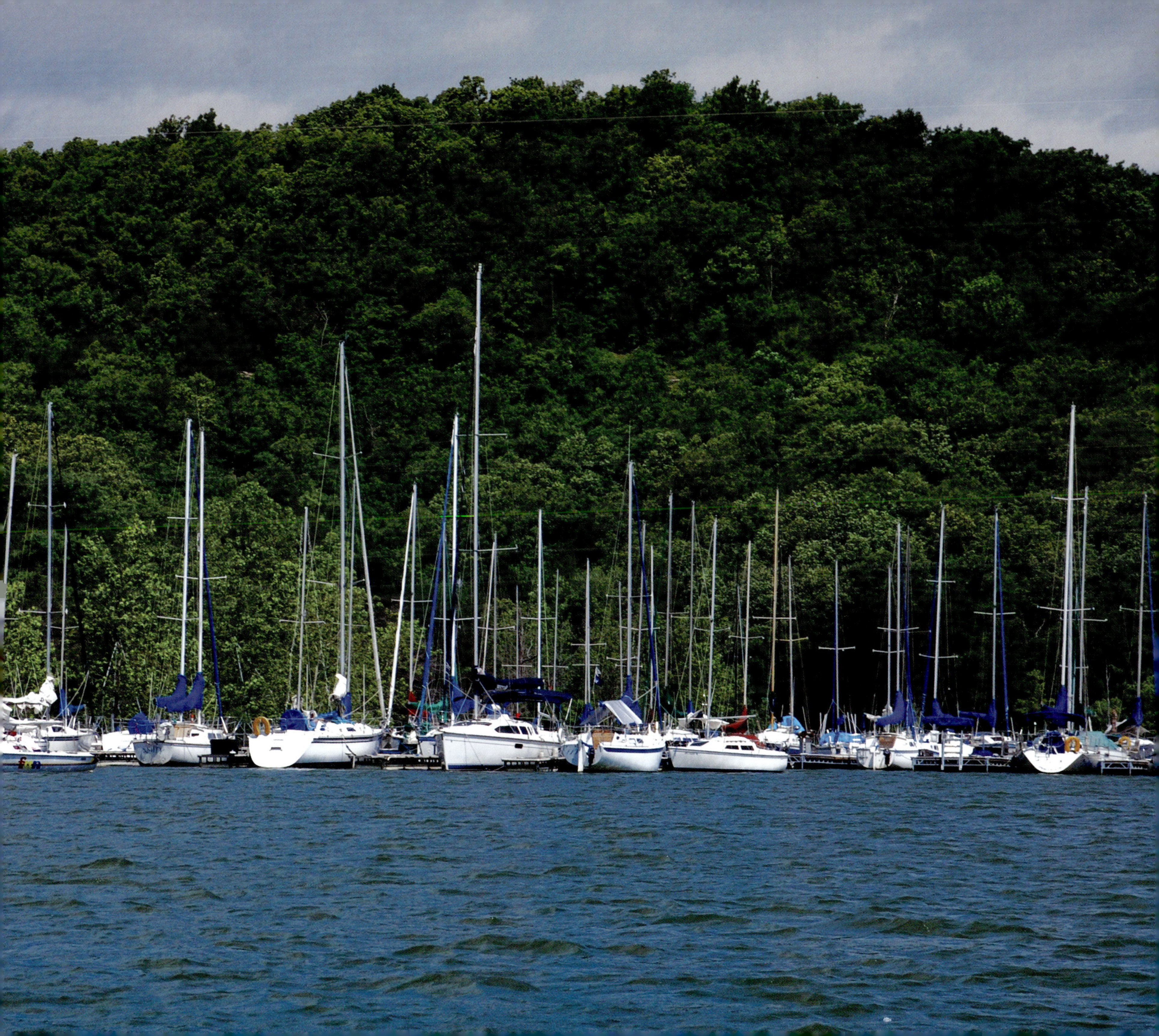

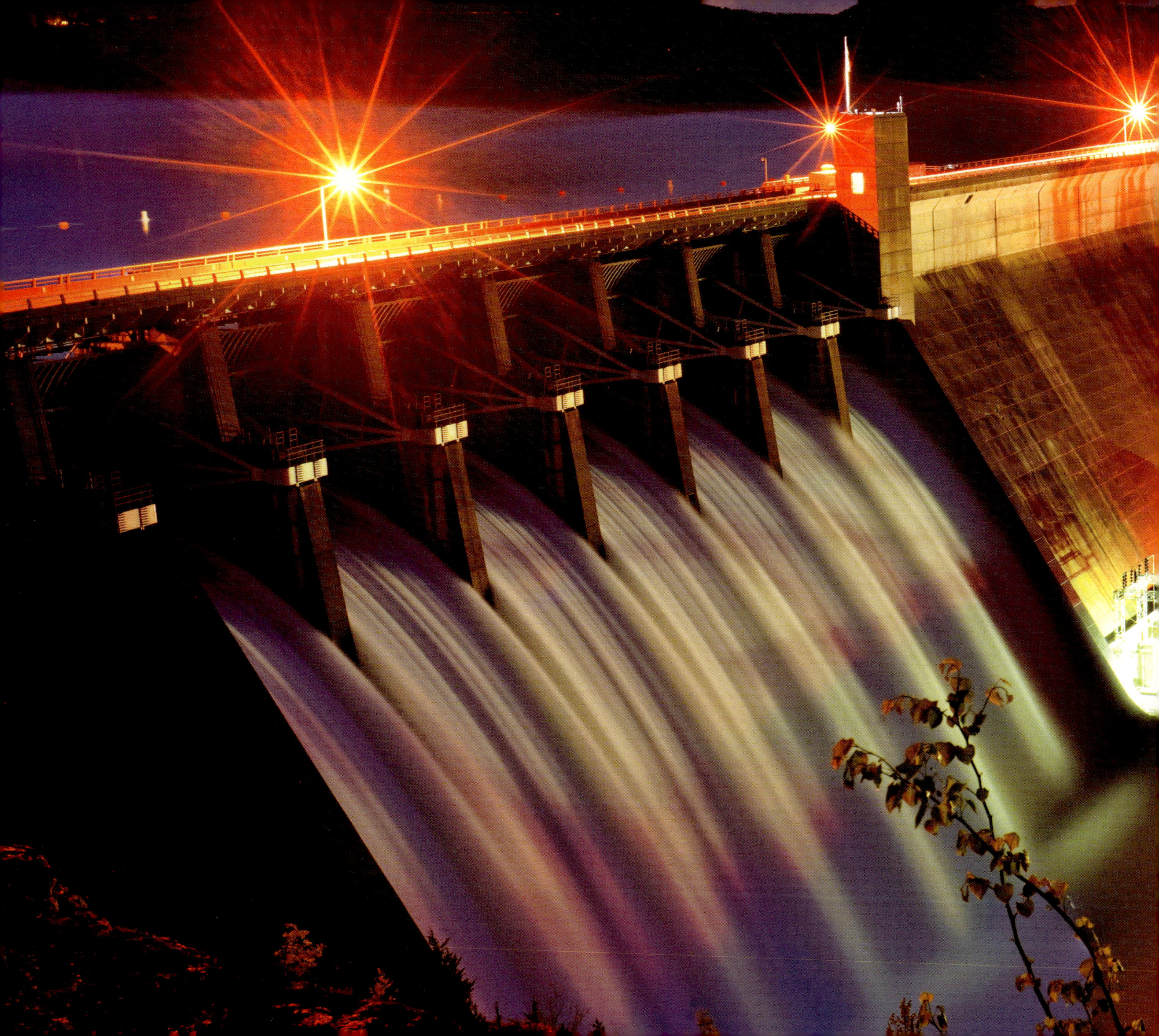

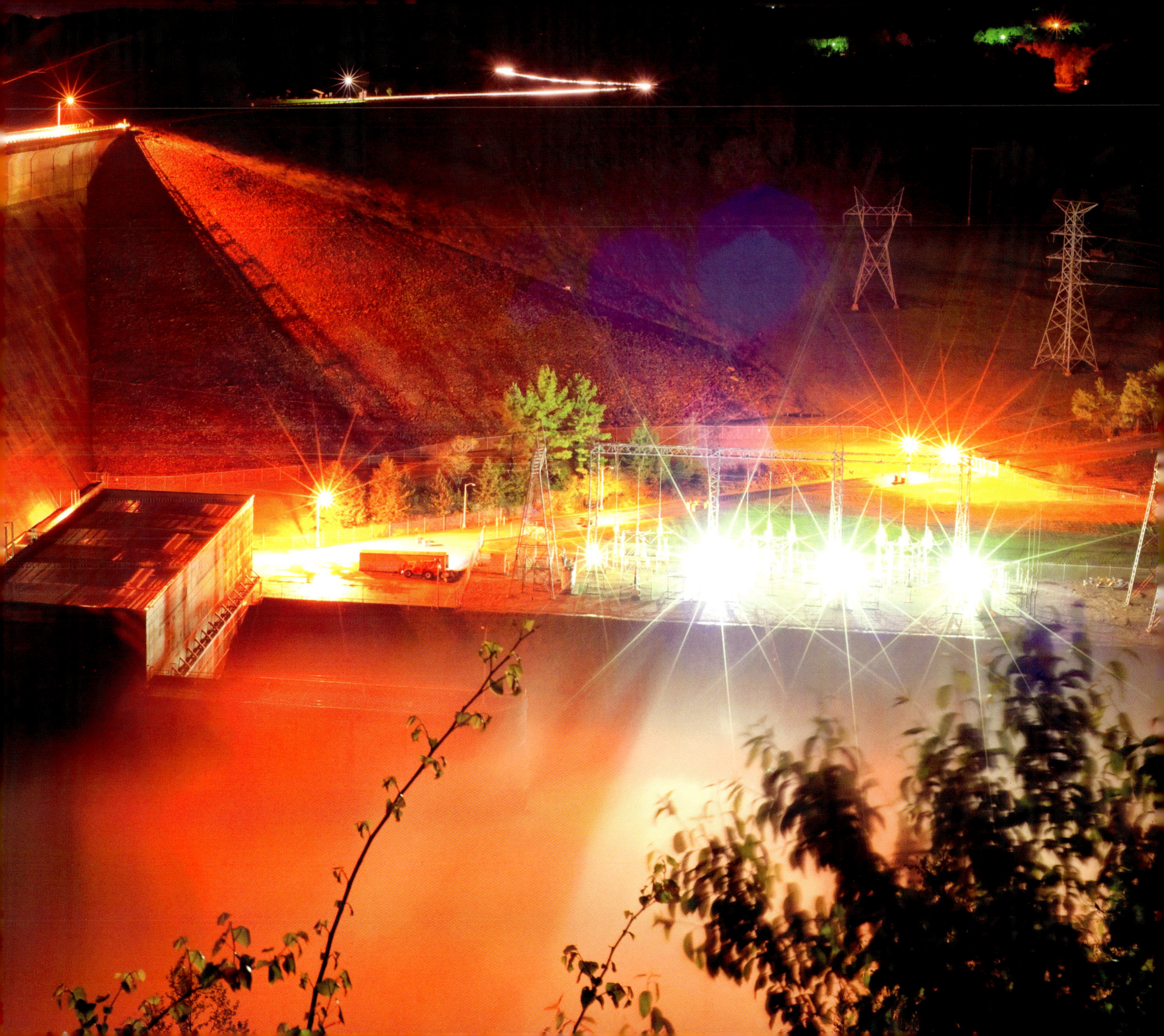

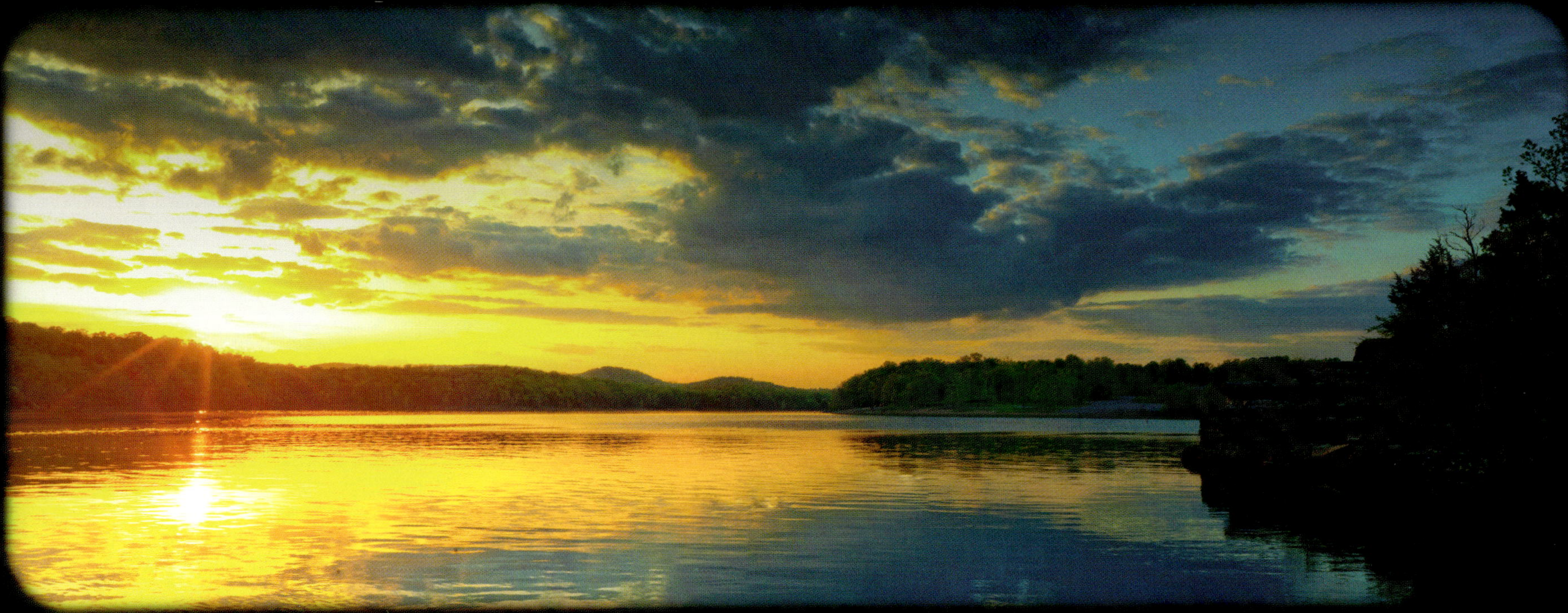

N 36°31.316'
W 093°43.438'
Elevation 875'

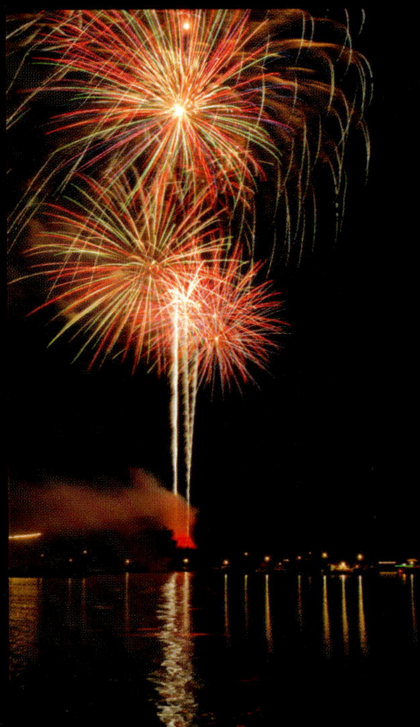

Named after a rock formation along a stretch of Hwy. 165, Table Rock Lake was authorized under the Flood Control Act of September 3, 1943. The man-made reservoir of Table Rock Lake was created by Table Rock Dam, constructed by the U.S. Army Corps of Engineers between 1954 and 1958 along the White River in the Branson, Missouri area. With a surface area of 43,100 acres, the lake spans between Arkansas and Missouri (the majority lying in Missouri) and draws swimmers, boaters, and fisherman from surrounding areas to its 745 miles of shoreline. The White, Kings, and James Rivers flow into the lake, and only the White River outflows. Lake temperatures vary from 42 degrees to 90 degrees, depending on the season.

N 36°31.539'
W 093°43.625'
Elevation 942'

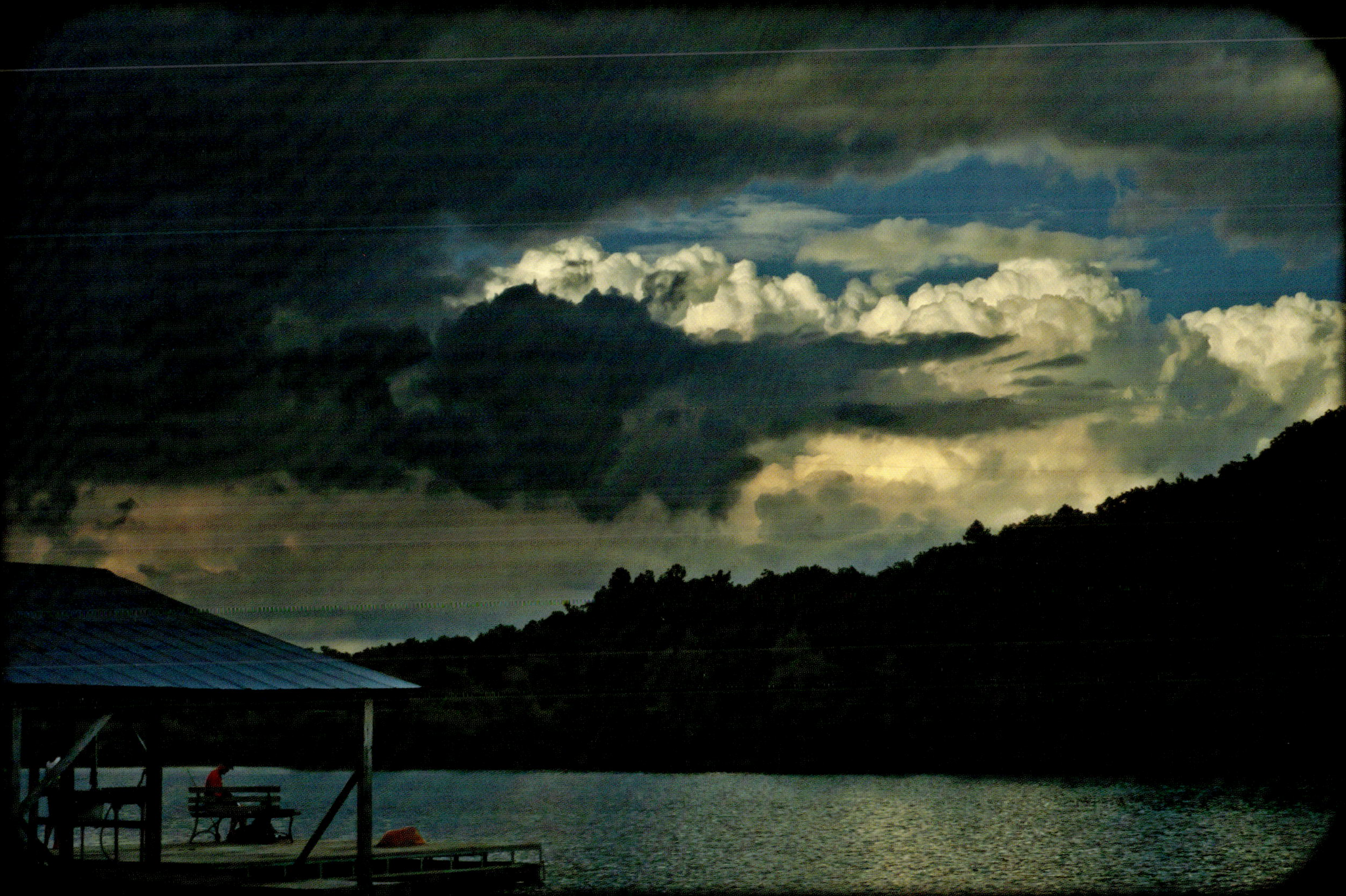

Natural free flowing springs feed the 85 acre lillypad-laced Lake Leatherwood – held back by one of the countries largest hand laid and locally cut
Natural free-flowing springs feed the 85-acre, lily pad laced Lake Leatherwood. One of the country's largest hand-laid and locally-cut limestone dams holds the lake water back. Lake Leatherwood sits on a wooded 1600 acres, and has numerous hiking and biking trails, camping sites, cabins, a marina, and tons of great fishing. The park hosts one of Eureka Springs' largest outdoor sporting activities, the annual Xterra races, among many others. The waters hold blue gill, bream, catfish, crappie, and largemouth bass. The park is also a hot spot for bird watchers through the year. The park, built in the 1940s, is located just west of Eureka Springs and is listed on National Register of Historic Places.

N 36°26.077'
W 093°45.553'
Elevation 975'

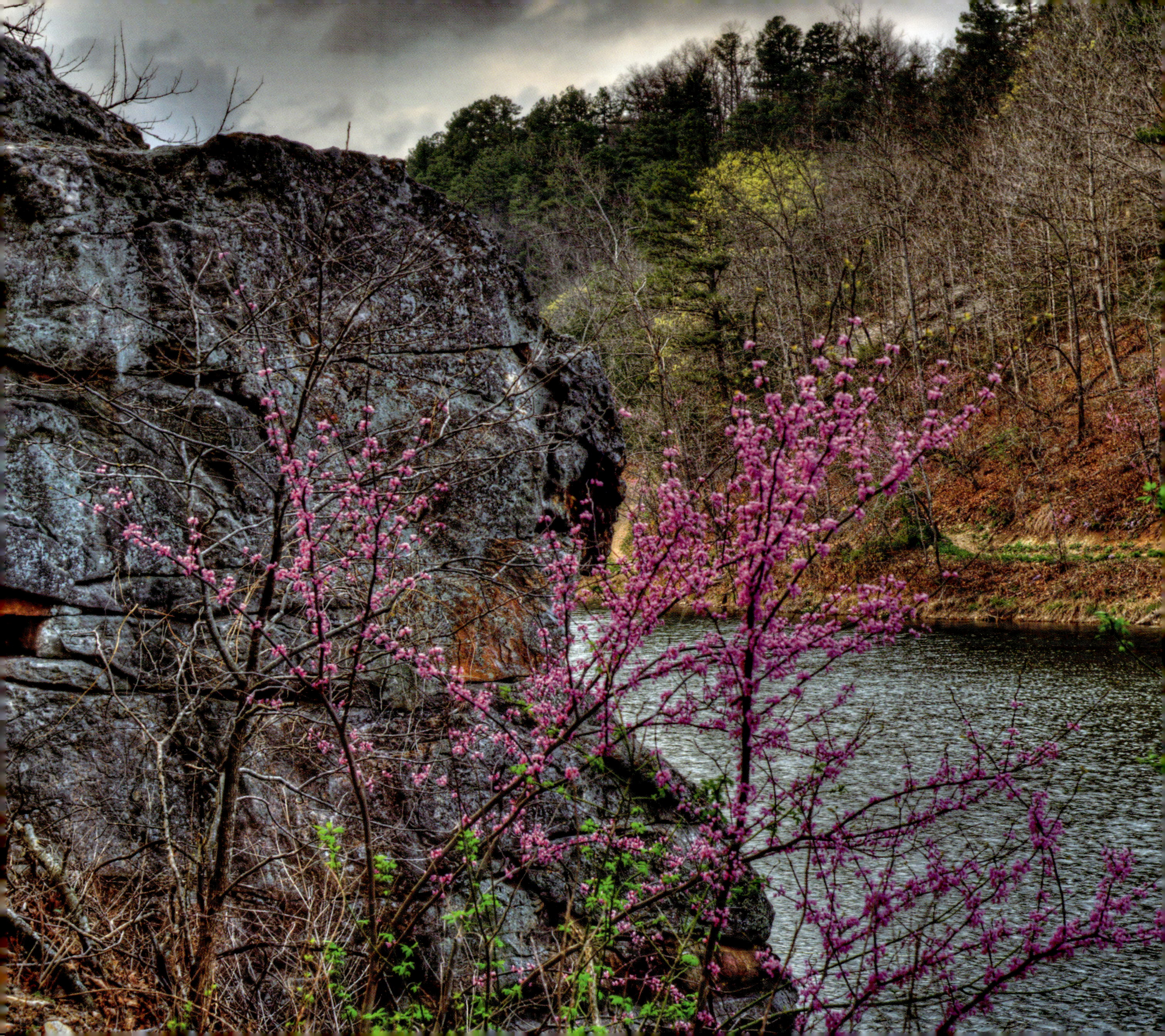

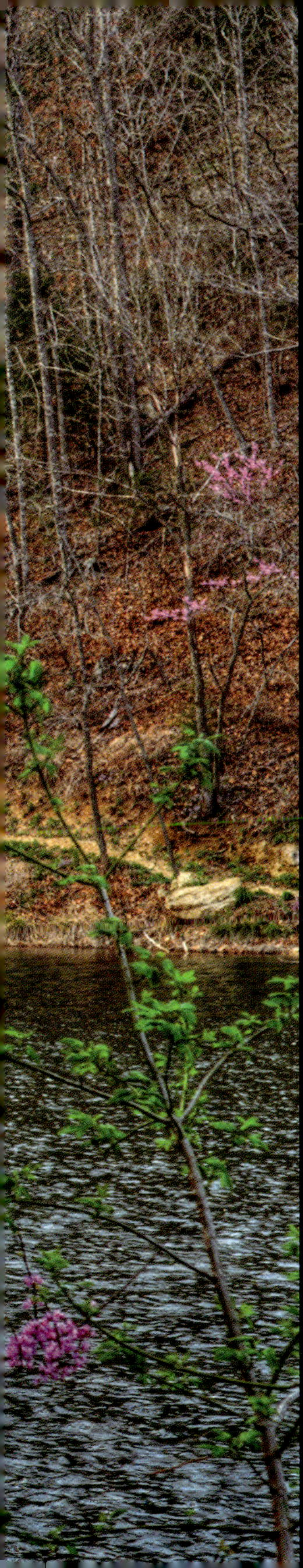

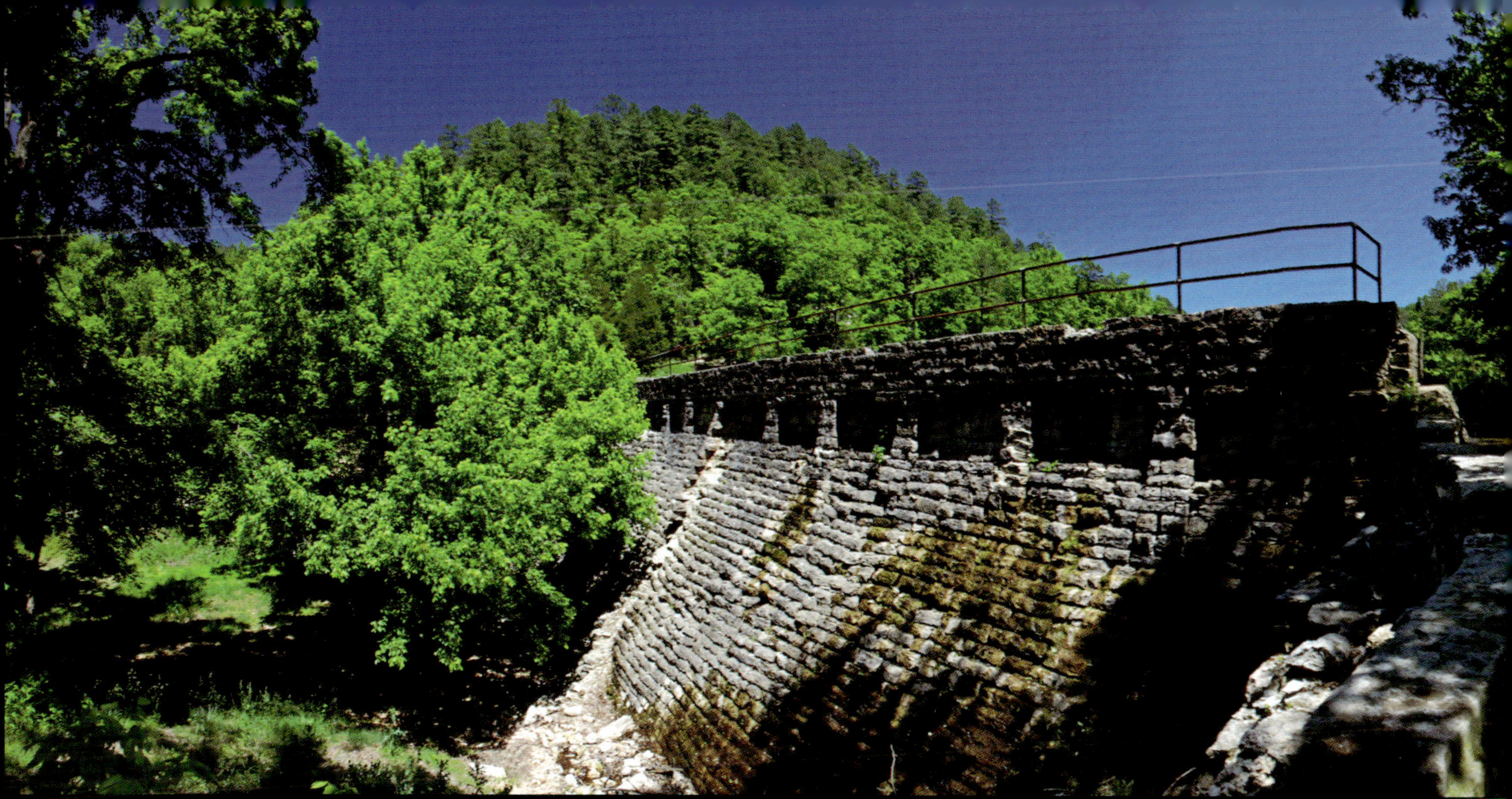

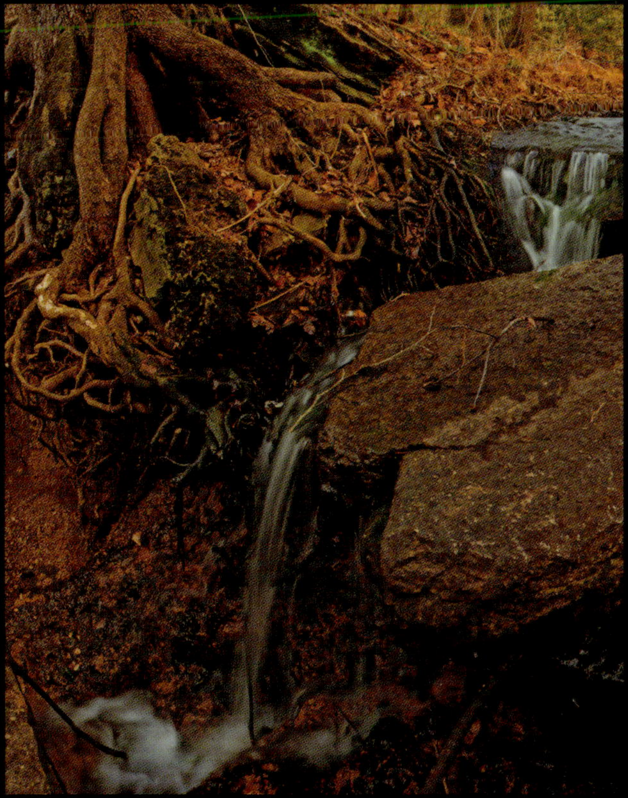

Black Bass Lake and Dam is located the end of Oil Springs Road in Eureka Springs. Around 1894, after Eureka Springs had suffered a set of four major fires between 1883 and 1892, construction began on a 150 foot long, 12-foot high limestone dam fed by Arsenic, Oil, Saucer, and Sycamore Springs. In 1916, an addition to the top of the existing dam added another 450 feet in length, and another 56 feet in height. The reservoir was Eureka Springs' sole drinking water supply into the 1960s. Hikers, fishers, canoers, and kayakers cherish the park for its year-round beauty. Pictured at far left is the aptly-named Standing Rock along the Standing Rock trail. Another rock formation, the St. Joe limestone outcropping, lies along the upper Bluff Trail.

N 36°23.560'
W 093°44.860'
Elevation 1153'

*(Following pages) Pictured is the recently-constructed Oil Spring Trail that connects with the other trail systems.*

N 36°23.768'
W 093°45.054'
Elevation 1249'

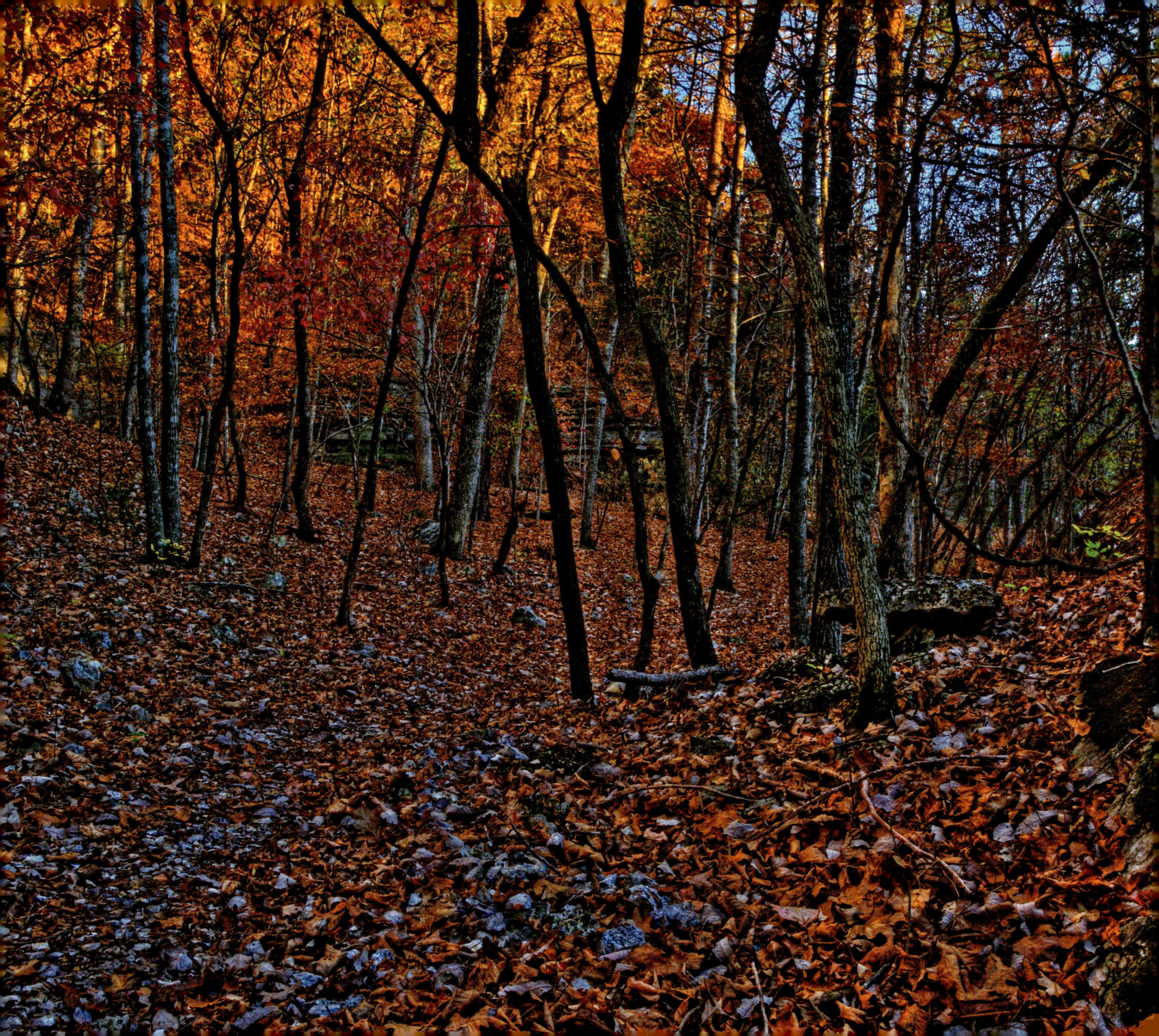

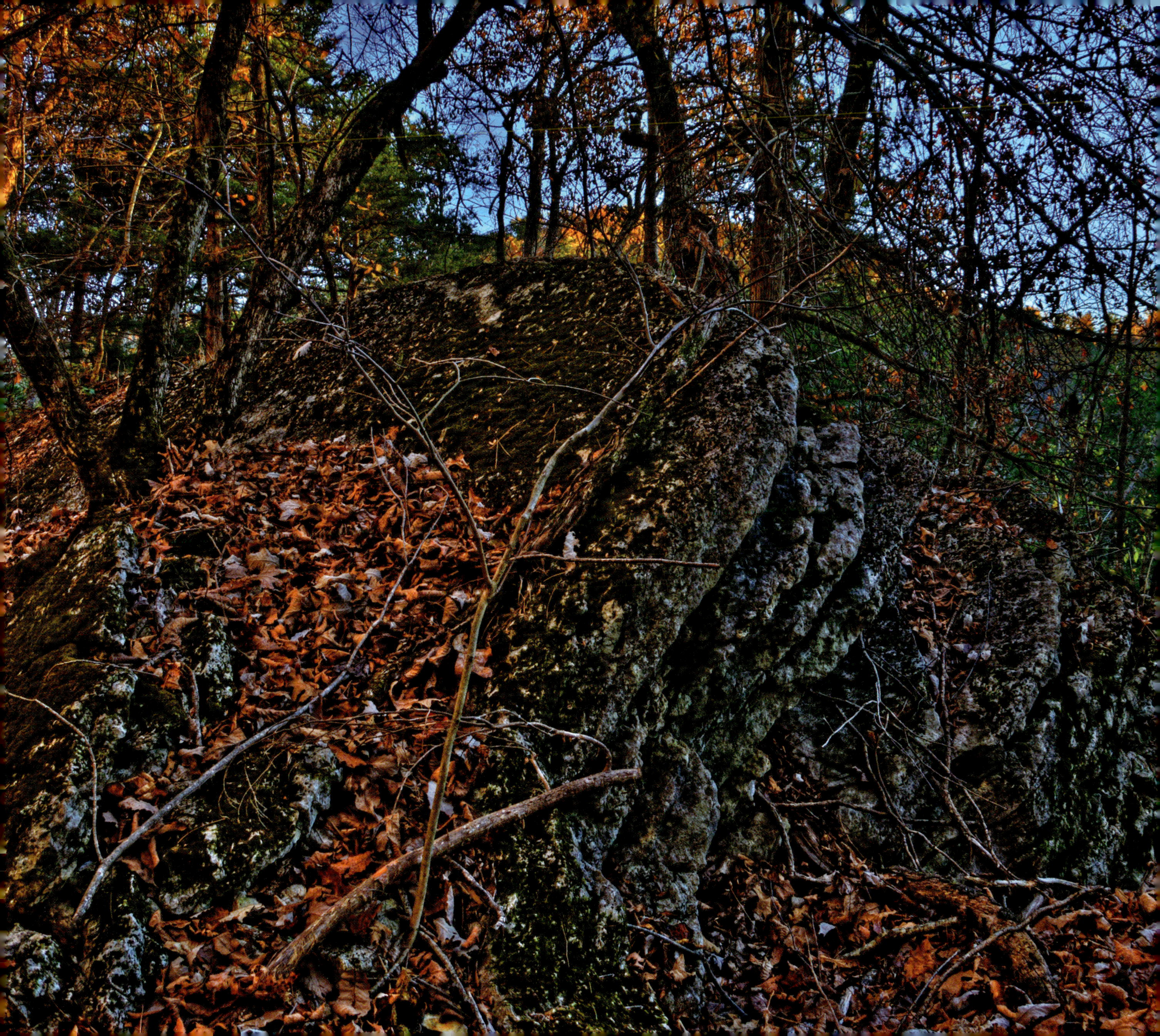

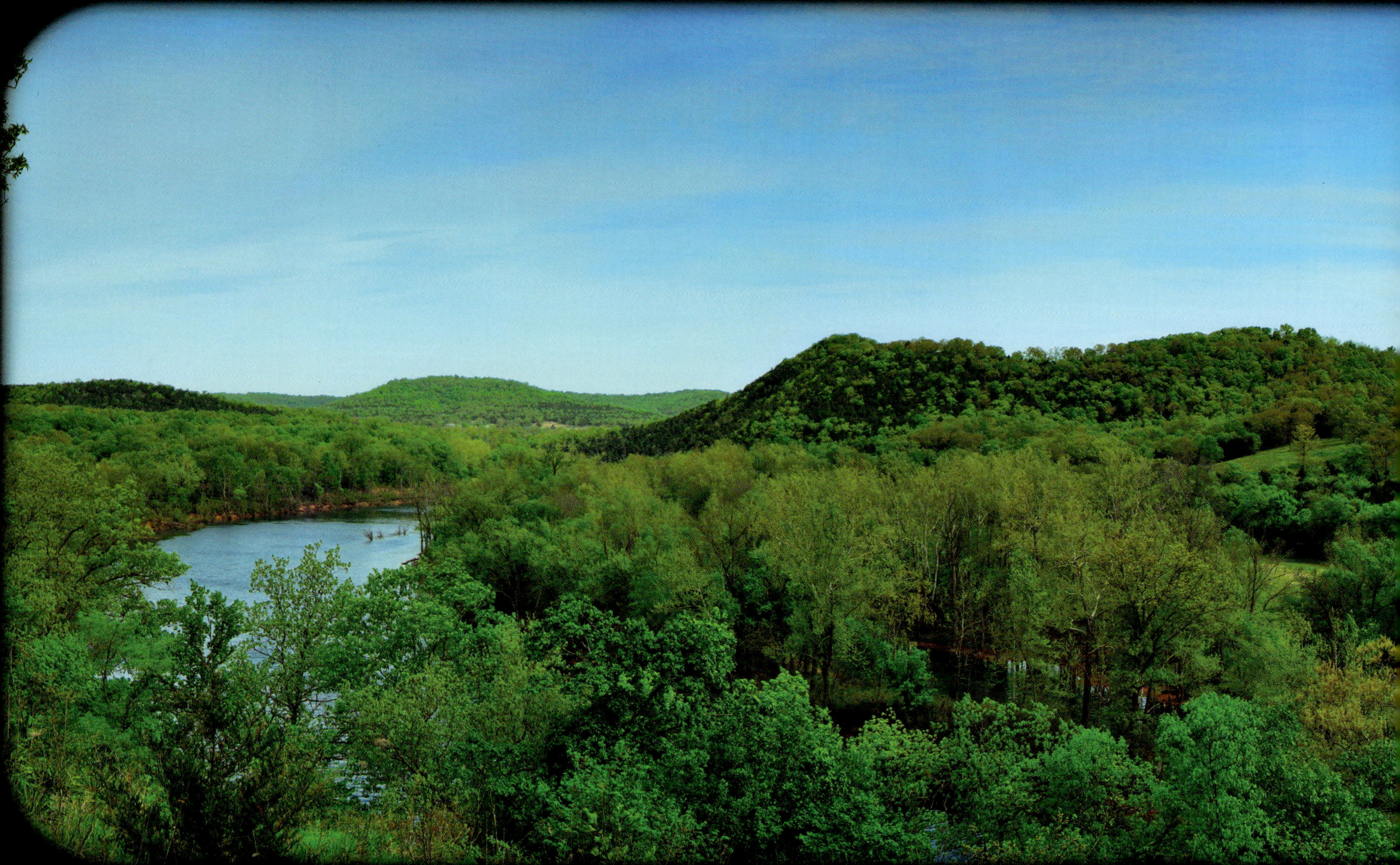

A trout angler's heaven is the White River. Starting in the Boston Mountains deep within the Ozark-St. Francis National Forest, the river flows 685 miles (some sources list 690 miles and others record 722 miles) through Missouri and Arkansas before its mouth touches the Mississippi River in Desha County, entering the floodplain around Newport, Ark. The section just below the Beaver Dam draws trout anglers from across the county, flicking flies across the river's surface. The river pushes over 8,200 cubic feet of Ozark water per second under normal conditions.

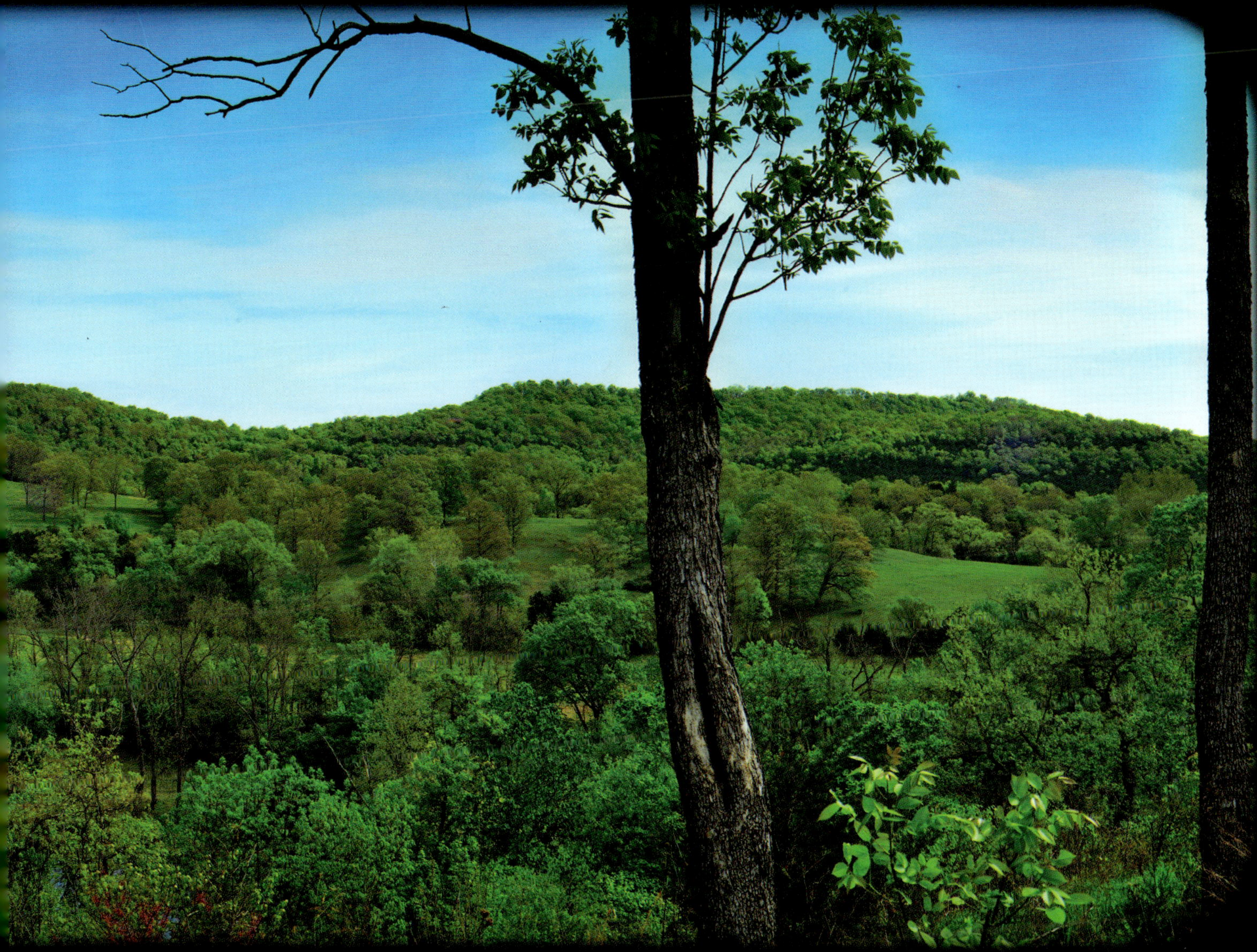

N 36°27.721'
W 093°48.453'
Elevation 998'

*(Following pages)* The White River makes a big turn in front of Can-U-Canoe Riverview Cabins, just above Blue Springs Heritage Center west of Eureka Springs. Tributaries to the White River are the Buffalo, Cache, Little Red and North Folk rivers. Six separate dams control the chilly river as it winds through Arkansas.

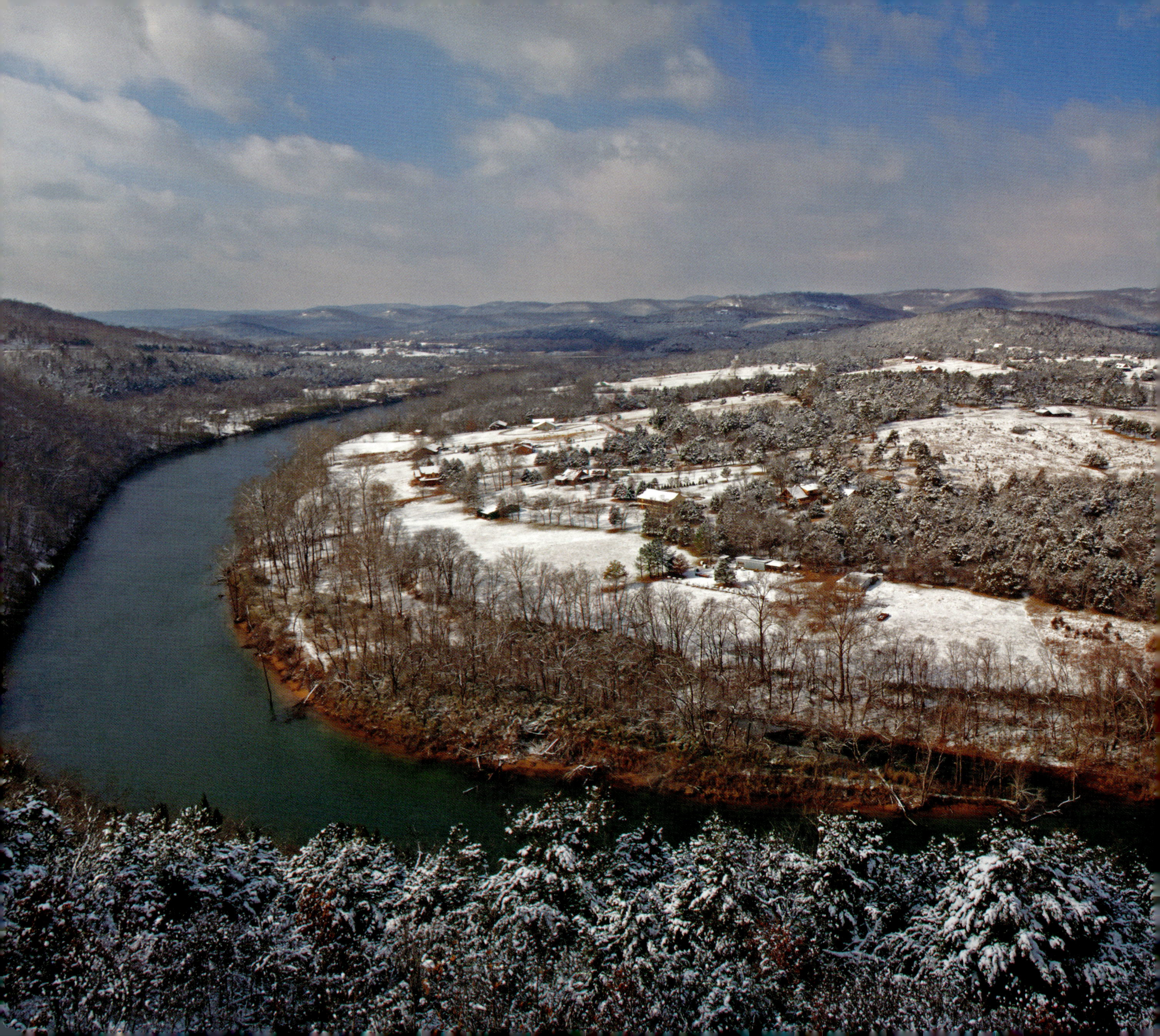

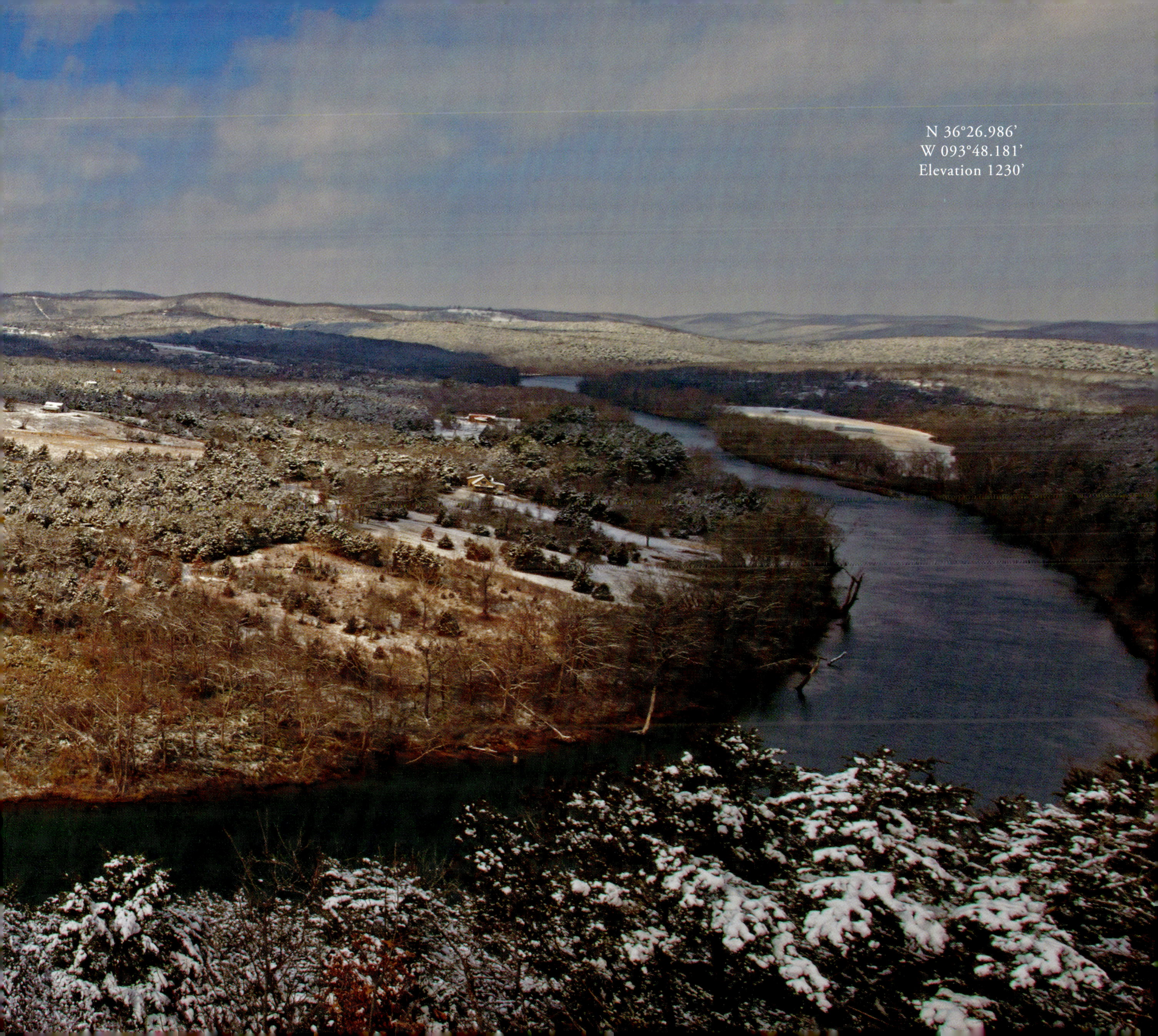

N 36°26.986’
W 093°48.181’
Elevation 1230’

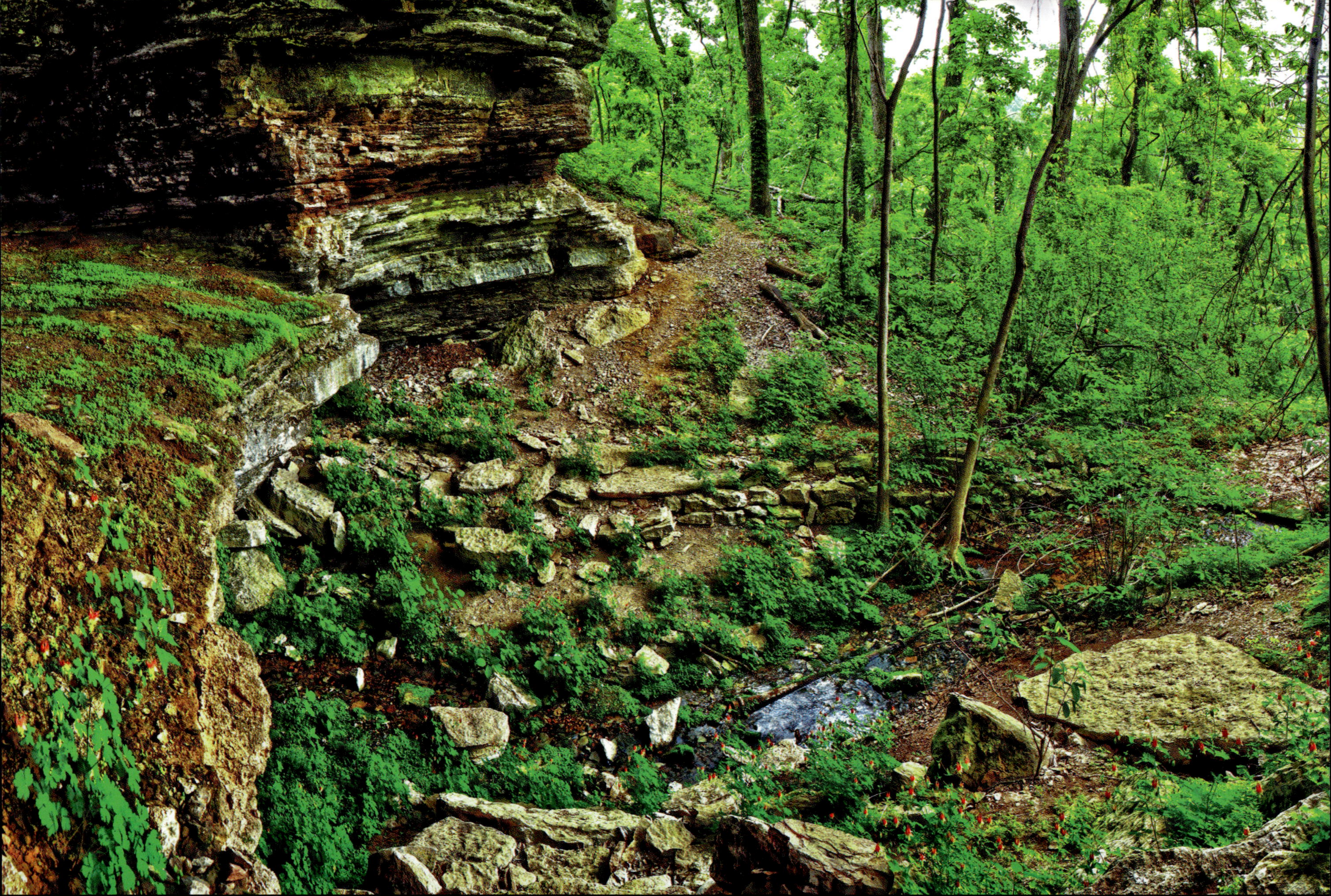

Nestled along the eastern side of Pension Mountain along CR 501, south of neighboring Berryville, is Johnson Spring. The spring at one point helped to supply water to Berryville, but now sits within an elaborate hiking, biking, and ATV trail system spanning some 385 acres. The trail system that leads to the spring winds across large bluffs with views of the surrounding area before opening into small groves and leading down through dense forest to the head of the spring.

N 36°17.912'
W 093°35.853'
Elevation 1510'

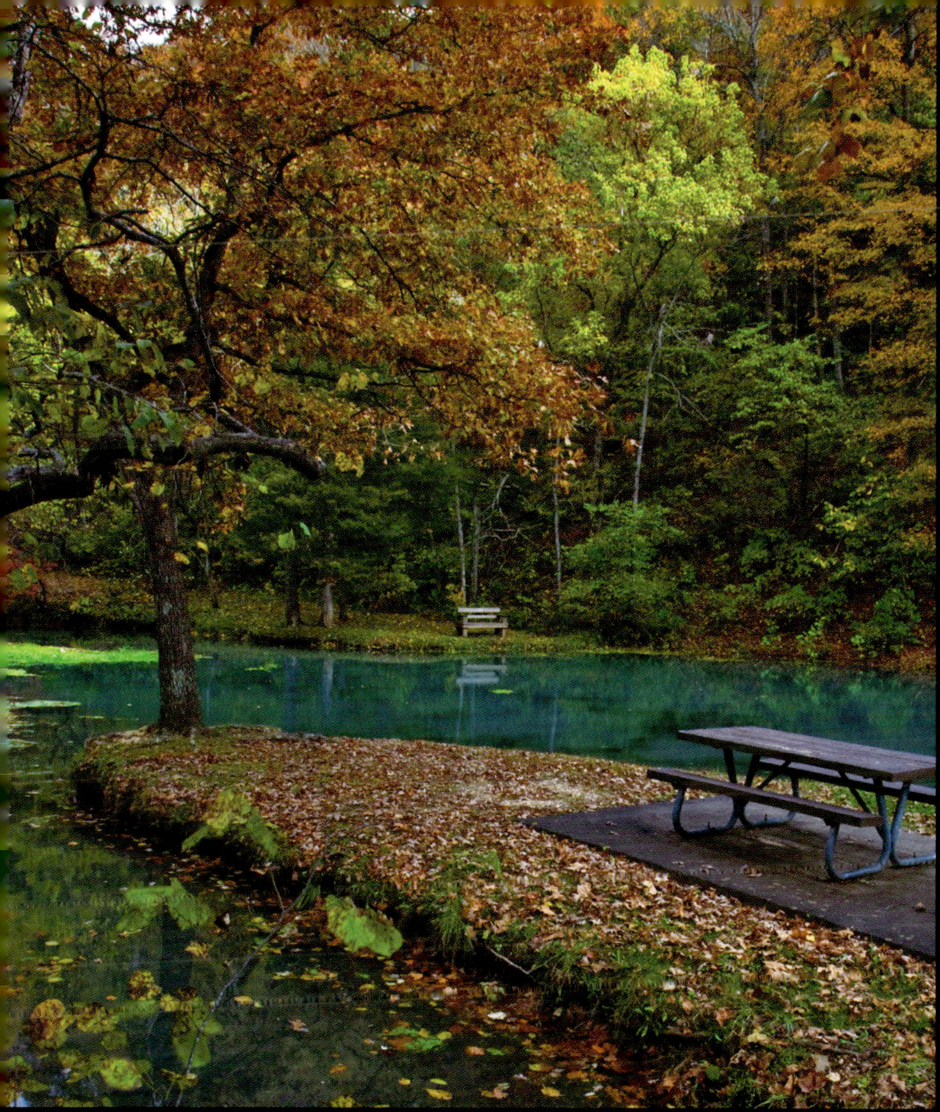

N 36°09.329'
W 093°44.061'
Elevation 1241'

The 21st State Park in Arkansas, Withrow Springs State Park, sits five miles south of Huntsville in 786 lush acres of wilderness. The spring releases a constant fifty-four degree flow of water that feeds a series of pools spanning the dense park. The park acquired its name from early gristmill operator, Richard Withrow. The waters dive underground after flowing for a little over a hundred feet, sprouting back up in War Eagle Cavern before feeding into War Eagle Creek.

N 36°09.373'
W 093°43.993'
Elevation 1250'

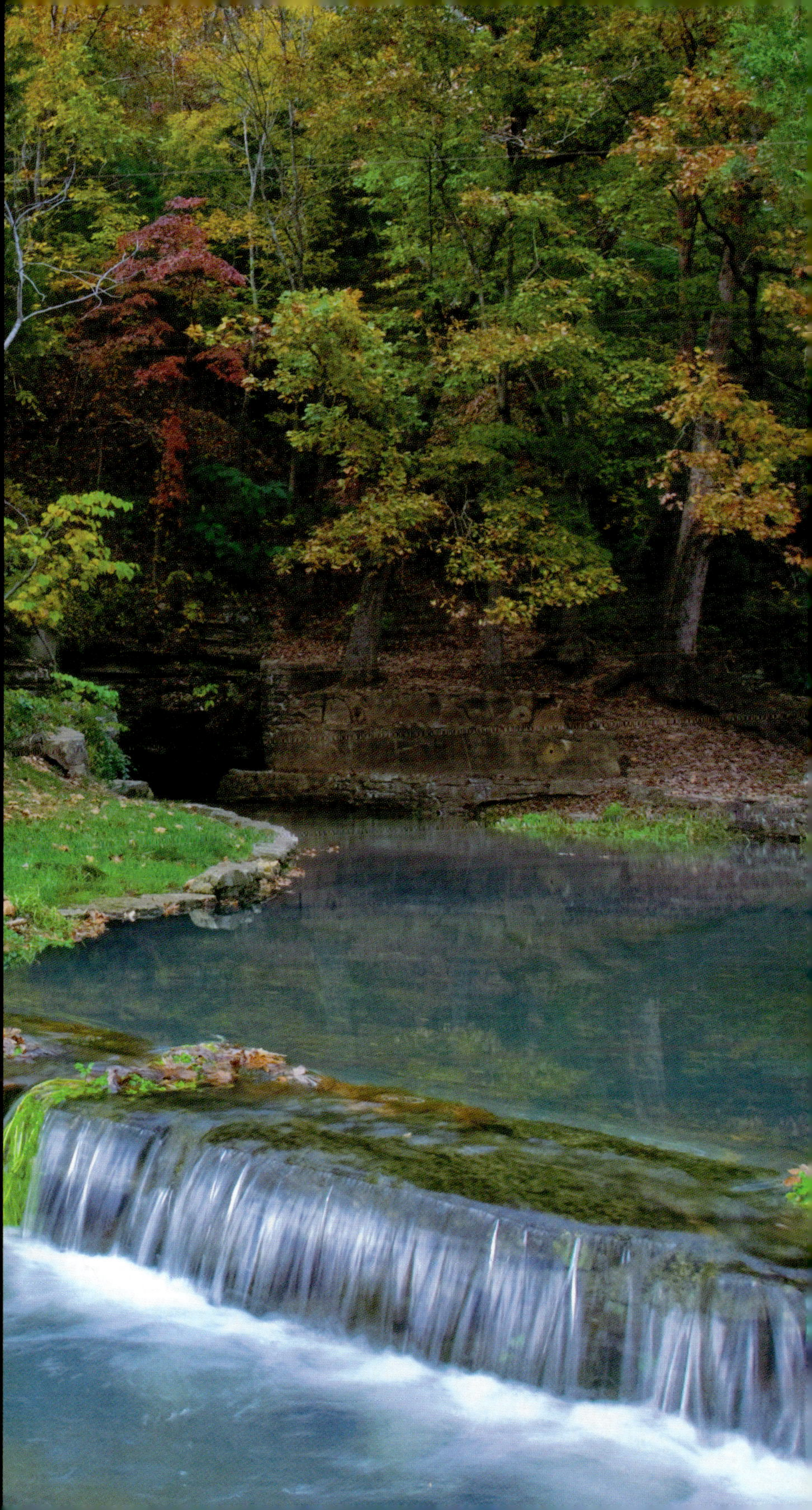

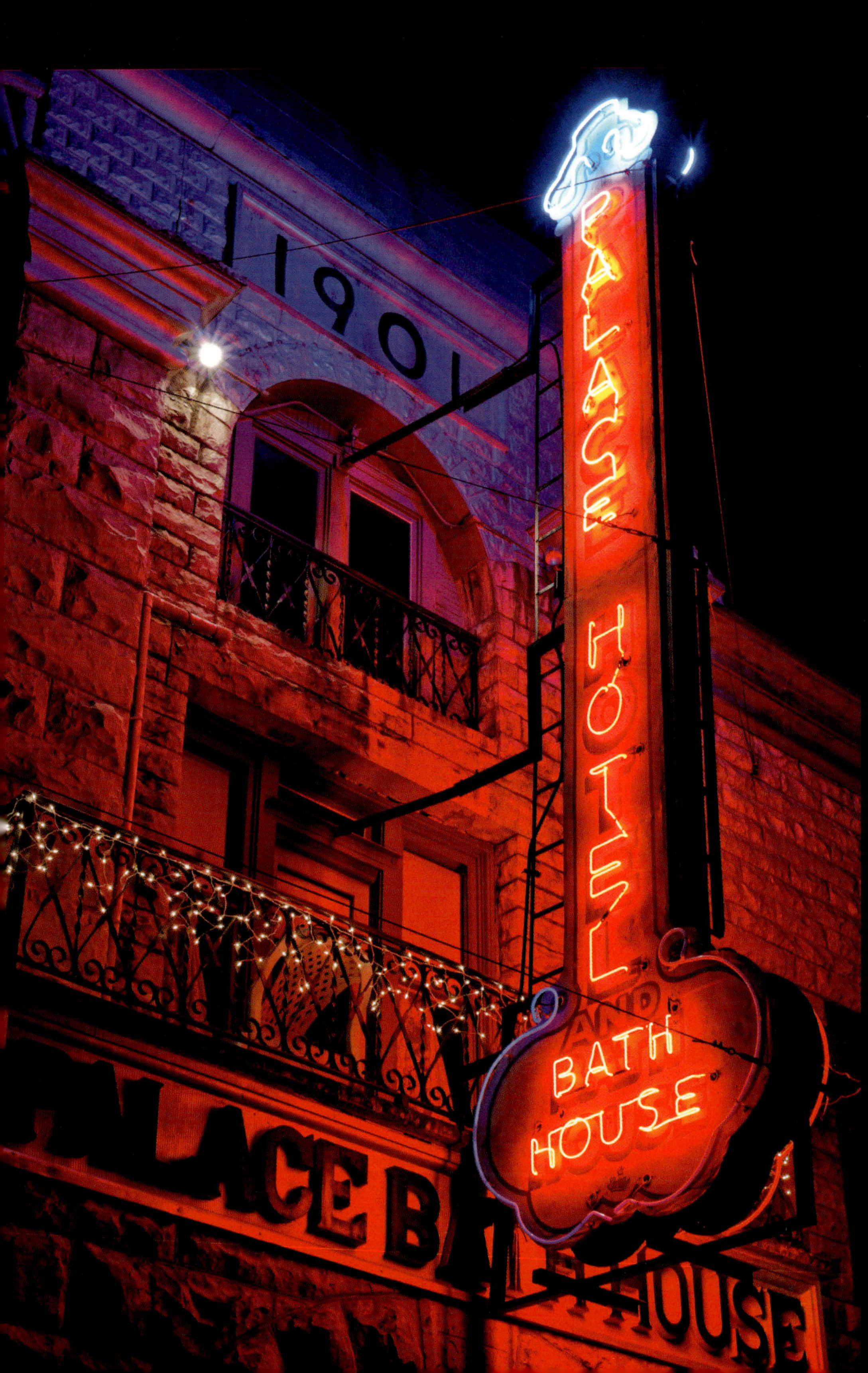


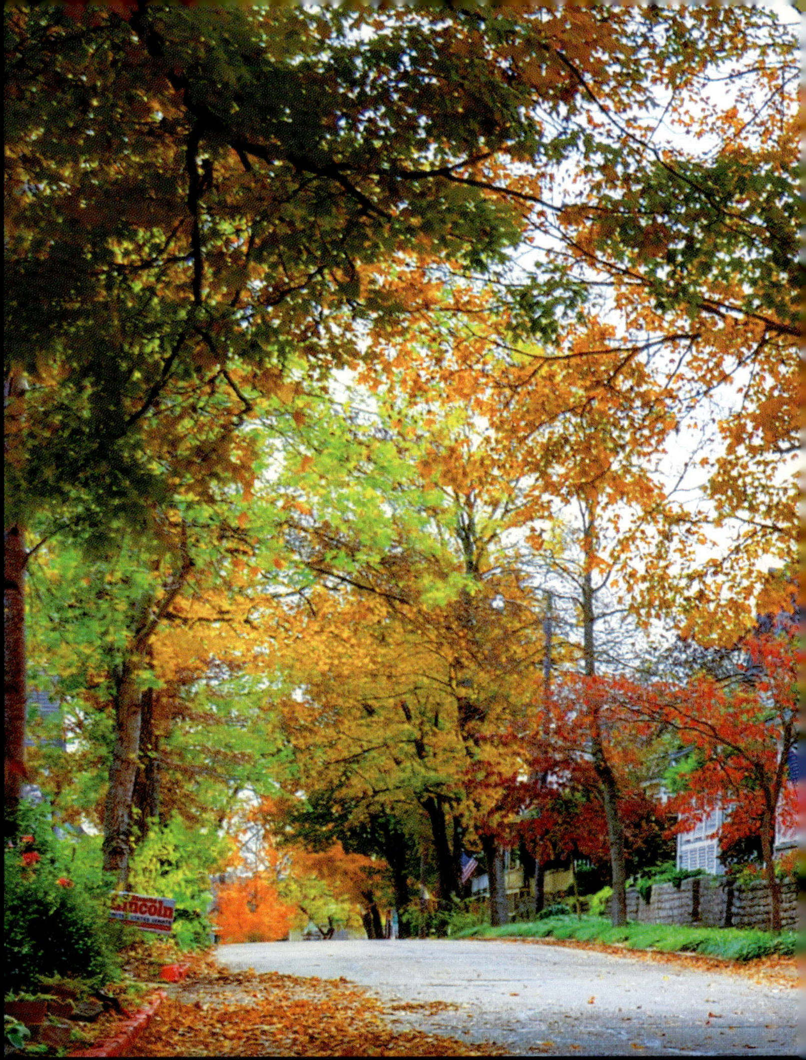

*(Pictured at left)* The Palace Hotel & Bathhouse, originally built in 1901 and rebuilt in 1983, chose the waters of Harding Spring (or Sweet Spring depending on who you ask) in the 1900s to fill the baths in their elegant spas. The erect neon sign was the first of its kind west of the Mississippi River. Once dubbed the "Swellest Place in Town," this historic registered hotel opened with around 15 rooms and utilized limestone from nearby Beaver. This beauty boasted an electric elevator, electric lights, steam-heated rooms, and over 13 various spa-related amenities.

N 36°24.297'
W 093°44.250'
Elevation 1277'

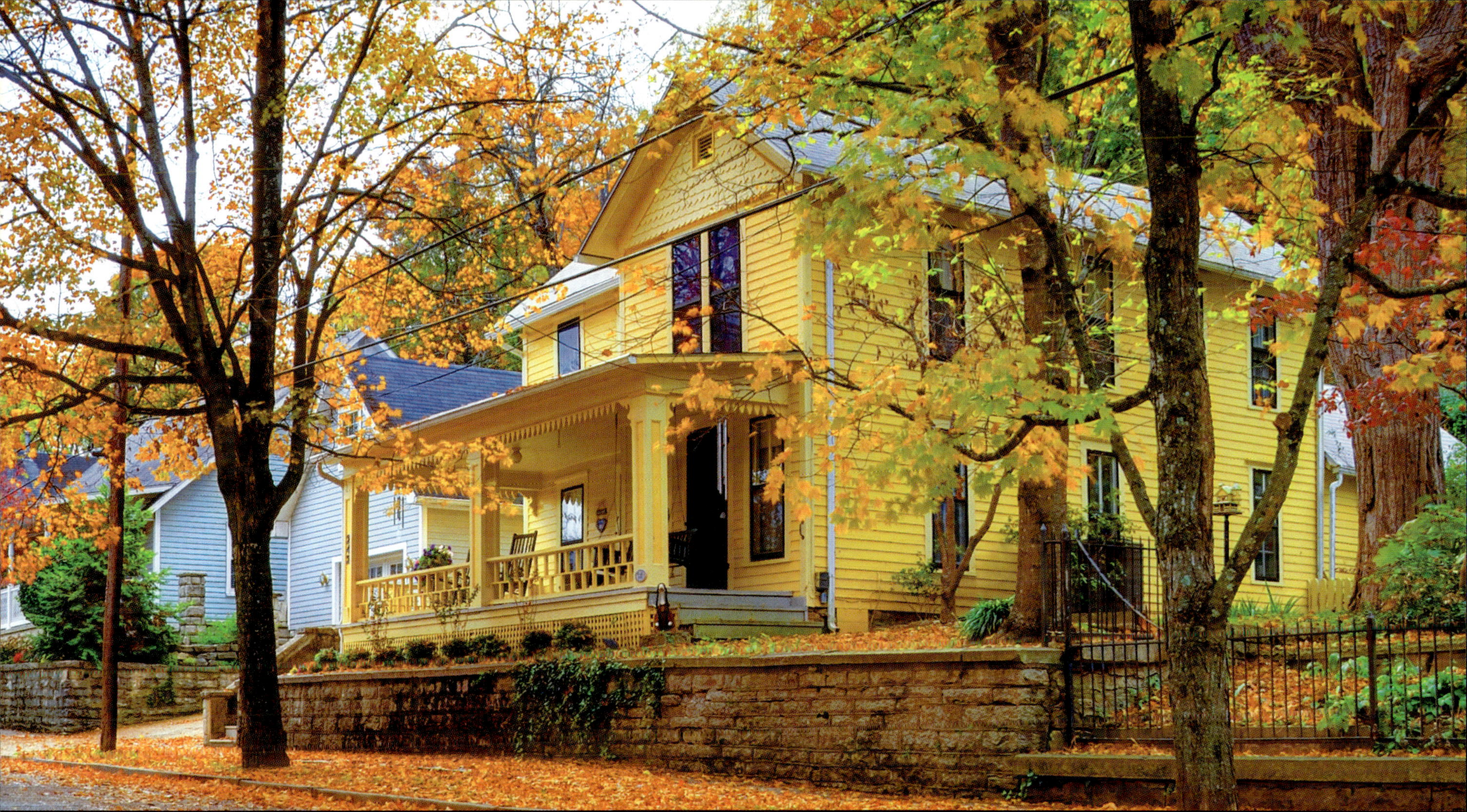

N 36°24.567'
W 093°44.133'
Elevation 1333'

# The Historic Loop

Upper Spring Street sits in the heart of Eureka Springs' Historic District. In 1970, The National Register of Historic Places listed the district, including a large portion of Eureka Springs, and extended the listing in 1979 to include the Eureka Springs Railroad Depot. The homes, which date back to 1880, are 19th and 20th Century Victorian Revival style and appear side-by-side along Spring Street in well-manicured landscapes. Horse drawn carriages saunter through on a daily basis, giving tourist passengers a feel for the era.

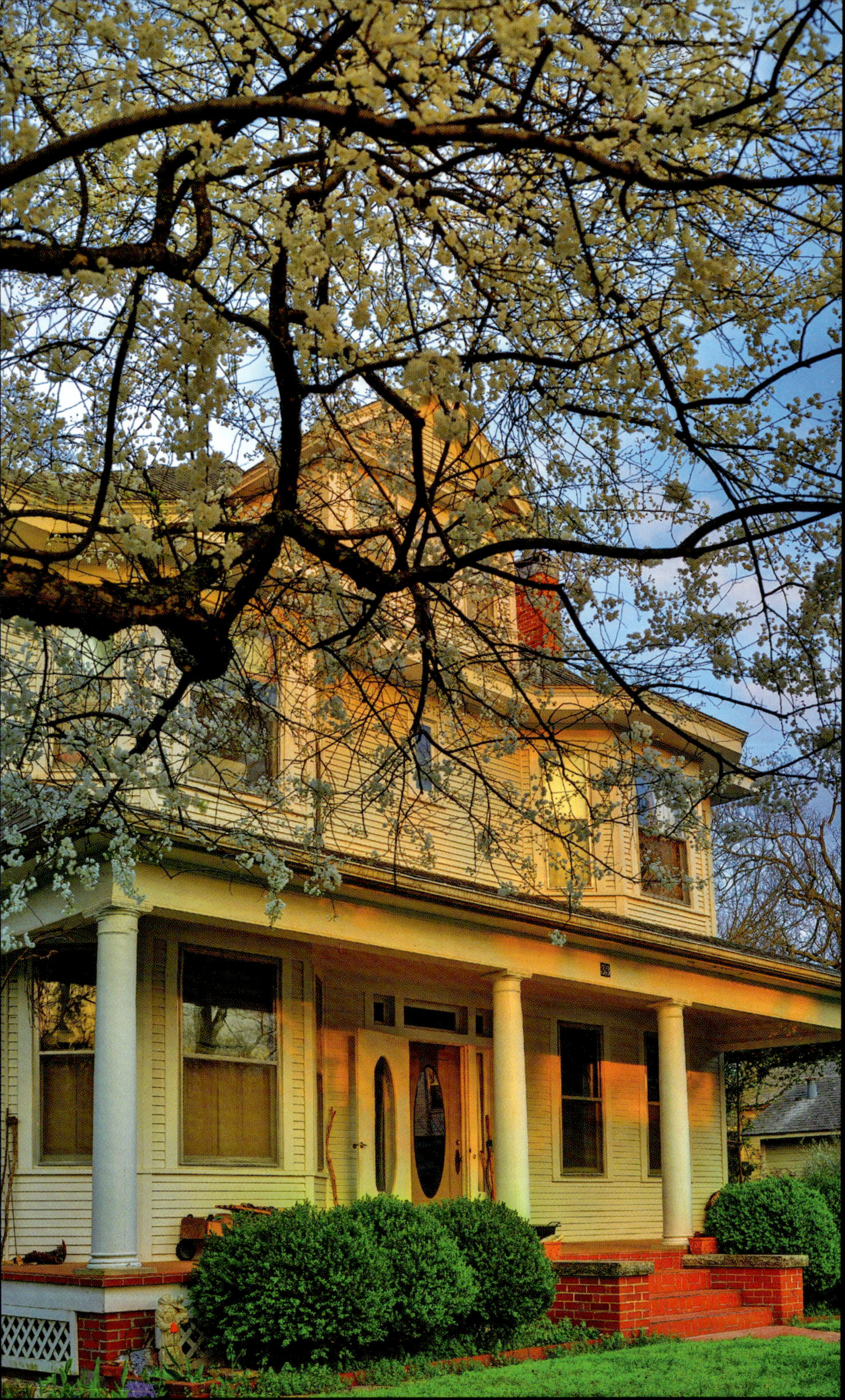

A home flanked by a blooming White Japanese Cherry tree.

N 36°24.446'
W 093°44.487'
Elevation 1471'

The Eureka Springs Rotary Club maintains a small gazebo on East Mountain Street called the East Mountain Lookout. The view from the site shows a section of downtown and the historic loop, and has a perfect view of the 1886 Crescent Hotel.

N 36°24.258'
W 093°44.028'
Elevation 1312'

*(Following pages)*
The gingerbread, Eastlake, and Steamboat Gothic home named The Rosalie House was constructed on spring Street in 1889 by J.W. Hill, who also built Eureka Spring's phone system and owned the Eureka Springs Livery & Stables.

N 36°24.699'
W 093°44.158'
Elevation 1310'

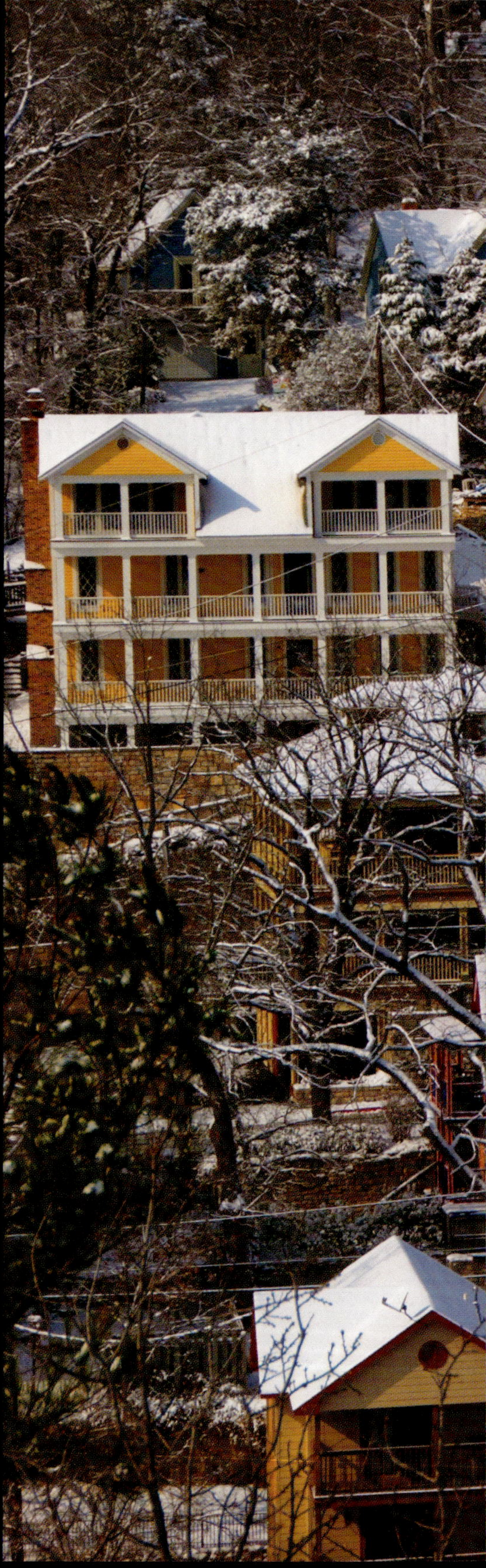

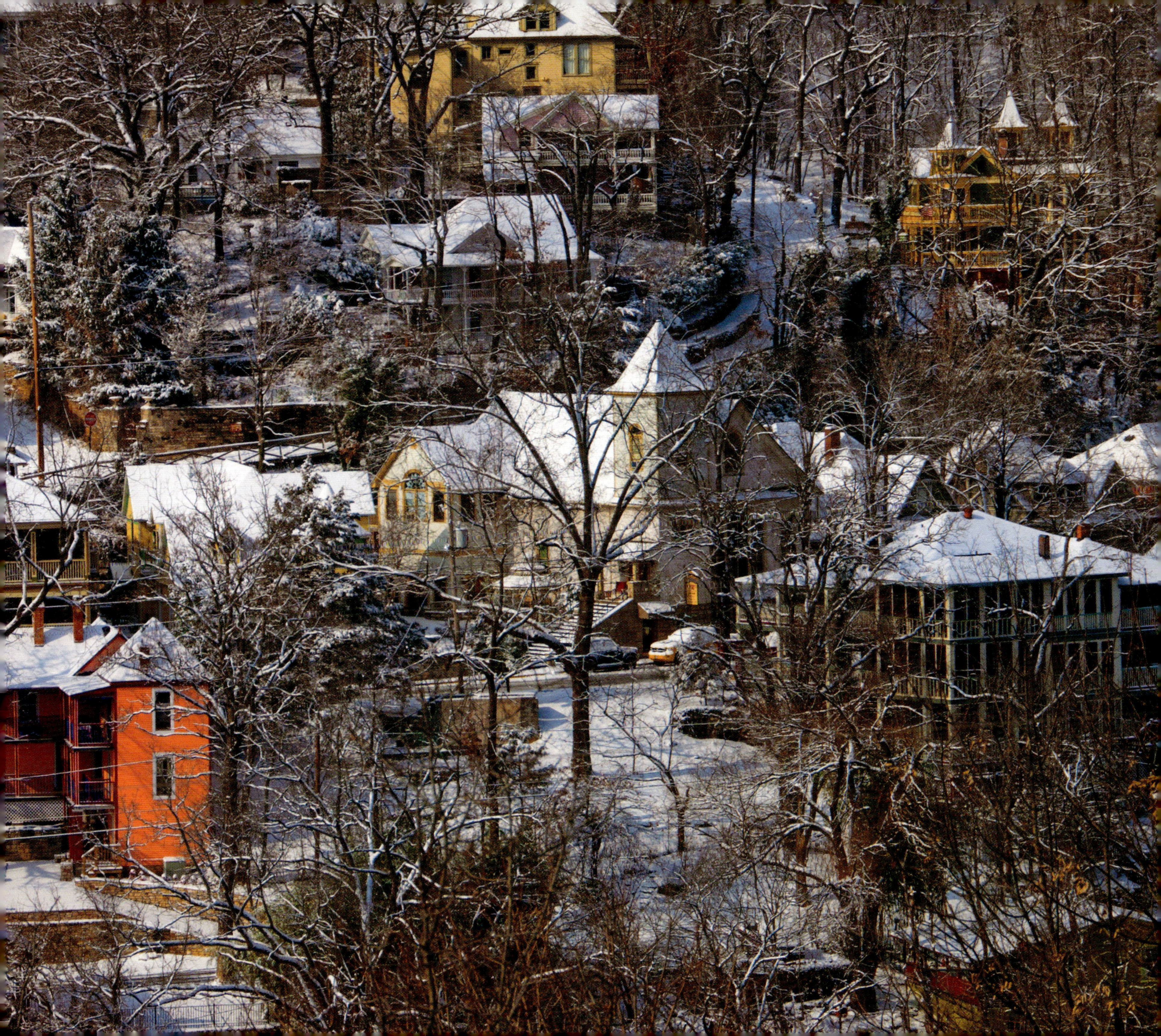

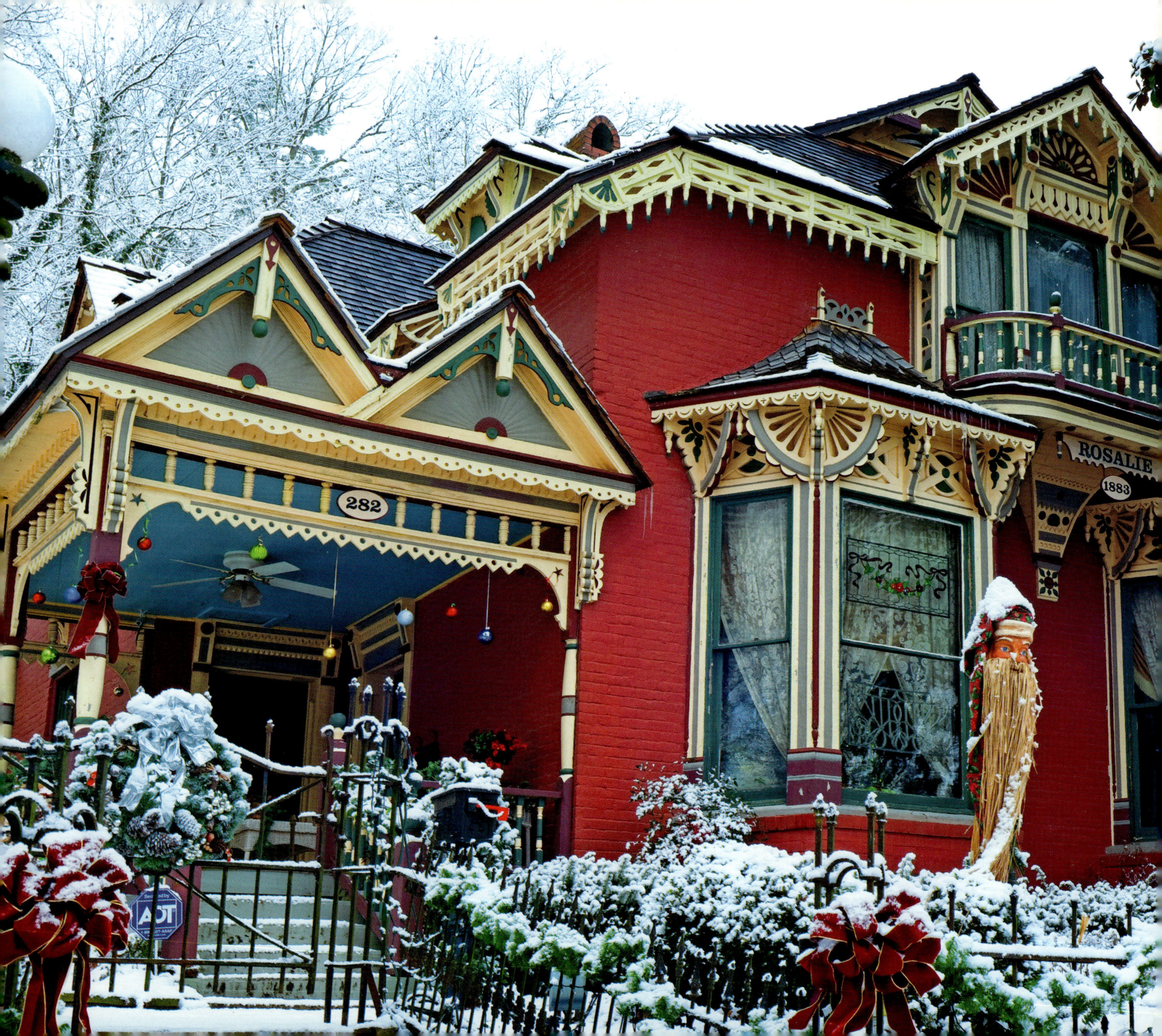
282
ROSALIE
1883
ADT

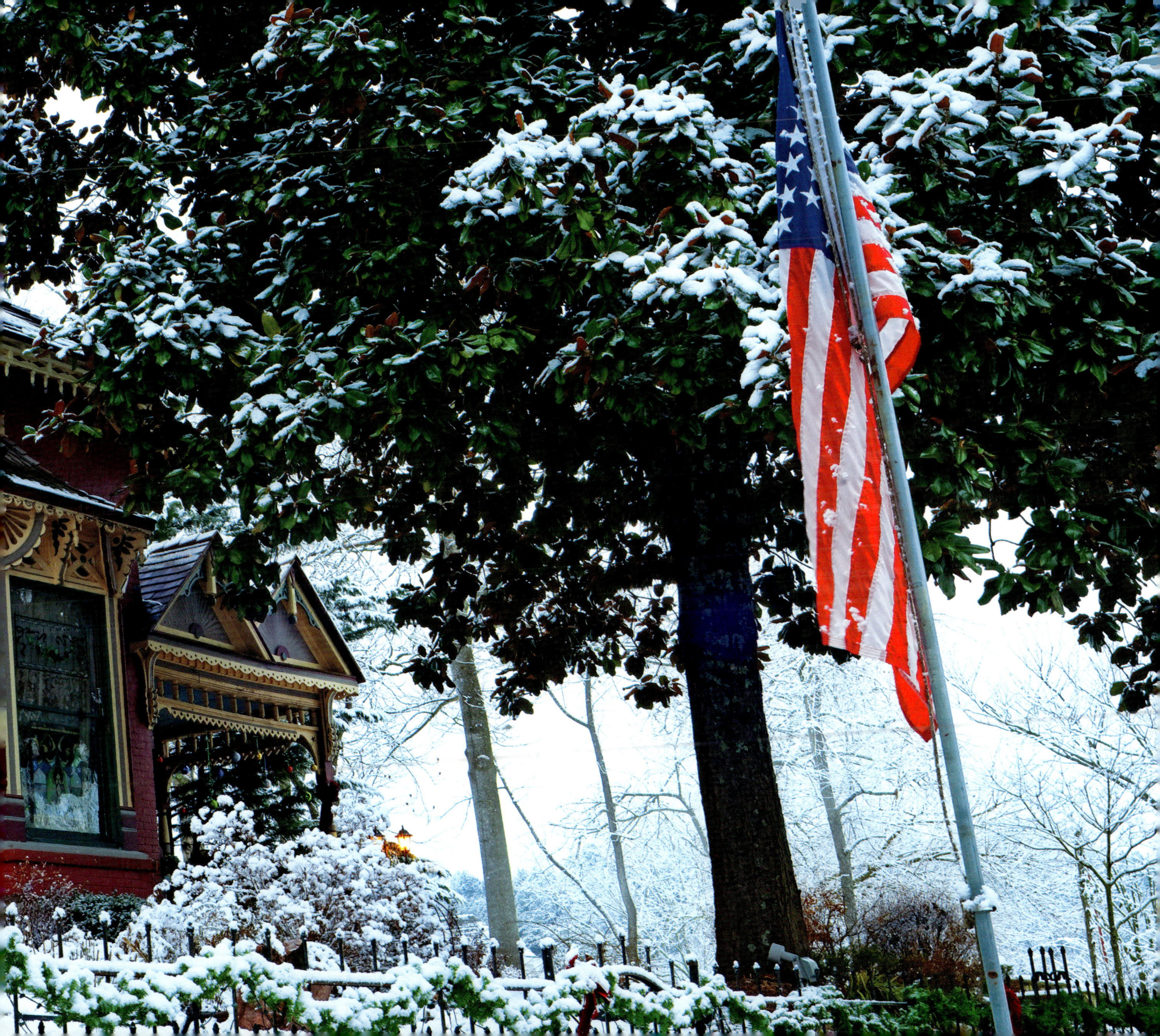

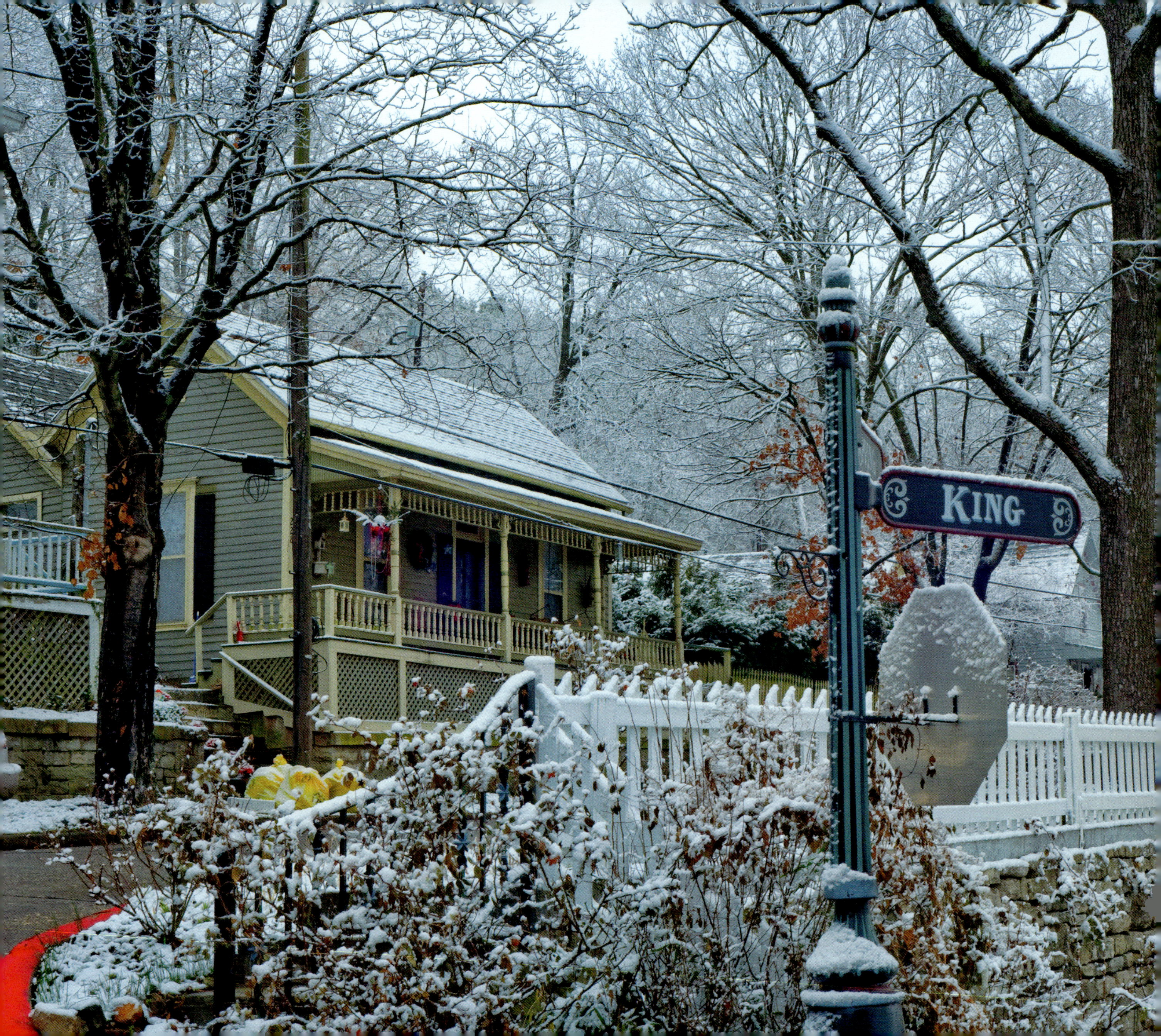
KING

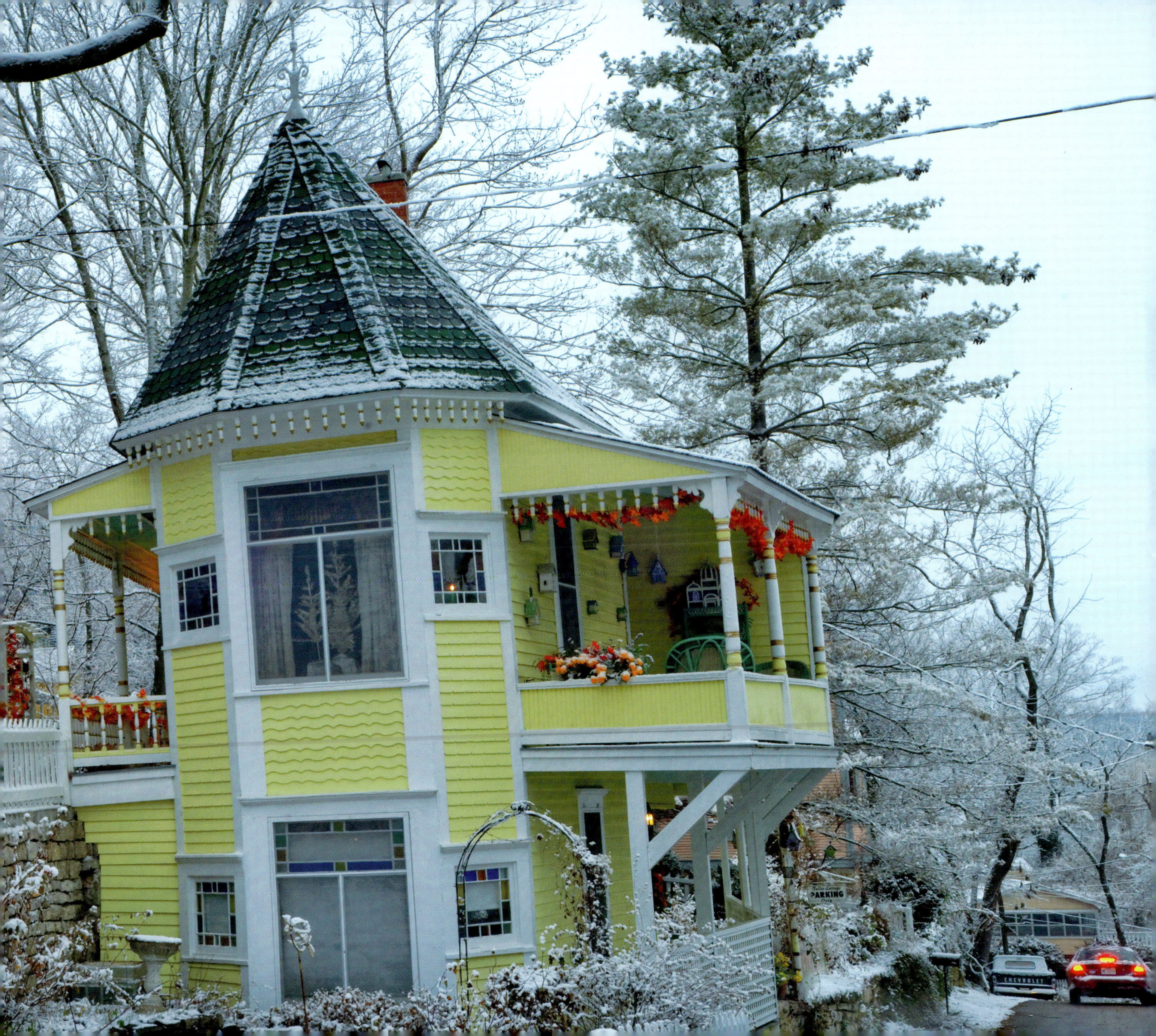
PARKING

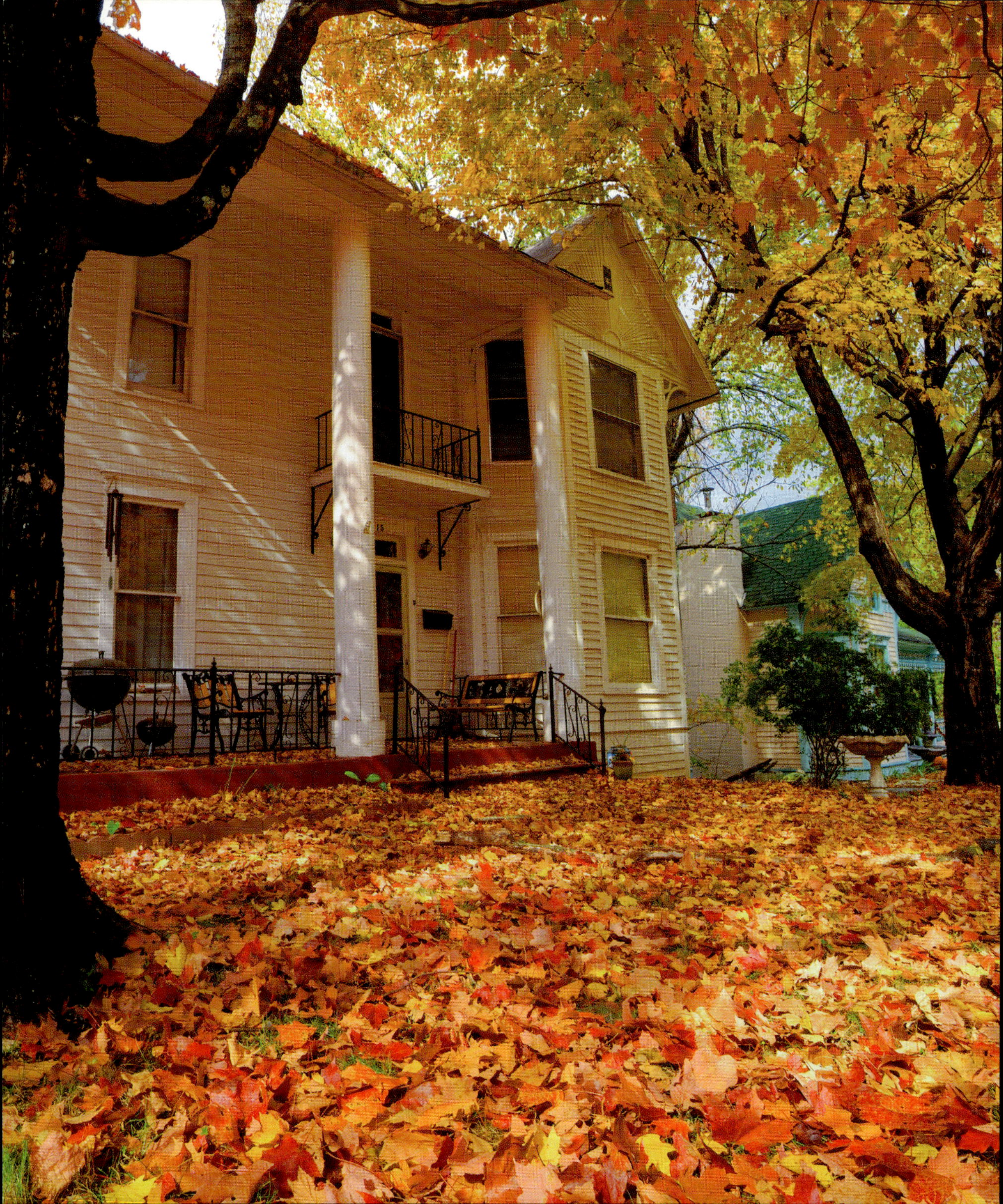

The historic loop is home to many different structures that span from vintage Victorian *(previous pages)* to contemporary modern and Colonial *(pictured at left)* to the down-right enlightening *(pictured below)*.

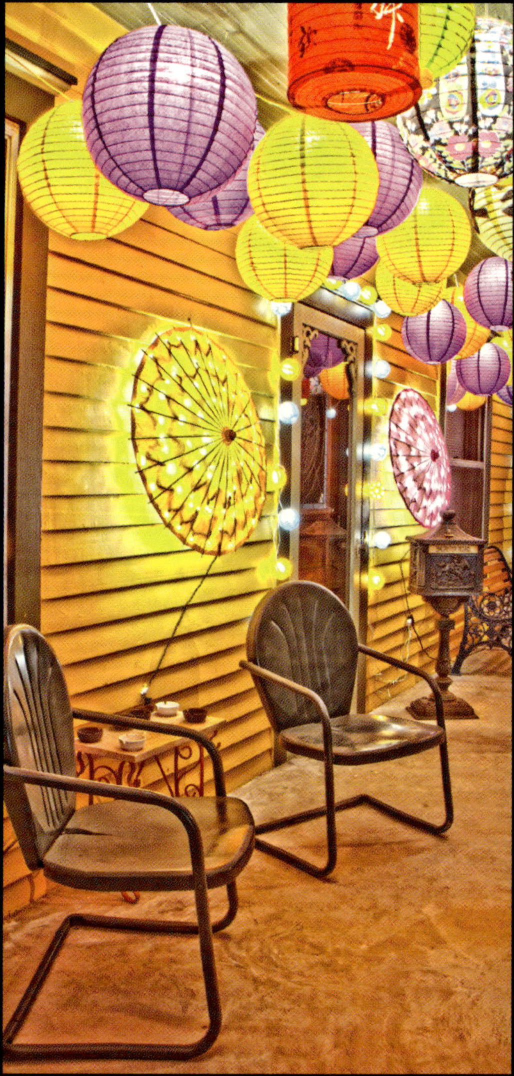

N 36°24.074'
W 093°44.697'
Elevation 1447'

This staircase ascends above Sweet Spring to a path winding through Spring, Hilton, Prospect, and Singleton streets before descending downhill to Harding Spring.

N 36°24.273'
W 093°44.295'
Elevation 1346'

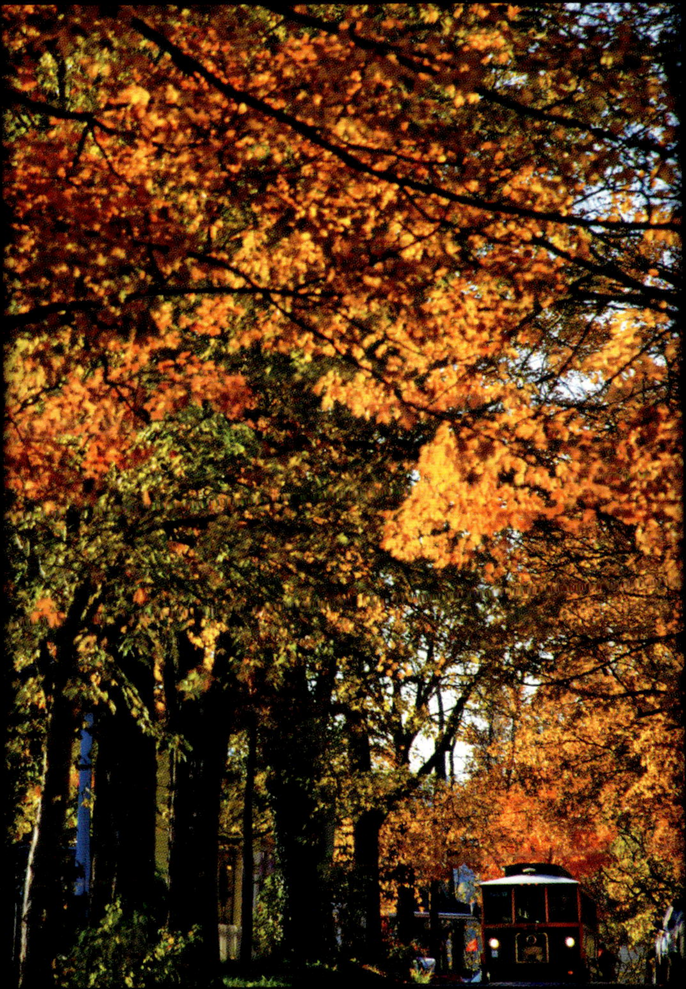

The Eureka Springs Public Transit System started with 10 streetcars on rails in 1891, becoming electric in 1898. Trolleys reach all sections of town with Red, Blue, Yellow, and Purple routes easily identifiable on the trolley route map.

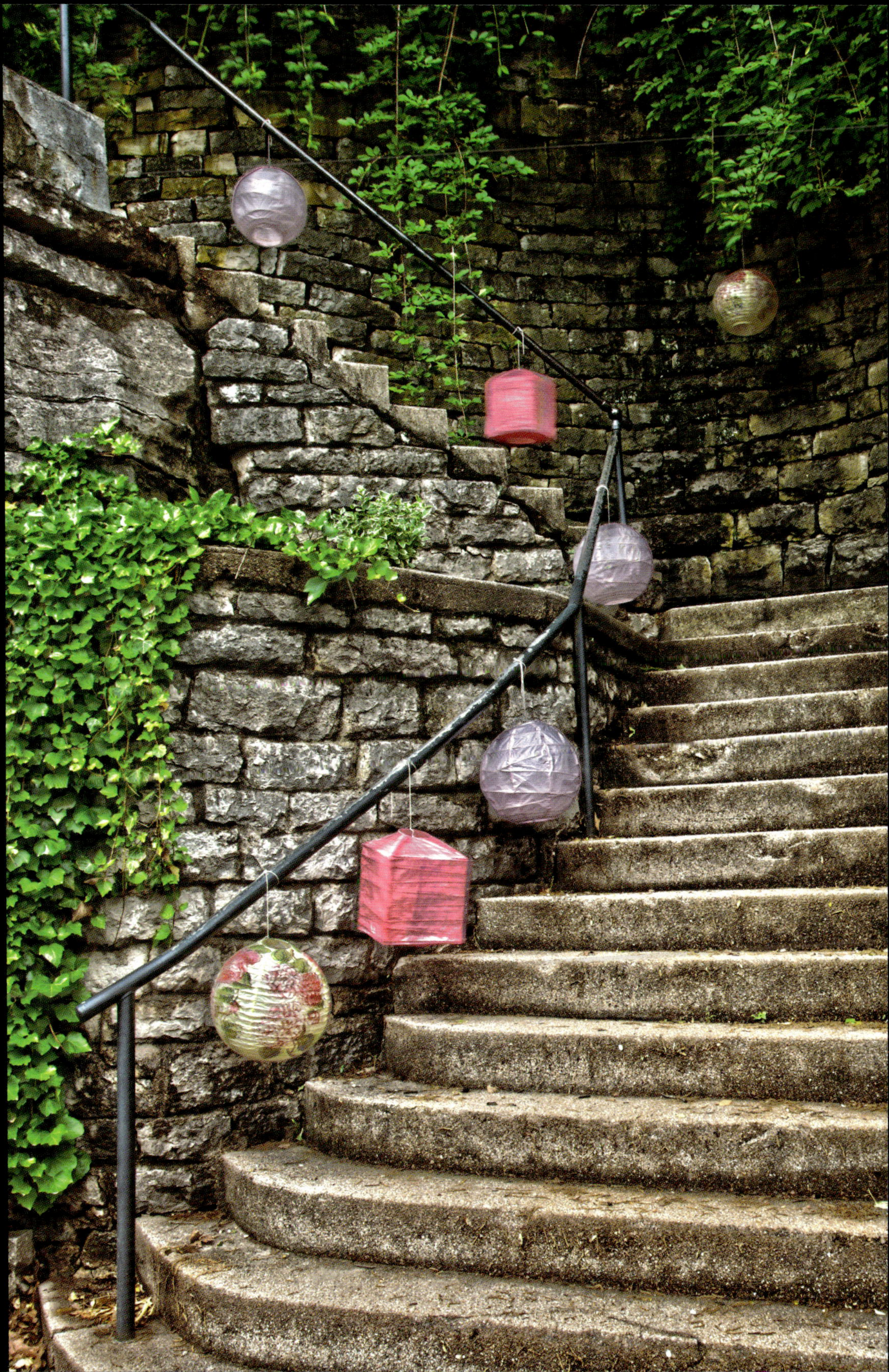

# Events Festivals & Parades

Eureka Springs loves a good parade and some span a mile in length. Others can last over an hour, always rolling through the downtown corridor and sometimes pausing in front of Basin Spring Park. Usually parades take place on Saturdays, most beginning around 2 p.m. A few occur during the cover of nightfall with lighted floats, and one even starts at 11:11 a.m. each November 11. One theme common to all parades is the essence of the area's colorful, creative people. At right is Margo Pirkle in full clown garb moments after the 2009 Mardi Gras Parade in February.

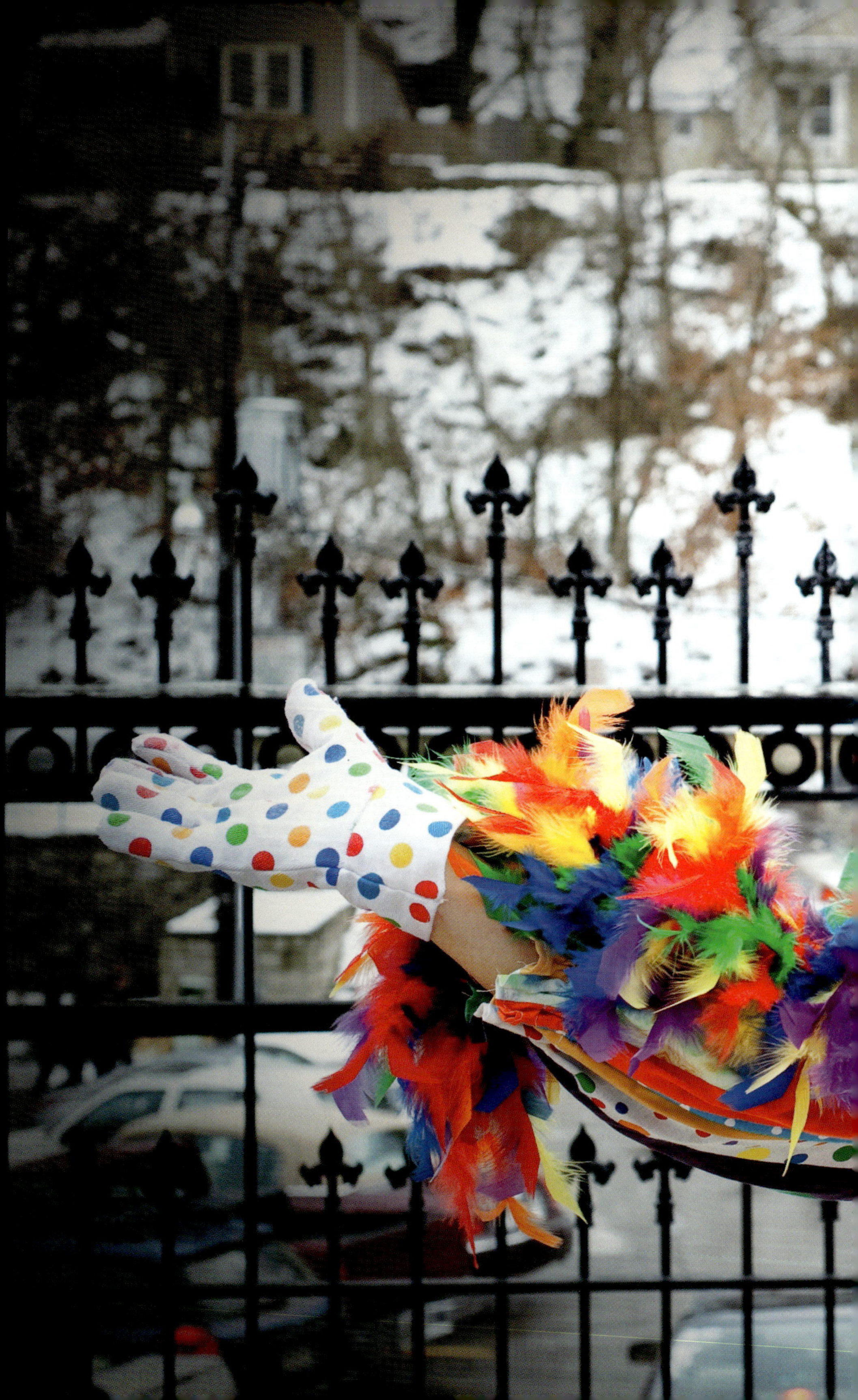

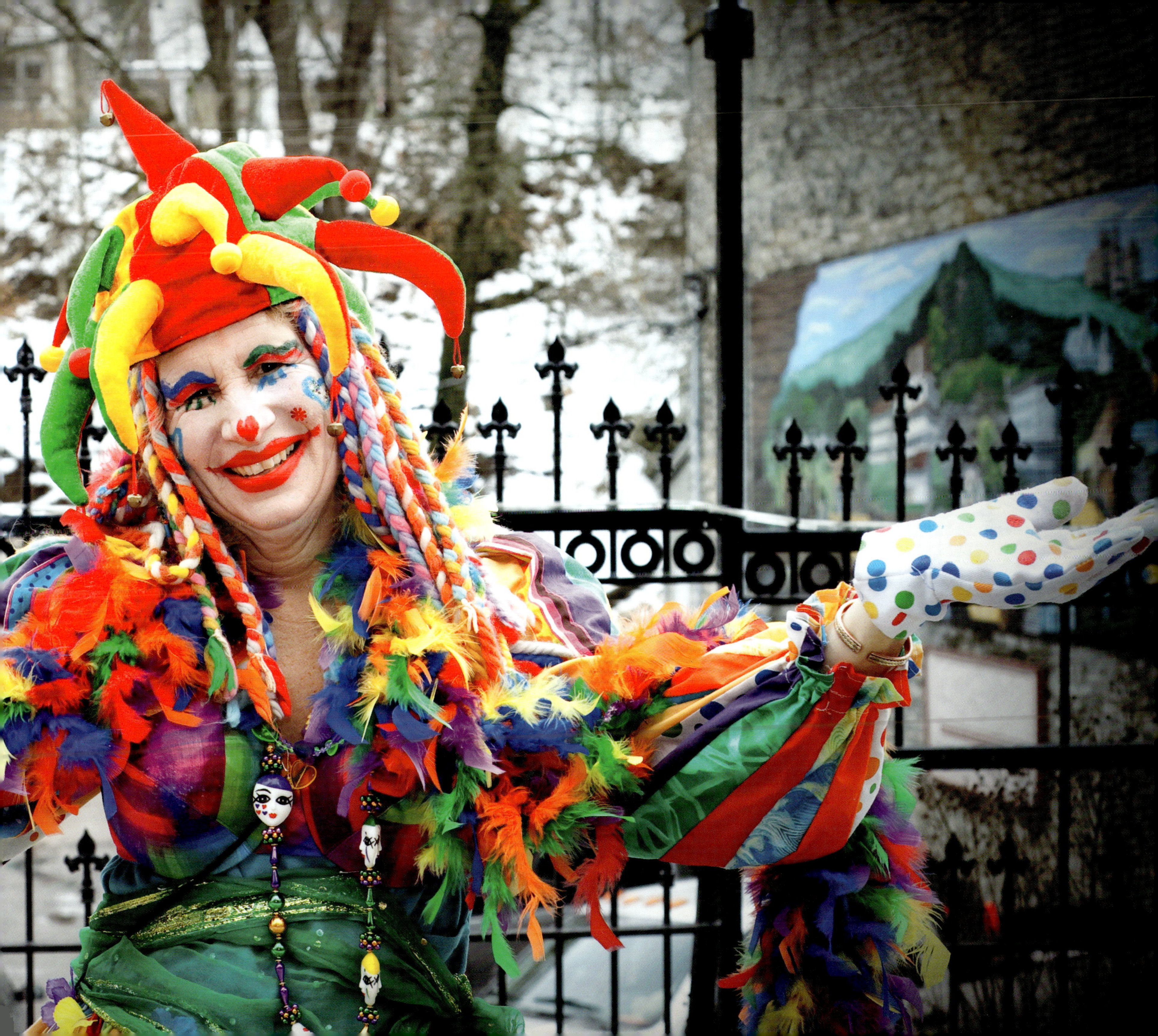

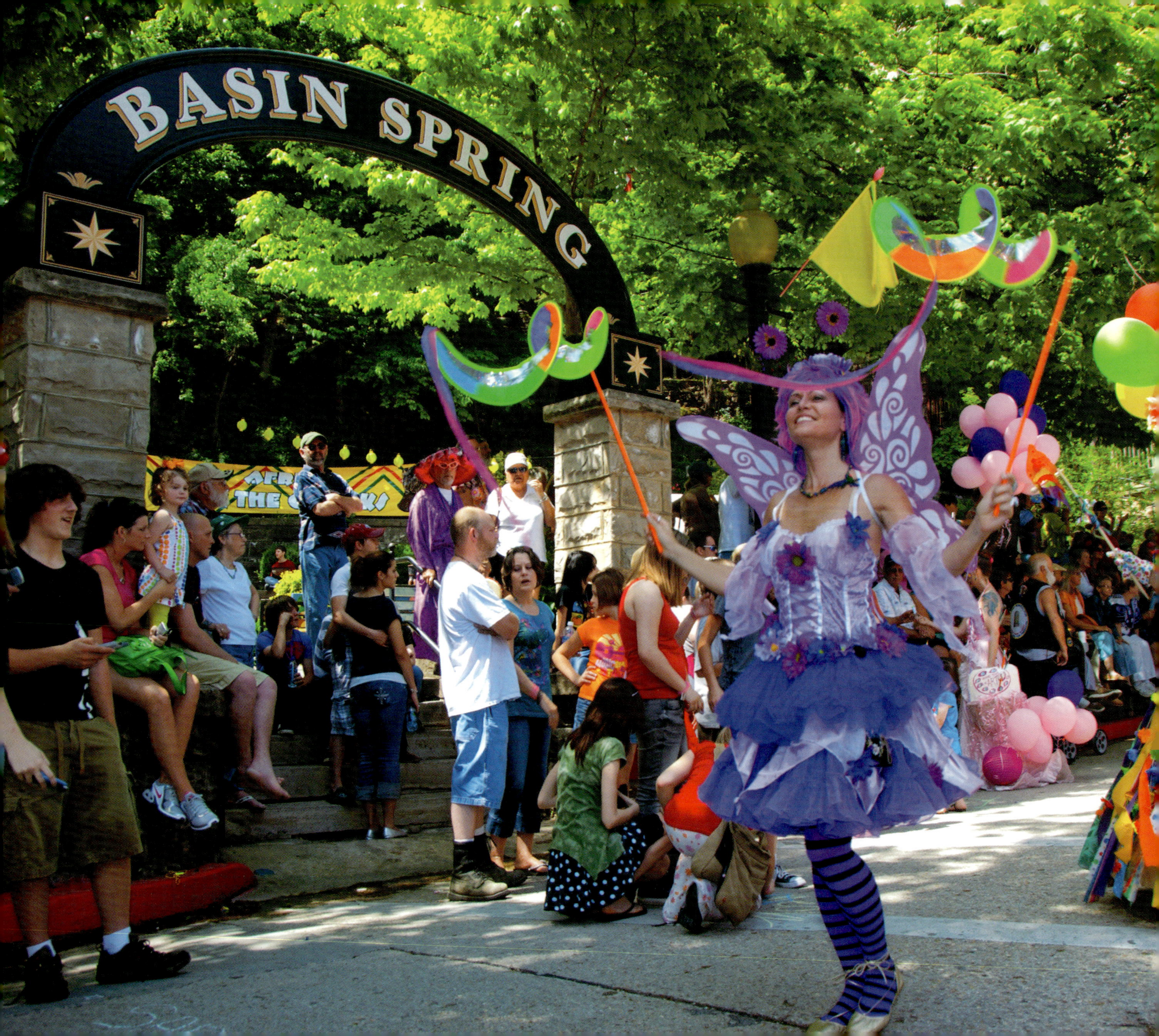
BASIN SPRING

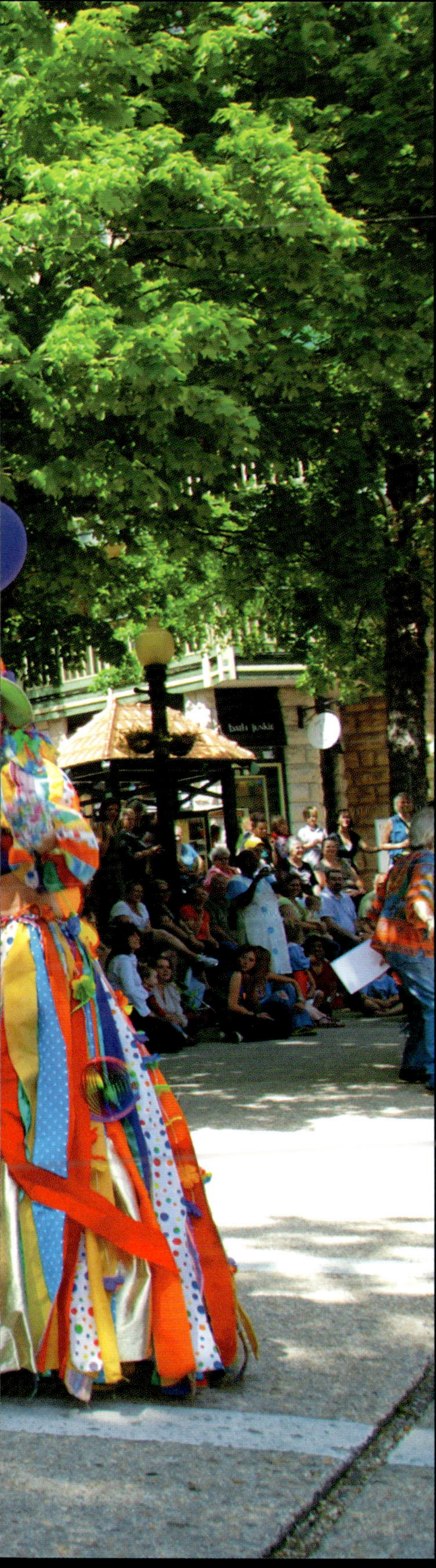

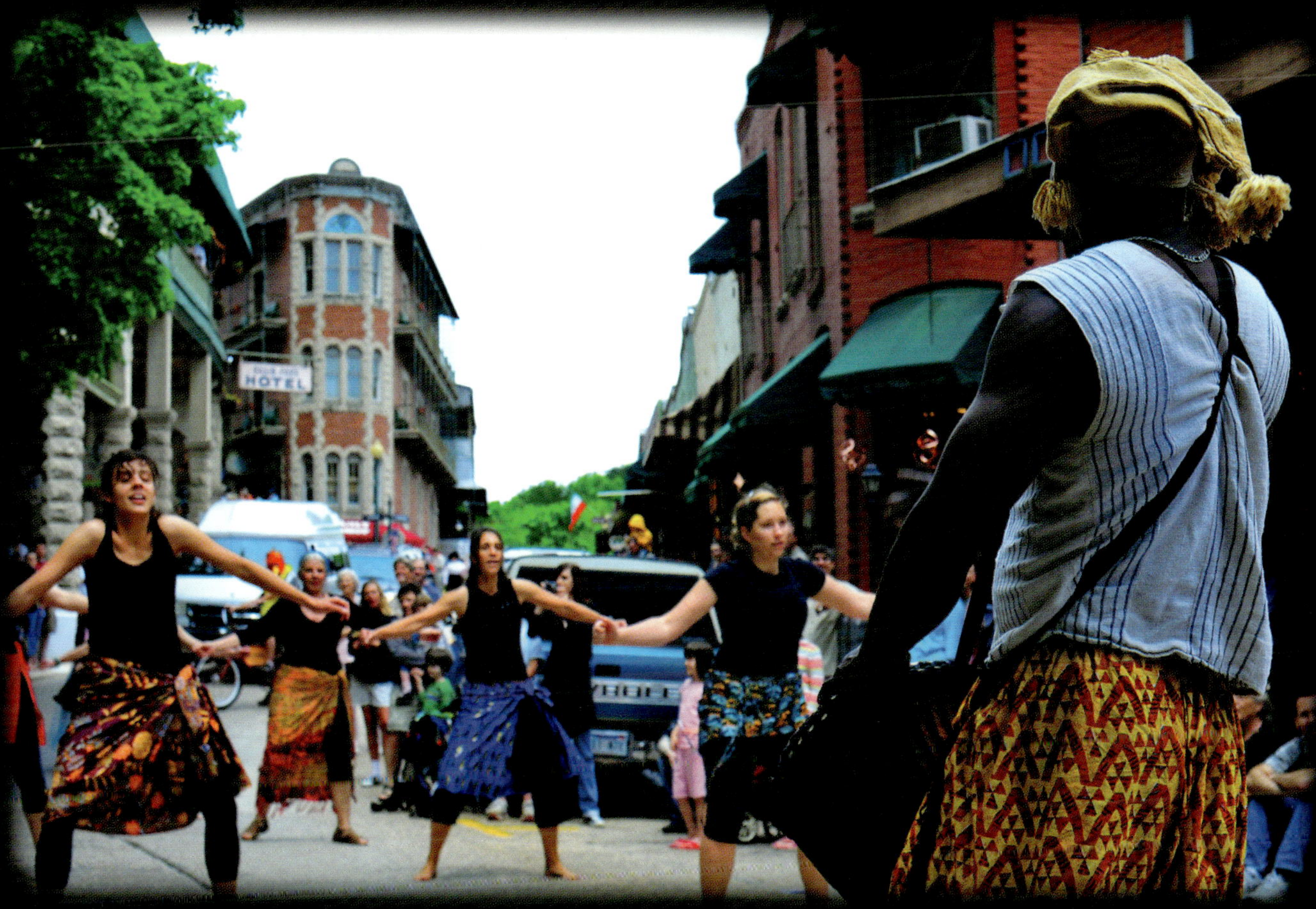


For many the official start of the Eureka Springs May Festival of the Arts is the ArtRageous parade. Flowing through historic downtown each year are clowns, fairies, human butterflies, and an ever-expanding sea of pure creativity. It is one of the many reasons for Eureka Springs' nationally-recognized arts culture. The town houses over 30 fine art galleries featuring more than 130 artists and their boundless mediums. The month boasts around 130 varying art-related events from art cuisine to gallery strolls. Art is everywhere, and many locals say it's even in their blood. Funding and promotion is provided by the Eureka Springs Arts Council and the Eureka Springs Chamber of Commerce for this month-long celebration of creative spirit, first organized in 1988.

N 36°24.115'
W 093°44.254'
Elevation 1298'

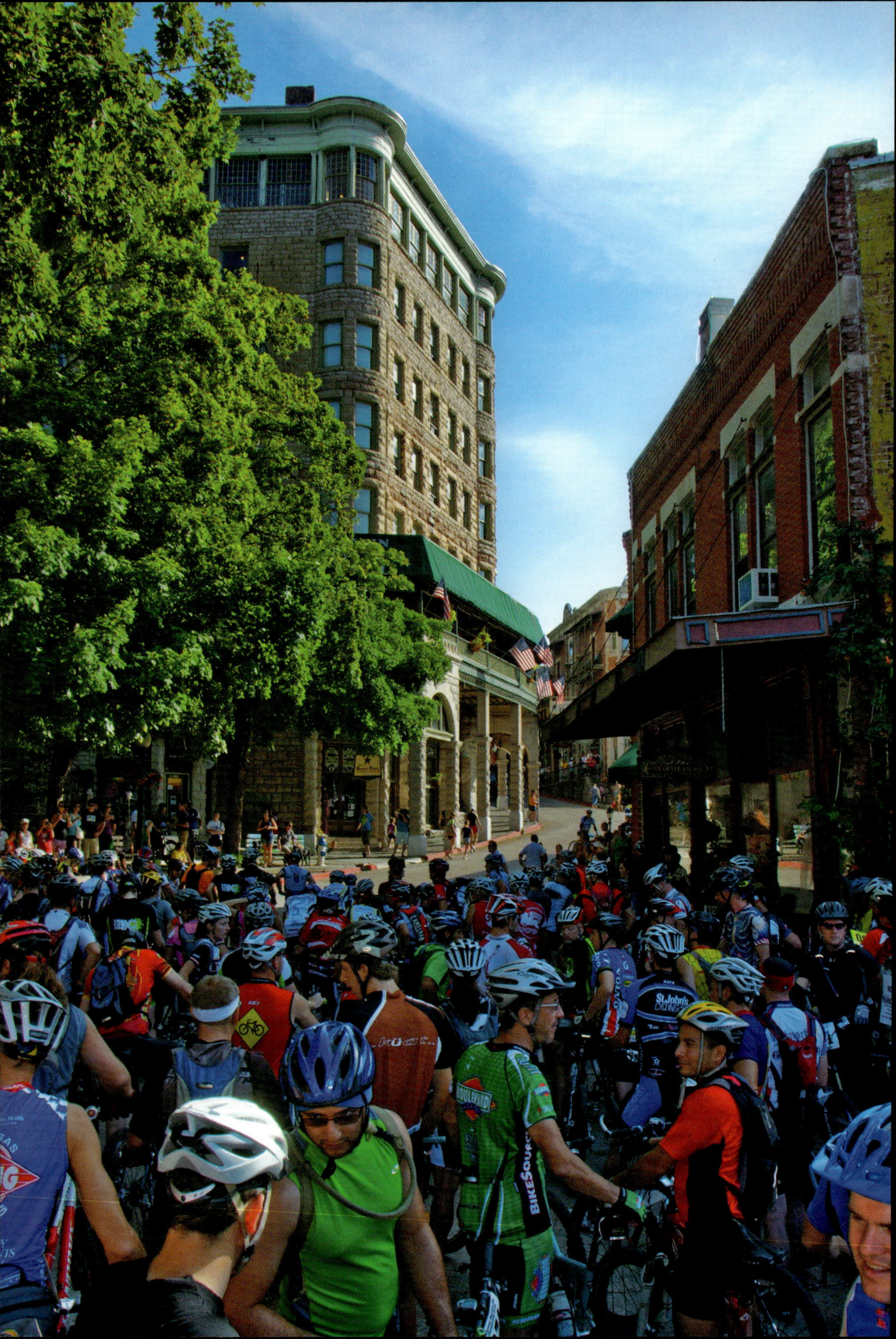

The annual Fat Tire Festival has off-road bicyclists rolling throughout the county, with Eureka Springs being the main leg.  Races include: "The Fatty" which hosts many separate races, the MX Race at Achord's Ranch which sends racers barreling through a narrow dirt track, Observed Trials forcing cyclists to hop and balance tough courses in Harmon Park, The XC Race to the Lake sending racers from Basin Spring Park through the Historic District and out to Lake Leatherwood, and kid's races held throughout most staging areas.

N 36°24.115'
W 093°44.257'
Elevation 1288'

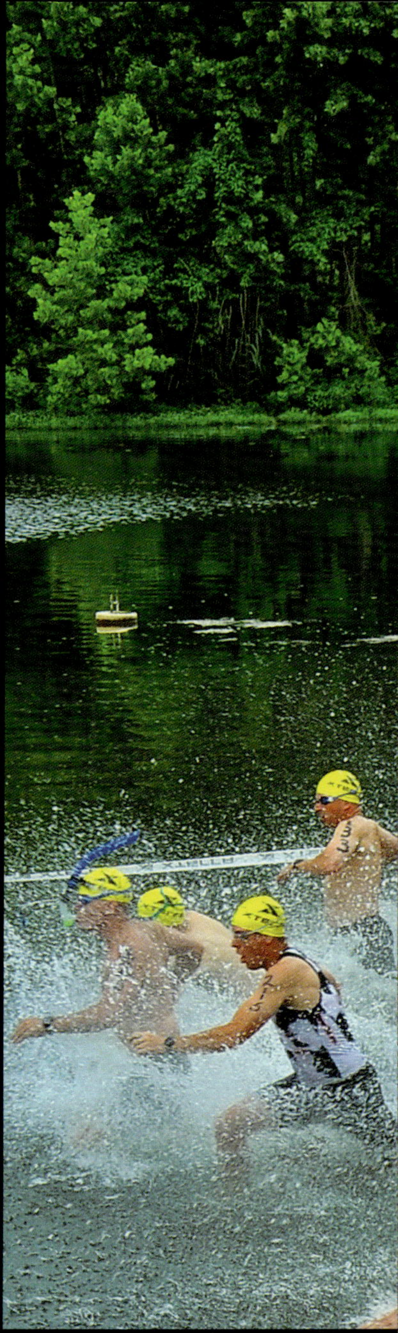

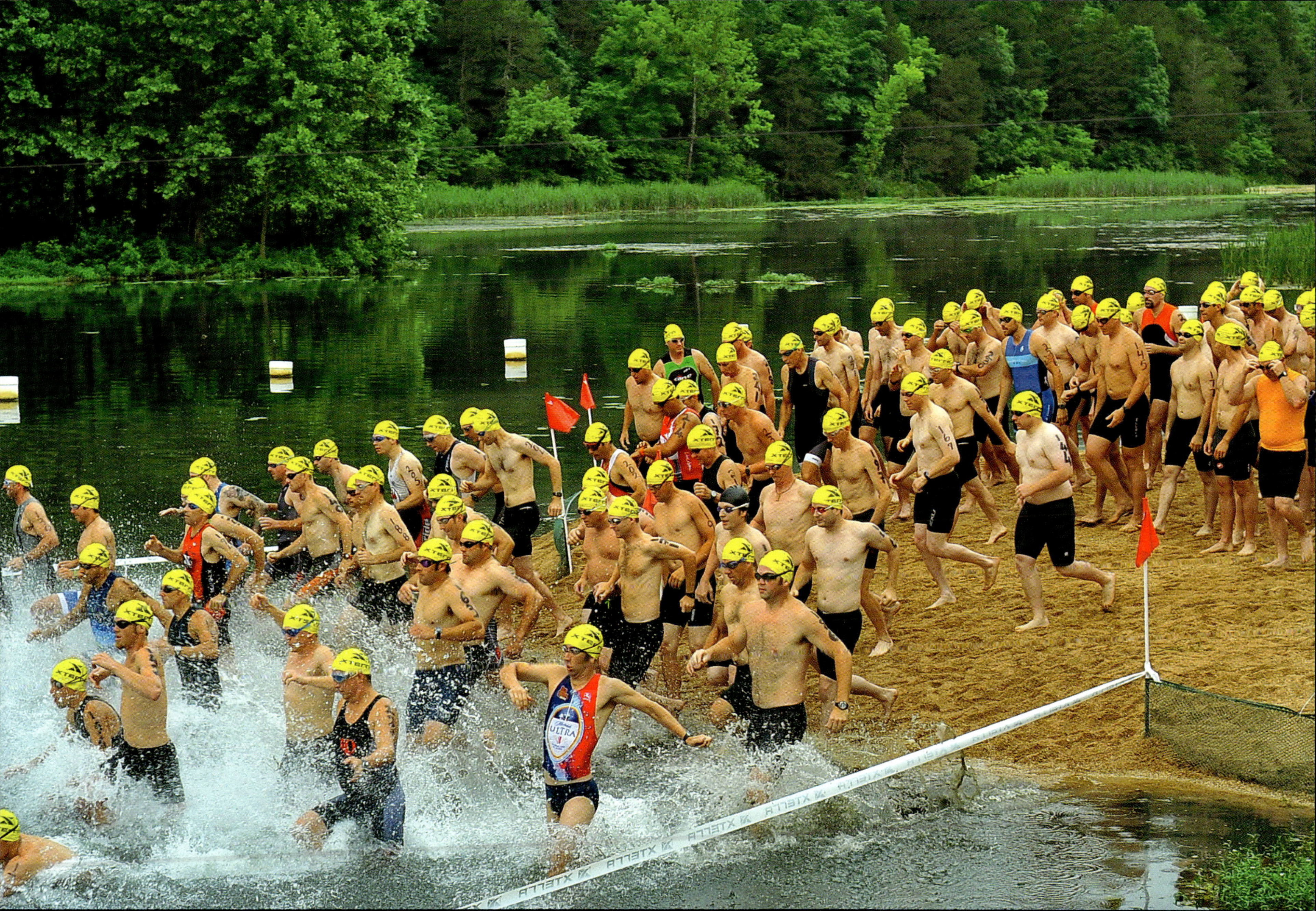


The kickoff of the 2009 XTERRA Eureka Springs is held at Lake Leatherwood, one of the loveliest of the 60 locations along the XTERRA America Tour. The event is usually held in June with hundreds competing in a triathlon; swimming (.5 miles), running (5 miles), and biking (13 miles) through a difficult course within Lake Leatherwood Park.

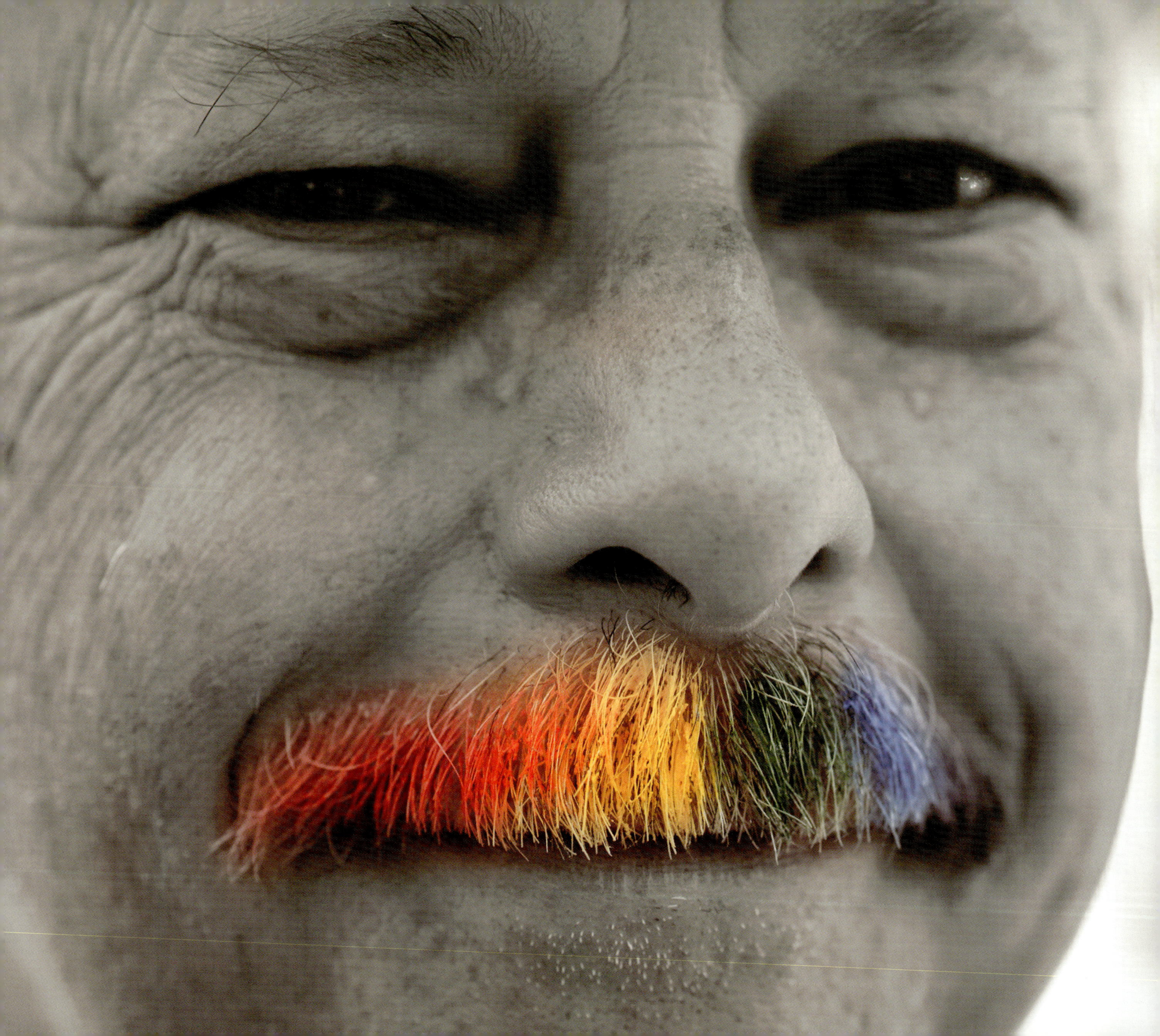

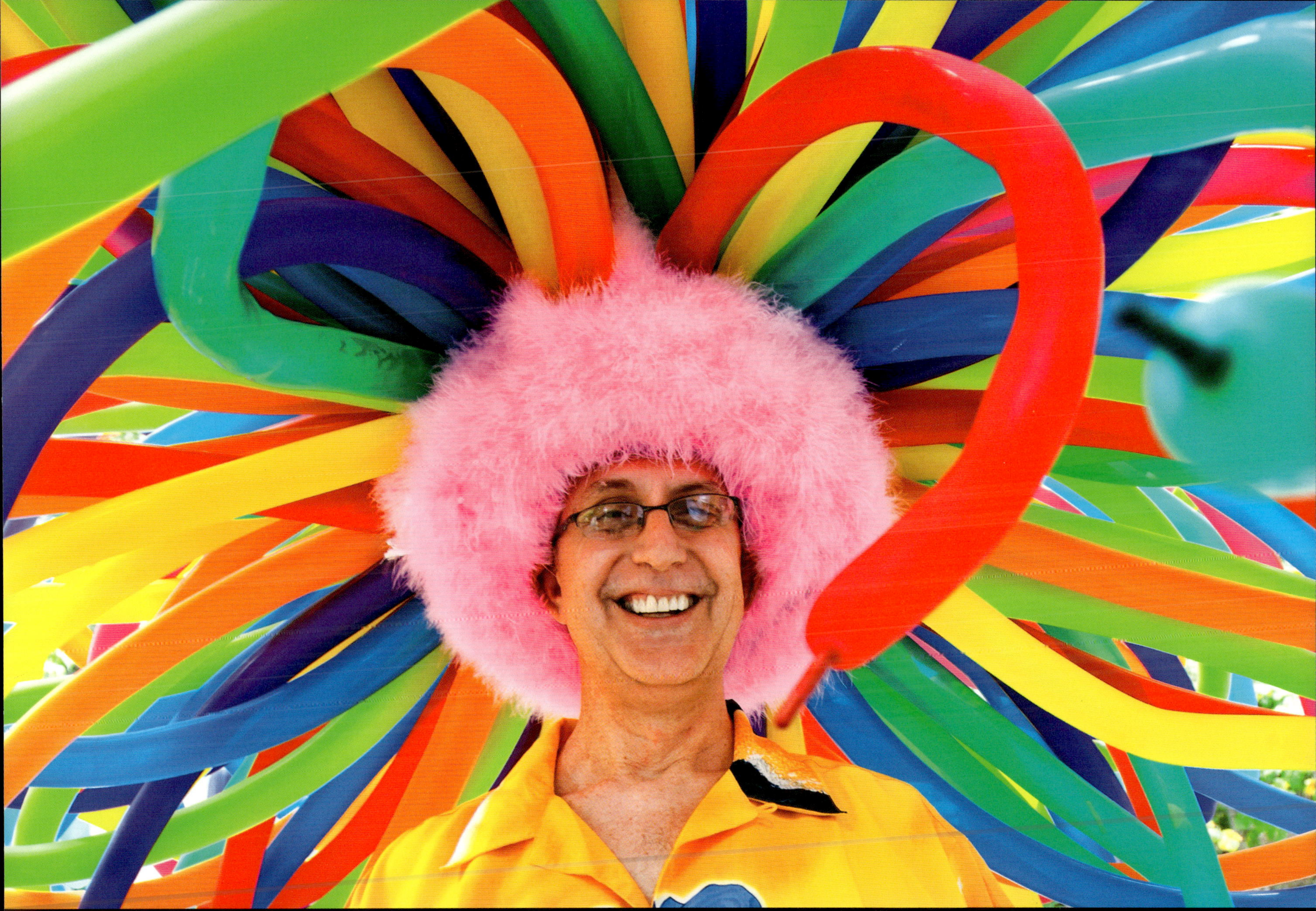

The only city in Arkansas with a Domestic Partnership Registry, Eureka Springs celebrates Diversity Weekend with two weekend events every year, one in summer and one in fall, dedicated to celebrating peace and equality for all. The PDA, art shows, motorcycle rides, and many other events are ongoing across town during the weekends with people coming from surrounding states to honor equality.

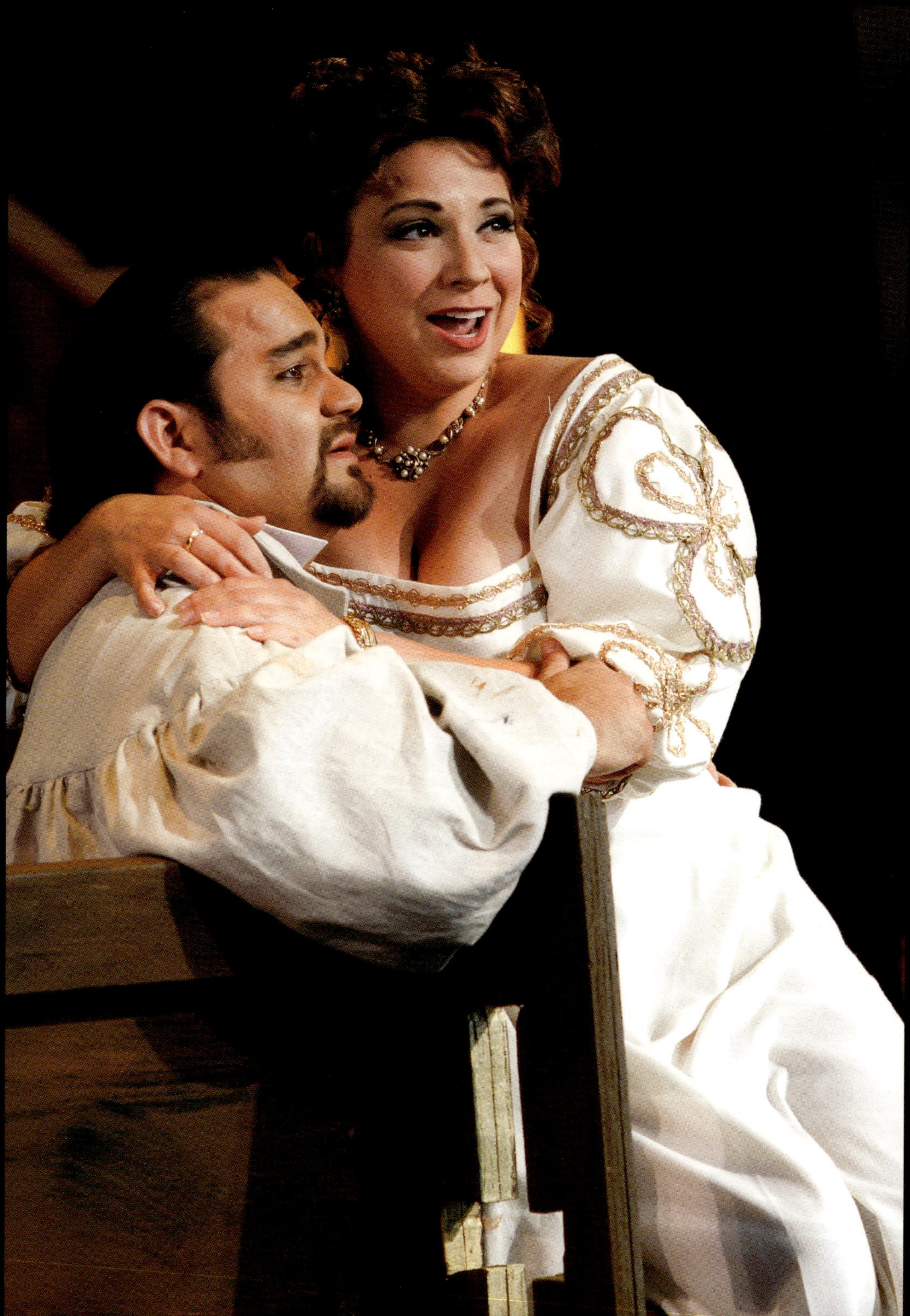

Opera in the Ozarks at Inspiration Point Fine Arts Colony is an intense summer training and performance program that lasts eight weeks each summer, with performers picked from national auditions. The result is one month of world-class opera performances. The organization formed in 1950, and the group's alumni have graced the stages of all major opera venues across the globe. The 2011 season showcased *Die Fledermaus, Le Nozze di Figaro, Little Women*, and a touring version of *The Pirates of Penzance*.

N 36°26.780'
W 093°48.027'
Elevation 1317'

The month of December is a sight to behold in Eureka Springs. The town goes all-out, decorating everything from its Courthouse to its Victorian Painted Ladies in a kaleidoscope of color and lights. The temperate climate zone presents a strong possibility of snowflakes. The city and many of its businesses host Christmas-related events and functions every day throughout the month. Contests are held for best Christmas decorations across a number of categories. Other events range from the elegant annual Tour of Homes to the annual Running of the Santas. However, nothing is quite like the annual lighted evening Christmas Parade, which lasts in the neighborhood of an hour and consists of floats from a vapor-spewing mechanical dragon to dancing elves.

N 36°24.136'
W 093°44.229'
Elevation 1286'

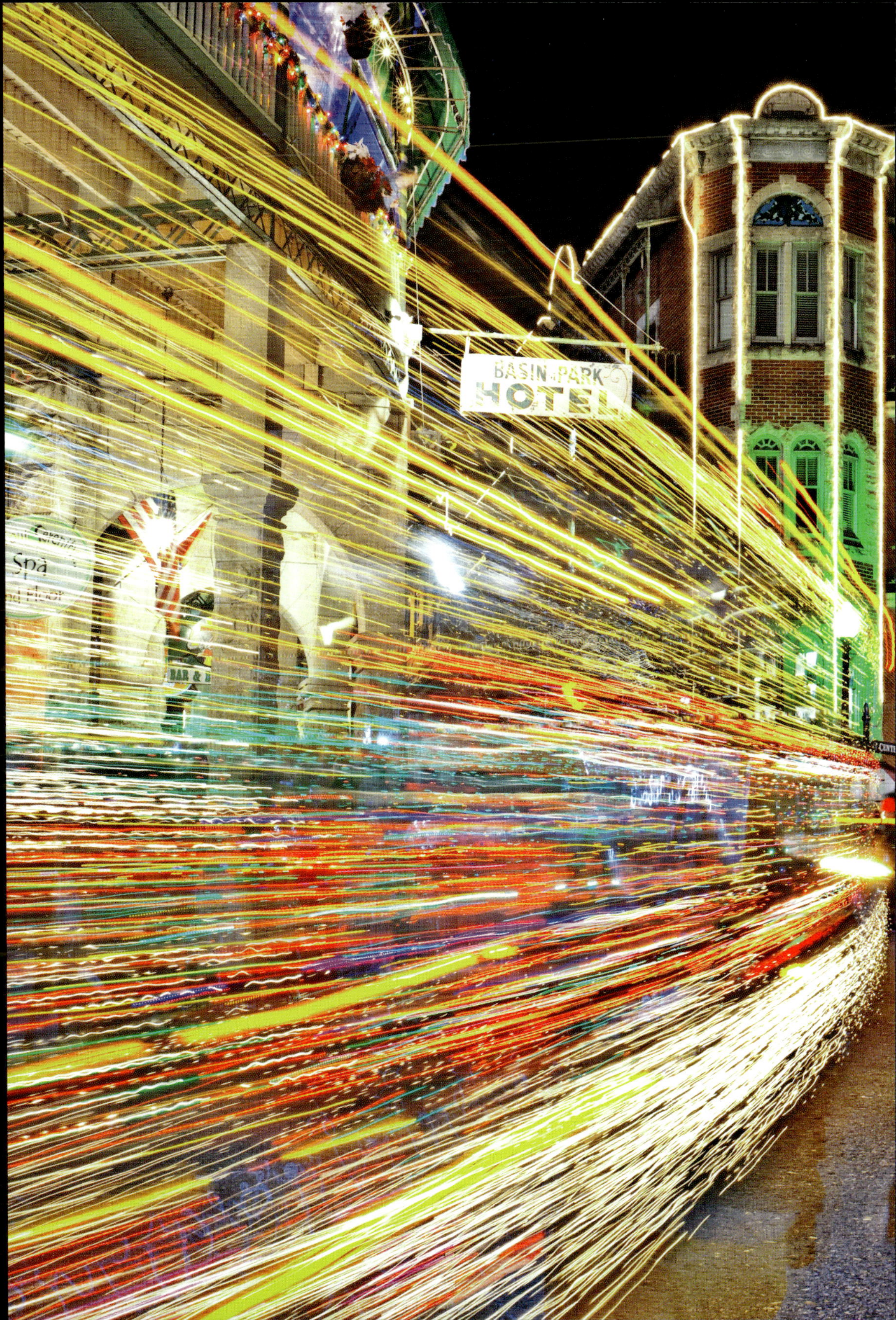

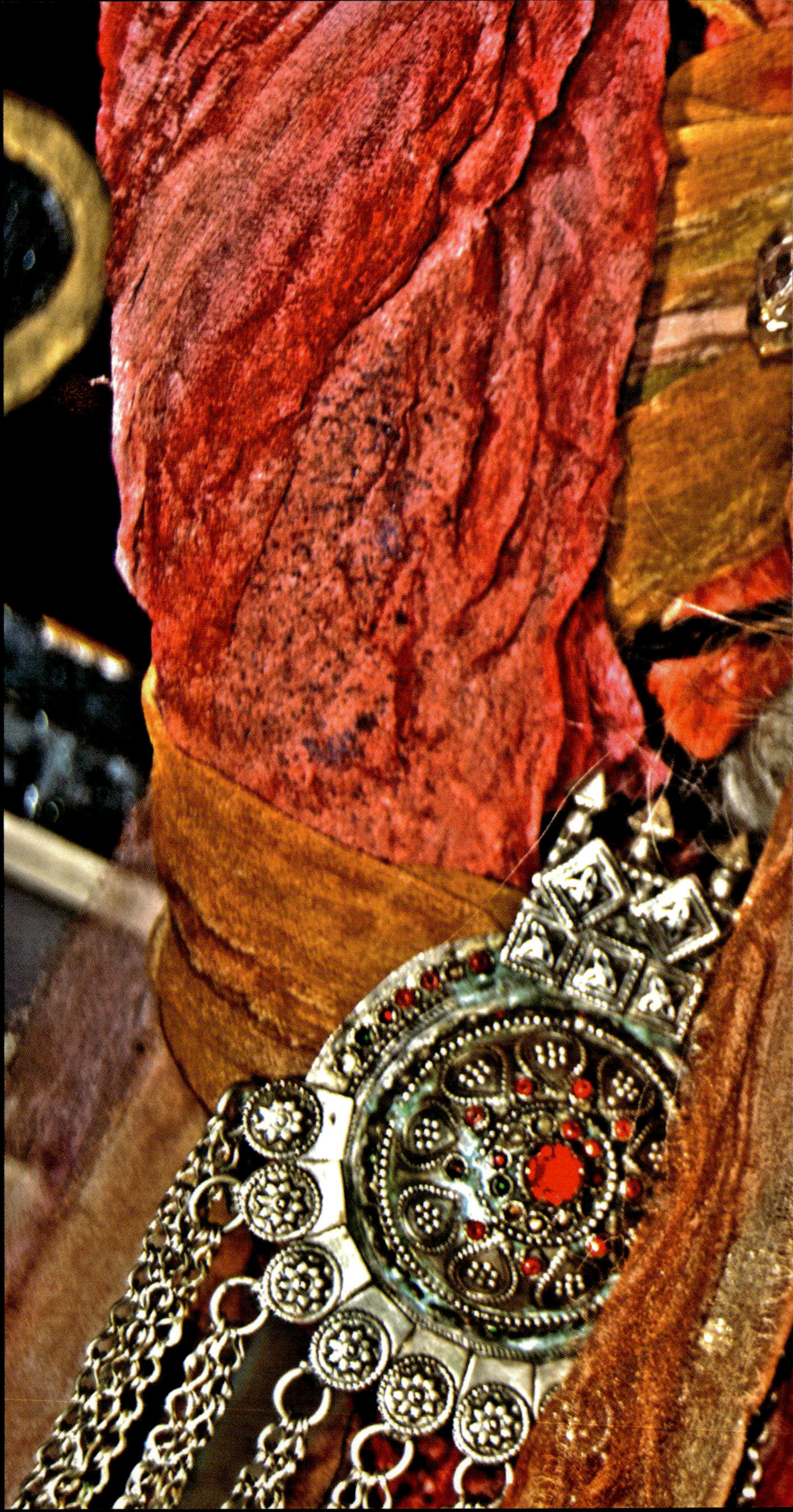

The Eureka Springs School of the Arts, founded in 1998, hosts the annual Mad Hatter Ball in October. Attendees to the fundraising event held in the Crystal Dining Room of the 1886 Crescent Hotel wear hats of all shapes and sizes, some going all-out with a full costume and face paint while others just sport a customized fedora. There are live and silent art auctions with pieces from the area's top artists up for the highest bid. The first ball was held in October of 2003, and the event continues to gain in popularity.

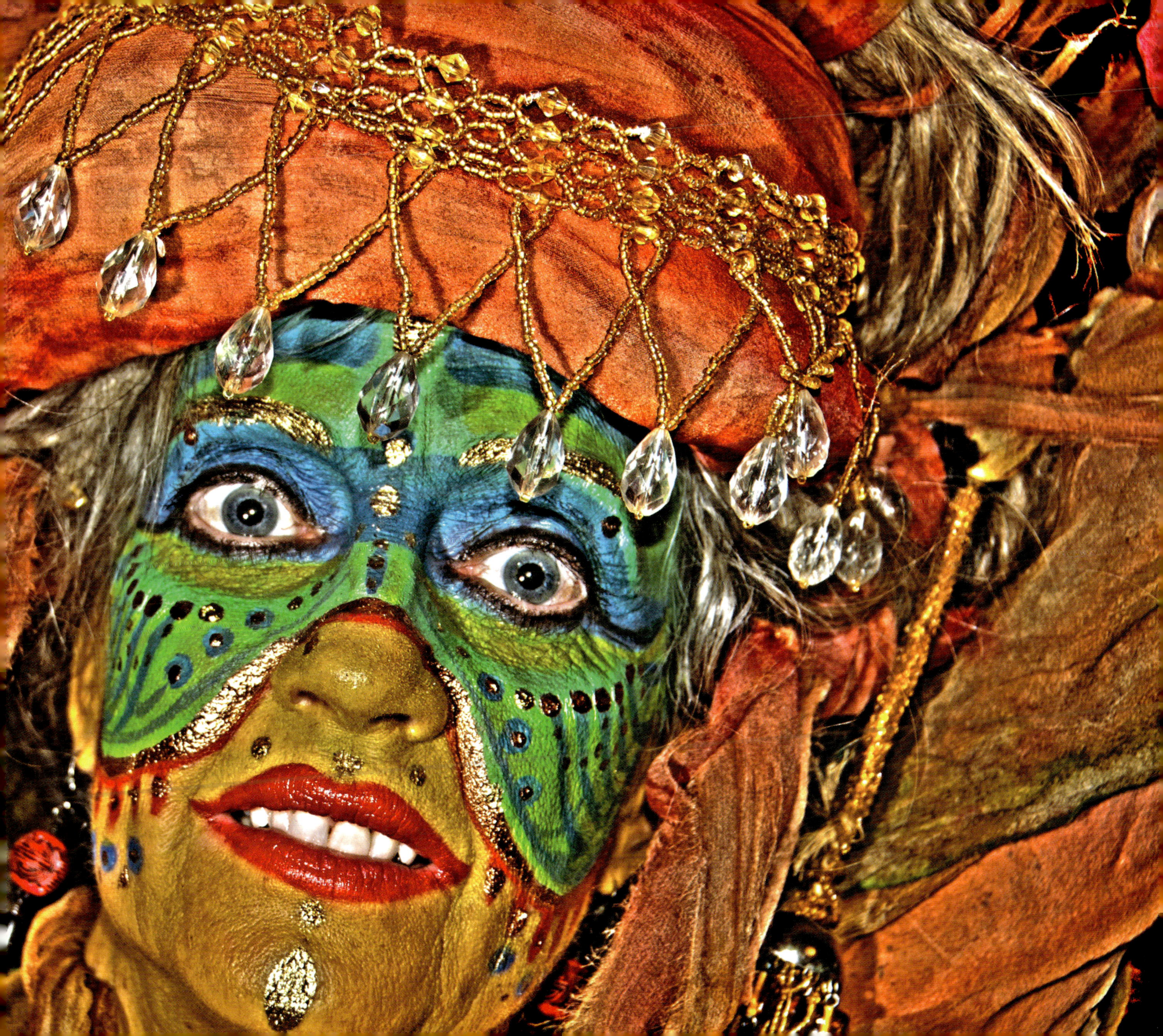

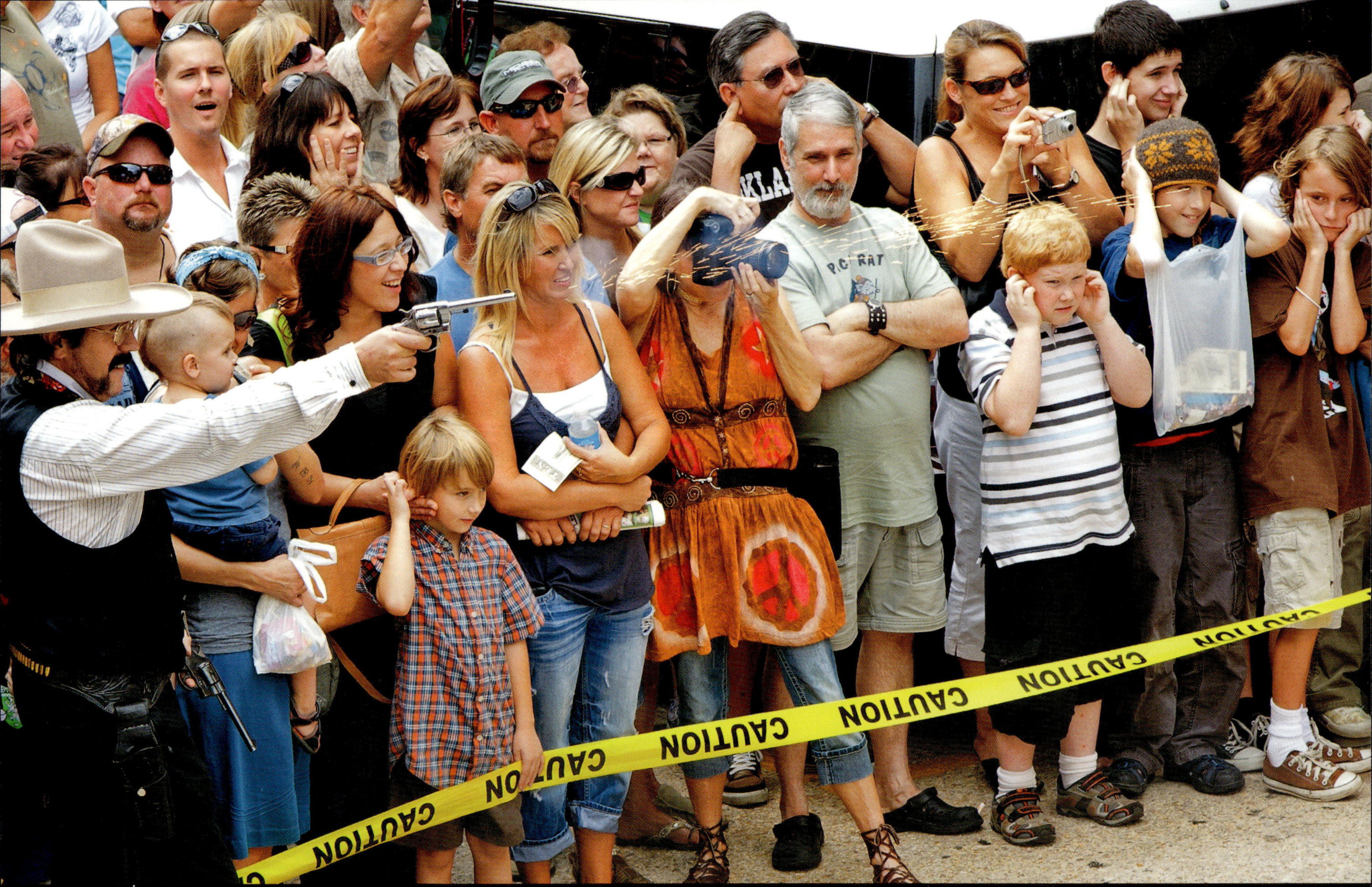
CAUTION
CAUTION
CAUTION

Five men, most from Oklahoma, driving a Model T Ford, robbed the First National Bank in Eureka Springs in the midmorning hours of September 22, 1922. Gunshots were a foreign noise in Eureka Springs back then, and the townsfolk were quick to react when alarms sounded. Just as the men thought they had scored $10,000 in cash and another $60,000 in Liberty Bonds, the man in the getaway car noticed locals heading his way with firearms in hand and tried to escape. The car started down Spring Street but locals opened fire upon the car until its driver lost control and smashed into a power pole. A firefight broke out between the remaining four bandits and many locals. It spilled from the bank into the streets and down a stairwell – and before the dust settled, the firefight left all the bandits dead or wounded. Two survived, and were both convicted. The day was marked as the bloodiest criminal act the town has seen to date. Each year Eureka Springs remembers the local heroes of that day with an Antique Car Parade and a reenactment of the infamous robbery attempt.

N 36°24.202'
W 093°44.220'
Elevation 1139'

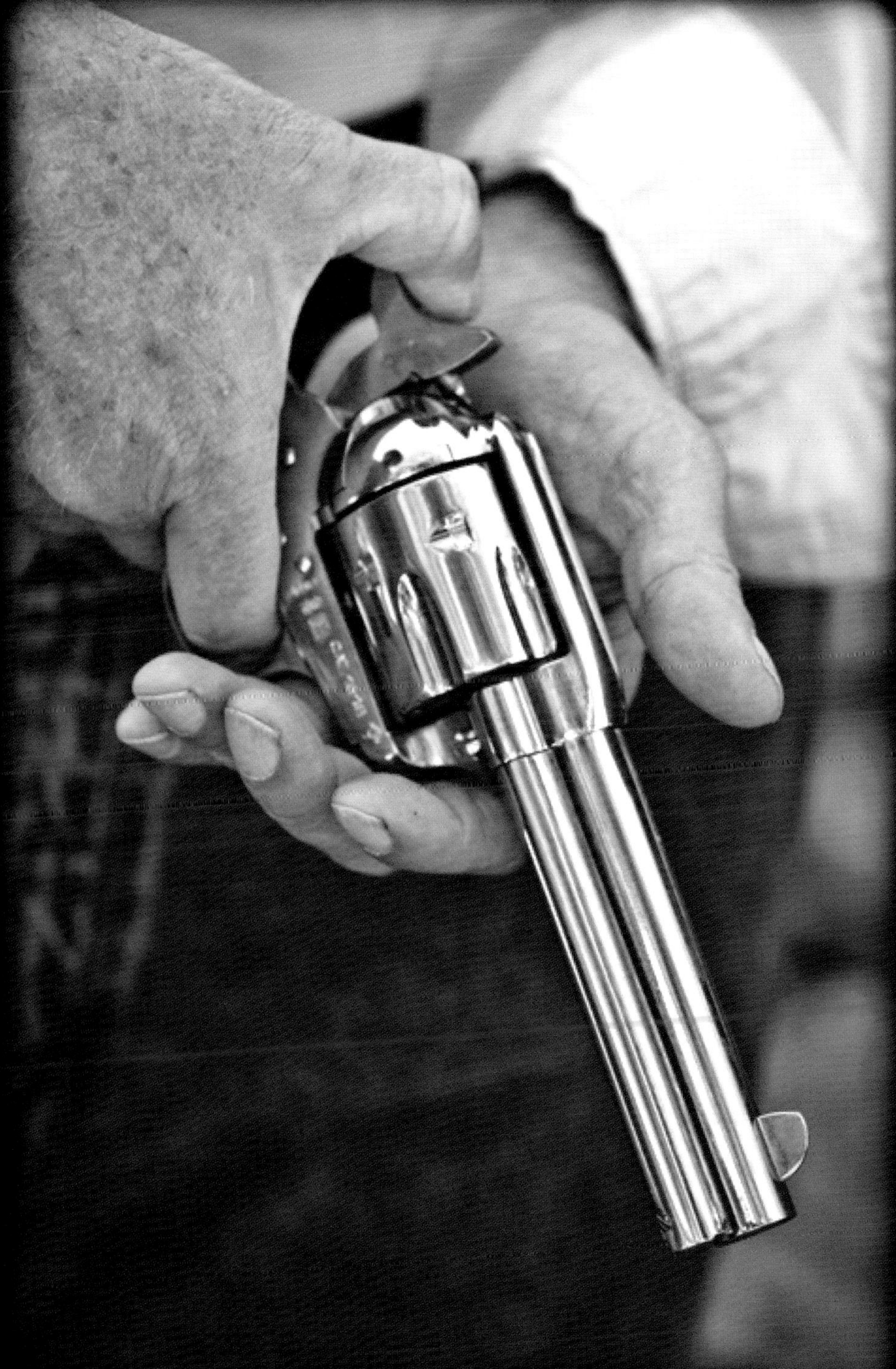

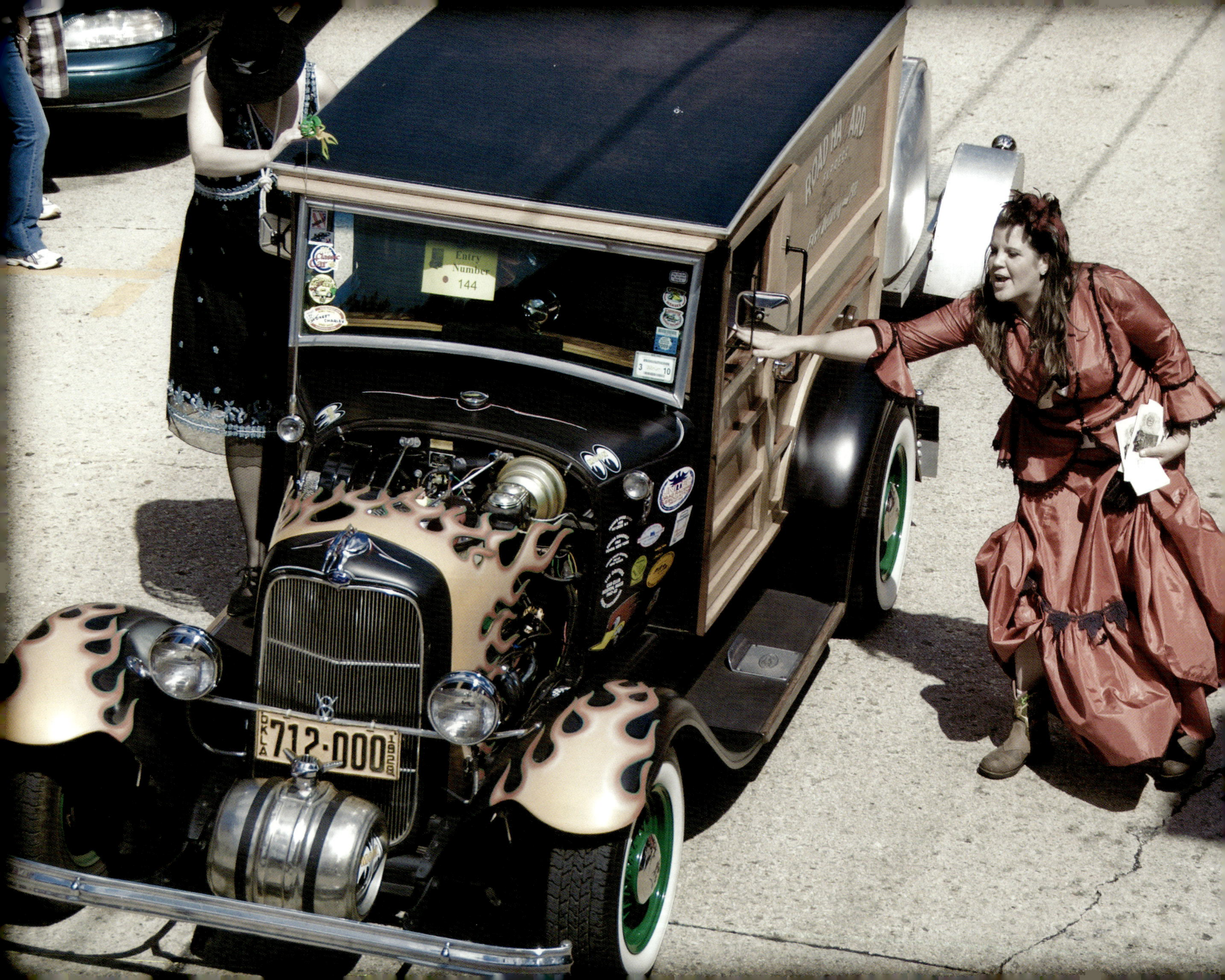
Entry
Number
144
OKLA
712-000
1928

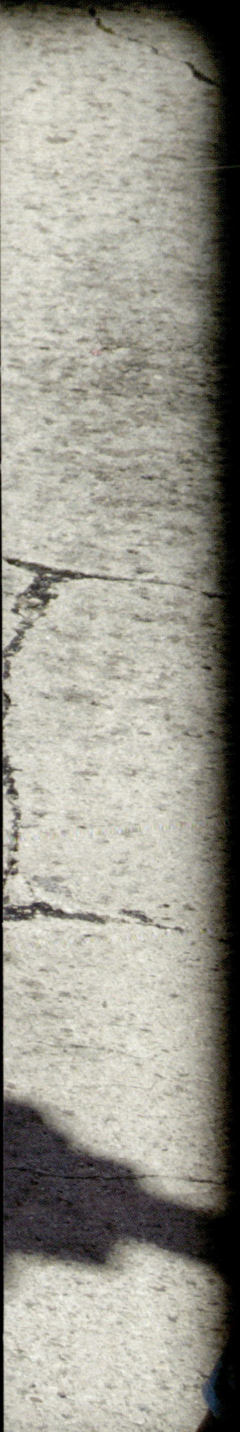

September welcomes the annual Eureka Springs Antique Auto Festival weekend. Vintage vehicles remain on display at the Pine Mountain Village shopping center over the weekend for viewing and contest judging. Model Ts, Mustangs, and Lead-Sleds compete across a wide array of categories for First Place. The cars tour the countryside in packs, so keep your eyes peeled for mini parades. The official parade, usually held on Saturday, can best be viewed at Pendergrass Corner *(pictured at right)*, Basin Spring Park, or from many points in between. Townsfolk gather at the local watering hole for a photo op just before the parade kicks off, then head downtown to work the crowds with their antics *(pictured at left)*.

N 36°24.202'
W 093°44.220'
Elevation 1139'

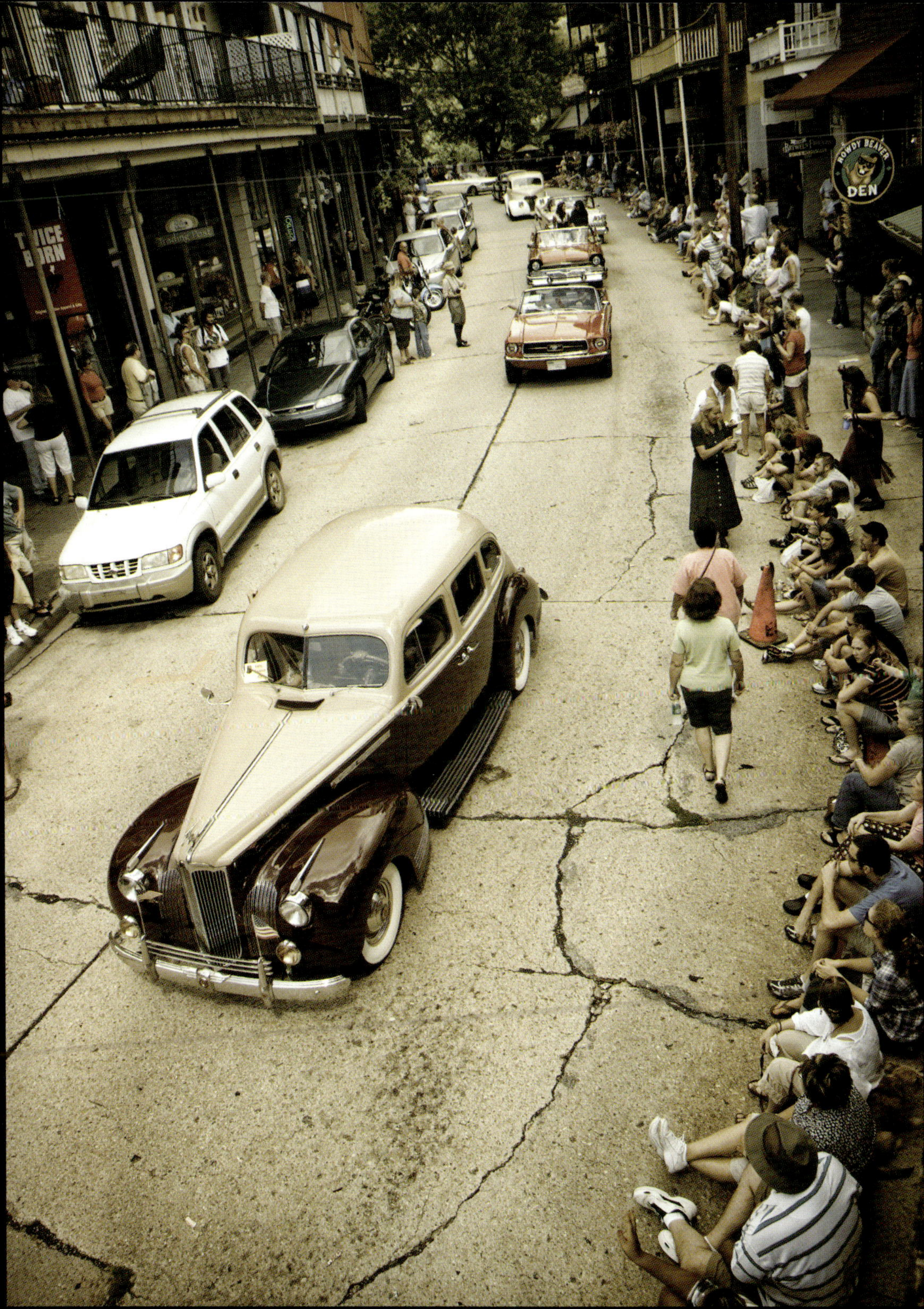

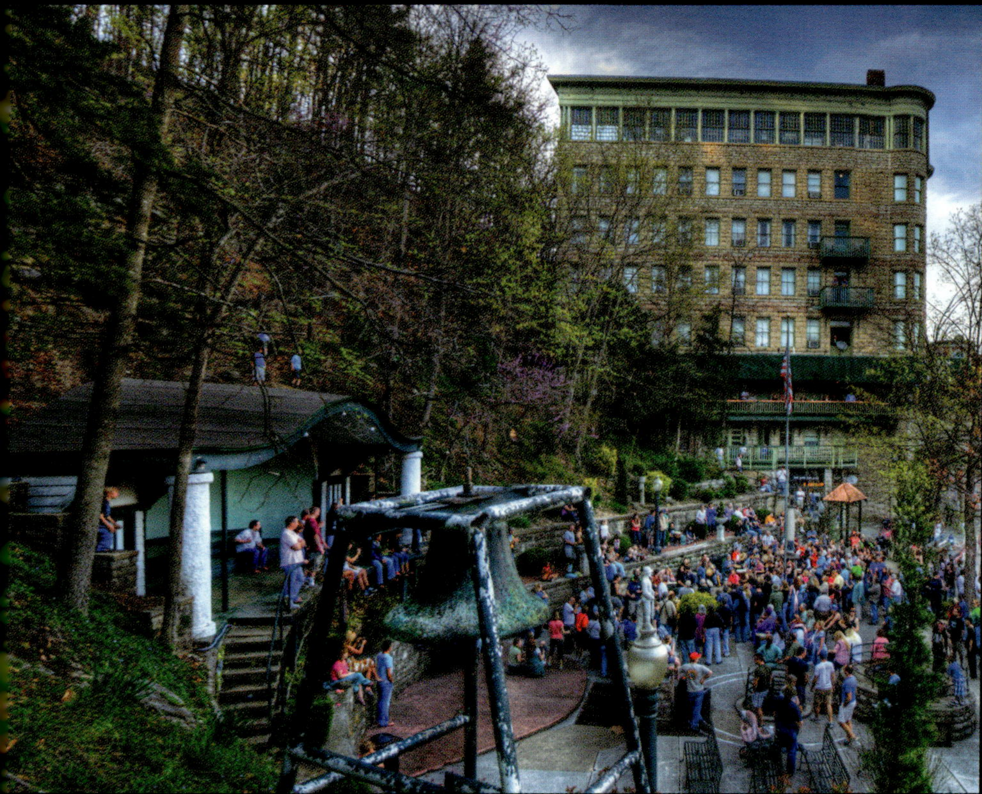

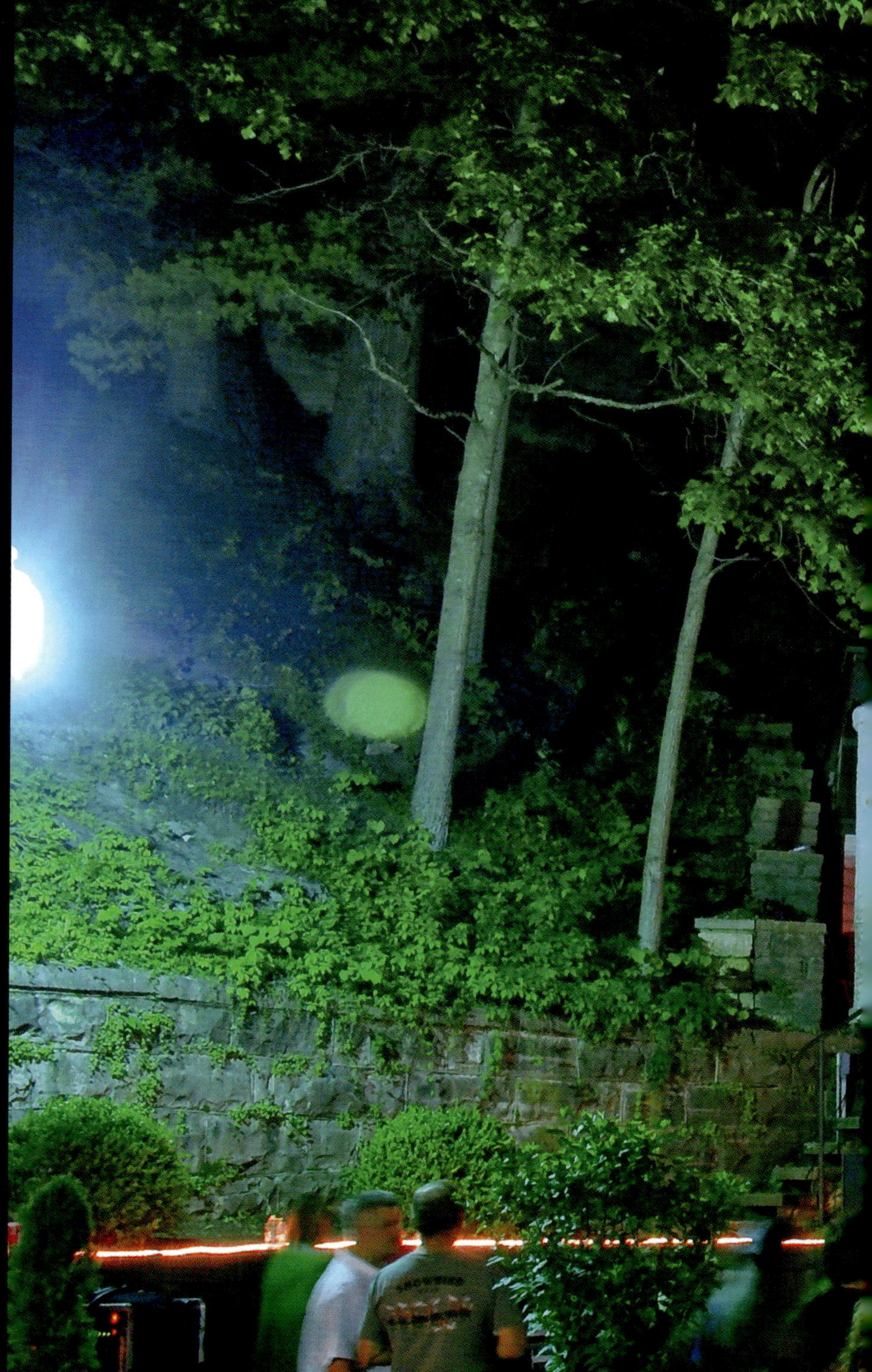

The heart of Eureka Springs, Basin Springs Park, comes alive with a bevy of performing arts from spring into fall. The bandshell, built in 1915, hosts a plethora of musical talents – all free to the public. Local brass bands were a familiar appearance in the 1920s, and these days the bands include anything from blues to afro-pop.

N 36°24.116'
W 093°44.258'
Elevation 1260'

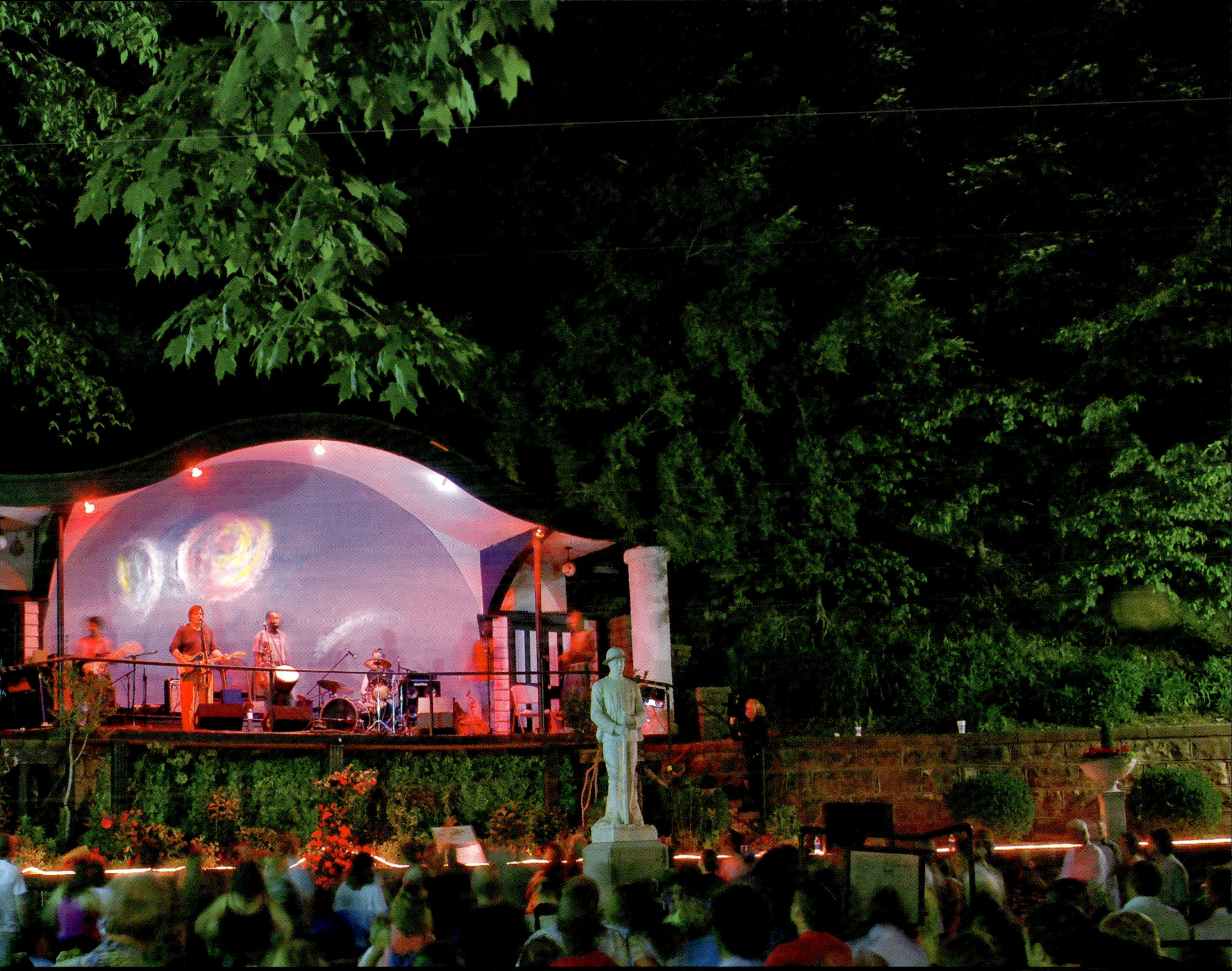

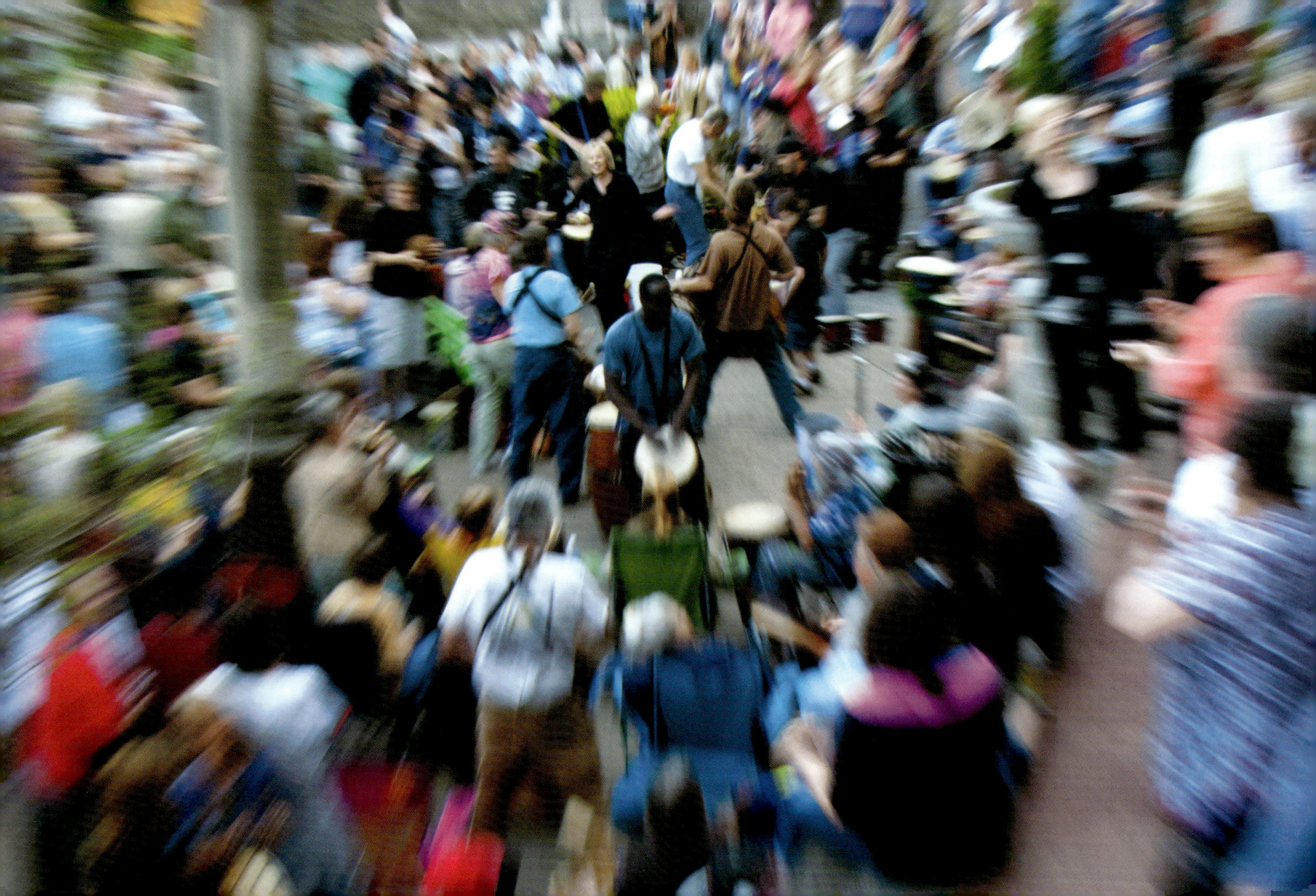

Angelo Yao lived in a village (Bouake) along the pristine Ivory Coast in Africa, and now lives in a village (Eureka Springs) in the pristine Ozarks Mountains. Yao joined the African National Dance Company in 1987 and toured the area until 1997, along with 8 others in the Troupe, when an opportunity led him to Yale University. He then traveled the states until meeting his wife in 2001. Yao moved to Eureka Springs around 2003 and worked for the Eureka Springs Police Department while in his spare time forming the afro-pop musical group, Ozakwaaba, and organizing Drumming in the Park and African in the Ozarks. Yao uses mostly deer skin drums that he fashions himself, and leads the drum circle held on first Saturday of each month in Basin Spring Park (or at an indoor location when the weather's too cold). He is a fixture in most parades, leading a large group of African drummers and dancers.

N 36°24.128'
W 093°44.257'
Elevation 1251'

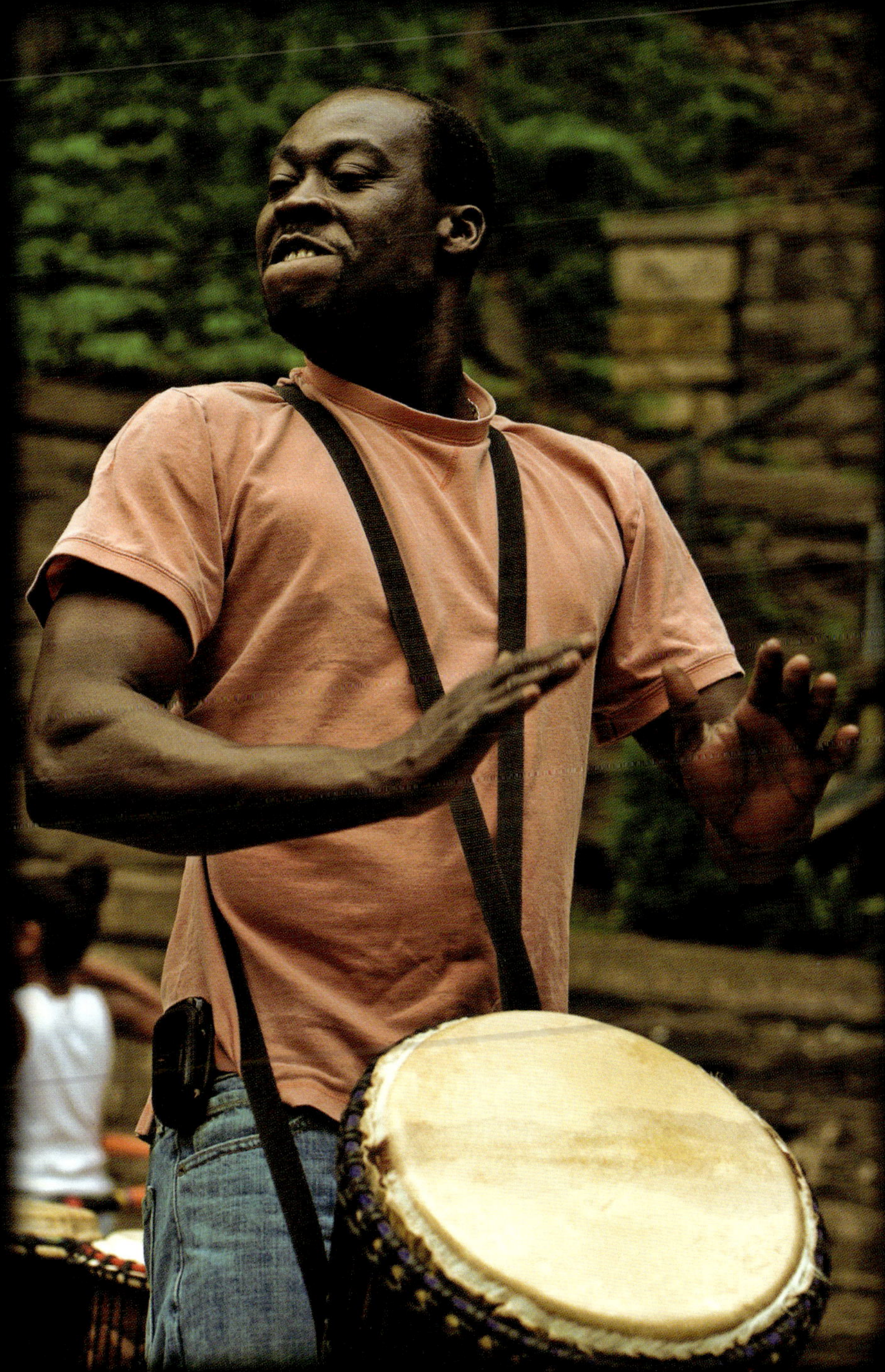

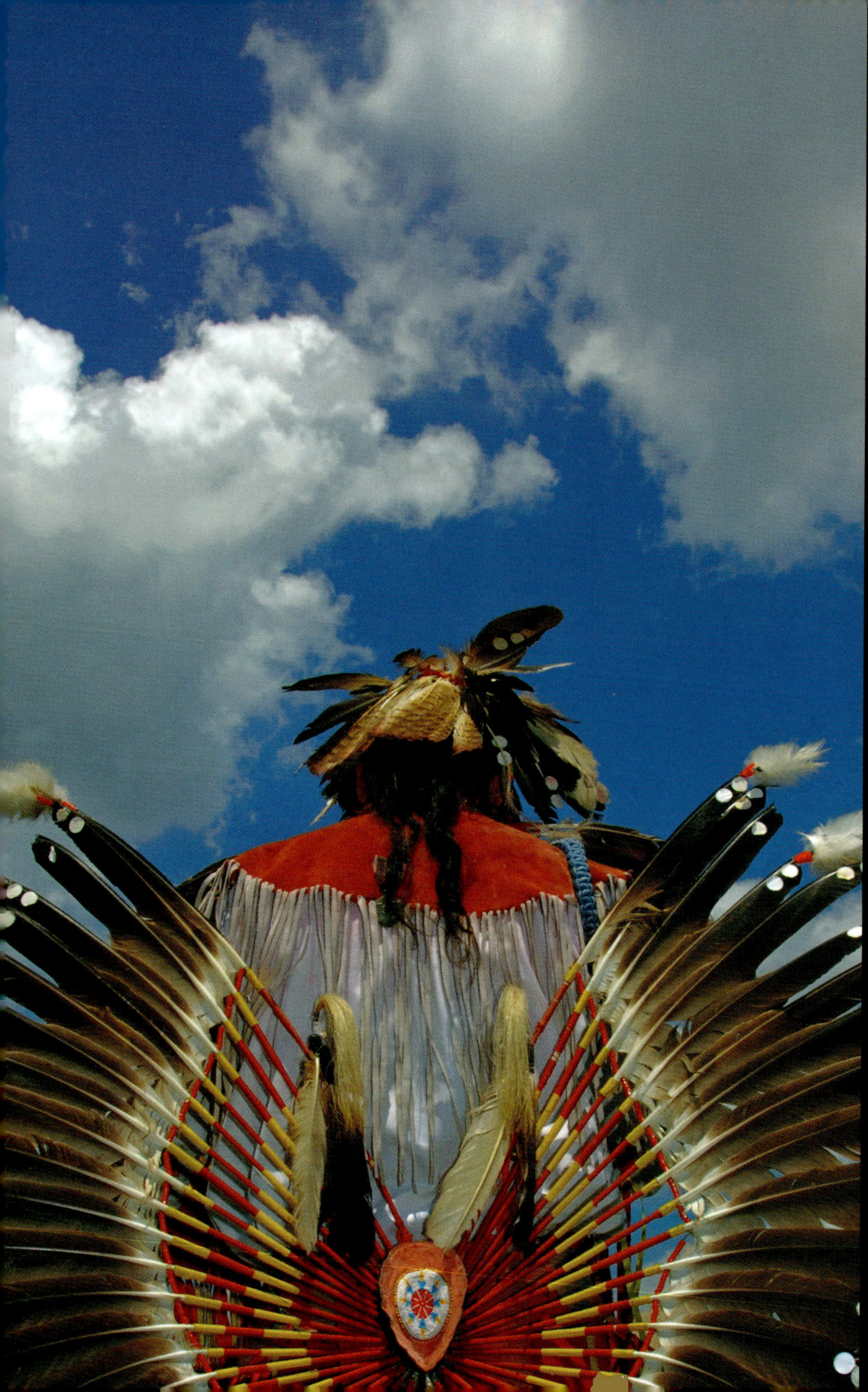

The annual Native American Pow Wow on Fathers Day Weekend is held at Turpentine Creek Wildlife Refugee. Booths of wares and edibles surround the circular performance area with a massive ceremonial drum at the center. Gourd, free-style, and ceremonial dances follow the Color Guard presentation, giving onlookers a taste of Native American heritage along with crafts and food.

Sponsored by Kaleidokites of Eureka Springs, the annual Kite Festival takes place each March at Turpentine Creek Wildlife Refuge and is free to the public. There is a different theme every year and there are always many different kites on riding the air. From five-foot tall dancing people to high-speed aerial stunt kites, there is something to wow both young and old.

N 36°18.637'
W 093°45.593'
Elevation 1606'

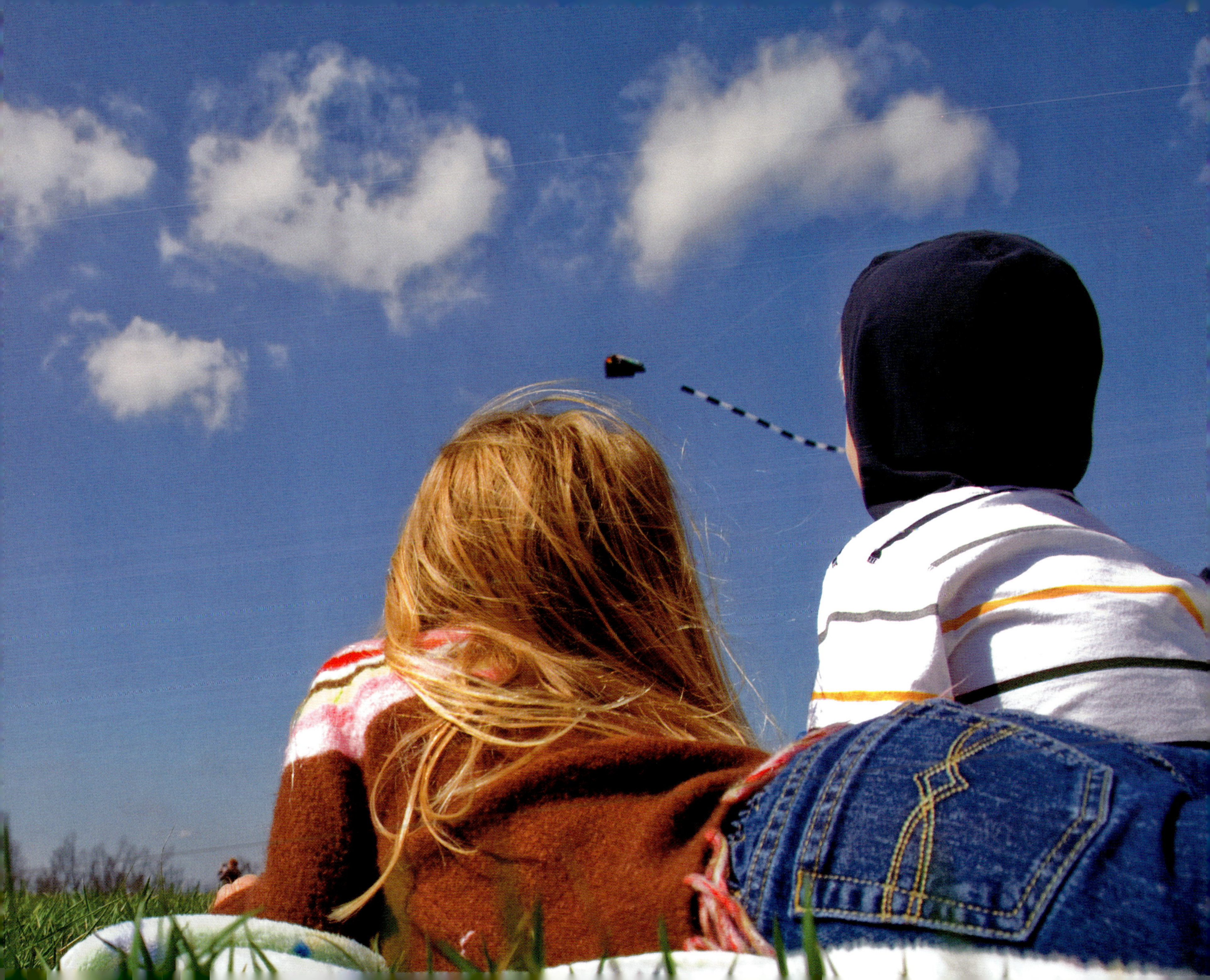

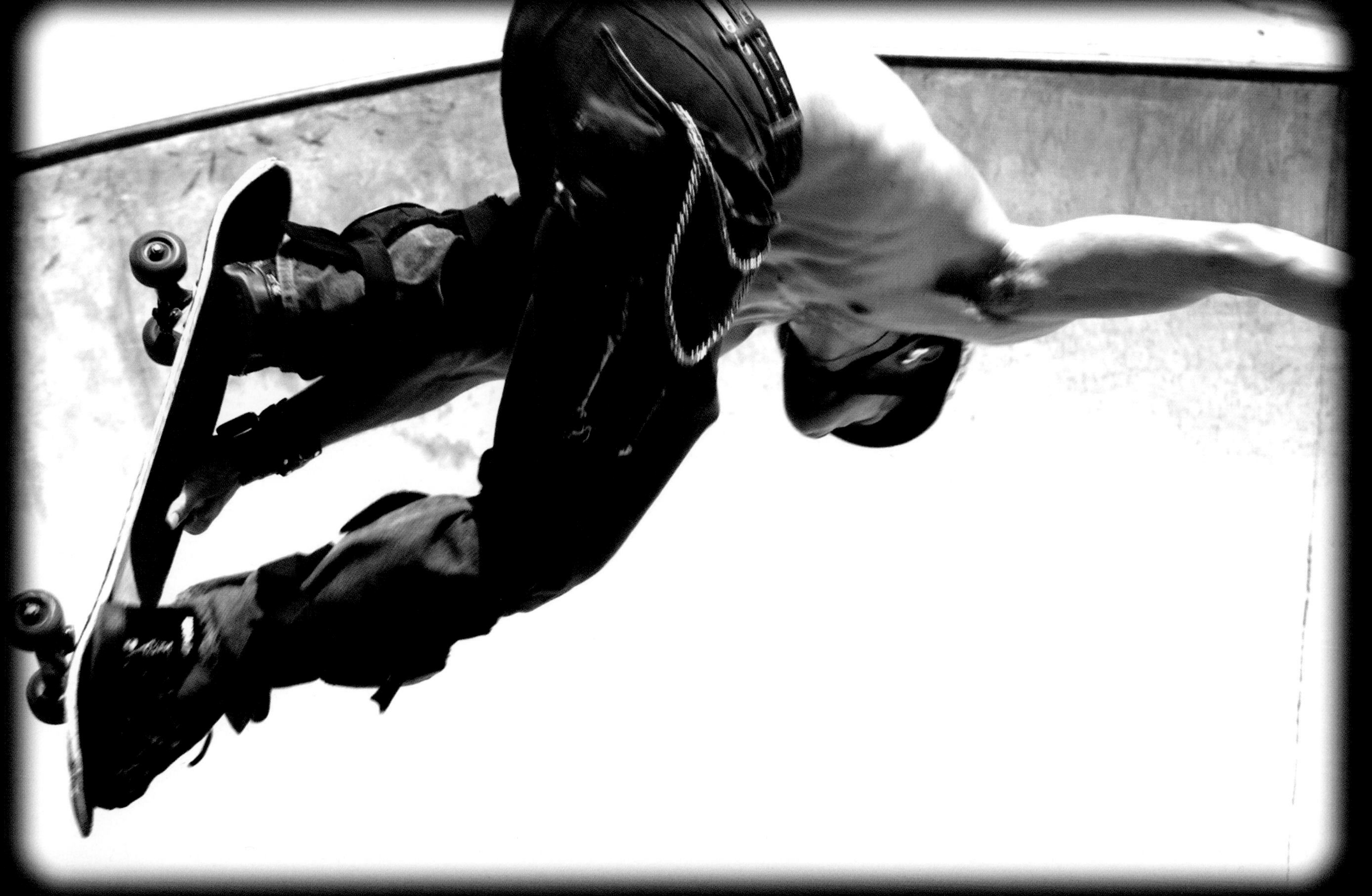

Originally called the Interstate Summer Normal and Educational Assembly Grounds, Harmon Park is the site of the Eureka Springs Parks and Recreation Commission's main office, located at the head of the park. Two charitable grant donations were made in 2004 and 2005 for the construction of a full skateboard park and bowl to go alongside a fully ADA-accessible playground.

N 36°24.619'
W 093°44.417'
Elevation 1242'

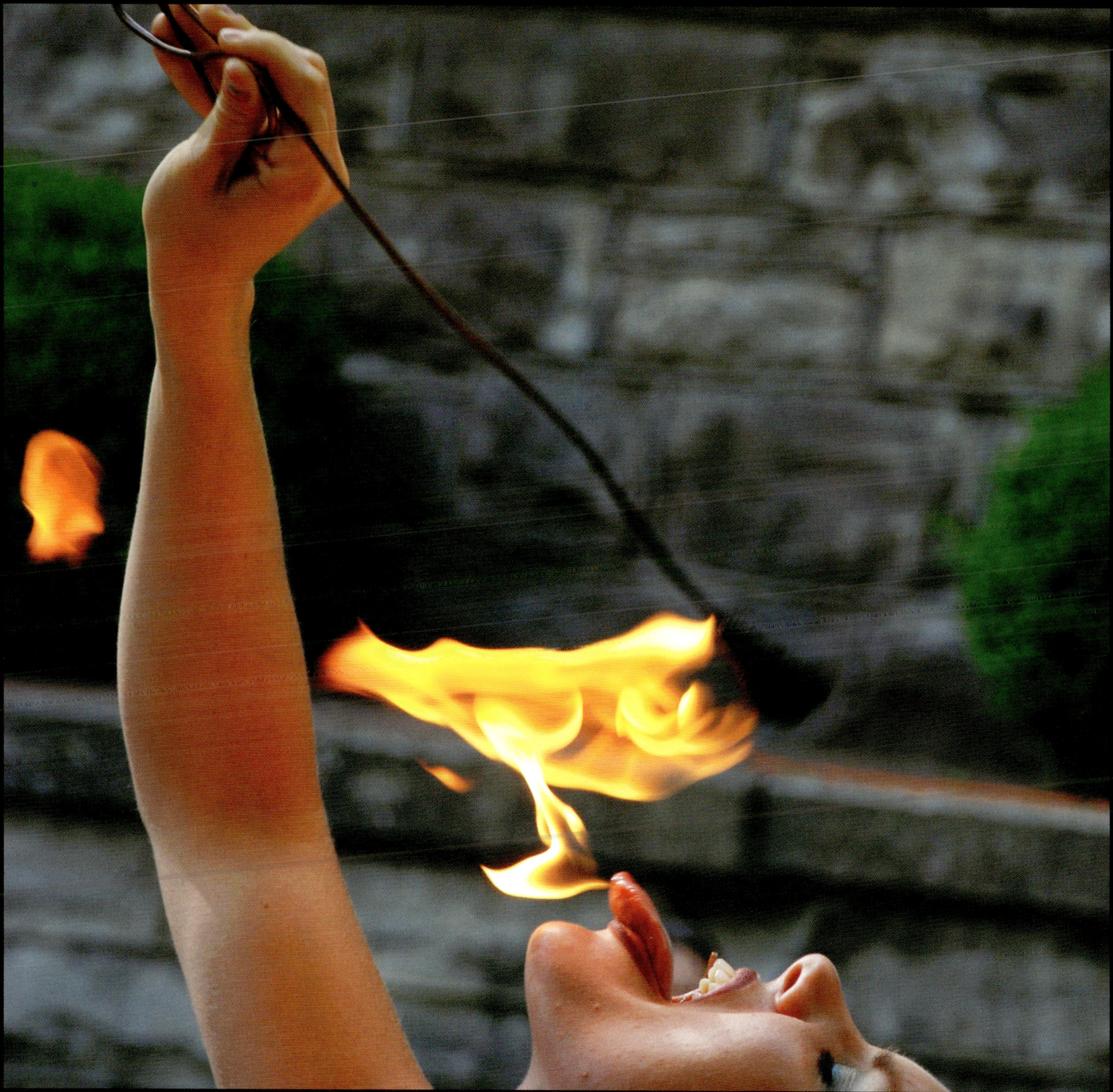

The sounds of banjos fill the hillsides during the Eureka Springs Bluegrass Festival in August. The events, primarily held in the Auditorium and Basin Spring Park, start midday and last into the night. A watermelon social kicks off the event on Thursday in Basin Spring Park. Picking sessions and shows continue across three or four days. During the social, musicians are encouraged to join in one of the many random jam sessions. Most local drinking establishments host live bluegrass-style music throughout the weekend as well.

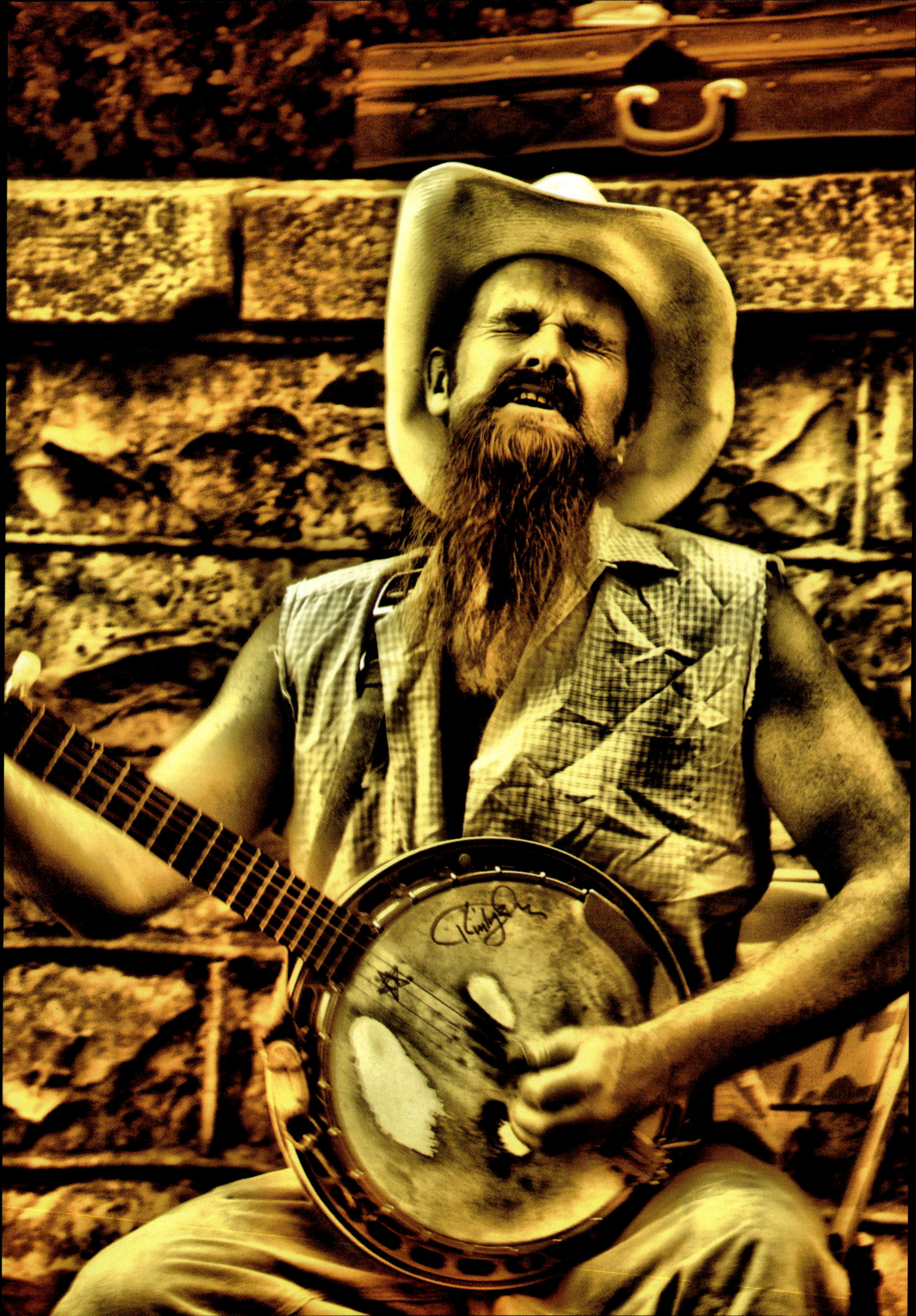

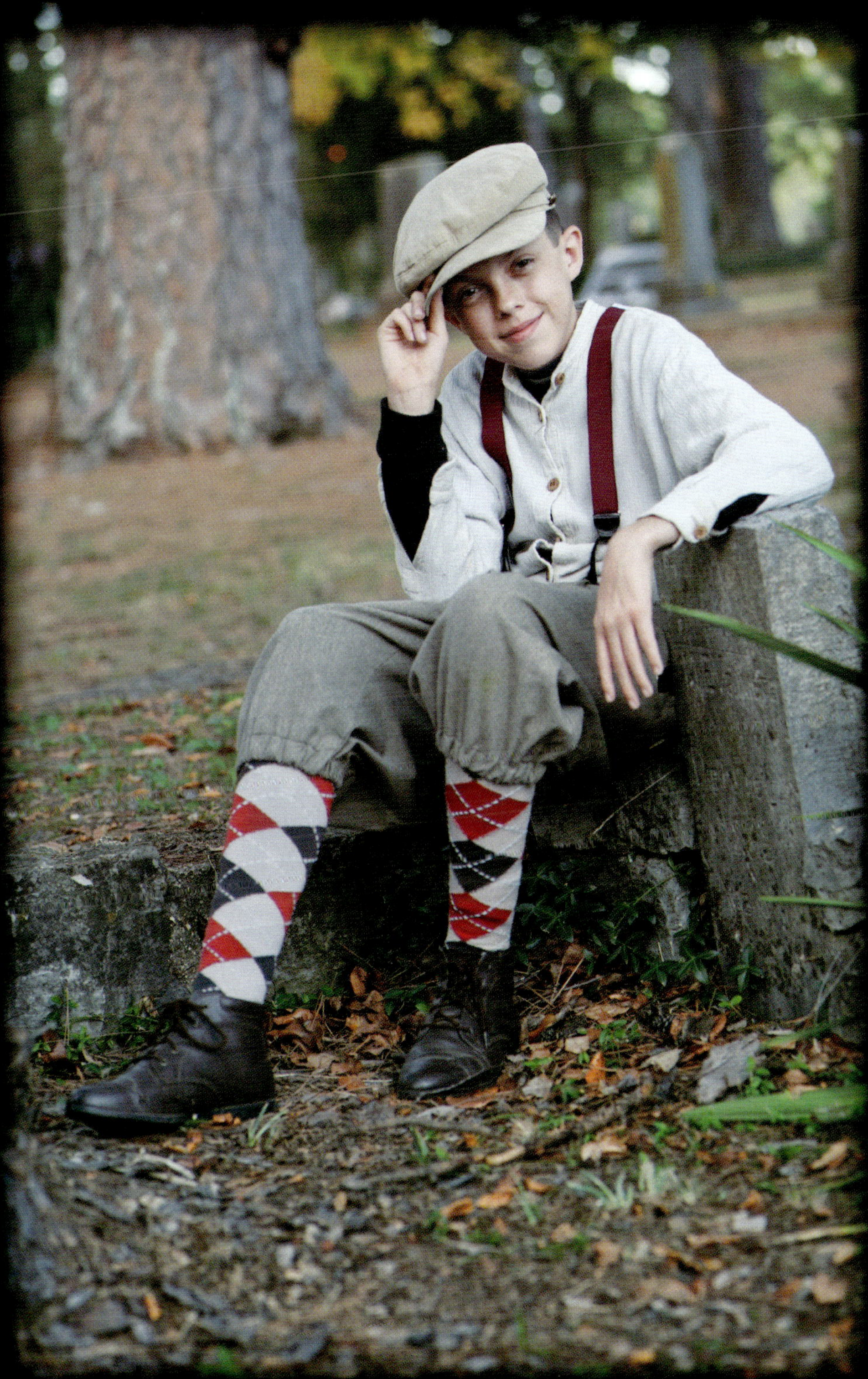

Eureka Springs' countryside is almost as unique as the people who populate it. Each October, the Eureka Springs Historical Museum hosts Voices from Eureka's Silent City at the Eureka Springs Cemetery. Volunteers don vintage garb and take on the persona of a deceased resident, most with an actual gravesite within the grounds. The tours start at dusk and the actors/actresses share first-person perspective stories amid candlelight. With hundreds of gravestones in the cemetery, new characters appear each year. The stories vary wildly from those of hanged murderers to scorned lovers.

N 36°23.820'
W 093°42.288'
Elevation 1528'

N 36°24.093'
W 093°44.218'
Elevation 1251'

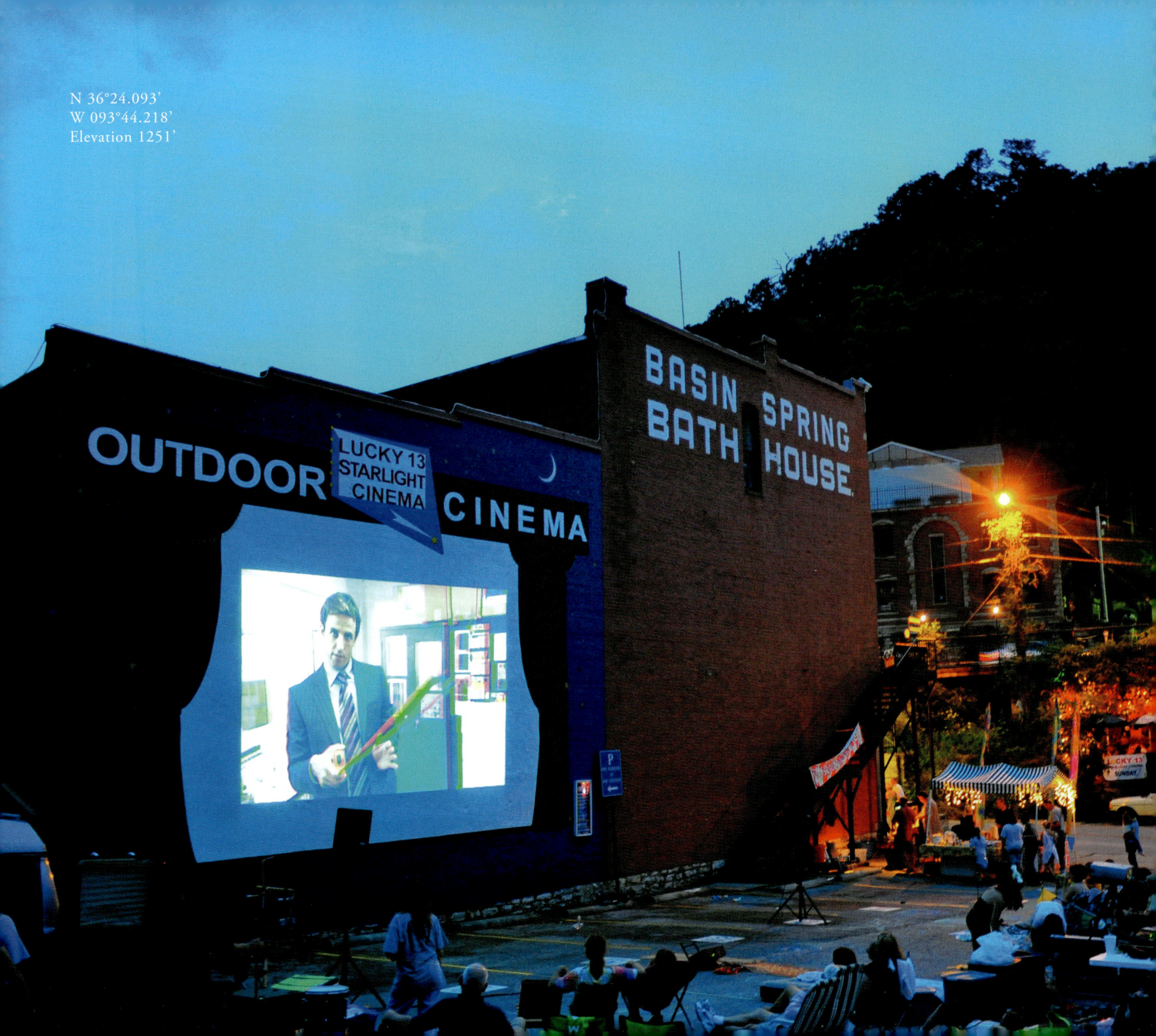

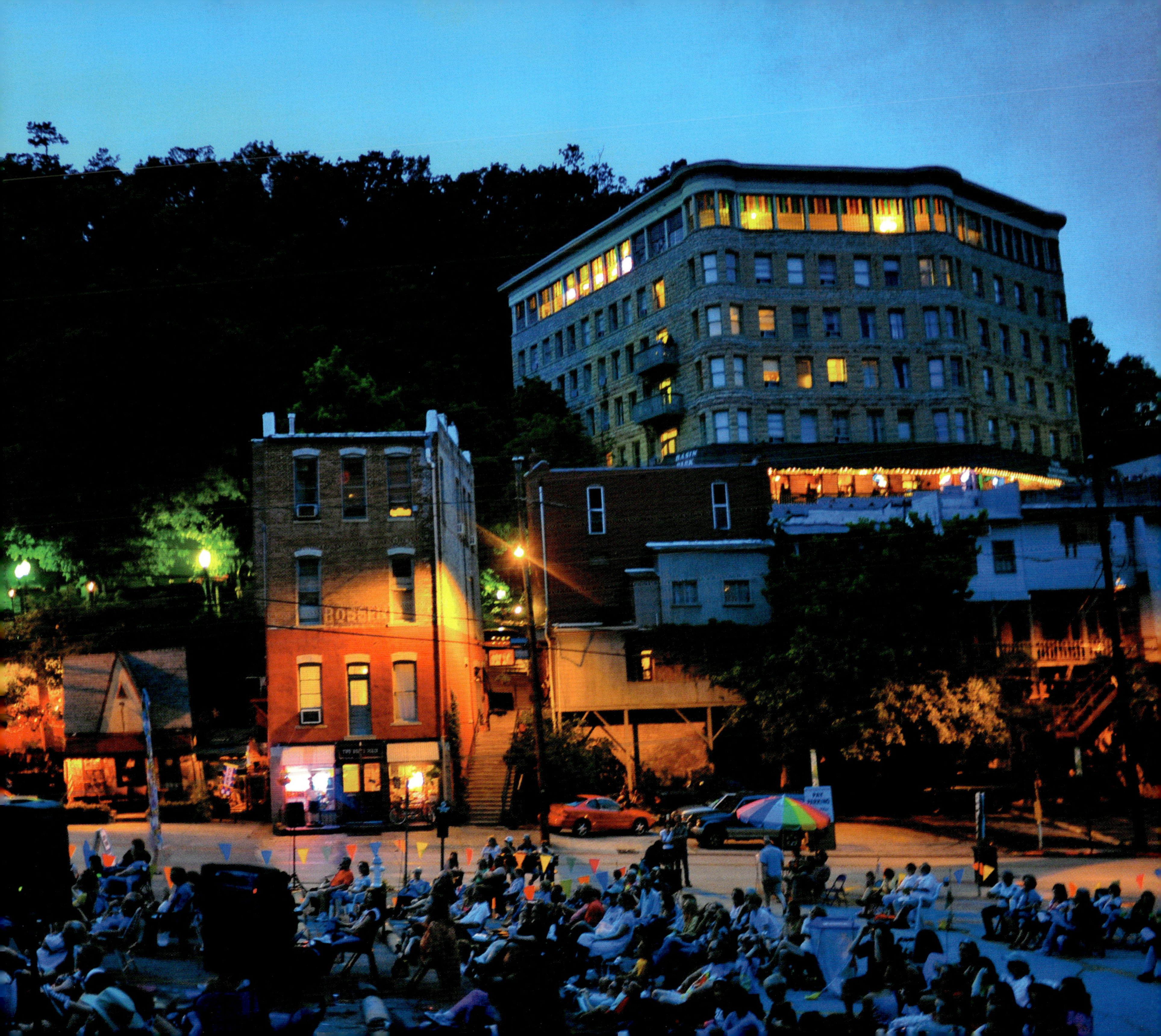

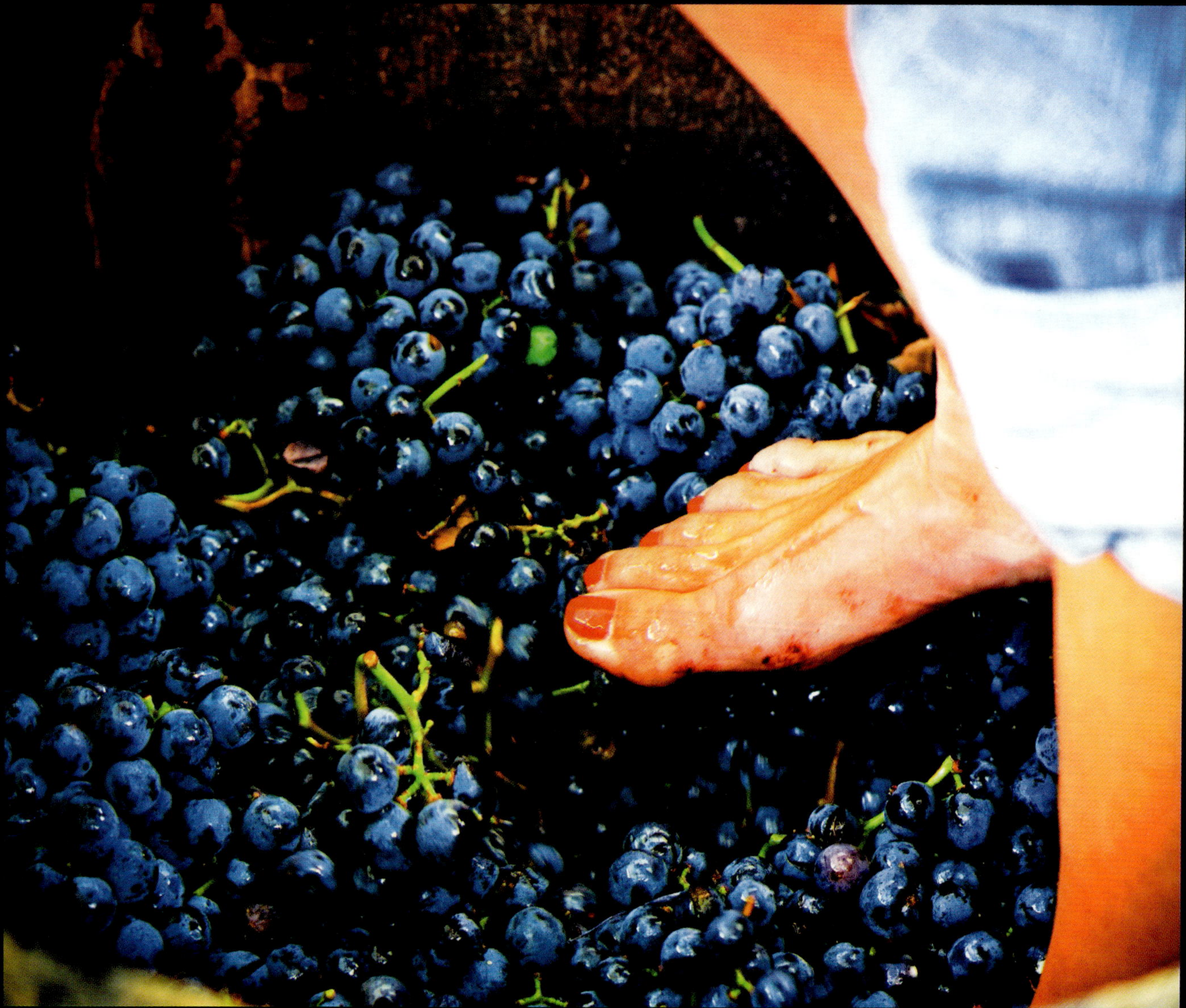

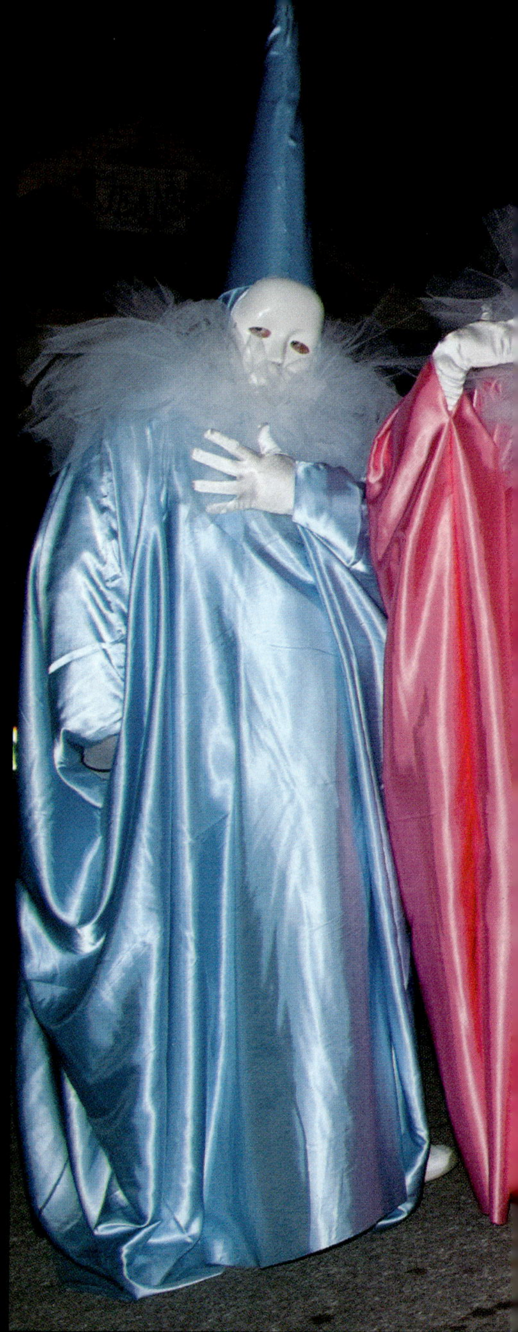

In 2006, wine production kicked off at Keels Creek Winery in Eureka Springs. Starting in 2004 with a span of about 10 sown acres, the grape vineyards grow along Keels Creek in the Rock House Road area. The winery storefront sells their mélange of wines alongside an upscale gallery (Keels Creek Art Gallery) showcasing the works regional artists. Pictured is a participant in the 2009 Grape Crush Festival.

N 36°23.393'
W 093°42.787'
Elevation 1501'

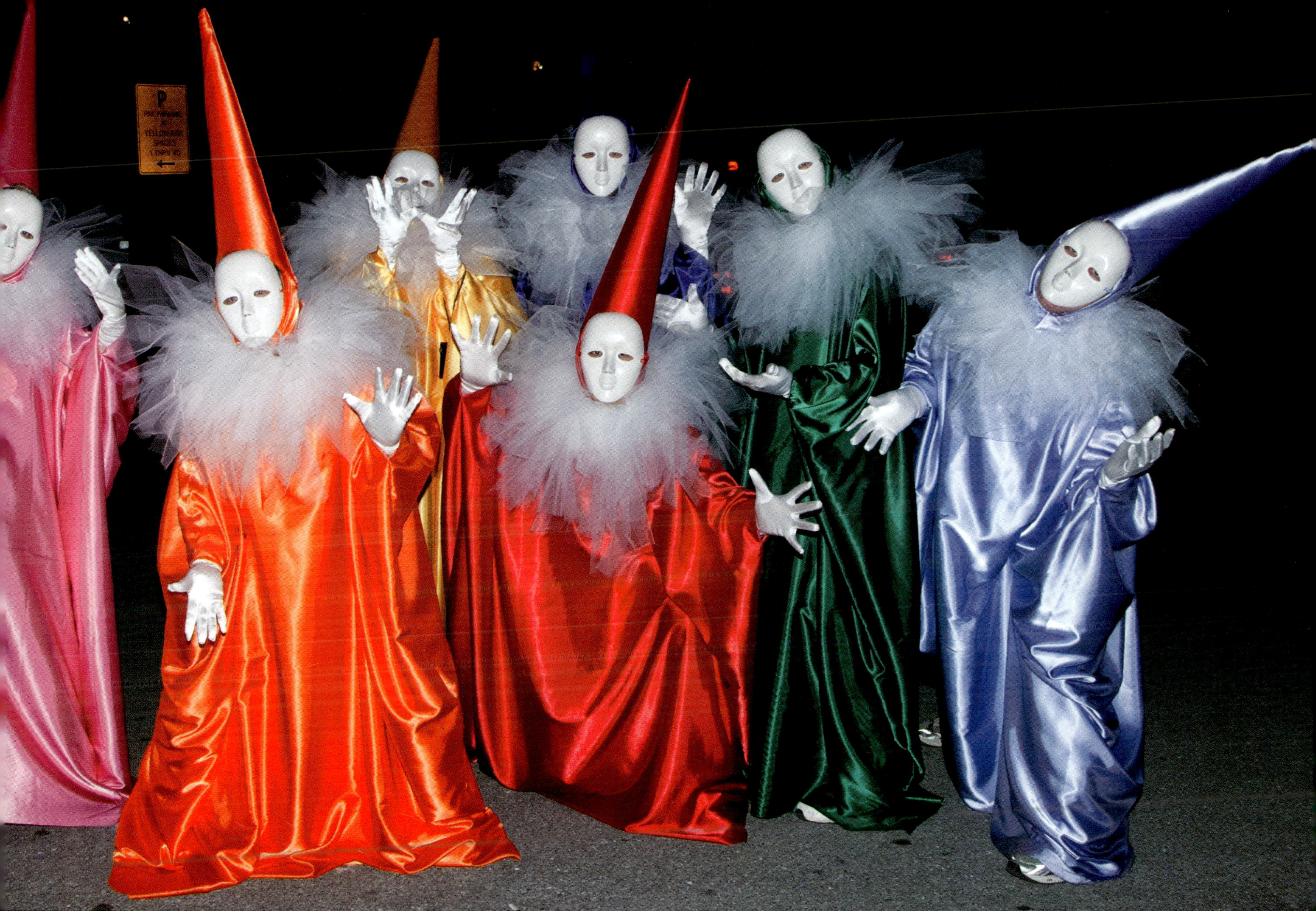

Halloween is over-the-top in Eureka Springs. Some residents and businesses along White Street in the historic loop have been known to prepare months prior to the day. Known through the surrounding counties as the best and safest place to trick-or-treat, White Street presents a very unique experience. Visitors and locals often shop and work downtown during the holiday in full costume.

N 36°24.128'
W 093°44.199'
Elevation 1186'

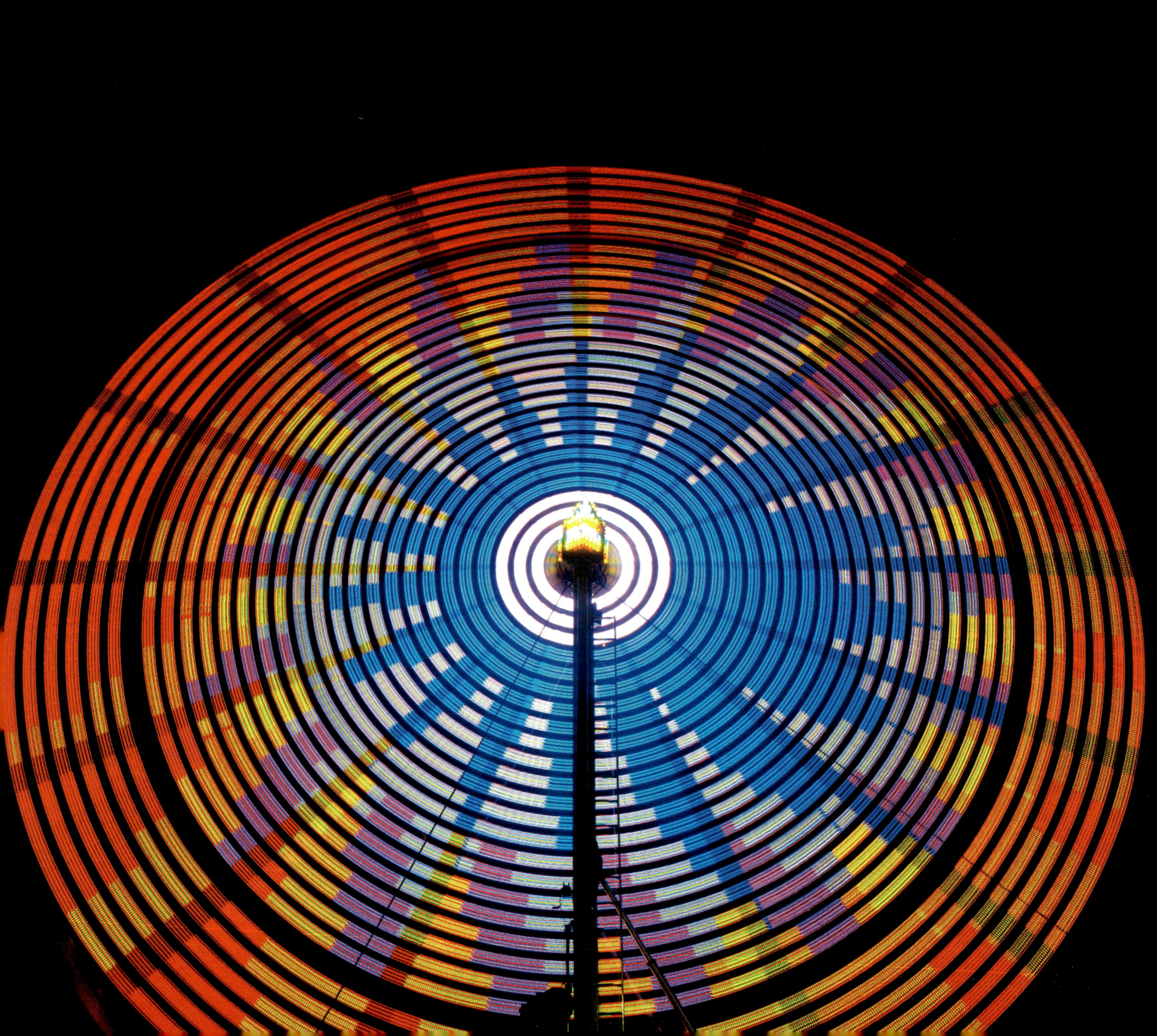

The annual Carroll County Fair held at the fairgrounds in Berryville hosts competitions from livestock shows and tractor pulls to art contests and beauty pageants. The fair also boasts quality State Fair rides and games that run into the evening.

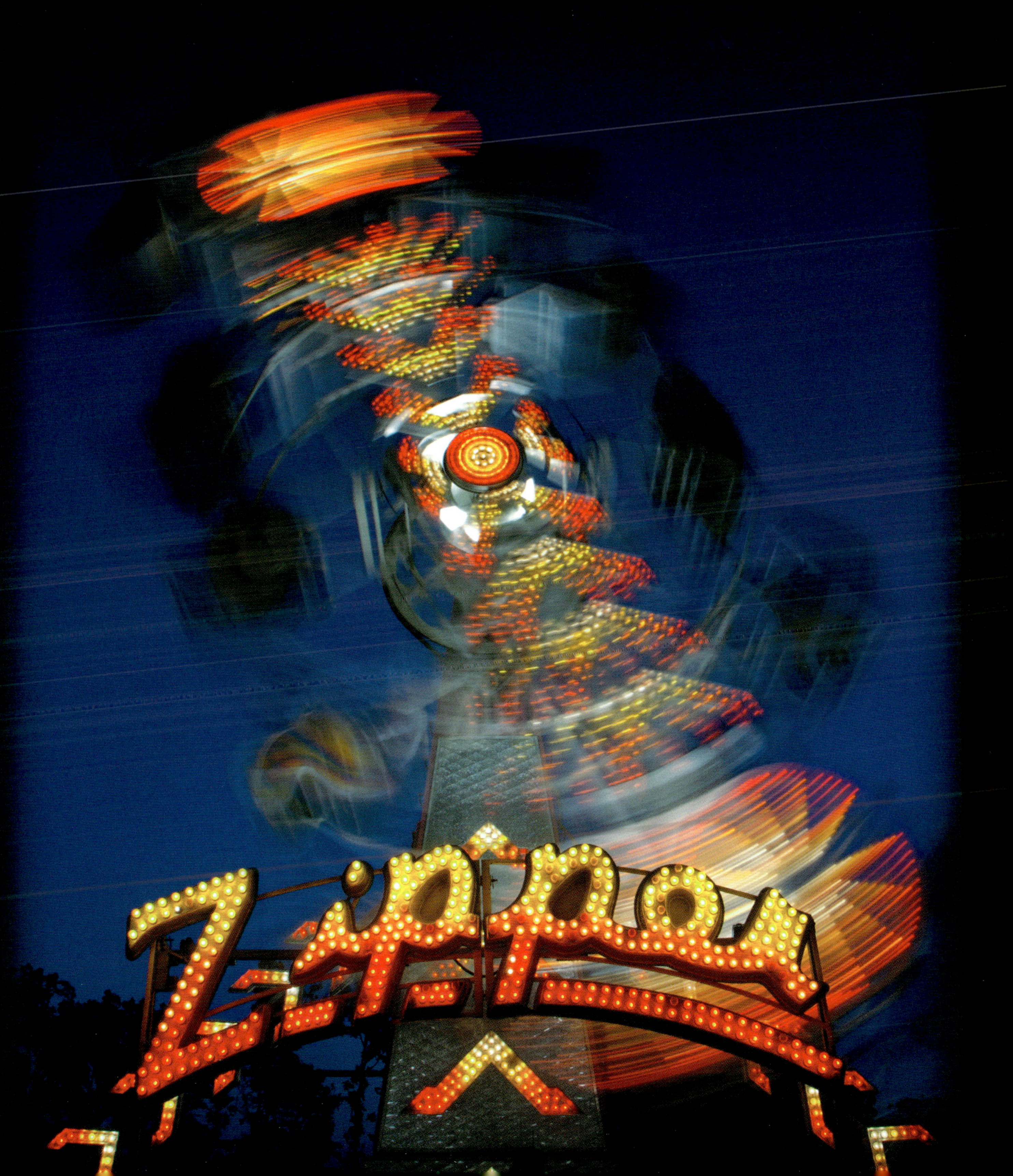

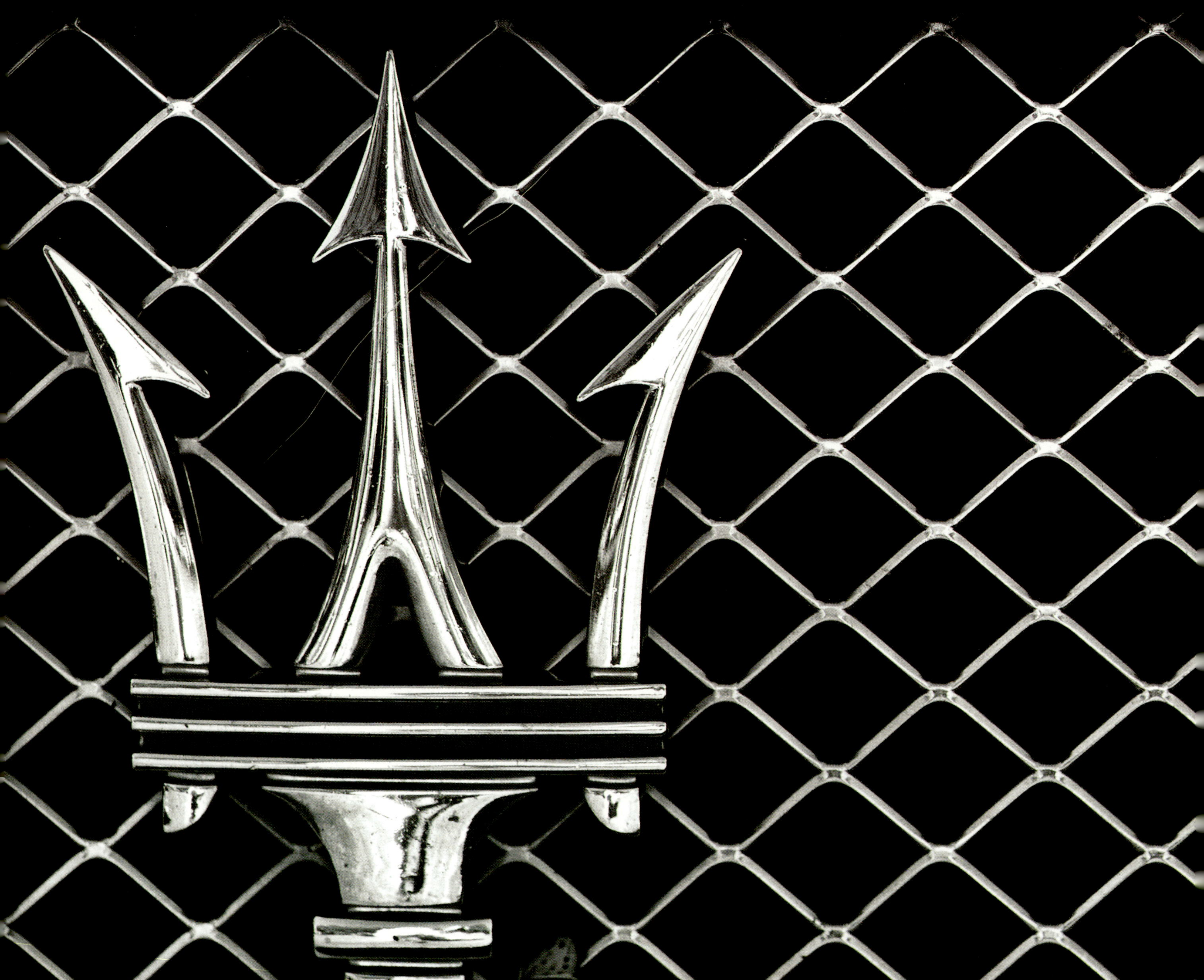

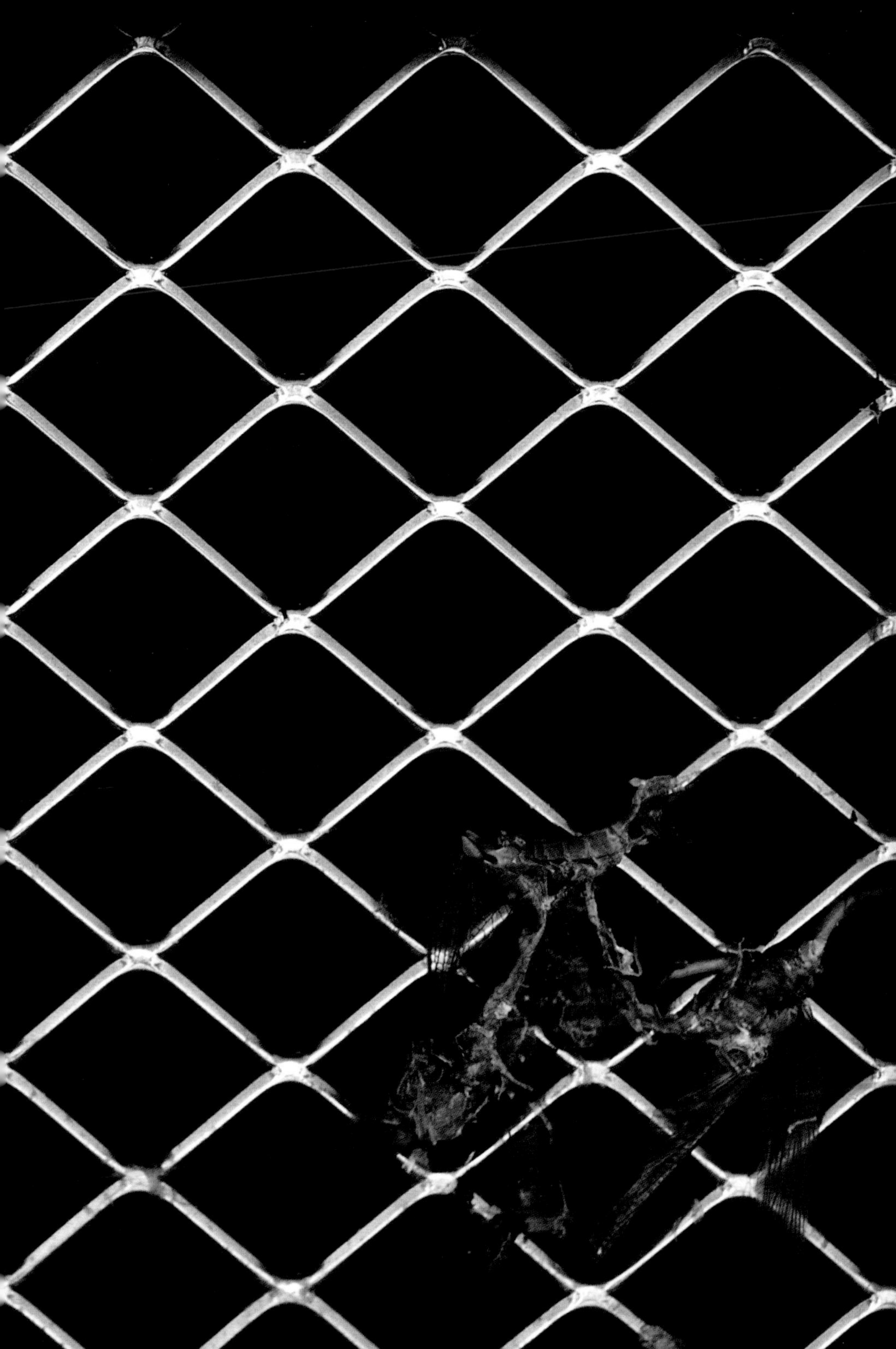

The Crescent Classic Car Show is a 5-day series of events that originate in Eureka Springs and expand beyond Carroll County. Some of the finest sports automobiles in the world flow into town and converge at the Crescent Hotel. The impressive display in the parking lot at the hotel welcomes many spectators. The Western County Courthouse also hosts a show of the cars on one day during the festival. One thing that sets this car event apart is the fact that all these high-end cars are driven to Eureka Springs from across the country - and driven hard.

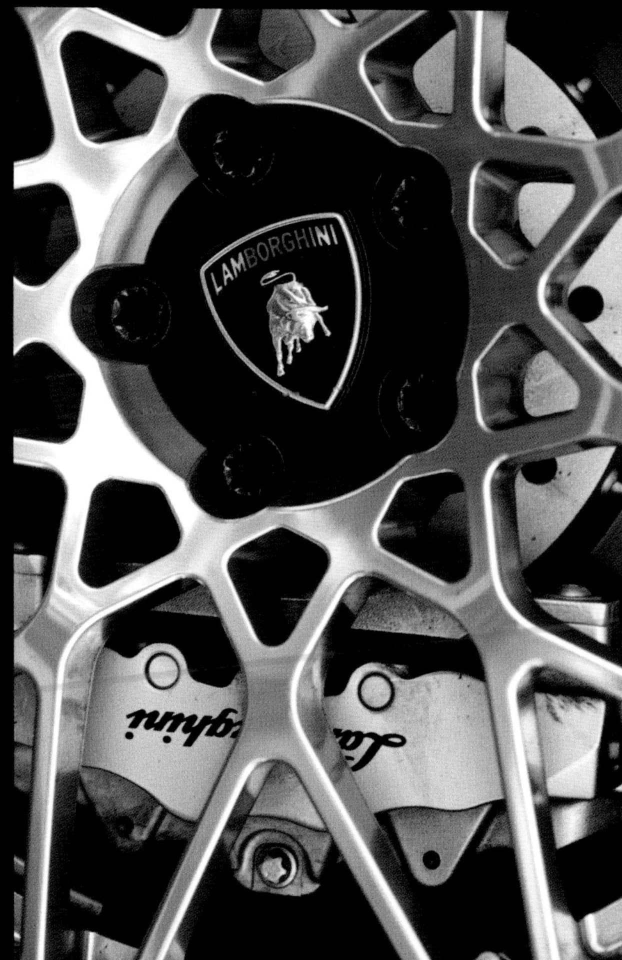

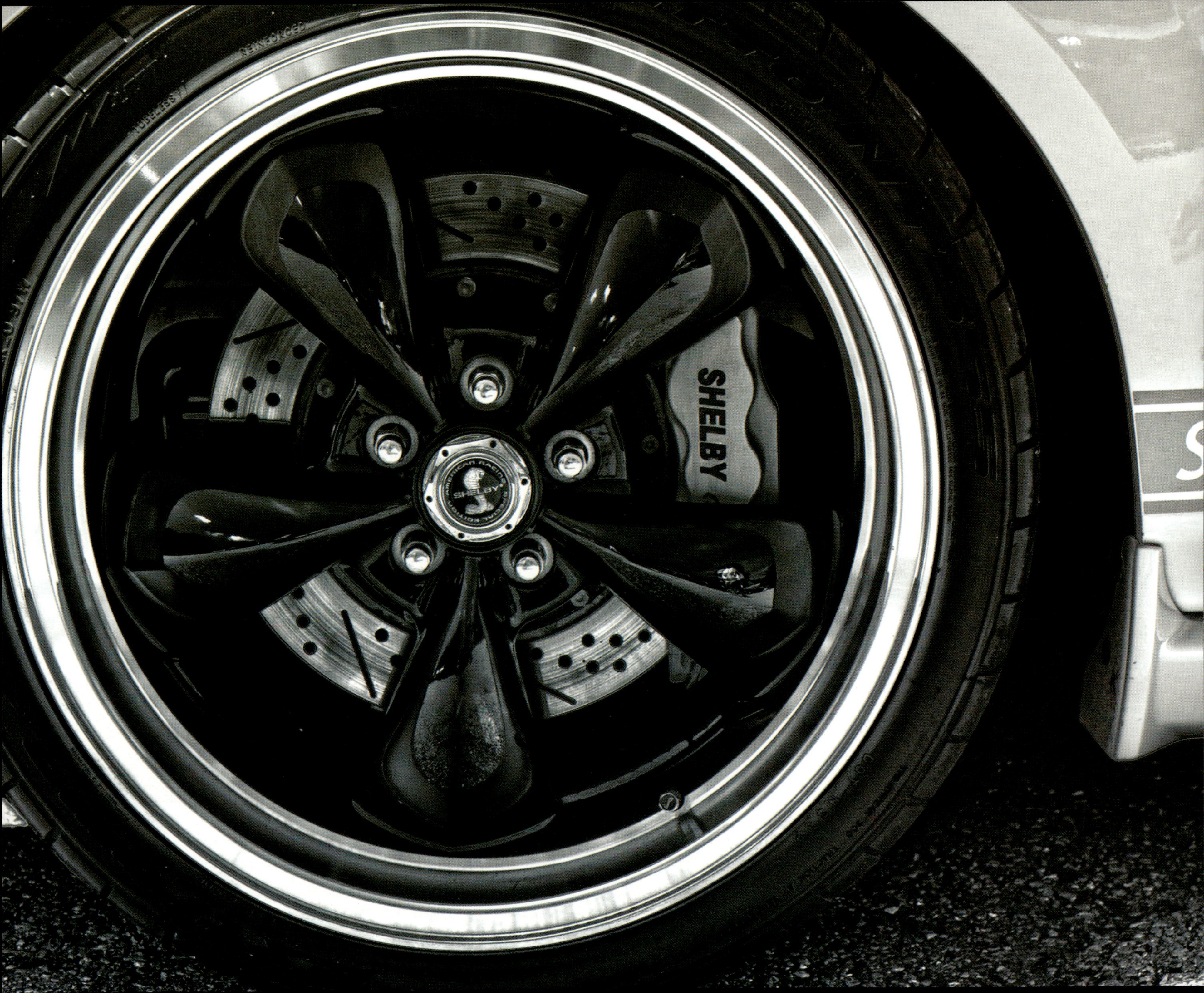
SHELBY
SHELBY

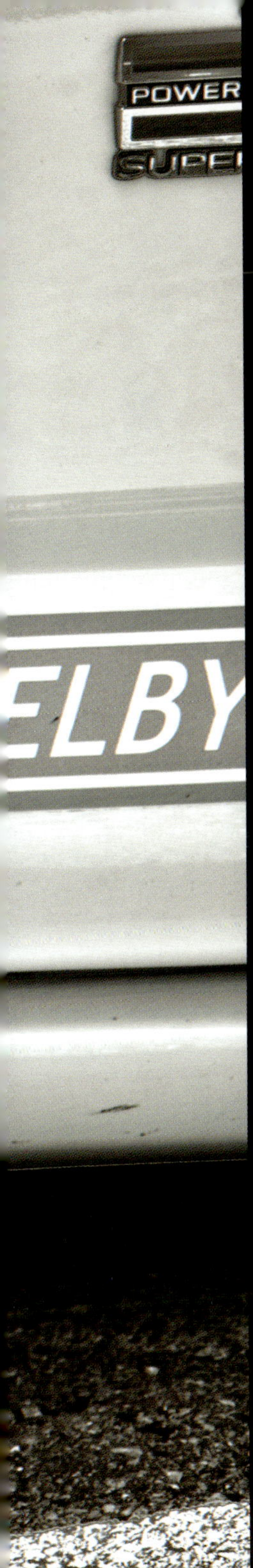


Porsche Club of America Palooza, or PCA Palooza, held in November at the Inn of the Ozarks Convention Center, registered over 205 cars with 360 attending in 2011 compared to a meager 57 Porches in 2005, its founding year.

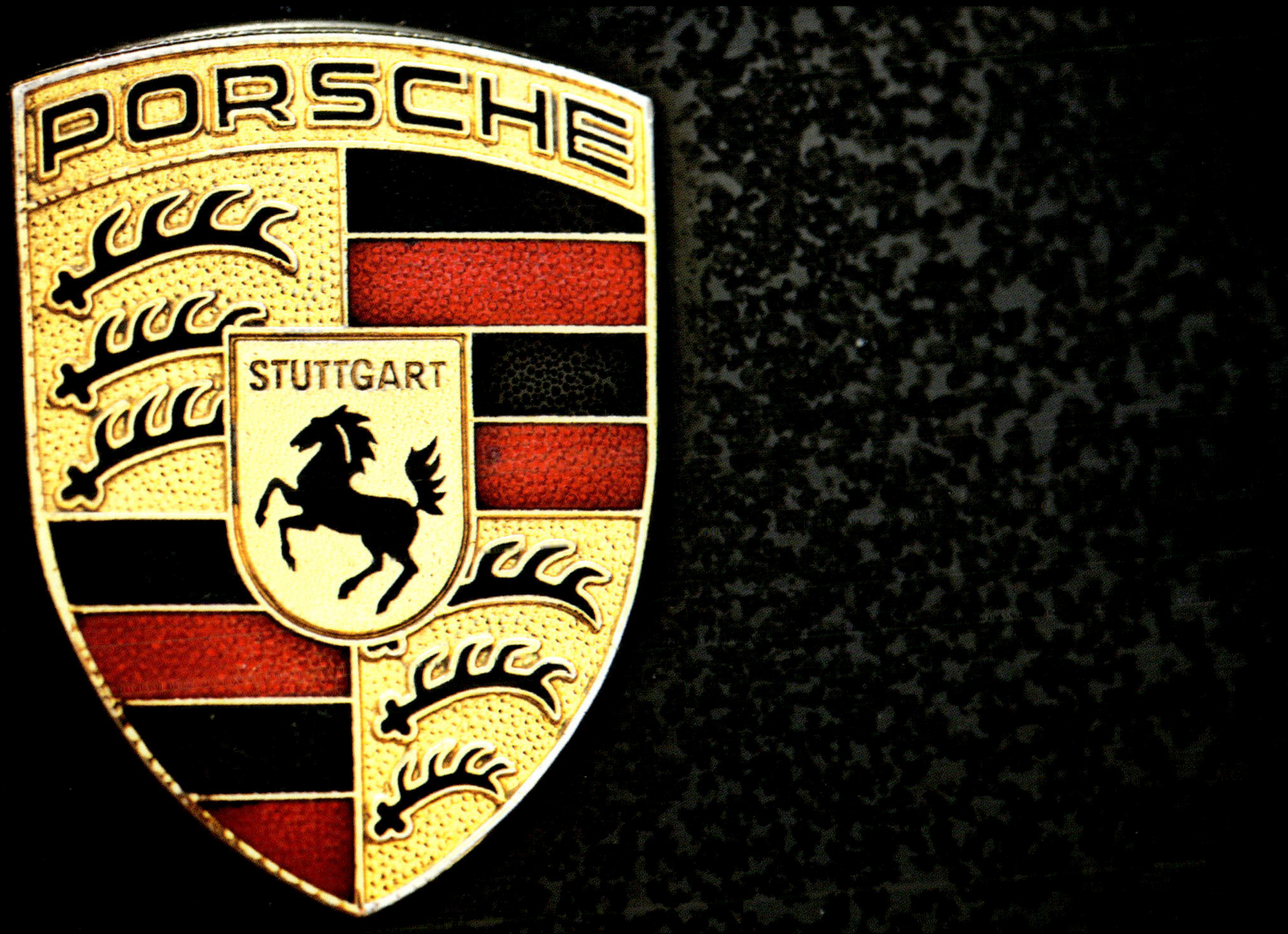


The first Eureka Springs Mustang Show, a three-day celebration of America's pony car, took place in 1994. The car show and competition is hosted in the parking lot of the Pine Mountain Village, and hundreds of Mustangs can be seen cruising the winding roads through town. Spectators are encouraged and attendance is completely free. The group also puts on one of the larger parades with the line of 'Stangs' stretching well over 1/2 mile as it winds through town past Basin Spring Park.

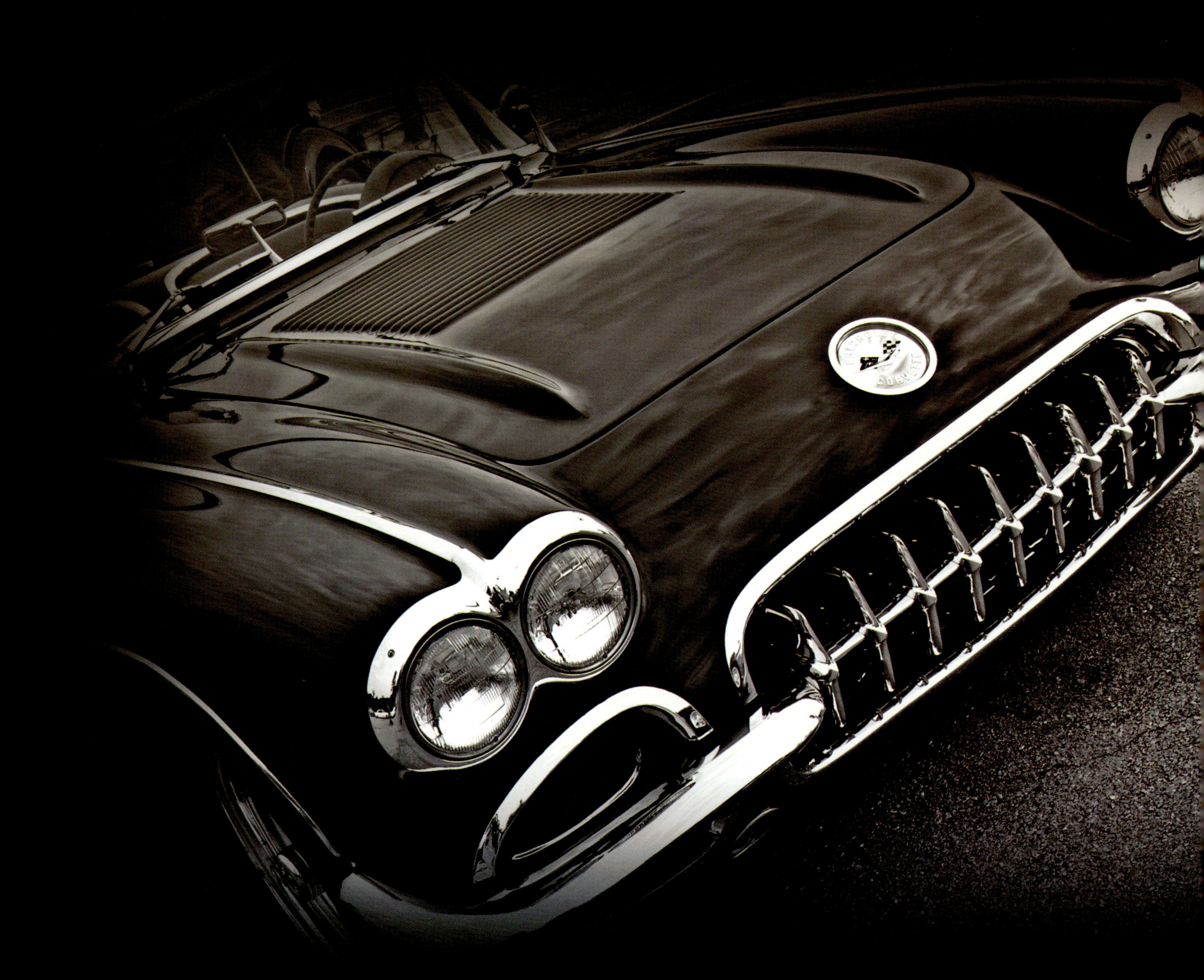

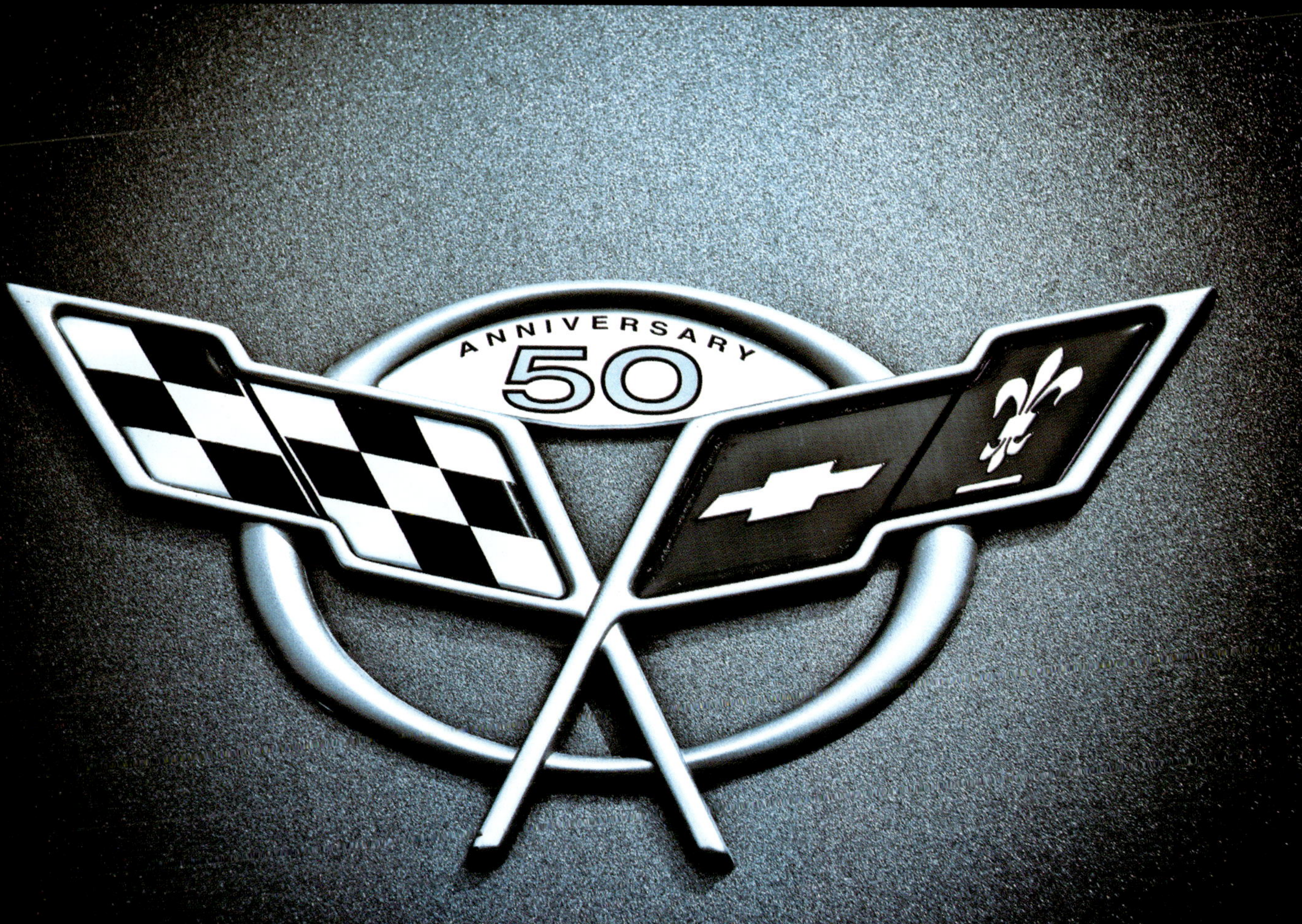


During the first weekend of October, Eureka Springs hosts the annual Corvette Weekend. The event started with a gathering of like-minded friends in 1991, and in 2010 had become an estimated 600 to 800 Corvettes cruising throughout Little Switzerland's winding roadways. With a totally volunteer workforce, this weekend is a true outing for those with a passion for Chevrolets' finest. The staging area is the Pine Mountain Village along U.S. 62W where cars are on display for onlookers and judges. Saturday marks the final judging along with a massive parade through the historic district and downtown, with Pendergrass Corner and Basin Spring Park being the favored viewing areas.

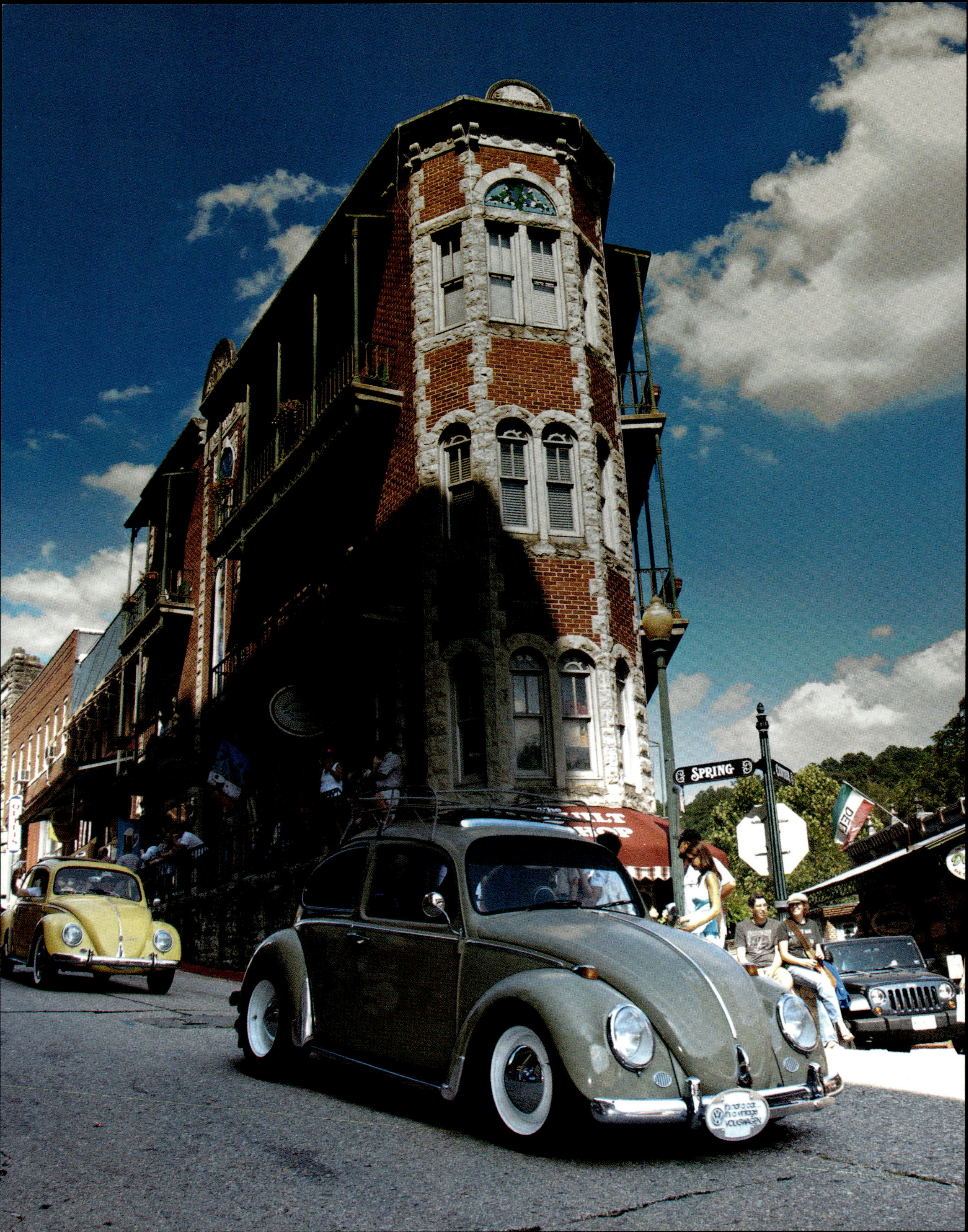


Michael Mountjoy, Dave Heilemann, Lee Ann, Scott Weaver, and the Eureka Springs Chamber of Commerce worked in conjunction to get this locally-beloved weekend started in 1992. A 3-day gathering celebrating all things Volkswagen, the annual VW Festival is hosted in August. Beetle, Cabrio, Corrado, Dasher, Eos, Golfs, Jettas, Karmann Ghia, Microbus, Passat, R32, Rabbit, Scirocco, Thing, Vanagon, and other models are on display during the car show at the Best Western Inn of the Ozarks Convention Center. They vie for first place in a wide array of competitions, as a sprawling swap meet offering parts of every kind runs adjacent to the polished VWs. Their 'tourcade' rides send them through the narrow roadways that snake through the Ozark countryside.

Established in 1980, the Kustom Kemps of America, or KKOA, comes to Eureka Springs to host the annual Kustom Kemps Modified Street Car Show in June, usually sharing the three days with Eureka Springs Blues Weekend. The group cruises their lead-sleds through the historic loop and past Basin Spring Park in a Saturday parade, after which many park their pre-1970 automobiles in the downtown area for display.

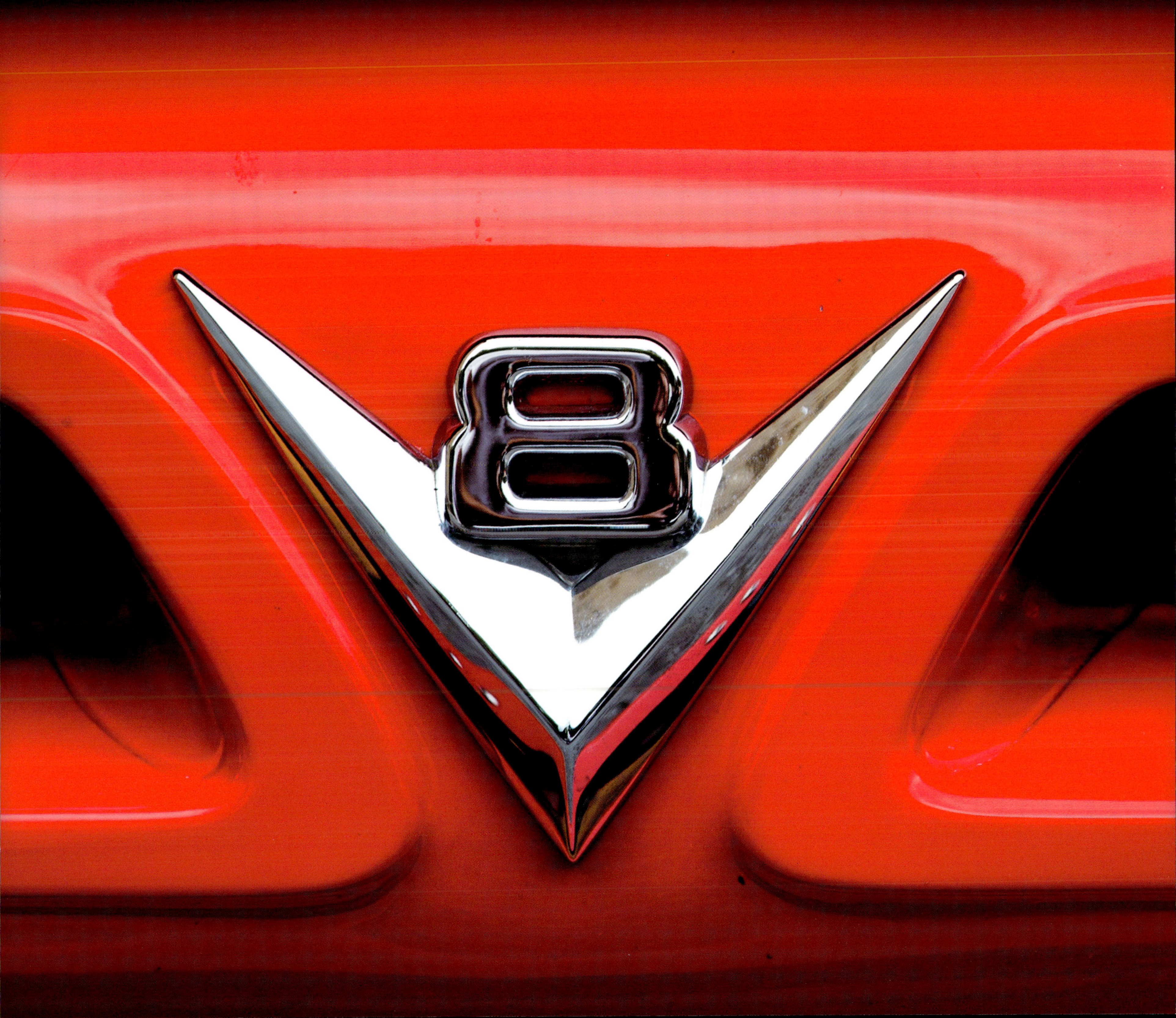

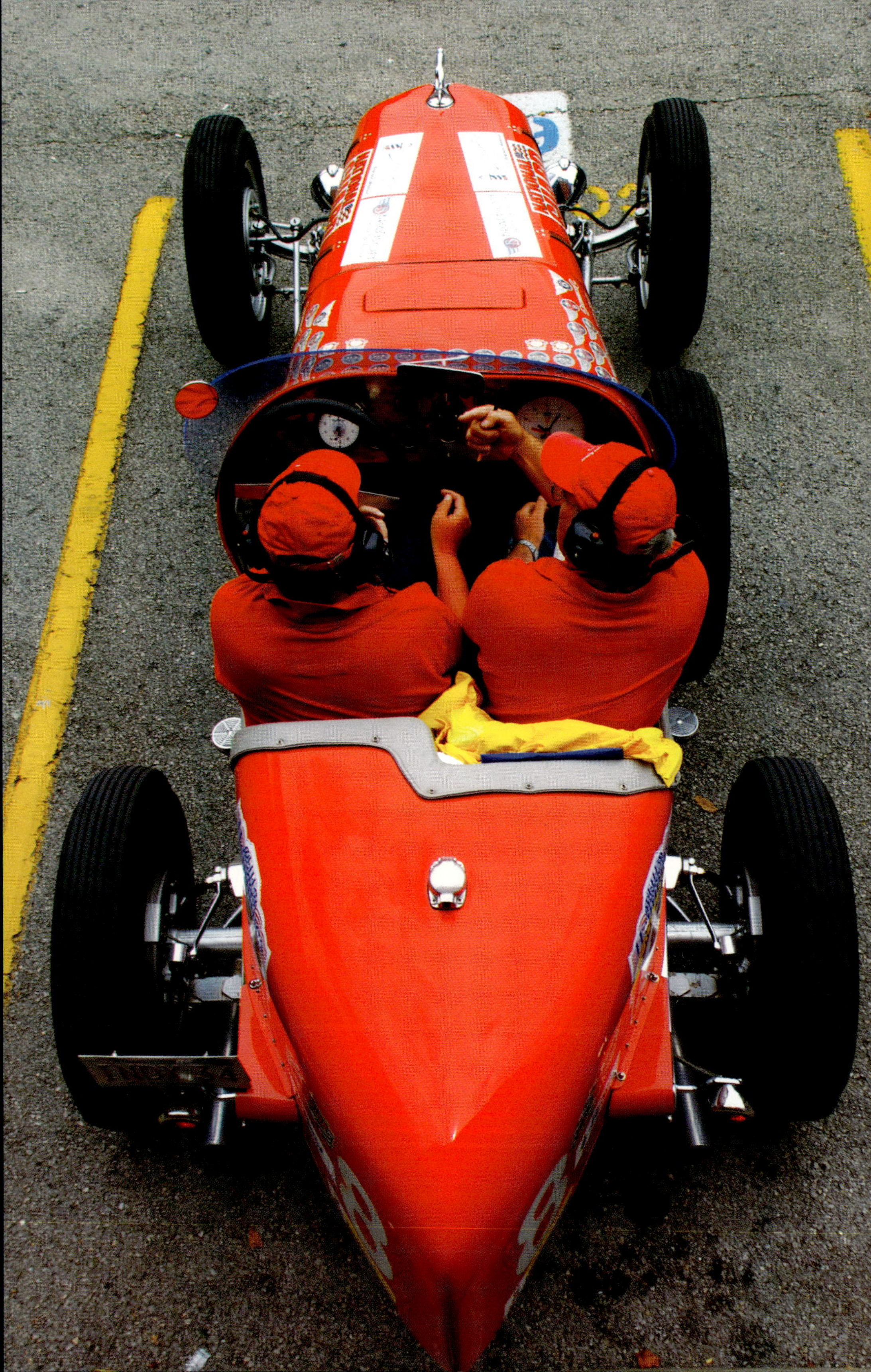

Eureka Springs and many rural parts of the county get overflow from other events and festivals held in the surrounding areas. An estimated 400,000 bikes from all 50 states converge in Fayetteville each year for the Bikes, Blues & BBQ benefiting local charity organizations and is the largest such event in county.

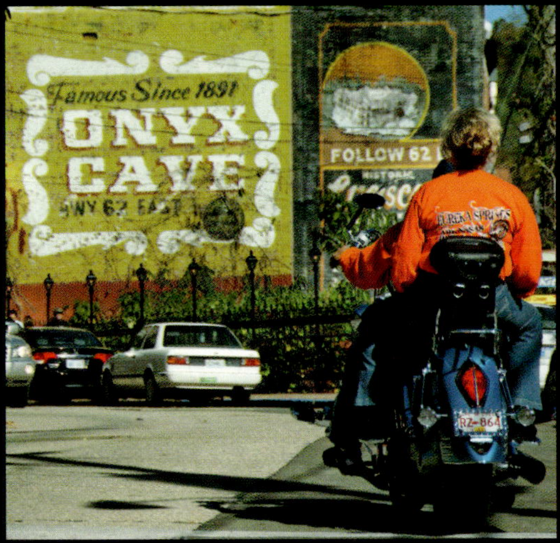


In 2008, another charitable event found itself barreling across the county in a race for first in a five-day series of races. Hemming's Challenge 2008 series, headquartered in Rogers and associated with the Vintage Car Rally Association, sends around 50 classic racing machines to the lower North Main Street parking lots to stage these automotive masterpieces.

N 36°24.105'
W 093°44.245'
Elevation 1256'

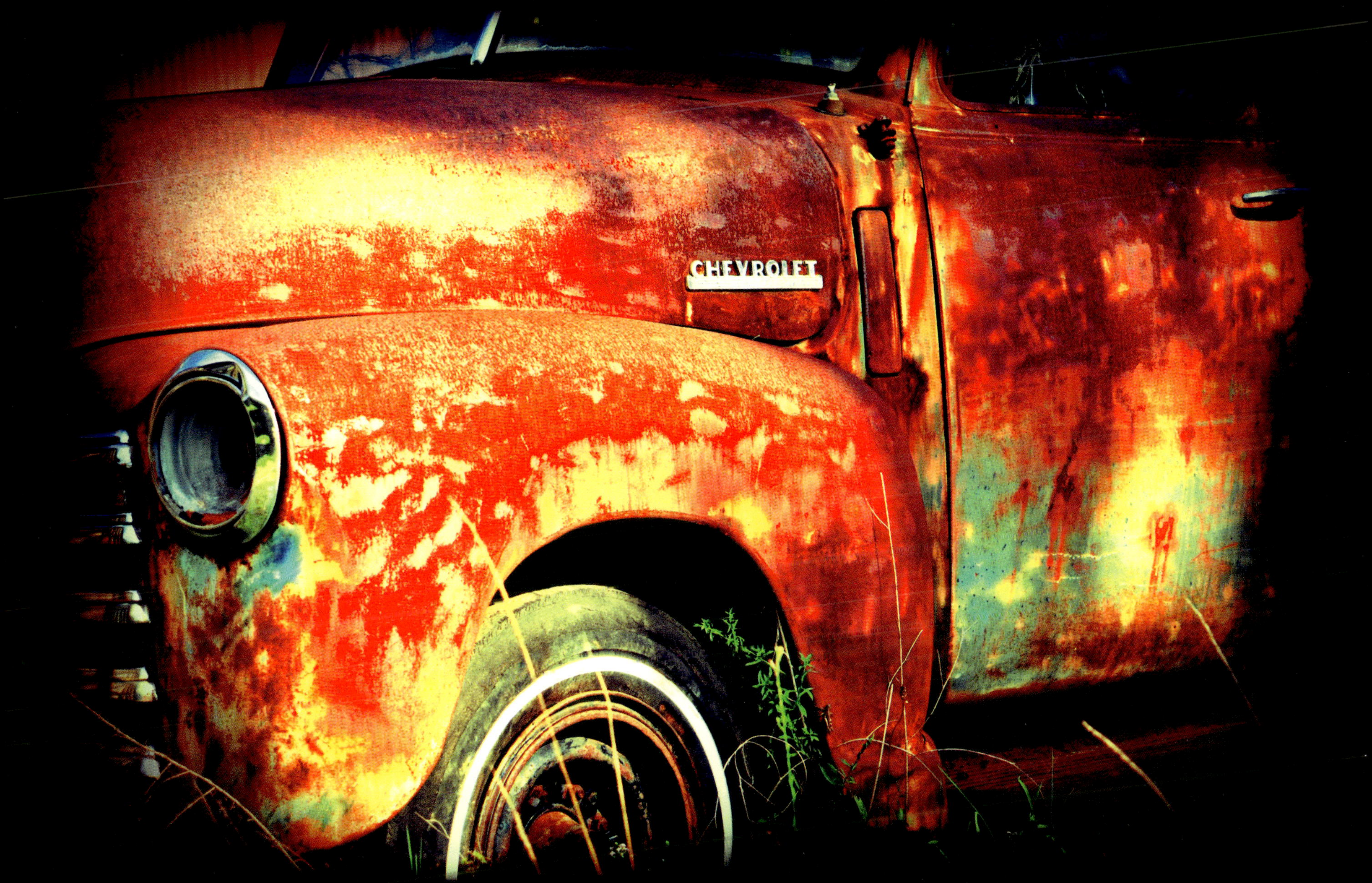


Vintage vehicles littered along roadsides throughout the county are now the dilapidated shells of eras long past, slowly fading into the wilderness.

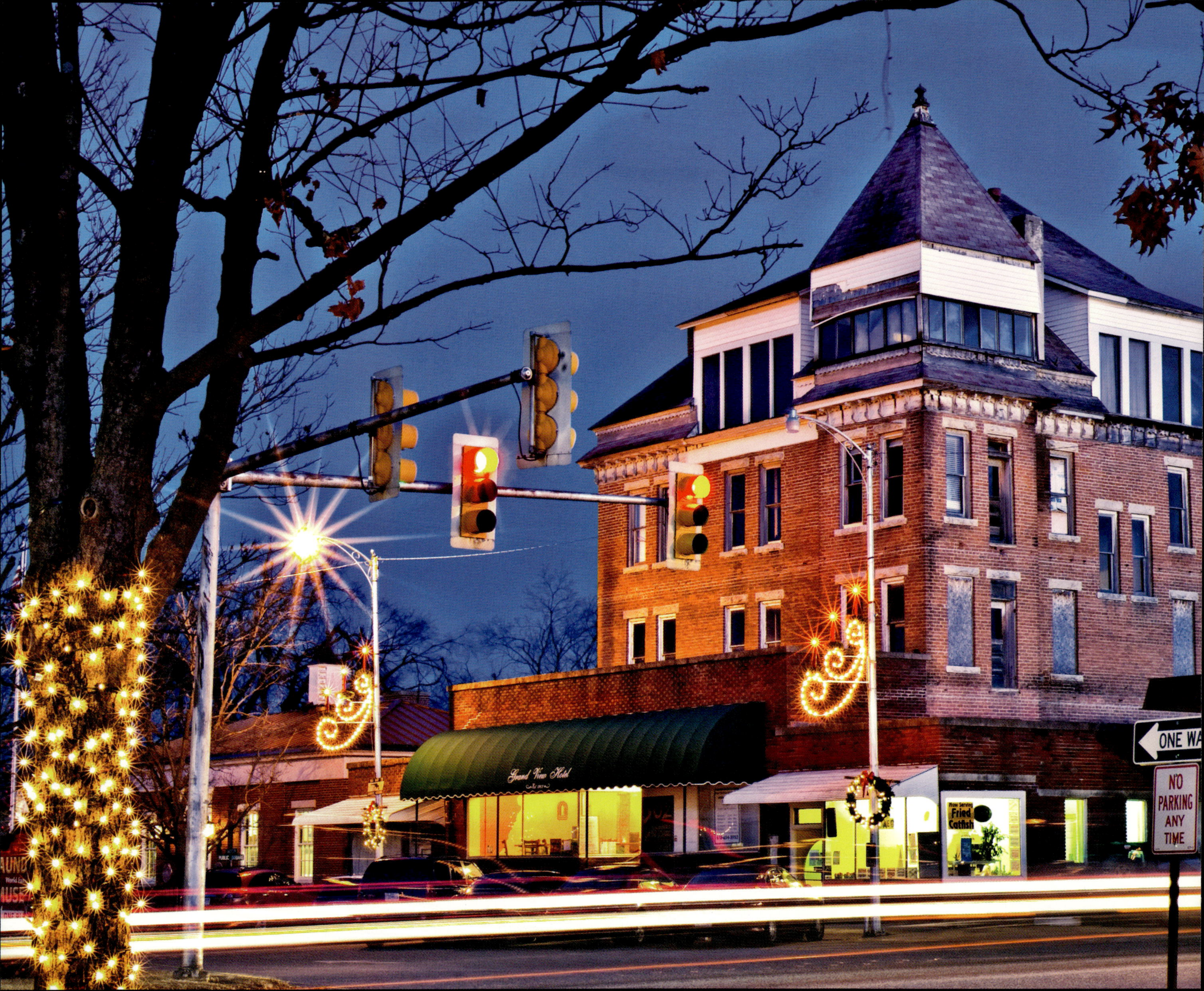
ONE WA
NO PARKING ANY TIME
Grand View Hotel
Fried Catfish

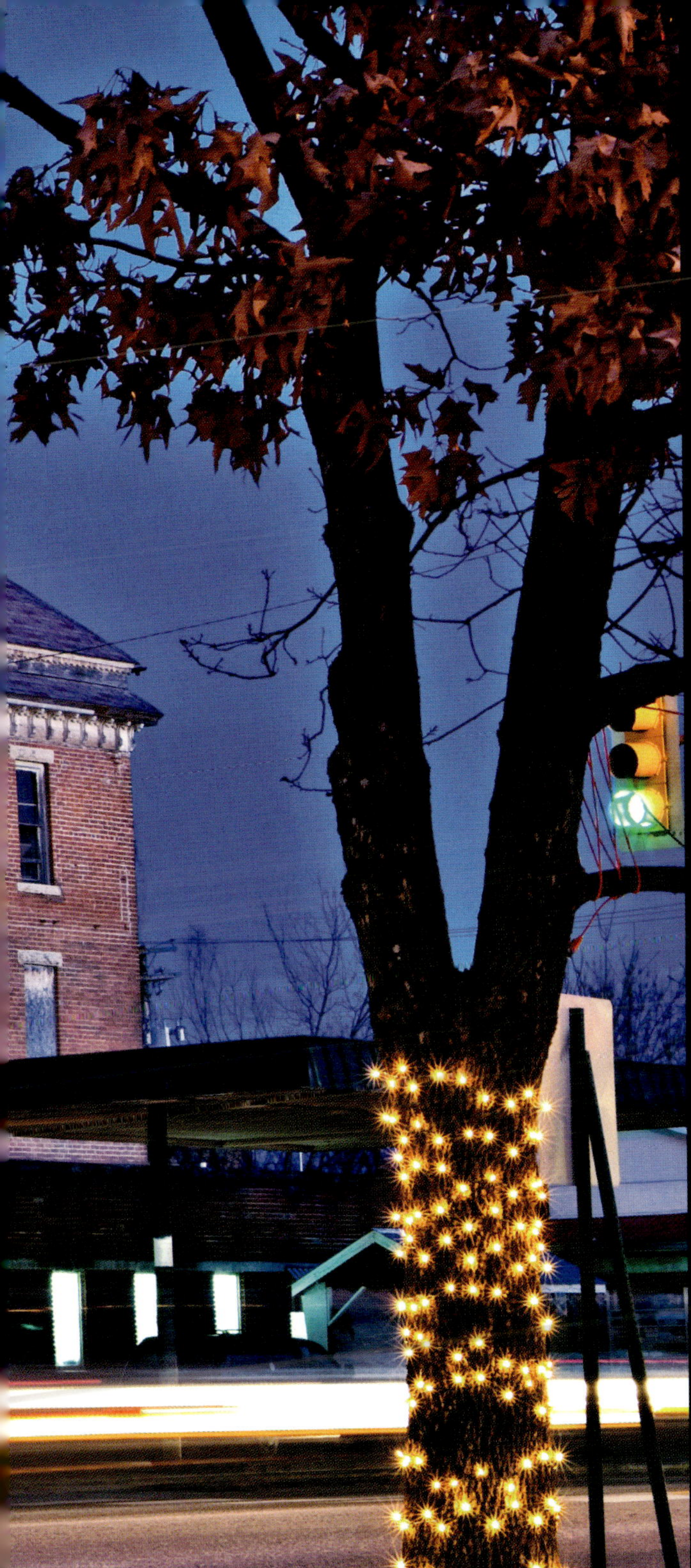

# Surrounding Towns

One of the many draws to Eureka Springs is the close proximity to an agglomeration of commodities in the form a diverse countryside.

Berryville, known for rich farming and hunting land, spans 4.4 square miles with a population 4,433. The first recorded white settlers to the area, Joel and William Plumlee, first set up camp and followed with a farm on what is now the town square (pictured). The area was once a trading post in the Ozark wilderness. Blackburn Henderson Berry of Alabama founded Berryville in 1850 and opened a store soon after purchasing the Plumlee's farm plot. With the help of former Carrollton blacksmith, Arthur A. Baker, Berry's work came to fruition with the incorporation of Berryville on March 23, 1876. In 1902, the Saint George Hotel was built on the square using locally-produced bricks. The structure had many different owners until 1926 when Mr. and Mrs. L.C. Smith took ownership and renamed it The Grand View Hotel, as it is known today. Since then, ownership has changed many times again, along with multiple attempts at restoration. Currently being renovated by Alexander Virden and Sandra Doss, there is now a full restaurant operating on the lower floor.

N 36°21.874'
W 093°34.039'
Elevation 1234'

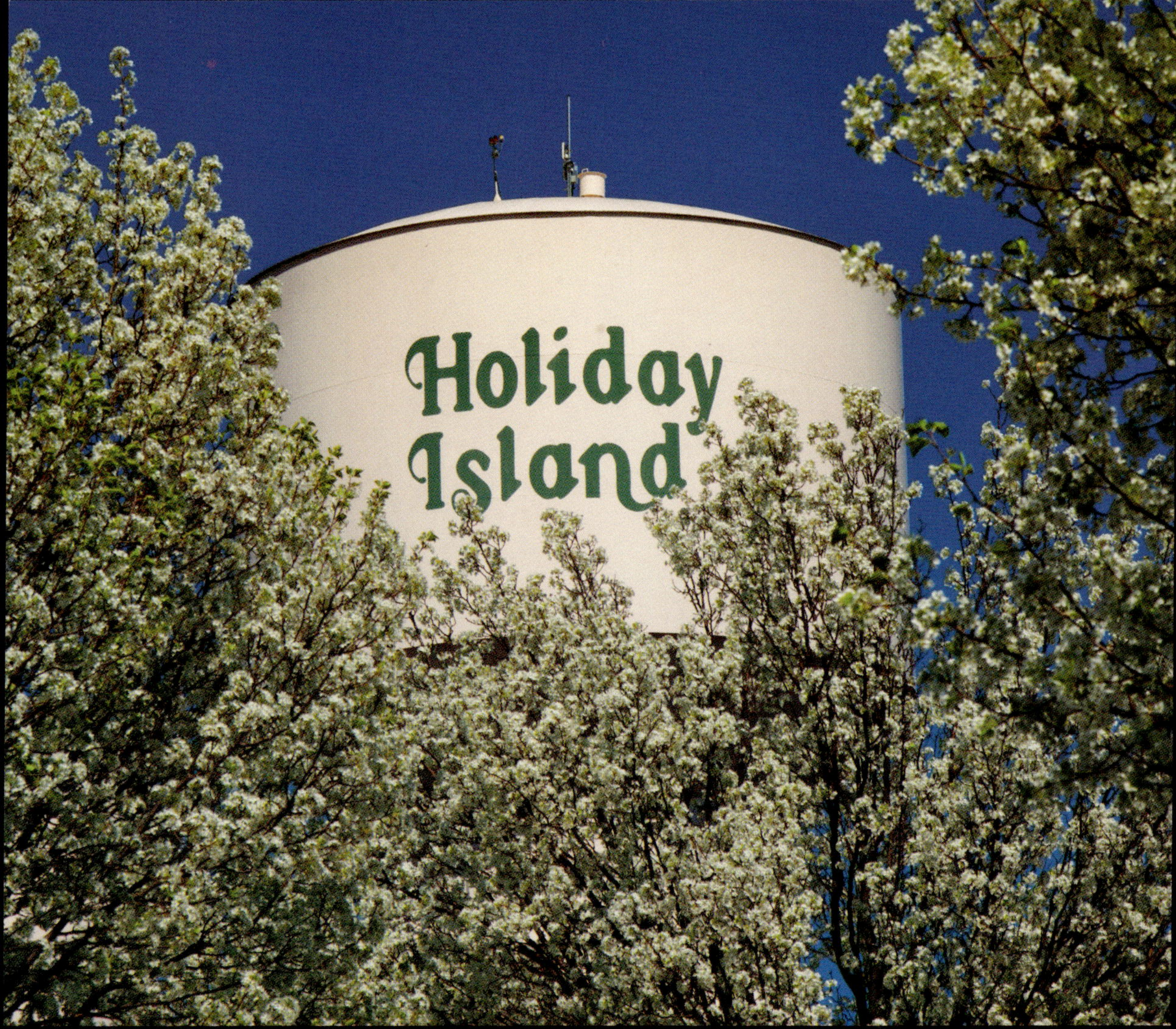


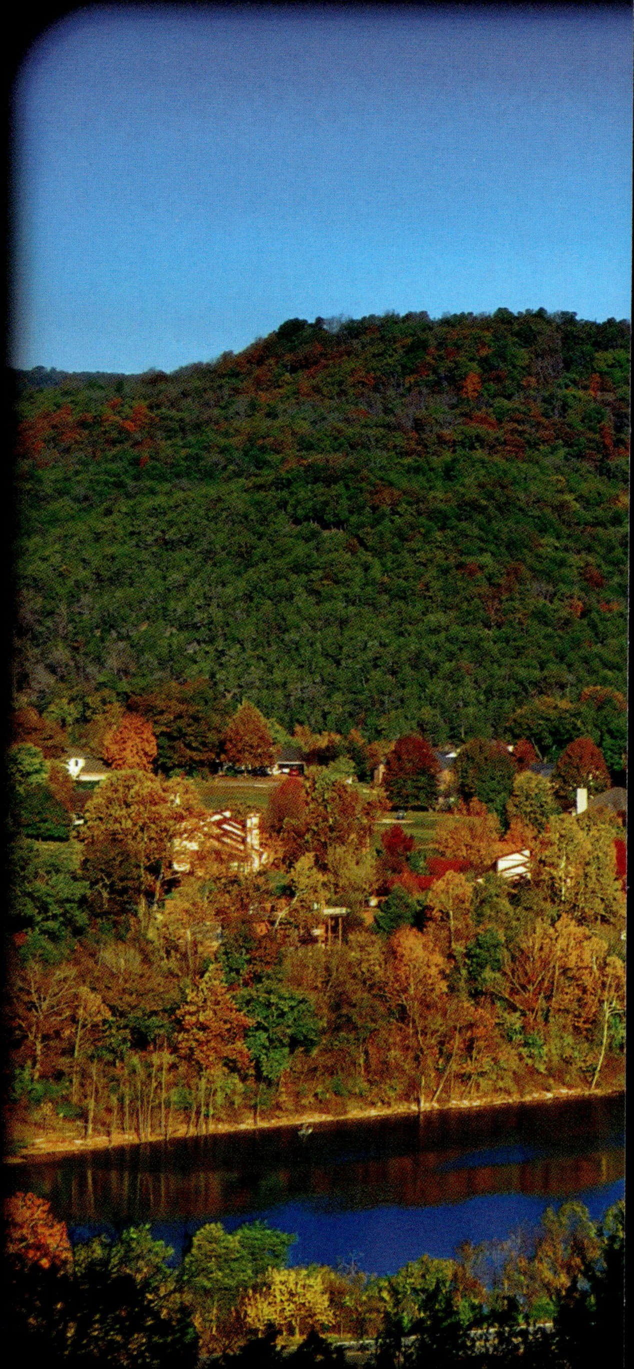

The 2,373 residents of Holiday Island enjoy some of the best vistas on Table Rock Lake the county has to offer. This recreation community comprises 4,500 acres that include two meticulously manicured golf courses (one 9-hole and one 18-hole), a recreation complex, a marina, and a shopping center complete with a grocery store, restaurants, and a fully stocked hardware store in addition to various business offices and medical services. Its estimated 800-acres is actually a peninsula that protrudes into in the southern waters of Table Rock Lake in close proximity to the Missouri-Arkansas state line. The community is protected by a fire department that boasts four fire stations throughout the sprawling hills, the first being formed in formed in 1974. Holiday Island has recently become an Arkansas Fire Wise Community.

N 36°27.302'
W 093°43.270'
Elevation 1521'

N 36°29.126'
W 093°45.365'
Elevation 1076'

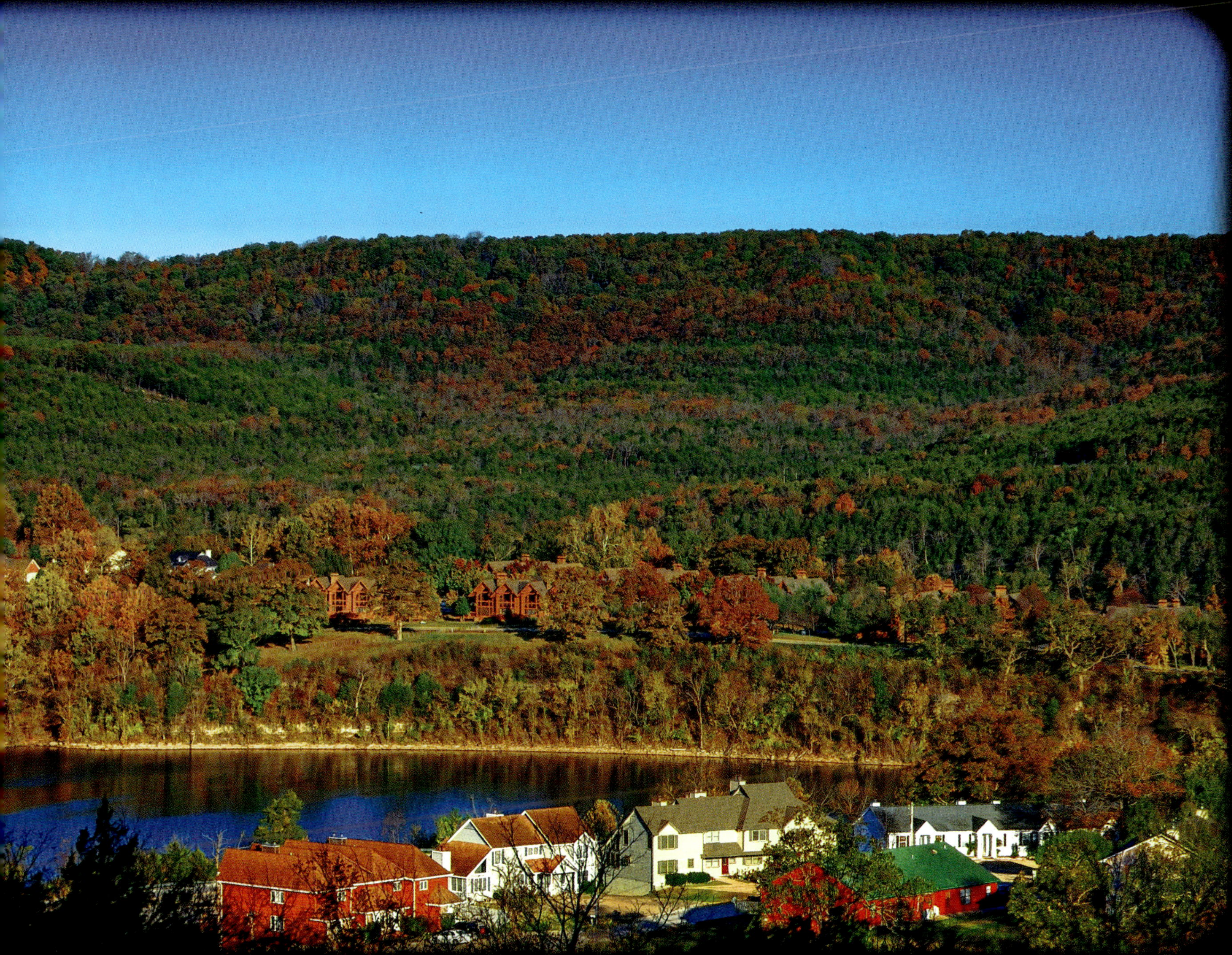

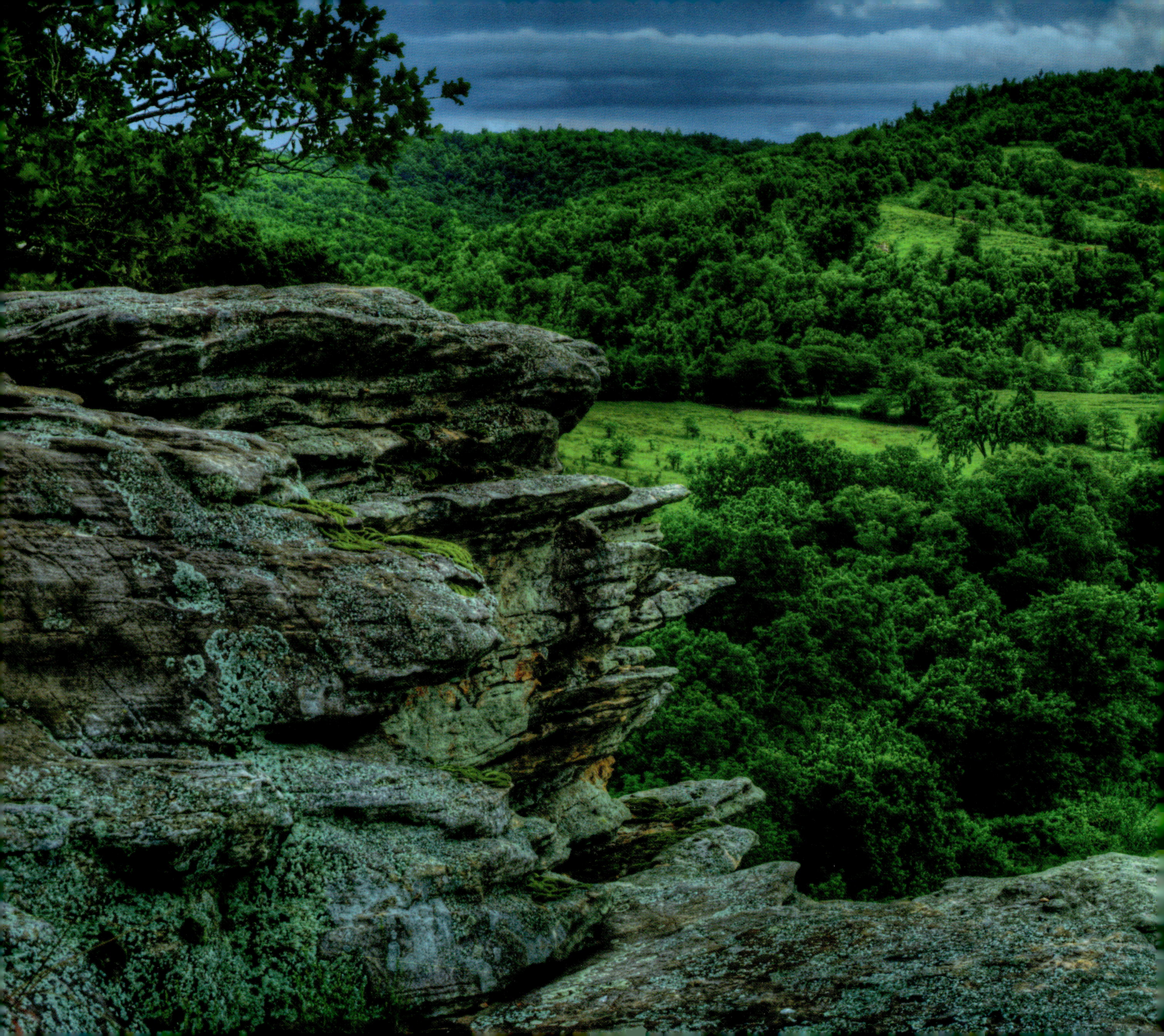

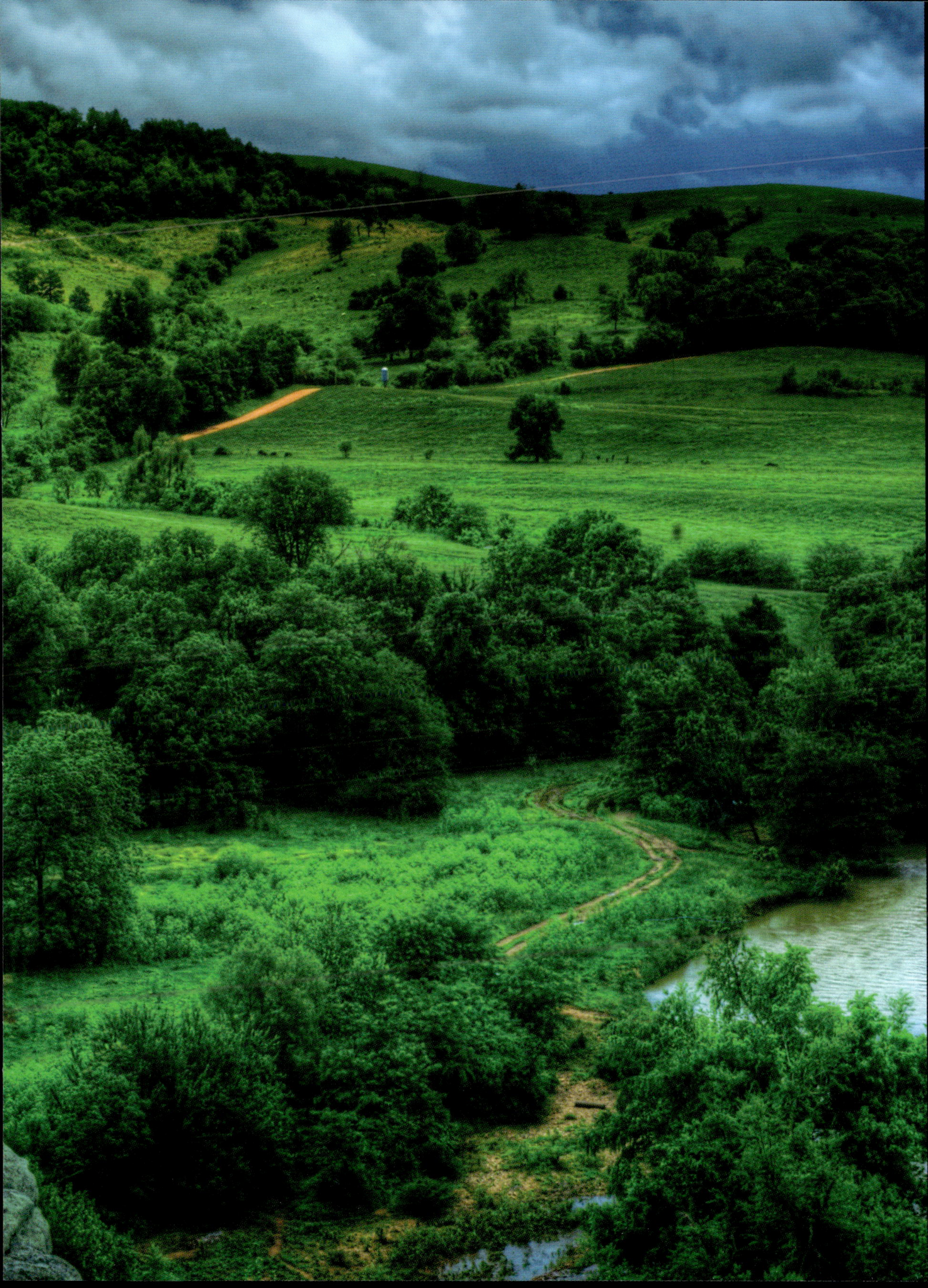

Green Forest's first early white settler, believed to be John Scott, came into the area in 1828 and his settlement later became known as Scott's Prairie. The town took its modern era name in 1895. The first home was built around 1860 and telephone service was incorporated in 1901. Pictured is a limestone bluff punching through the earth alongside CR 995 that partially hugs the Osage Creek.

N 36°14.858'
W 093°25.771'
Elevation 1369'

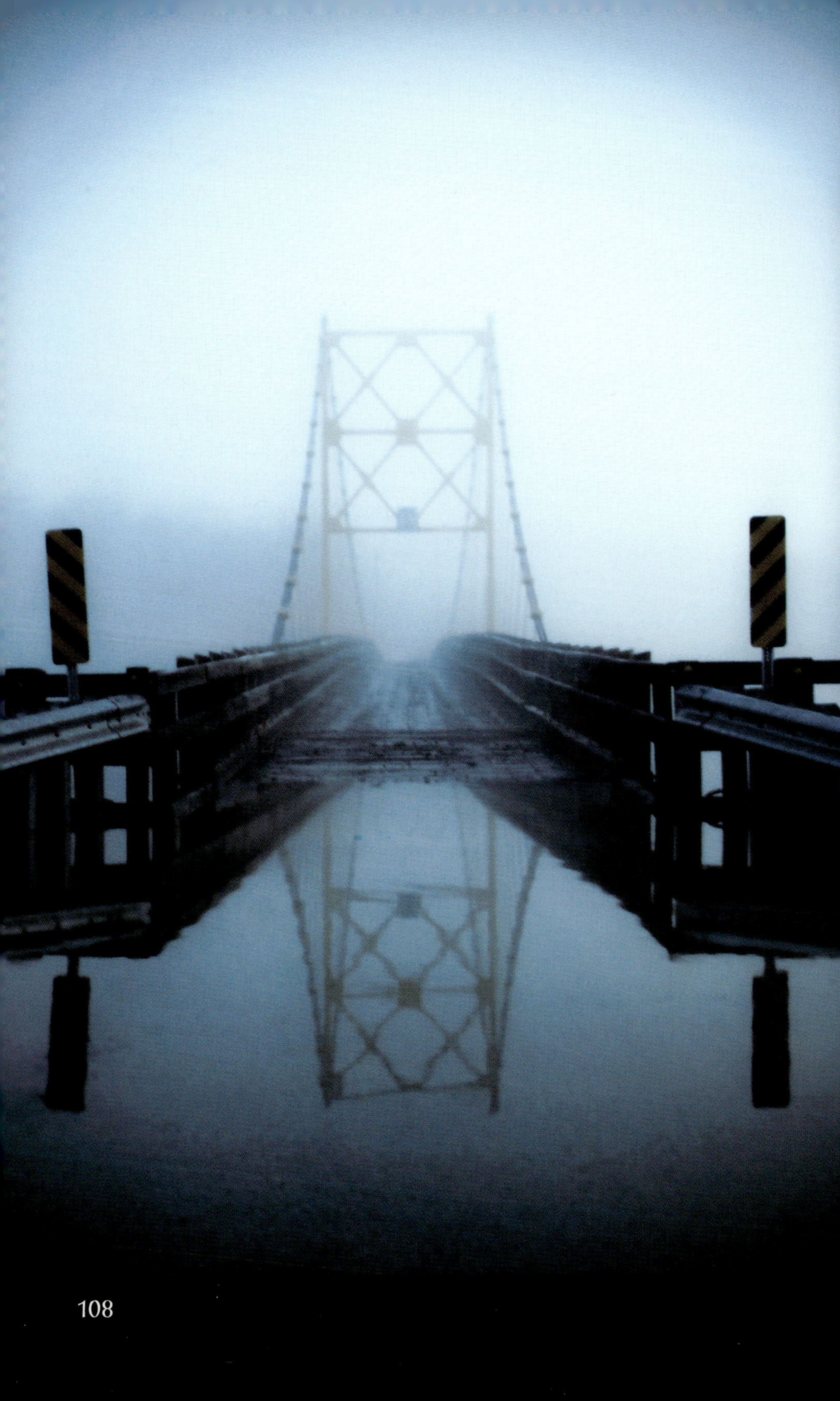

N 36°28.248'
W 093°46.116'
Elevation 921'

The "Little Golden Gate Bridge" has stood through thick and thin, all the while remaining a symbol of human persistence and perseverance in the rugged Northern Arkansas region. The bridge, constructed by 1949 under the direction of lead engineer W.E. Hicks, cost $107, 785.93 paying proficient laborers an estimated wage of $1 an hour. The bridge spans 554 ft. with a width of 11 ft., allowing only for one-lane traffic flow. If this bridge looks a little familiar, it's most likely due to appearances in the TV mini-series 'The Blue and the Grey' and the movie 'Elizabethtown.' The bridge stands steadfast even though suffering repeated blows to its structural integrity, including staying partially underwater for close to a month in 2008. Time and again, the residents of Beaver have saved their beloved bridge from being replaced by a modern concrete structure.

N 36°28.357'
W 093°46.116'
Elevation 903'

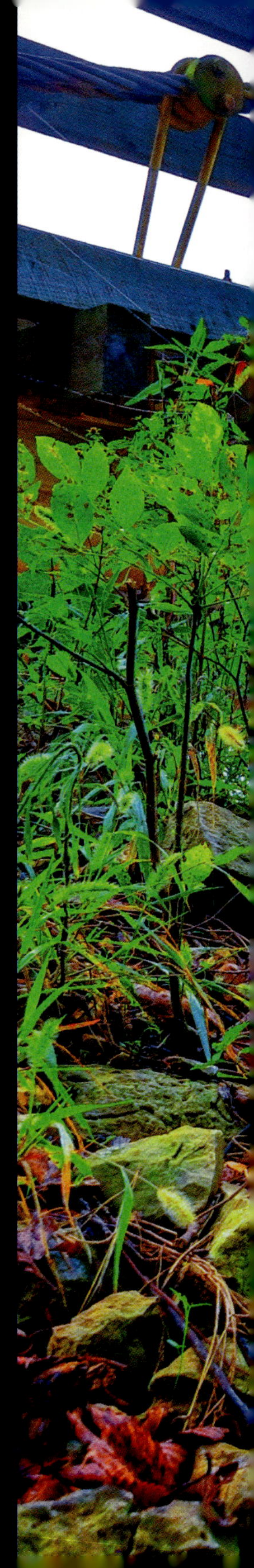

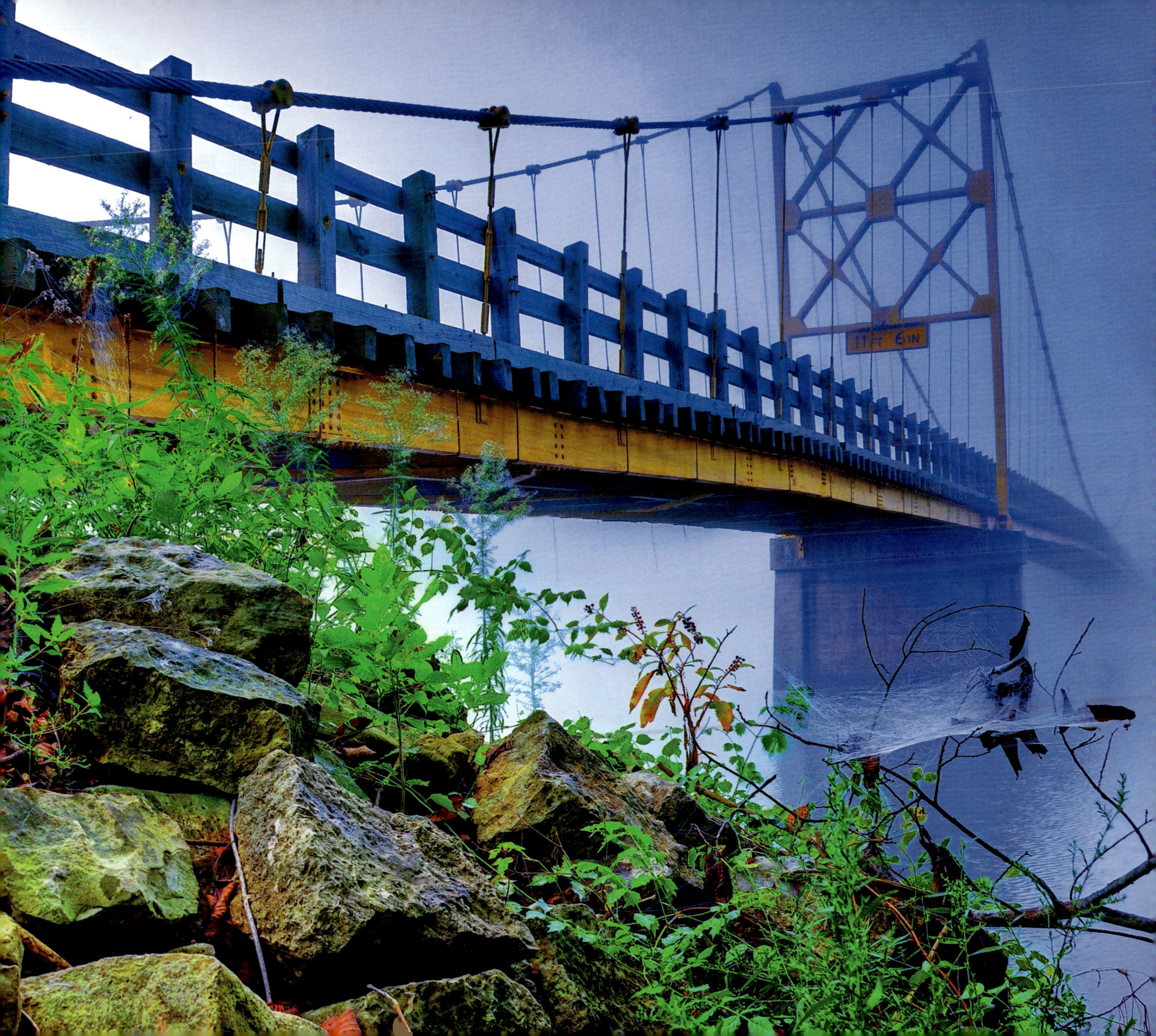
11 FT 6 IN

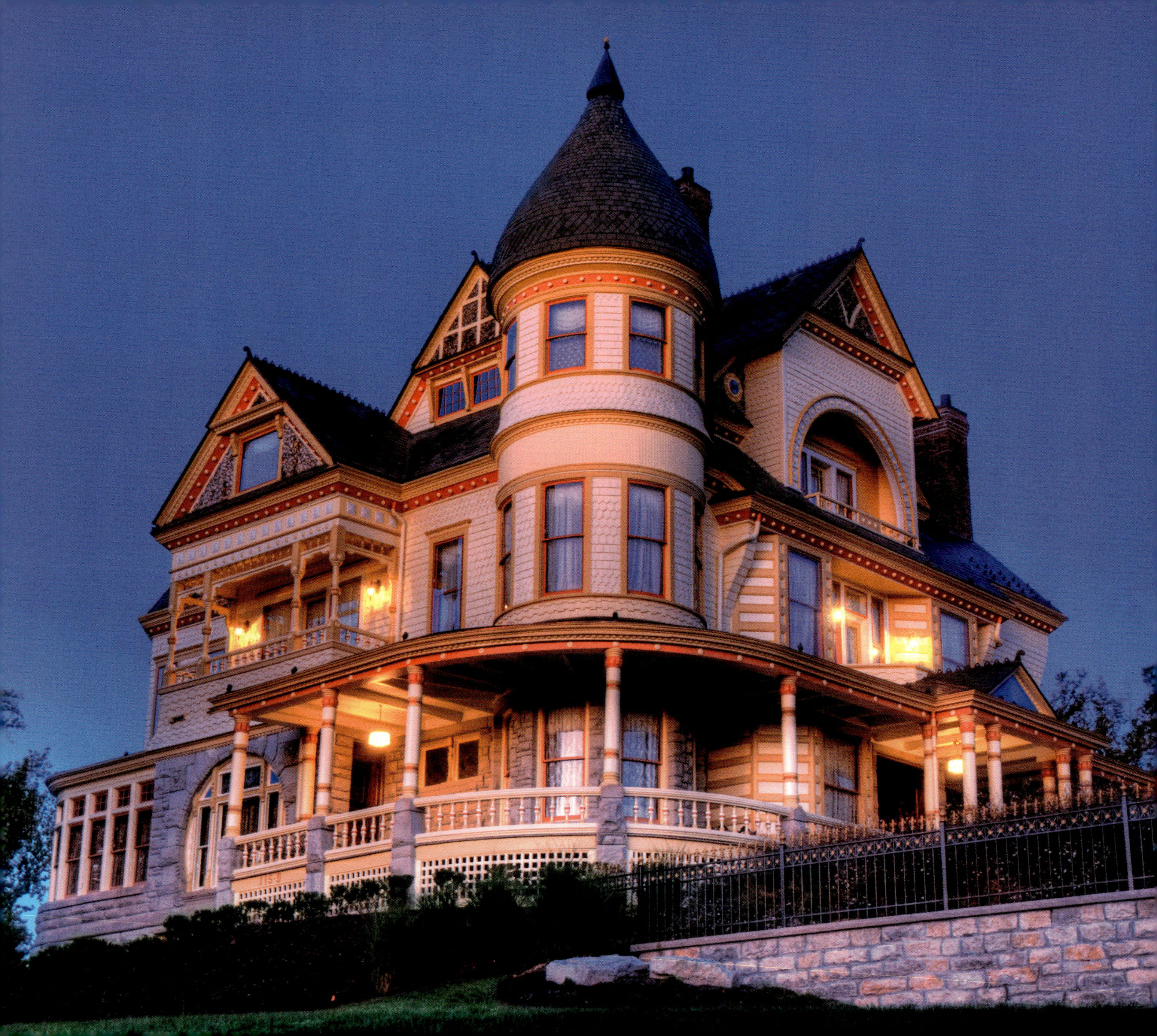

# Points of Interest

Eureka Springs has always catered to visitors and locals in anomalistic ways. The city and surrounding countryside host a long list of attractions.

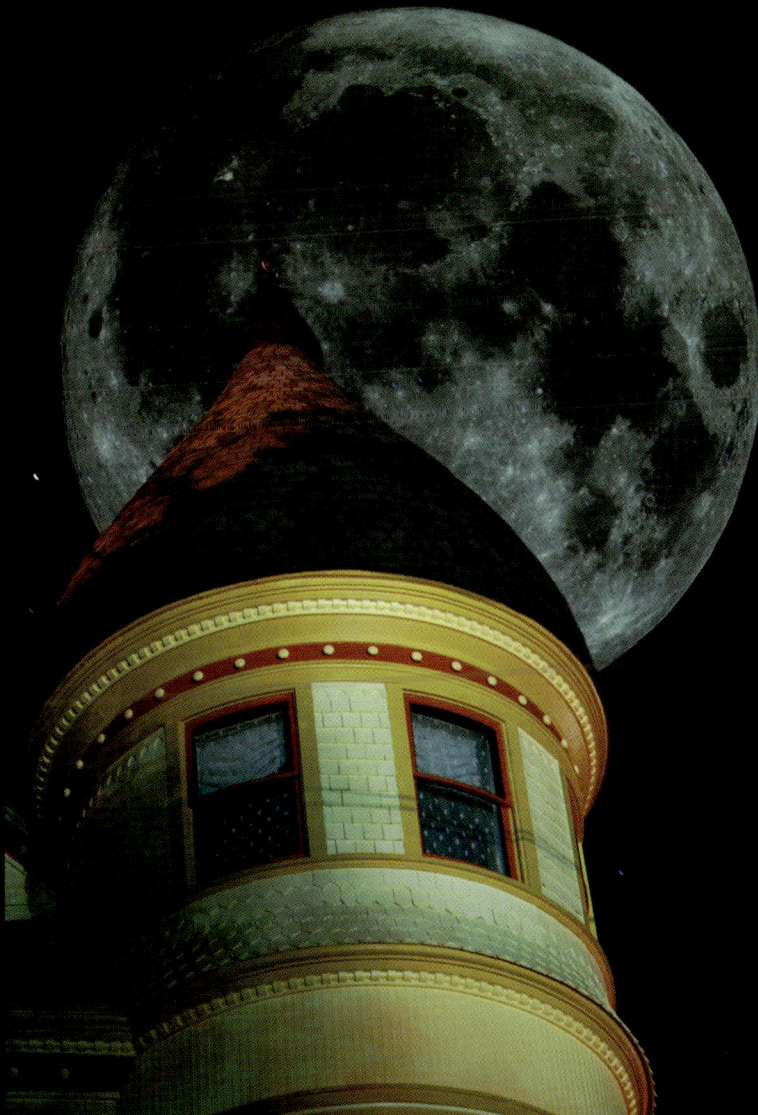

In 1891, an illustrious man named Curtis Wright, distant cousin to Orville and Wilbur Wright, built a magnificent Queen Anne style home in Carthage, Missouri. Wright owned a furniture factory in Indiana but was drawn to Carthage for the opportunity that the mineral rich deposits in the area presented to turn of the century entrepreneurs. Awestruck by the geology, Mr. Wright originally invested in lead and mineral mines and later opened the Carthage Stone Company, supplier of limestone for public buildings across Missouri. He promised to build a most superior mansion for his wife, Nira and their eight children. The Wrights constructed a 22 room mansion, with every inch having an ostentatious flair. For 20 years the Wright family entertained a multitude of guests, both famous and family, in their home on Macon Street. Once the Wrights no longer owned the mansion, it changed ownership several times. In 1984, the Evans family purchased the home with the intent of moving the entire structure to Eureka Springs, Arkansas. The massive oak and cherry wood structure was dismantled and moved piece by piece to its current location in Eureka Springs. The Queen Anne operated for years as a tour home under Evans. Steve and Lata Lovell purchased the property in 2005 and undertook a five-year complete restoration on the 12,000 square foot home and the neighboring 1888 Victorian cottage original to the property.

N 36°23.654'
W 093°44.593'
Elevation 1423'

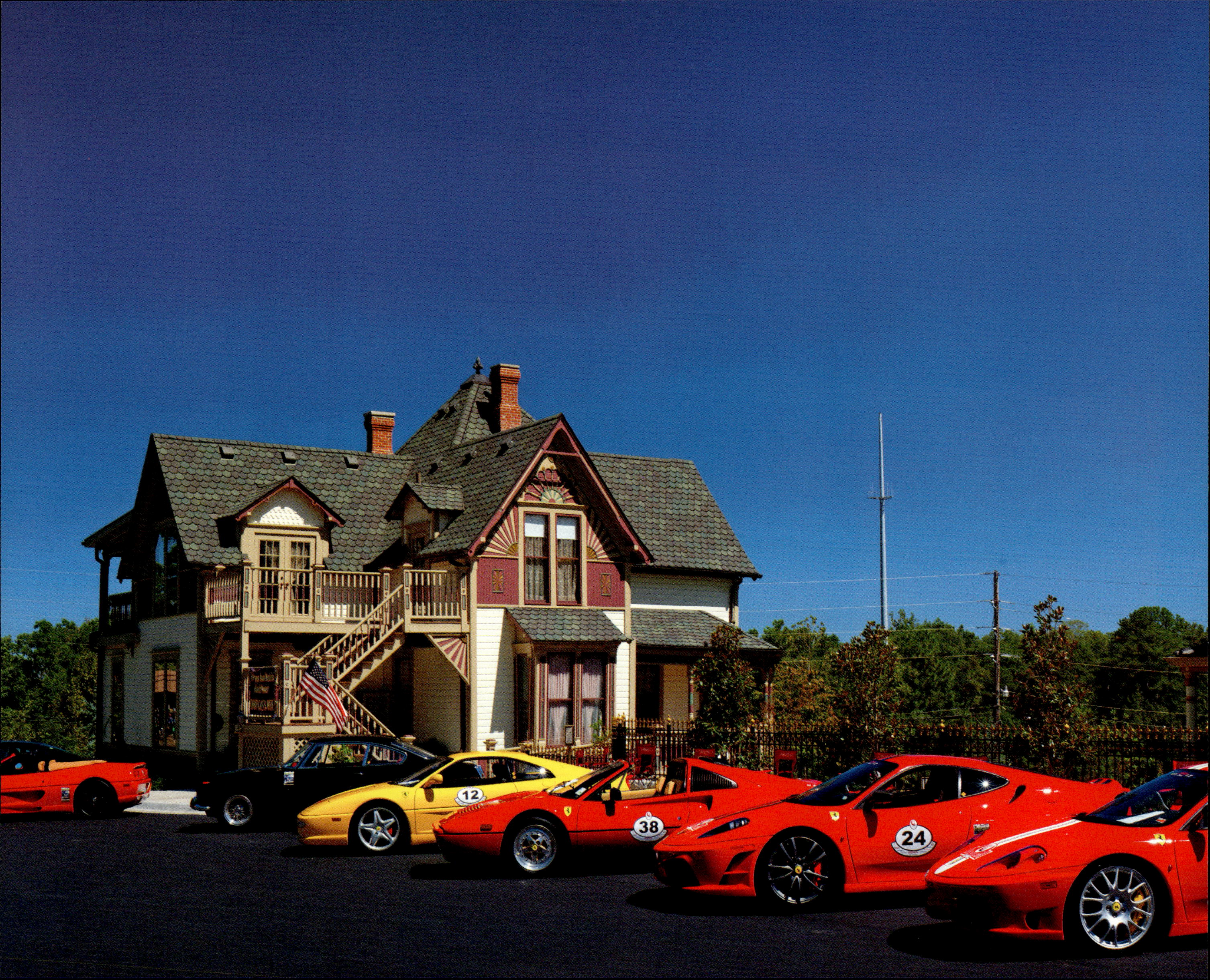
12
38
24

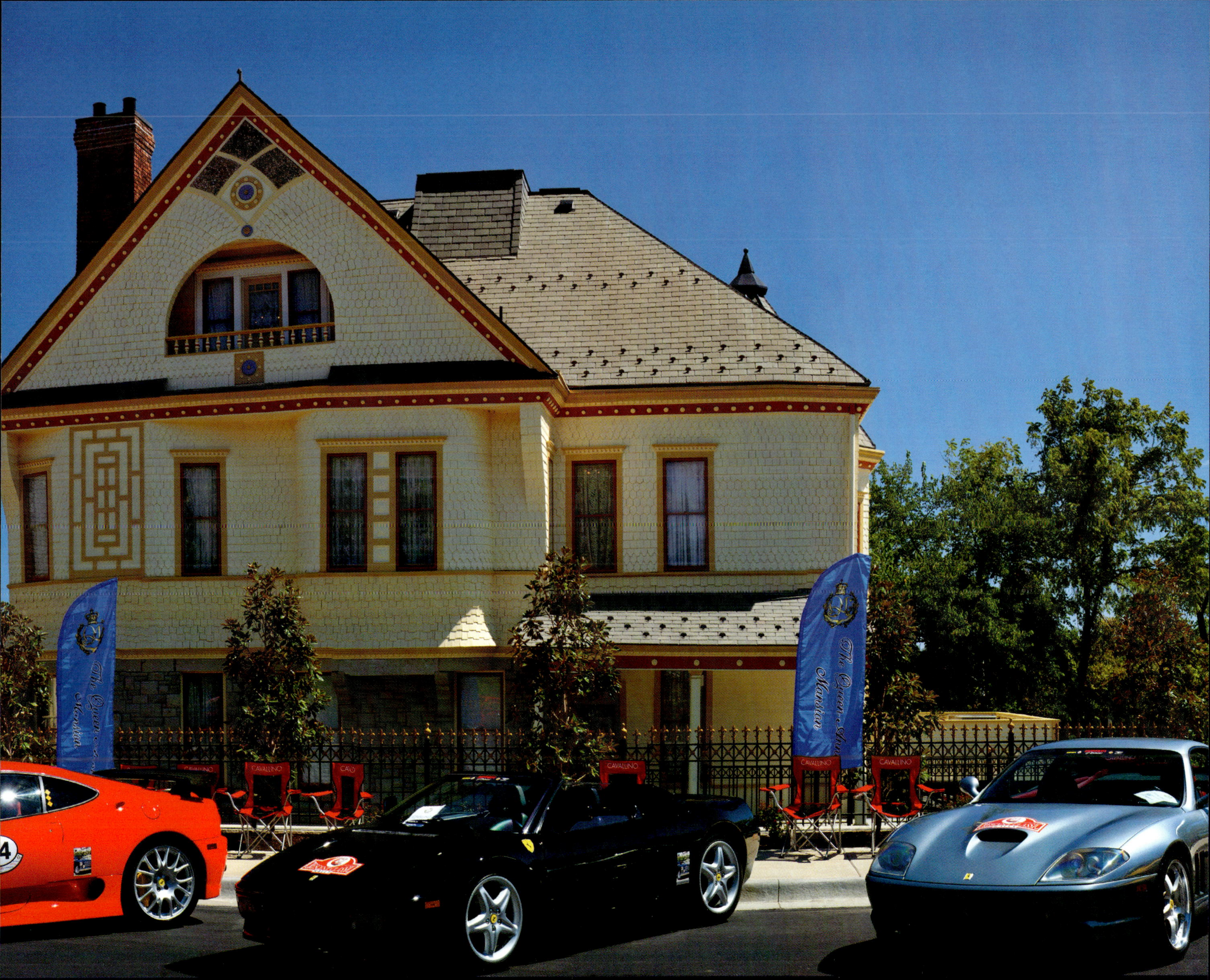
The Queen
Mansion
CAVALLINO
CAVALLINO

*(These pages and following page)* Once a memorial chapel for the family of Richard C. Kerens, St. Elizabeth's Chapel sits just behind the Crescent Hotel. In 1908, the chapel's donation to the community led to the Sisters of Mercy abandoning their old church for this pristine setting. The entrance hall holds four statuary pieces as the only remnants of the old church. Ripley's Believe It or Not notes it is the only church with an entrance through the bell tower.

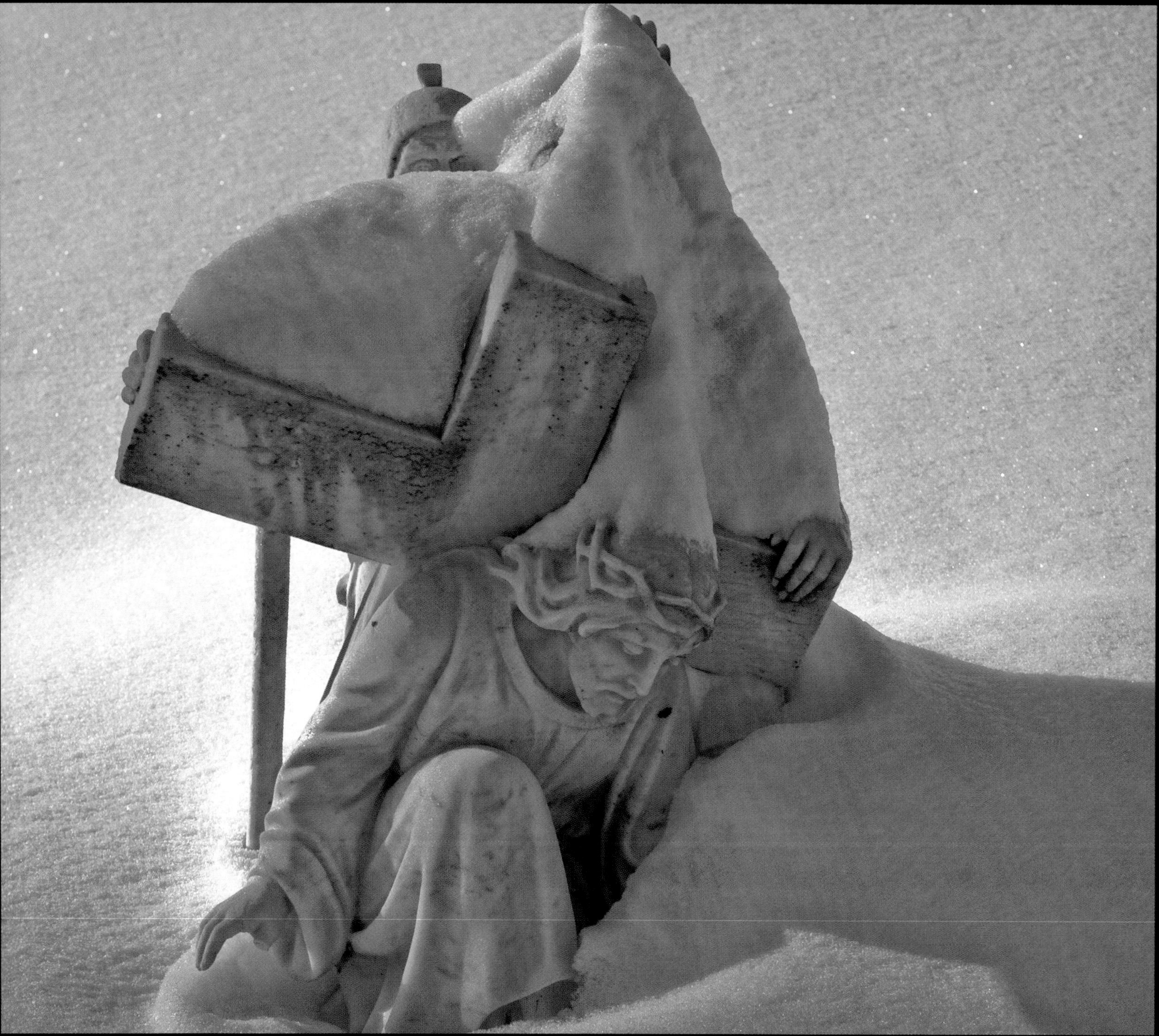

N 36°24.500'
W 093°44.223'
Elevation 1488'

N 36°24.272'
W 093°44.232'
Elevation 1428'

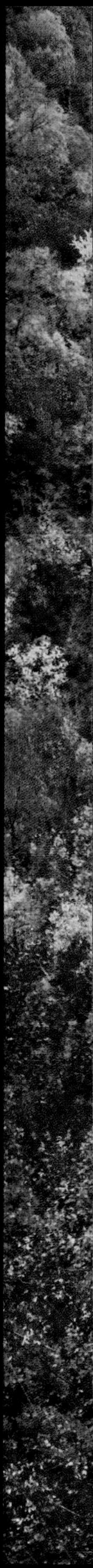

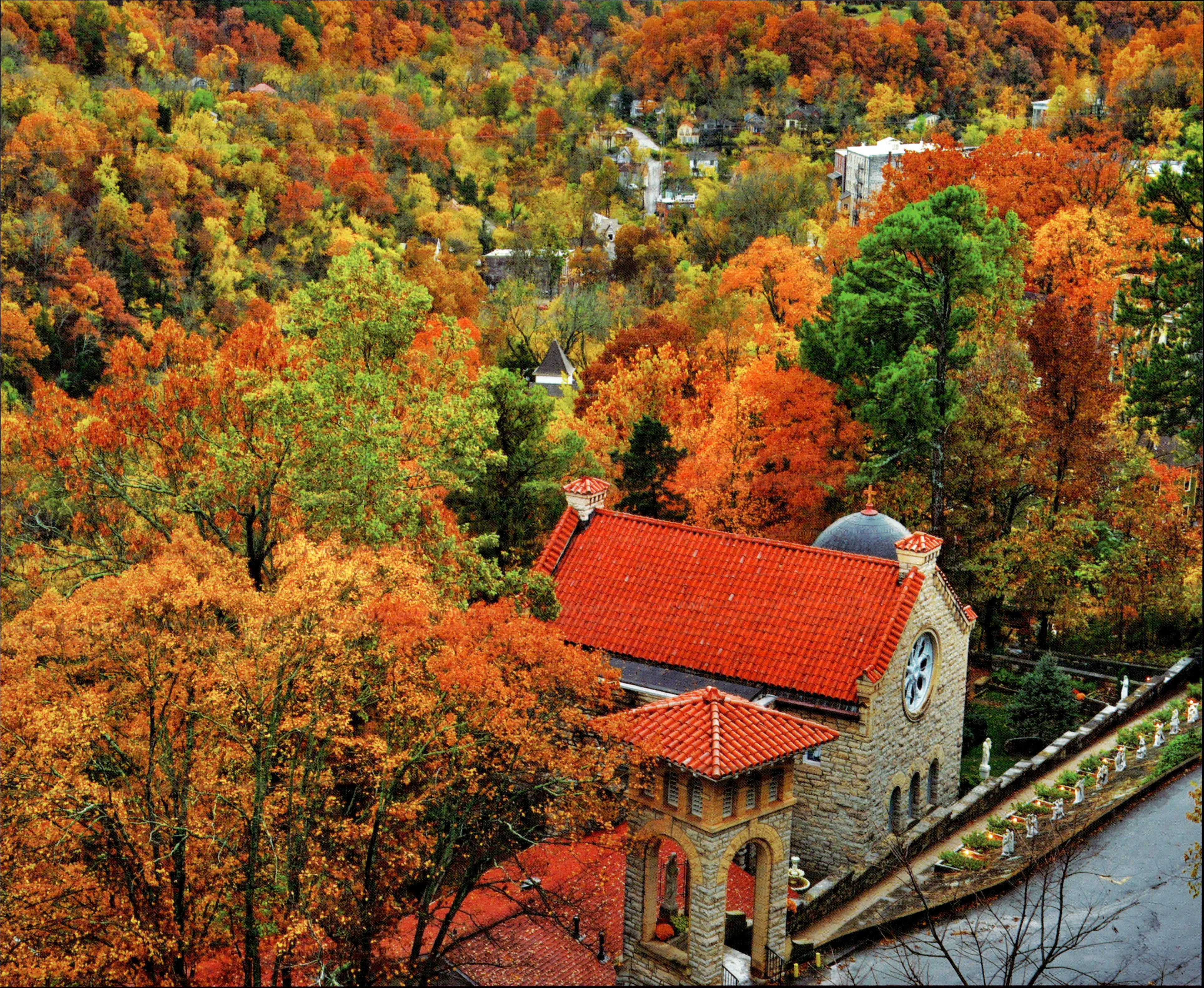

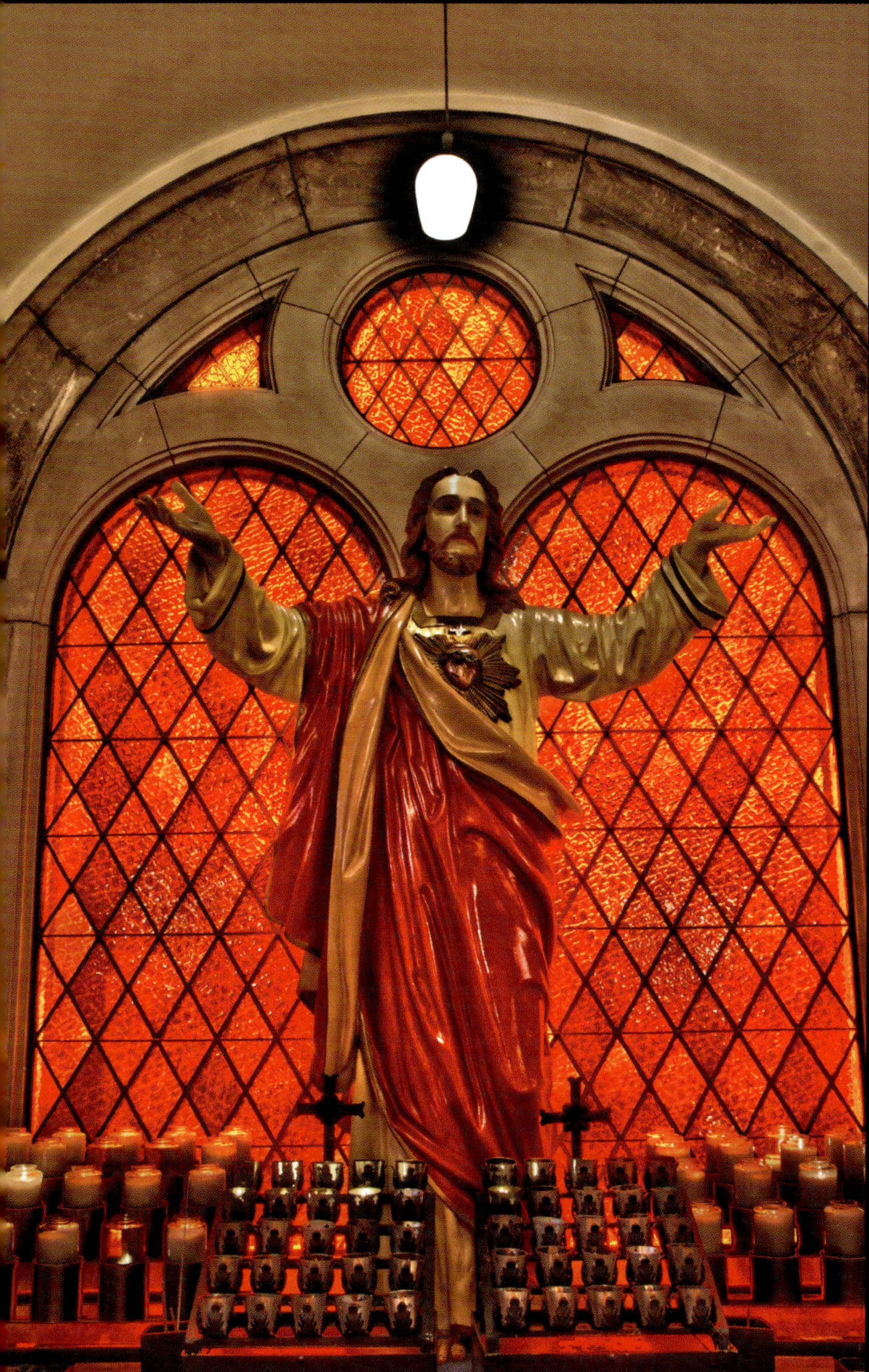

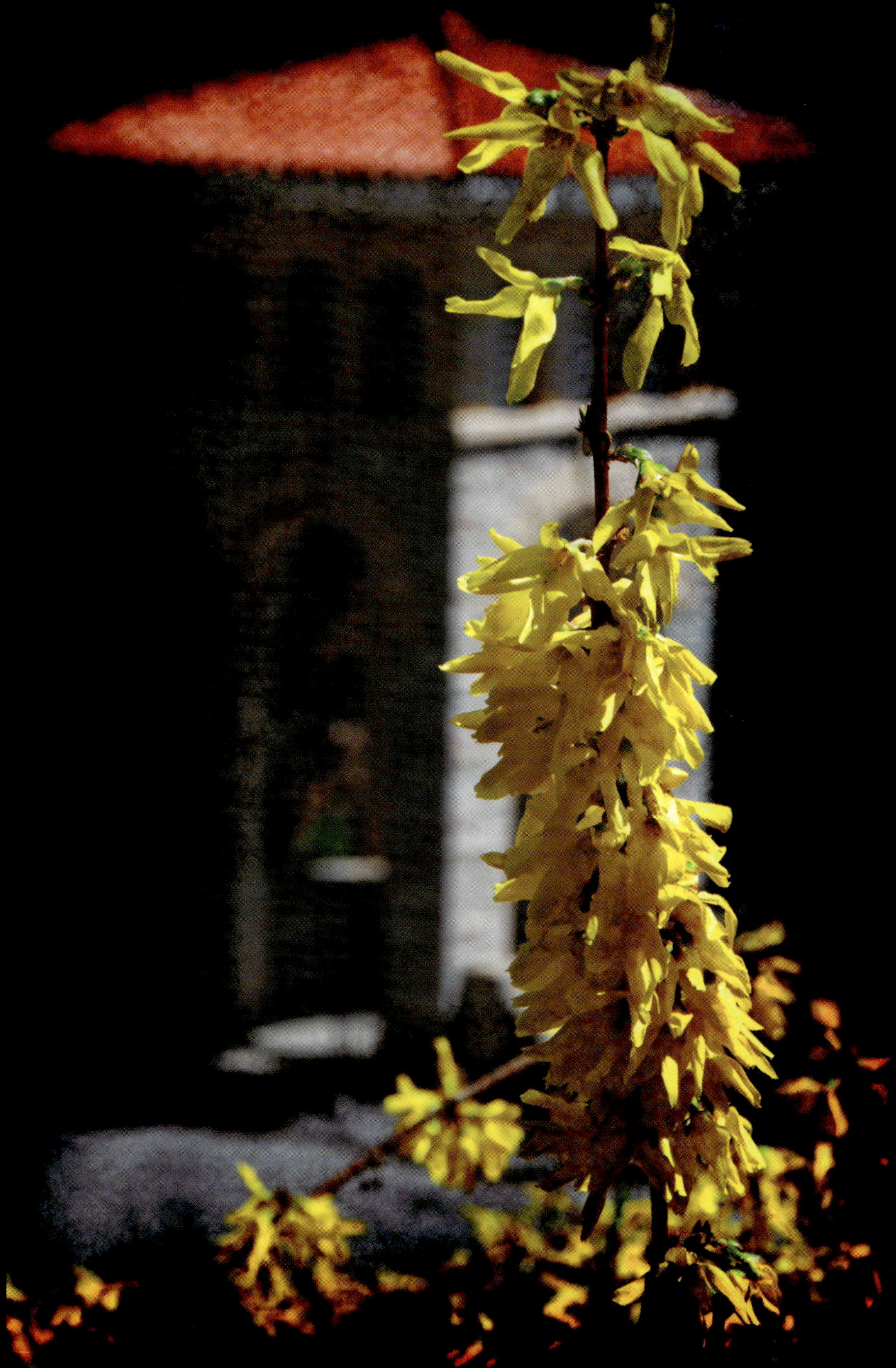

John Michael Talbot, an Oklahoma native, is a major Catholic music artist who is the founder, general minister, and spiritual father of the Brothers and Sisters of Charity at Little Portion Hermitage. The group moves away from mainstream materialism and excessive consumerism and embraces the Franciscan lifestyle of simplicity. Around 40 individuals in search for a monastic place of worship live in the community Talbot built. In April 2008, a fire decimated the original hermitage and chapel. The brothers and sisters undertook a large reconstruction project and held the reopening ceremony for the new chapel in October 2010. It is now home to one of the area's more intriguing chapels.

N 36°27.085'
W 093°39.742'
Elevation 1182'

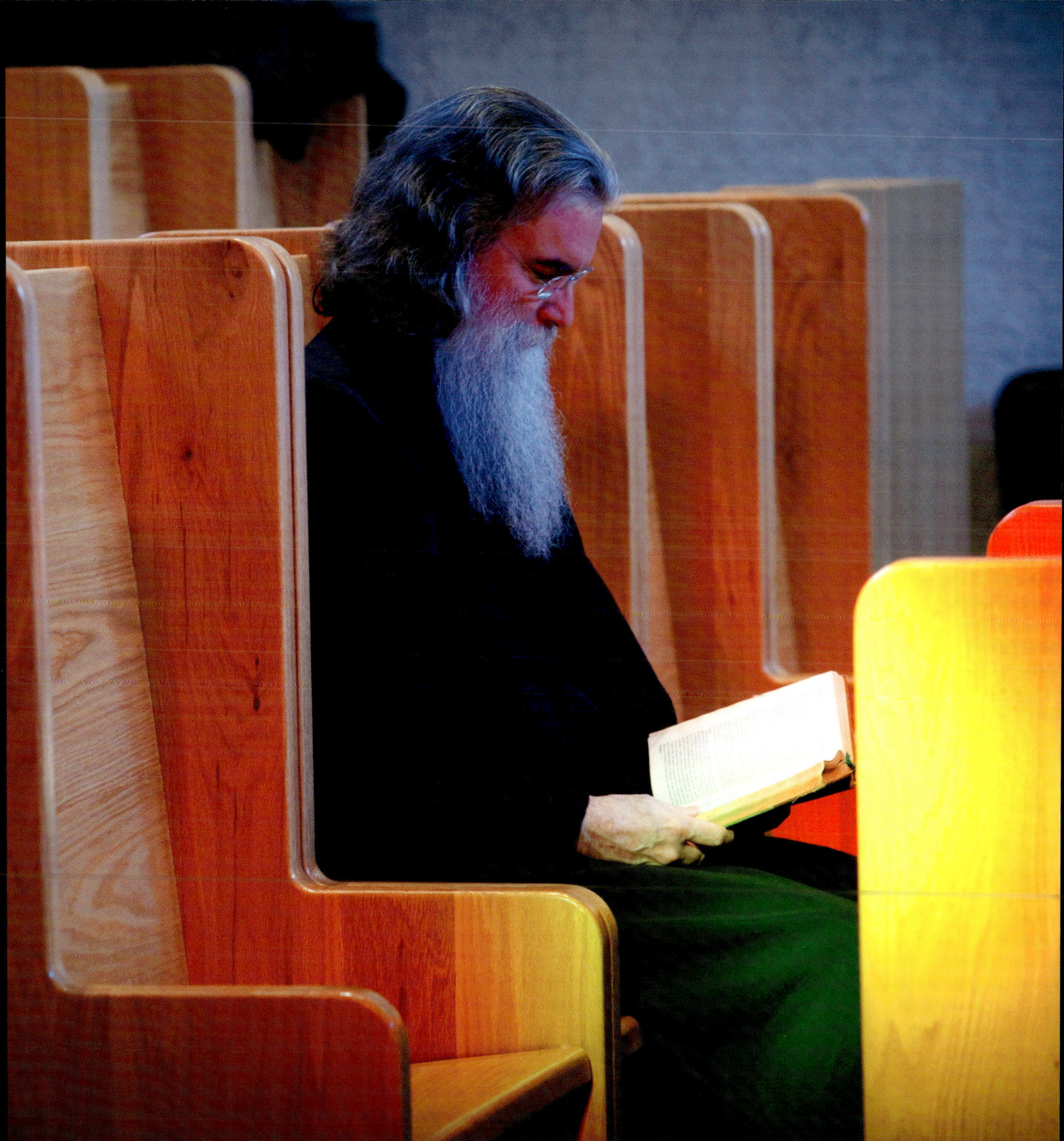

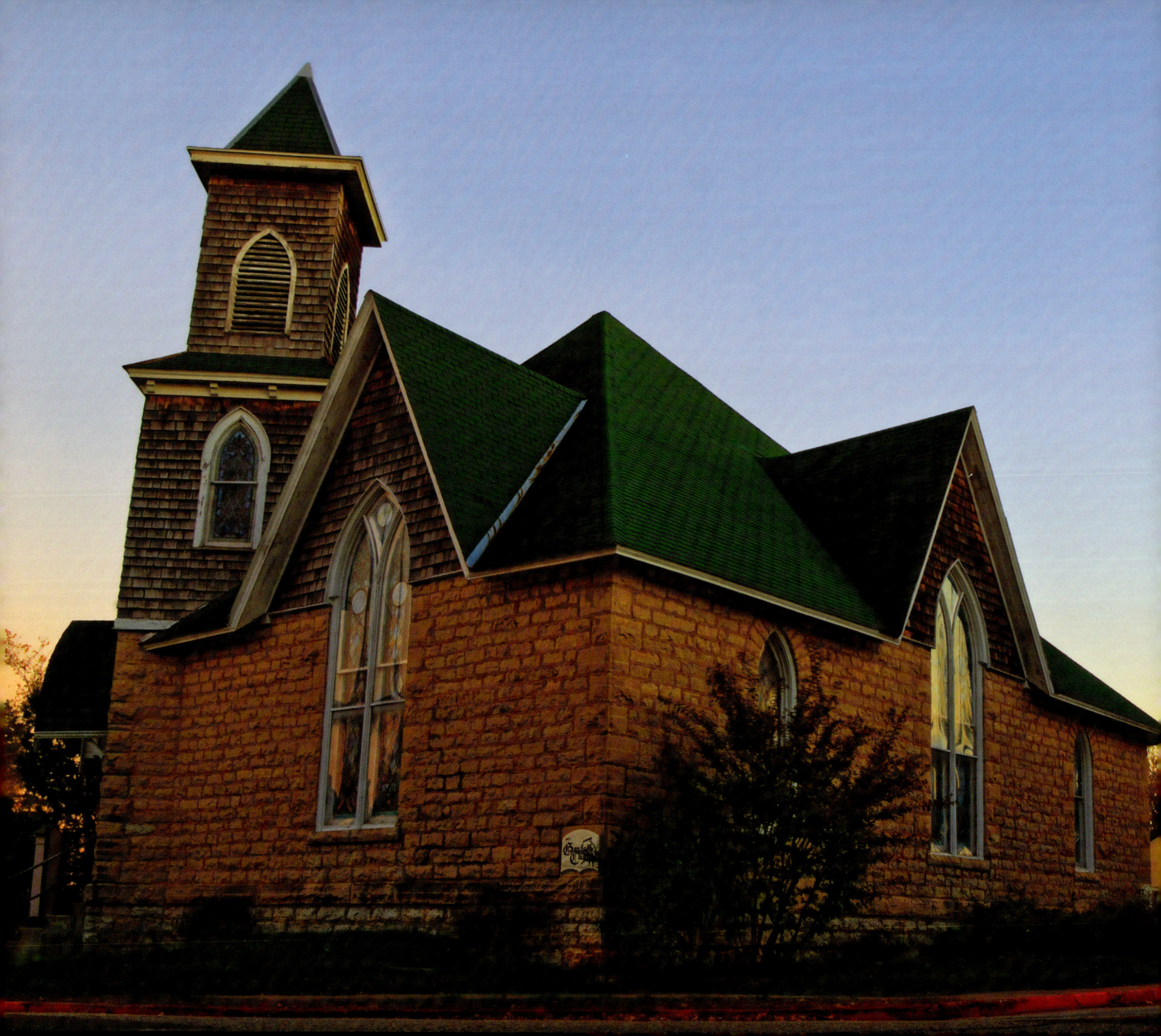

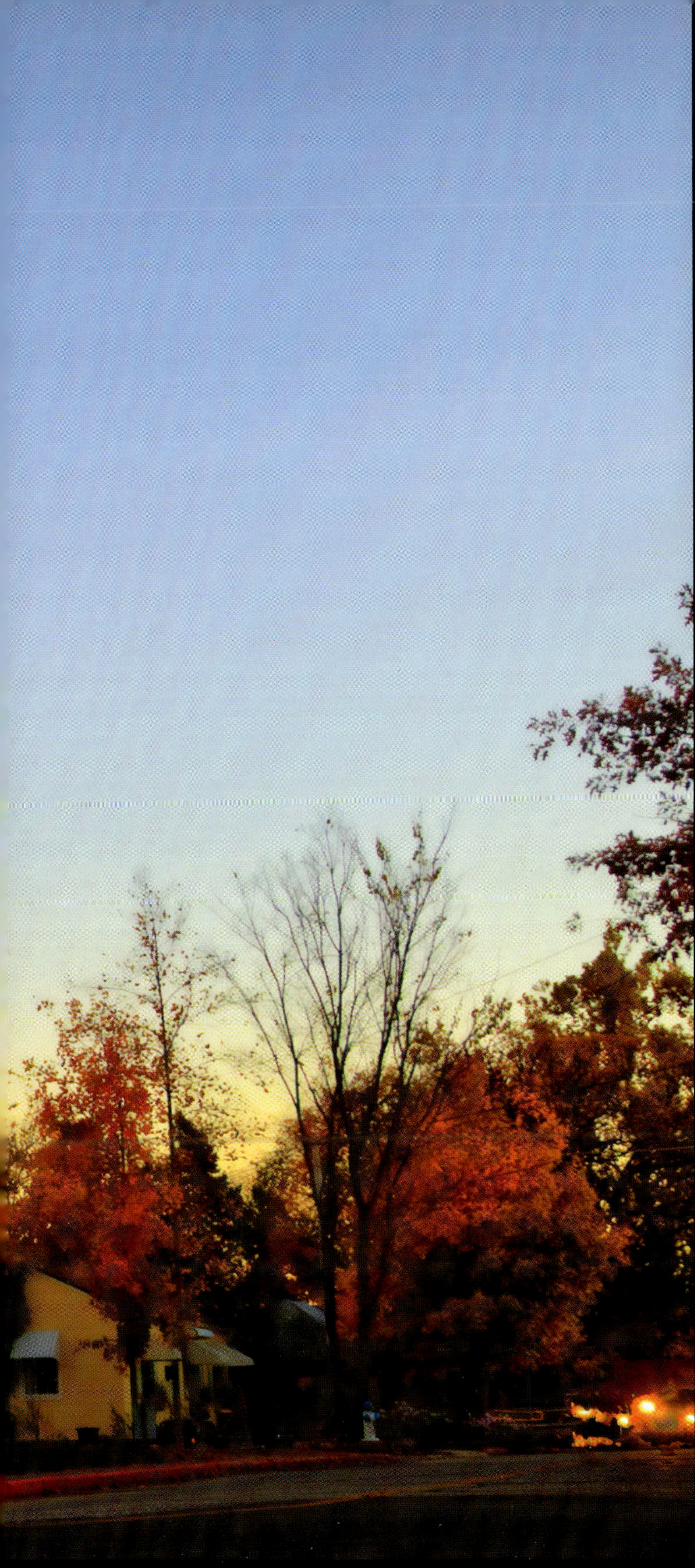

The limestone Gavioli Chapel houses a massive collection of vintage music machines. The chapel, built in 1901 on a plot originally chosen for the Emmanuel Baptist Church and later the First Christian Church, is a popular wedding and tourist attraction.

N 36°24.234'
W 093°44.556'
Elevation 1423'

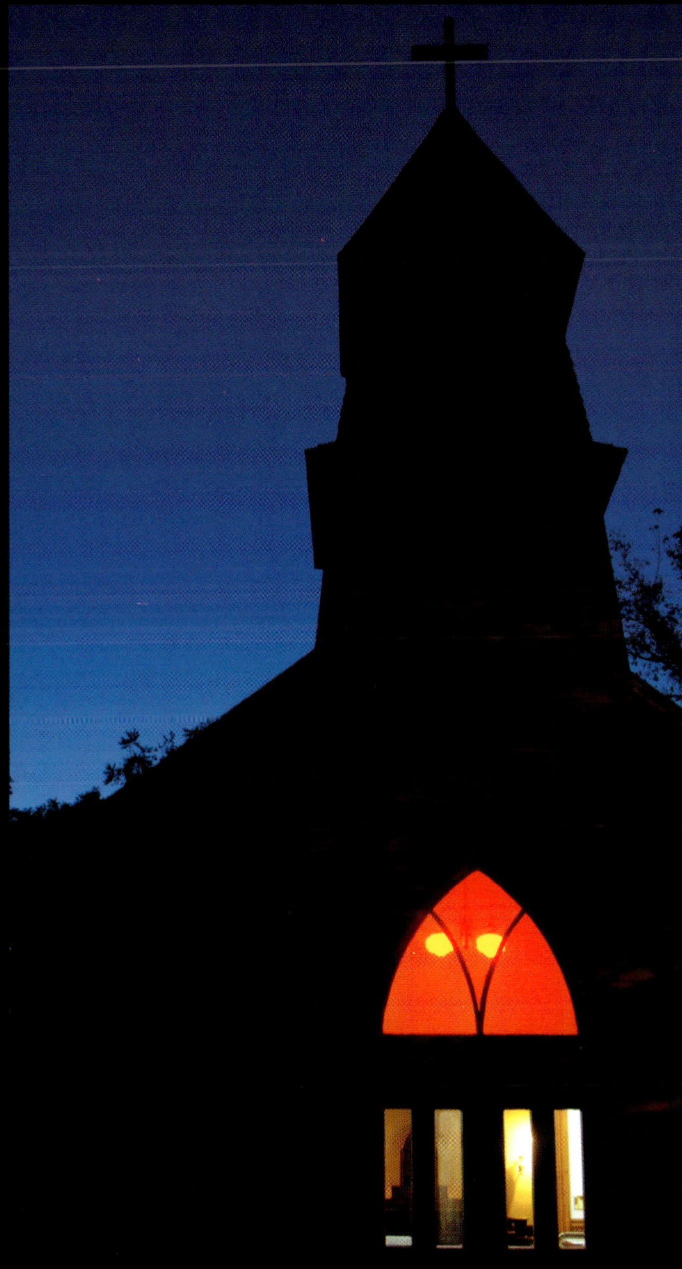

The 1883 St. James' Episcopal Church declared their congregation to be the first in Eureka Springs. The building went into complete disarray after World War I until renovation by congregation members in 1947. On August 24, 1962, a fire destroyed a portion of the church and the second oldest pipe organ in Arkansas. Repairs took eight months to complete.

N 36°24.420'
W 093°44.358'
Elevation 1415'

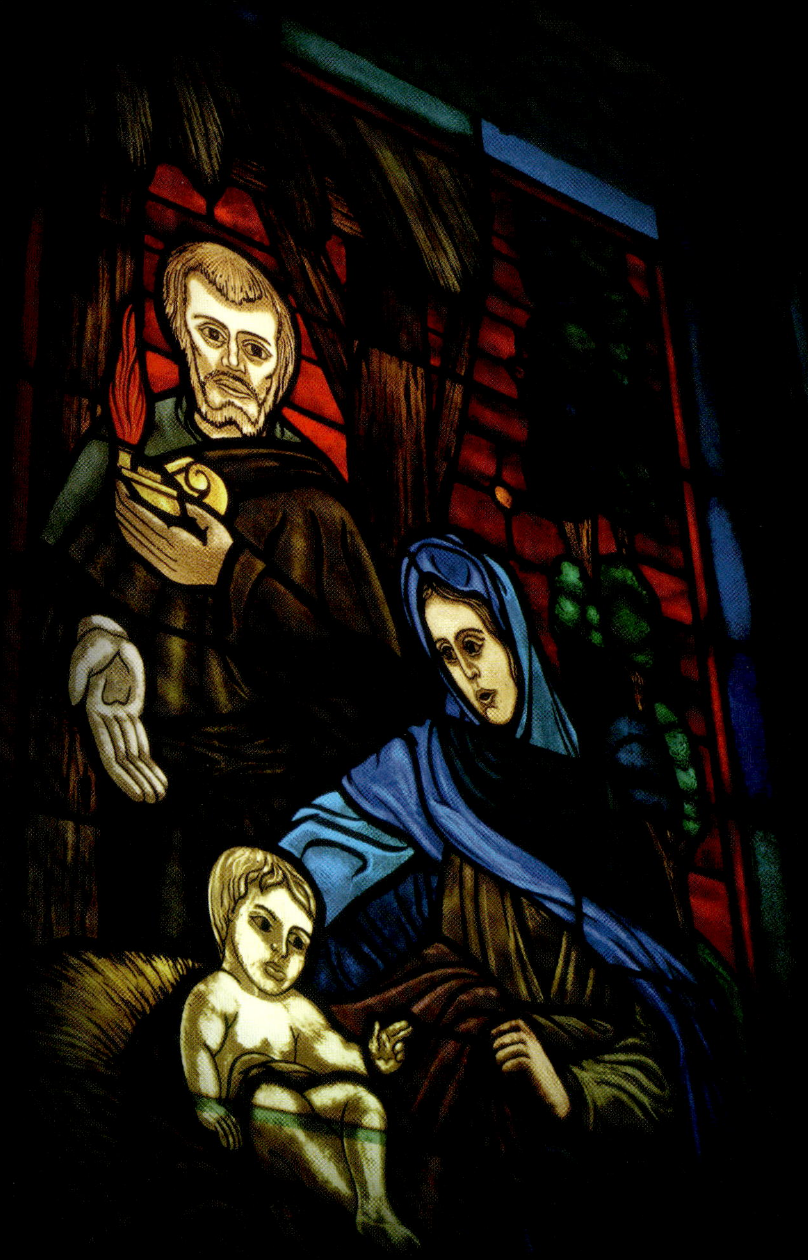

October 12, 1913, dates the dedication service for the Penn Memorial Church of Eureka Springs, named after western evangelist William Penn, who moved to Eureka Springs in 1888. Noted in Ripley's Believe It Or Not are the three addresses for each of the three streets it touches, and the fact that each of the four floors has a street level entrance.

N 36°24.226'
W 093°44.288'
Elevation 1326'

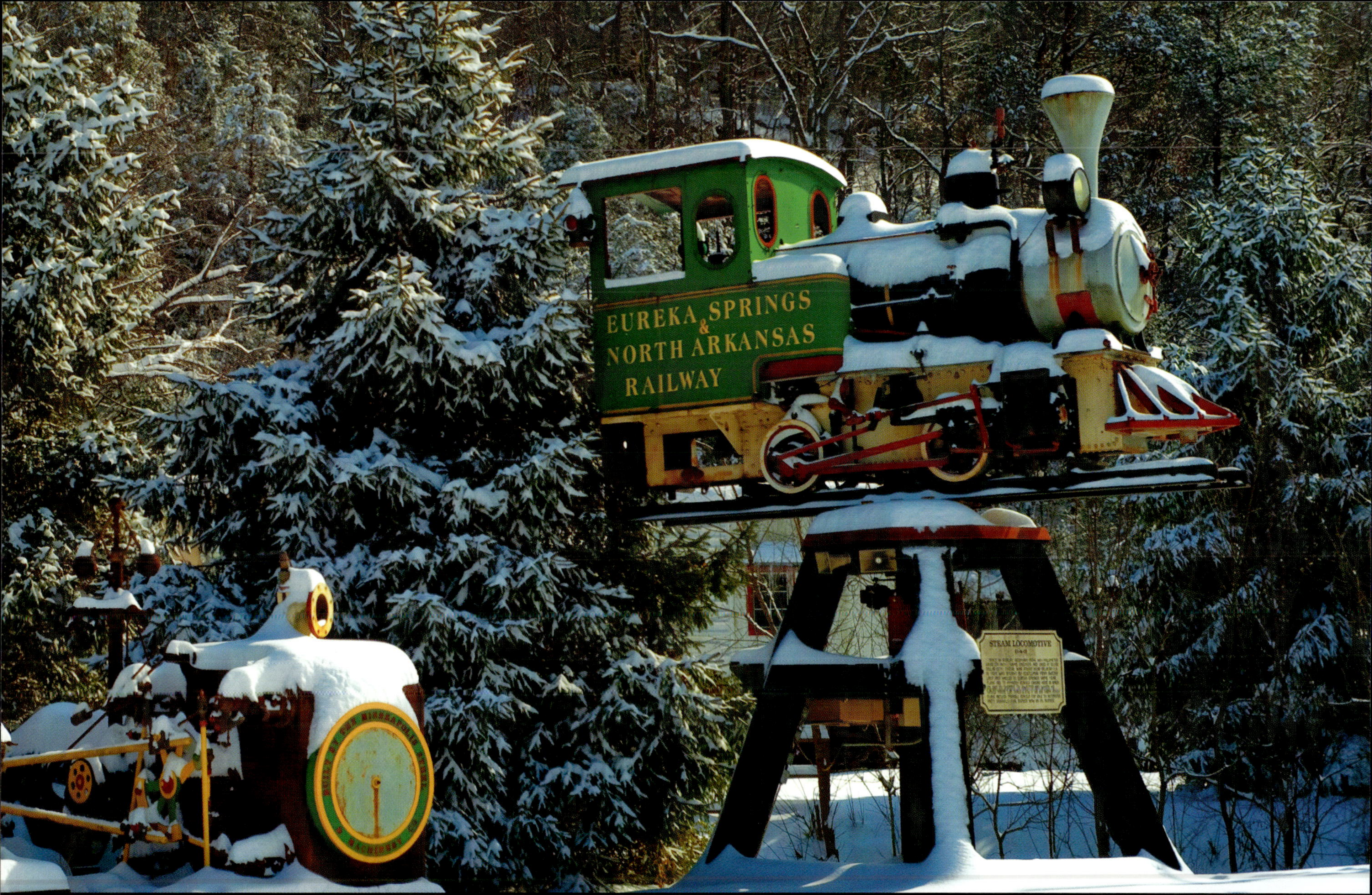


January 24, 1883, marked the completion of the rail line from Seligman, Missouri, to Eureka Springs and the opening of the depot there. What remains of the old truss bridge is visible from the shoreline in Beaver. Round-trip fare to Seligman form Eureka was $3.50. By the end of 1883, using first year profits, the fleet had expanded to two engines, a combination car, six flatcars, and a coach. In May, 1889, the organization of the St. Louis & North Arkansas Railroad was complete and work finally began on a line to Harrison. The Harrison – Seligman line opened in April of 1901 with daily service. On May 19, 1906, the St. Louis & North Arkansas Railroad was sold, and during the restructuring, was renamed the Missouri & North Arkansas Railroad Company. By 1909, the fleet consisted of 21 passenger cars, 9 passenger engines, and 11 freight engines.

N 36°24.825'
W 093°44.042'
Elevation 1067'

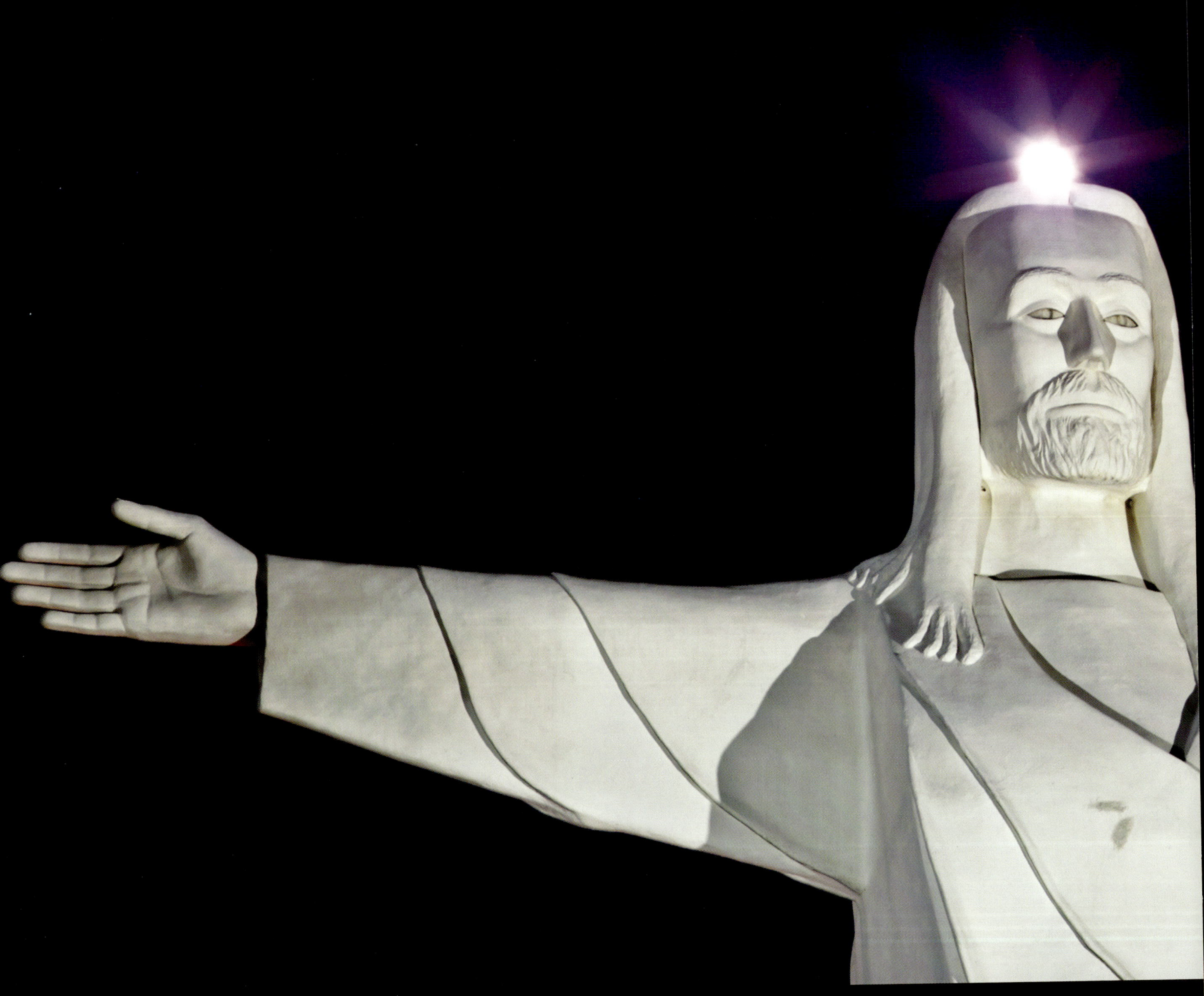

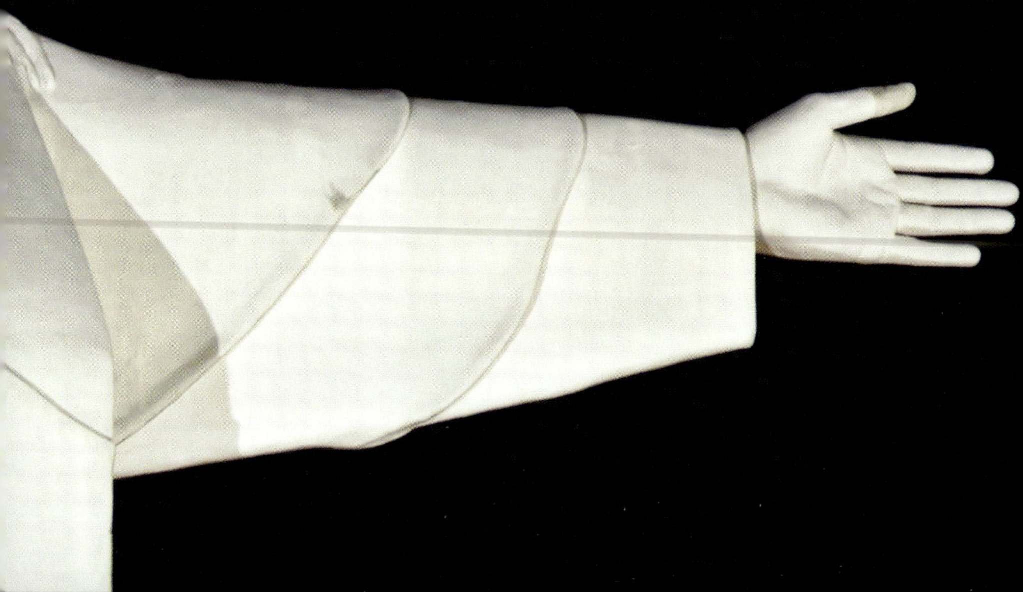

The Christ of the Ozarks statue stands 67 feet tall, shown here as a full moon arises in the night skies. The sculptor, Emmet Sullivan, who also worked on Mount Rushmore, completed the statue in 1966. The 340-ton concrete foundation supports 65-foot arms swathed in 27 layers of white mortar over a steel frame. The statue stands on a hillside at The Great Passion Play, which hosted their first play on July 15, 1968.

N 36°24.534'
W 093°43.524'
Elevation 1438'

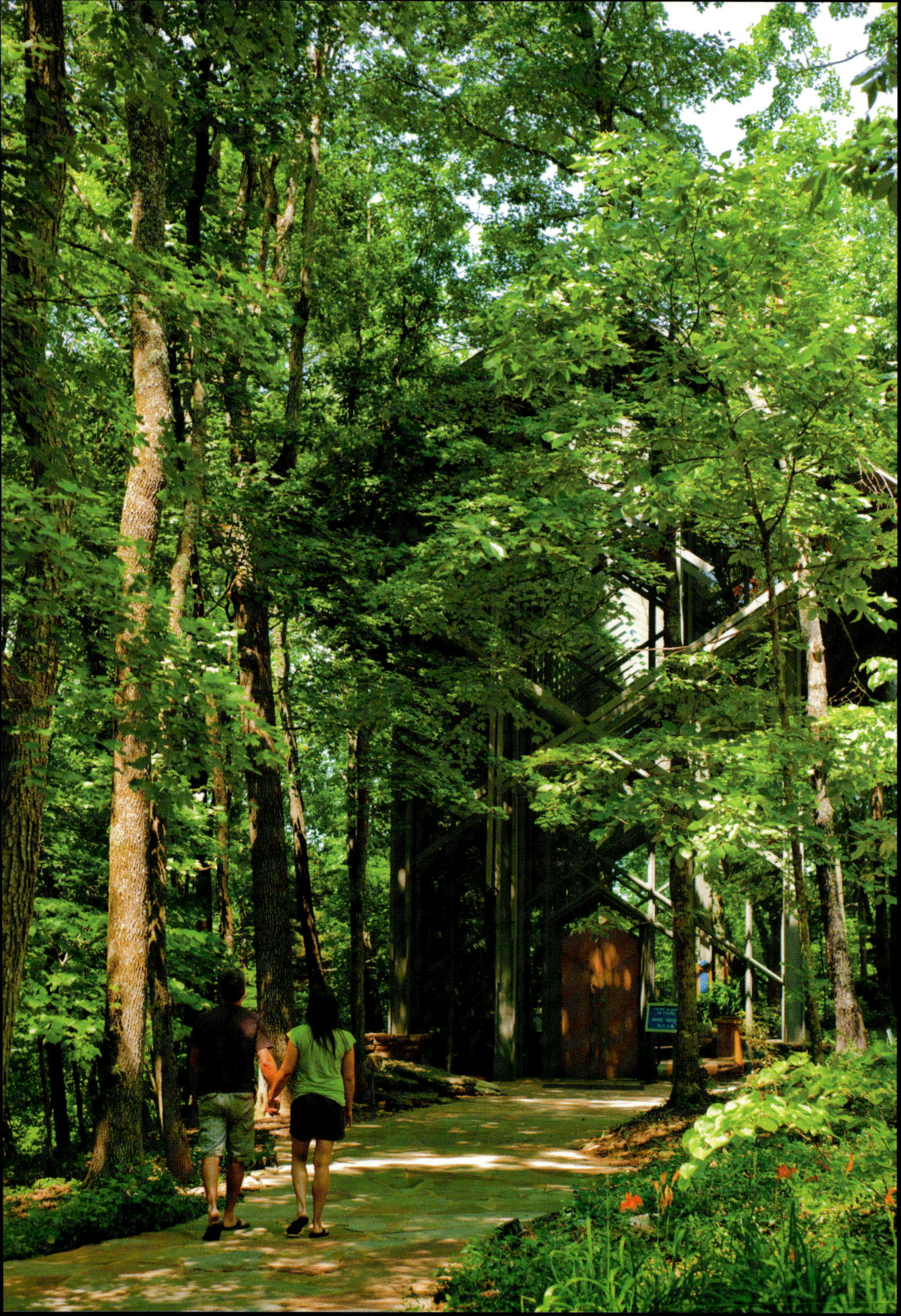

Onyx Cave stays a cool 53 degrees annually and boasts a range of various cave formations including boxworks, anthodites, helicites, and stalactites. "Dragon Rock" and "Witches Fireplace" are two of the more aptly-named formations along a self-guided tour route that takes around 20 minutes. One tale about the discovery of the cave is that the Huntsville sheriff stumbled upon the entrance while searching the land for a hidden cache of money stolen in an 1891 Huntsville bank robbery. The land belonged to civil war veteran Buck Robbins, who had no clue the cave system was below his feet.

Jim Reed enlisted architect E. Fay Jones to design Thorncrown Chapel, nestled in the mountains just outside of Eureka Springs. The chapel opened on July 10, 1980, allowing views of the woods through 6,000 square feet of glass in 425 windows. The chapel is surrounded with an estimated 100 tons of colored flagstone and native rock. It stands as one of the finest examples of a religious structure on the globe.

N 36°25.016'
W 093°46.312'
Elevation 1248'

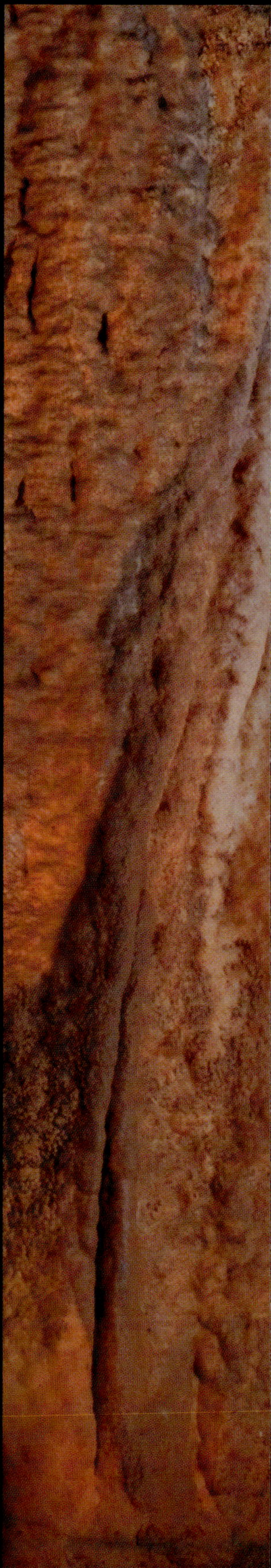

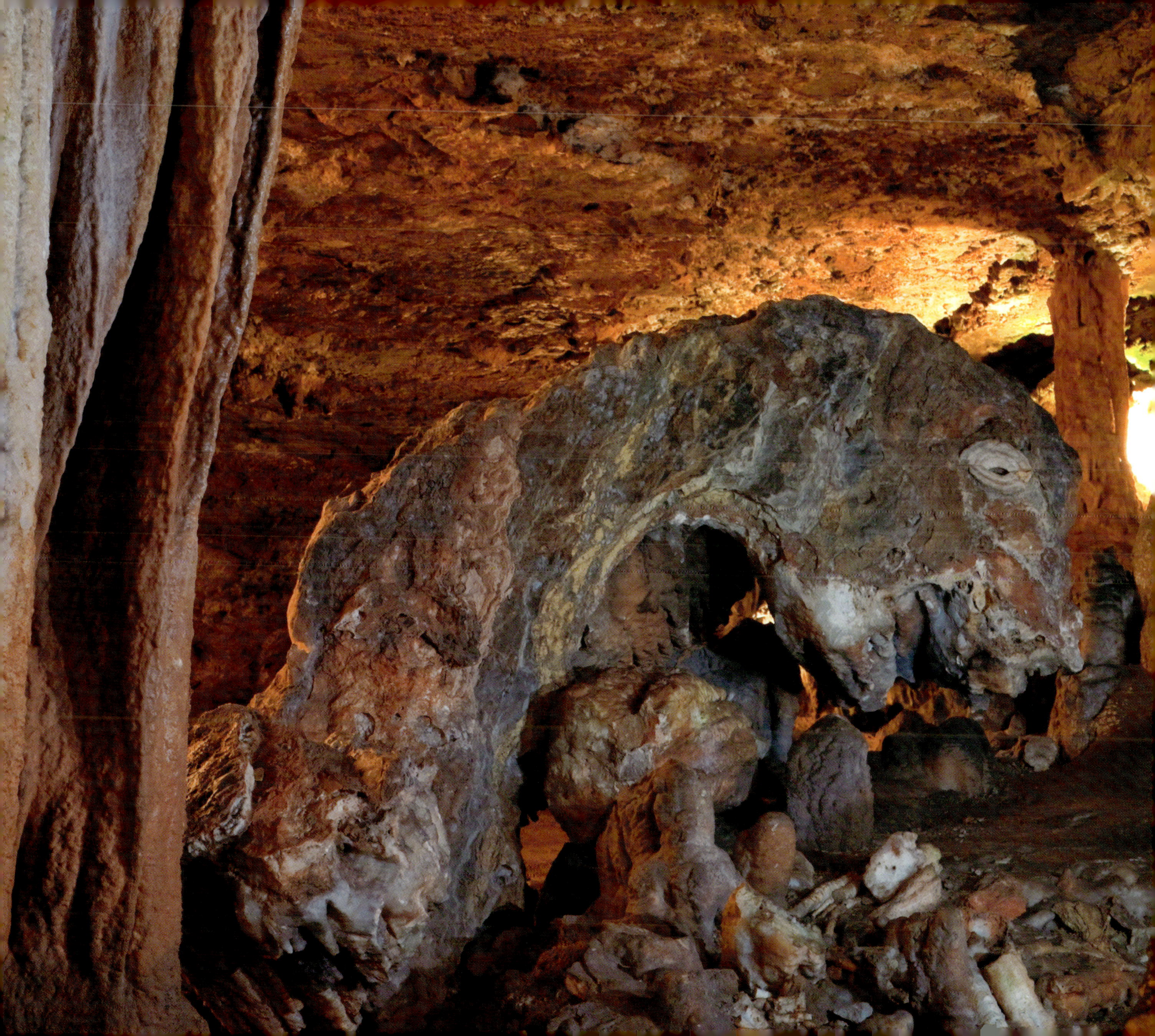

Persistent floodwaters along the King and Osage Rivers, which separate the county, forced a need for the Western District Courthouse. Eureka Springs acquired its county seat position on March 12, 1883, via the Arkansas General Assembly, but it was 25 years before for the 1908 completion of the courthouse.

N 36°24.046'
W 093°44.343'
Elevation 1243'

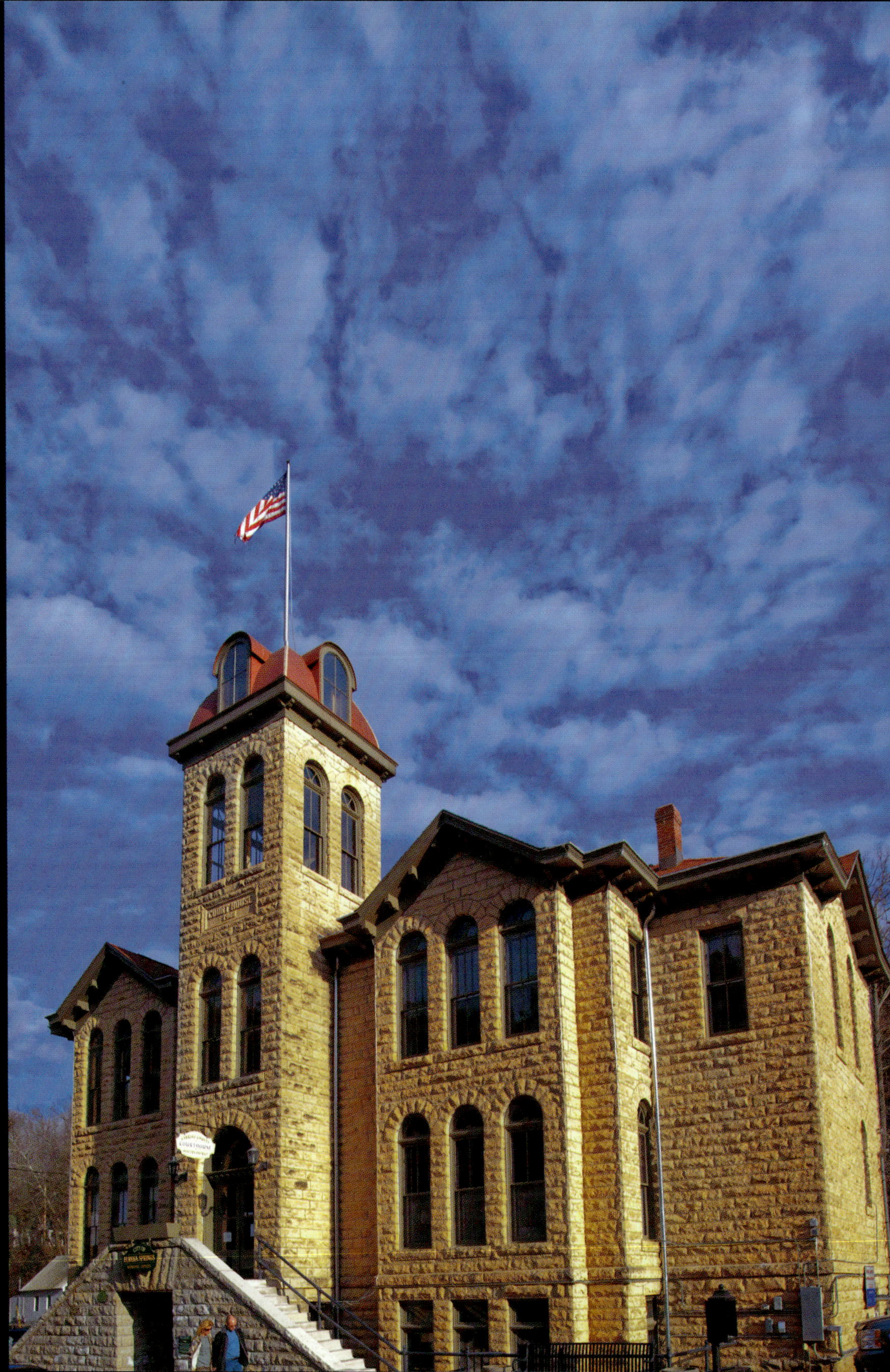

On September 13, 1929, John Phillip Sousa and his 67-piece Sousa Band was the first to perform at the Eureka Springs Auditorium, known as the 'Aud' by locals, fulfilling the dream of Mayor Claude A. Fuller. The venue over the years has hosted the likes of Willie Nelson, BB King, Bill Cosby, and a long list of other top performers.

N 36°24.057'
W 093°44.324'
Elevation 1245'

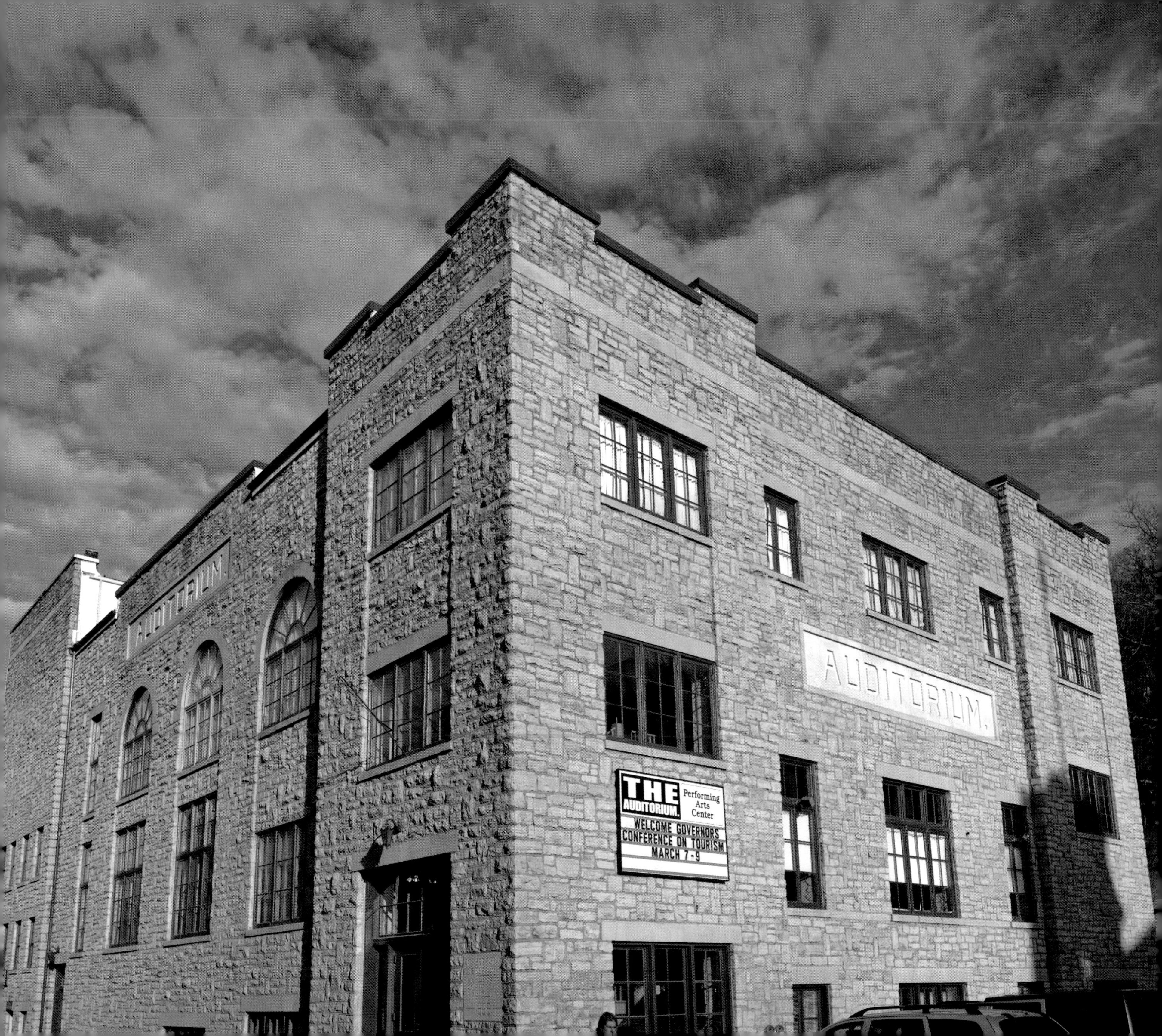
AUDITORIUM.
AUDITORIUM.
THE AUDITORIUM.
Performing Arts Center
WELCOME GOVERNORS
CONFERENCE ON TOURISM
MARCH 7-9

Roaring River State Park covers more than 3,403 wooded acres in Southern Missouri. Twenty million gallons of cool water flow forth from Roaring River Spring every day, making it the perfect environment for a trout fishery to thrive. The large spring has been the site of mills dating back to 1836. On December 6, 1928, Dr. Thomas Sayman donated the park to the state of Missouri for the purpose of a State Park.

N 36°35.299'
W 093°50.158'
Elevation 1043'

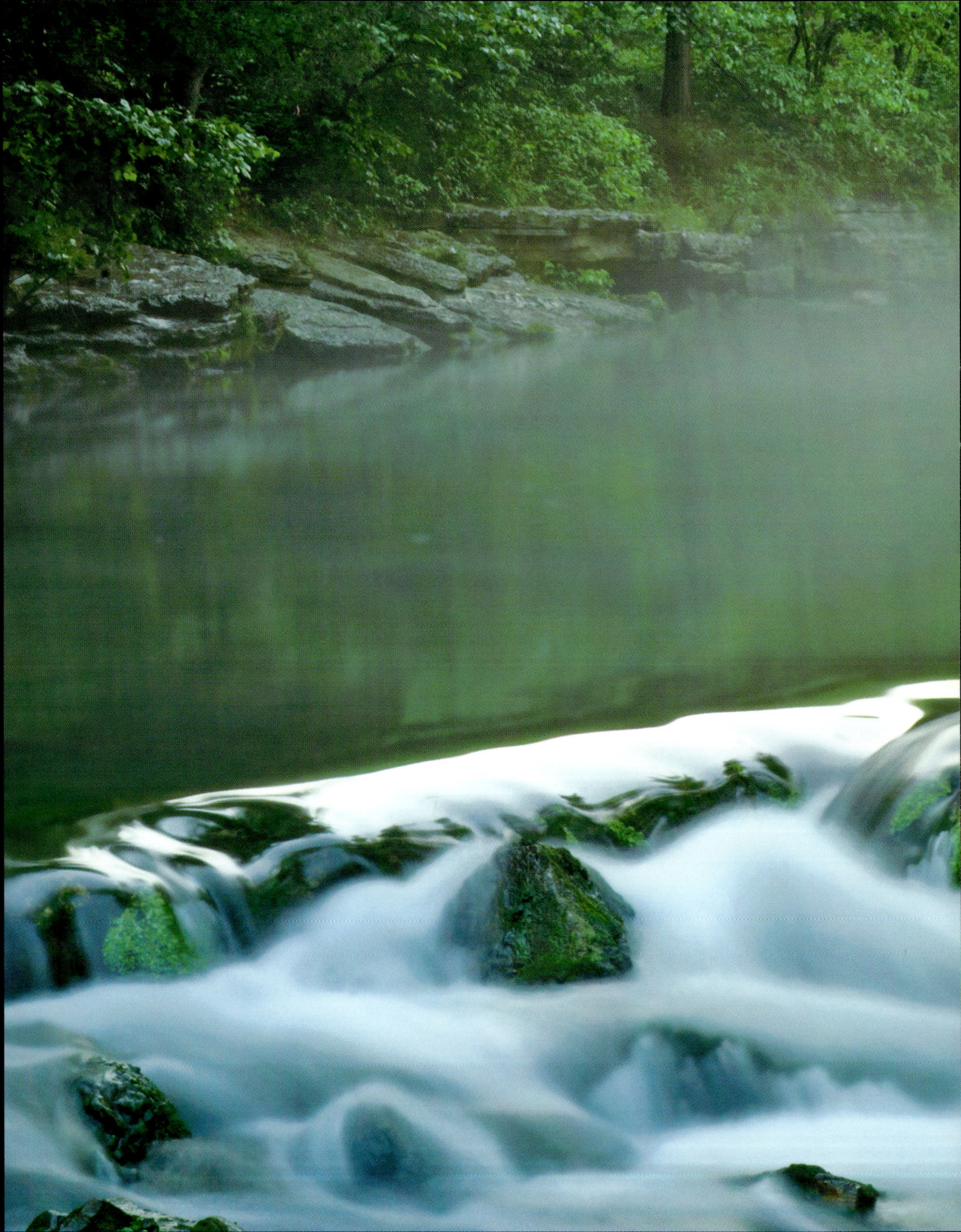

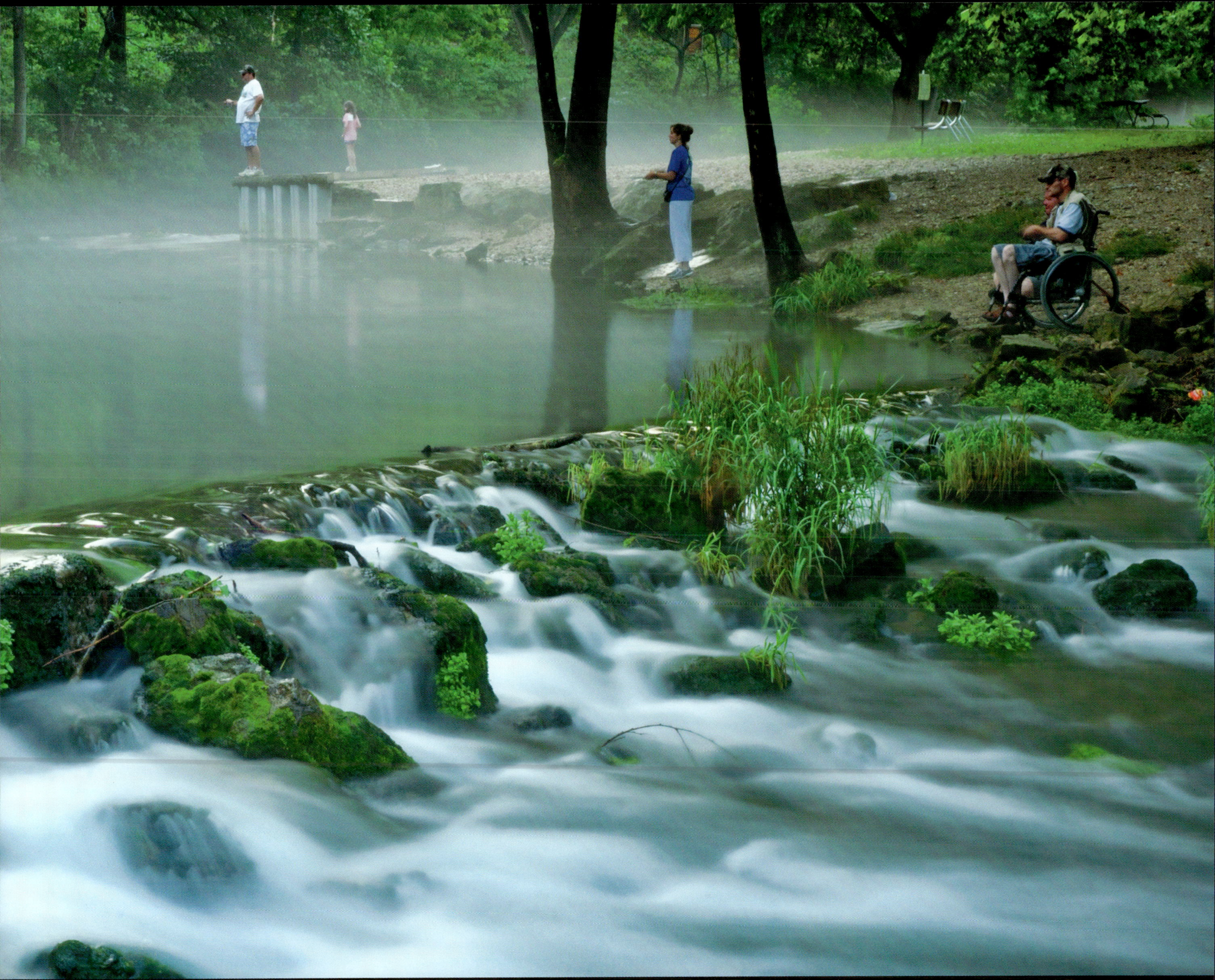

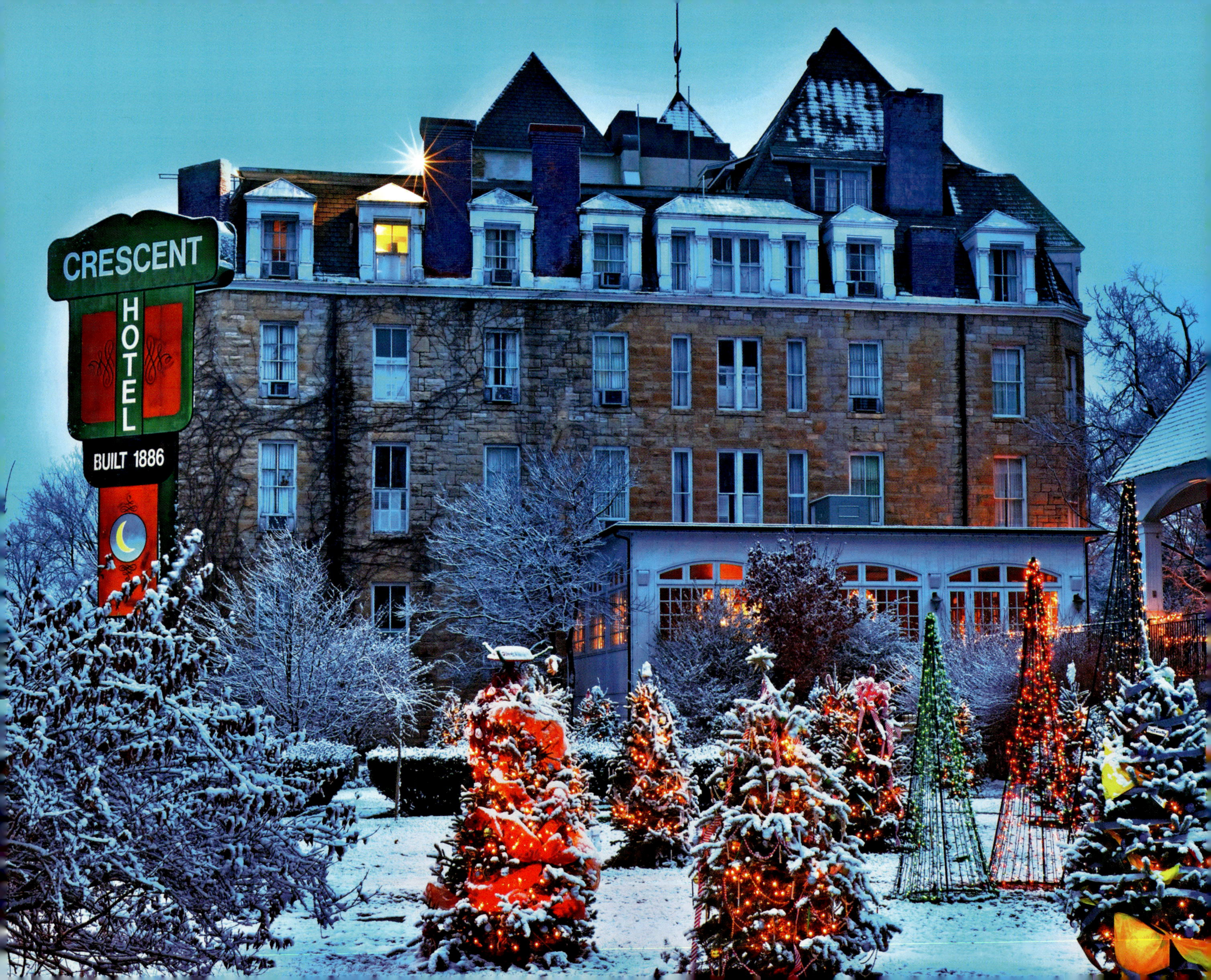
CRESCENT
HOTEL
BUILT 1886

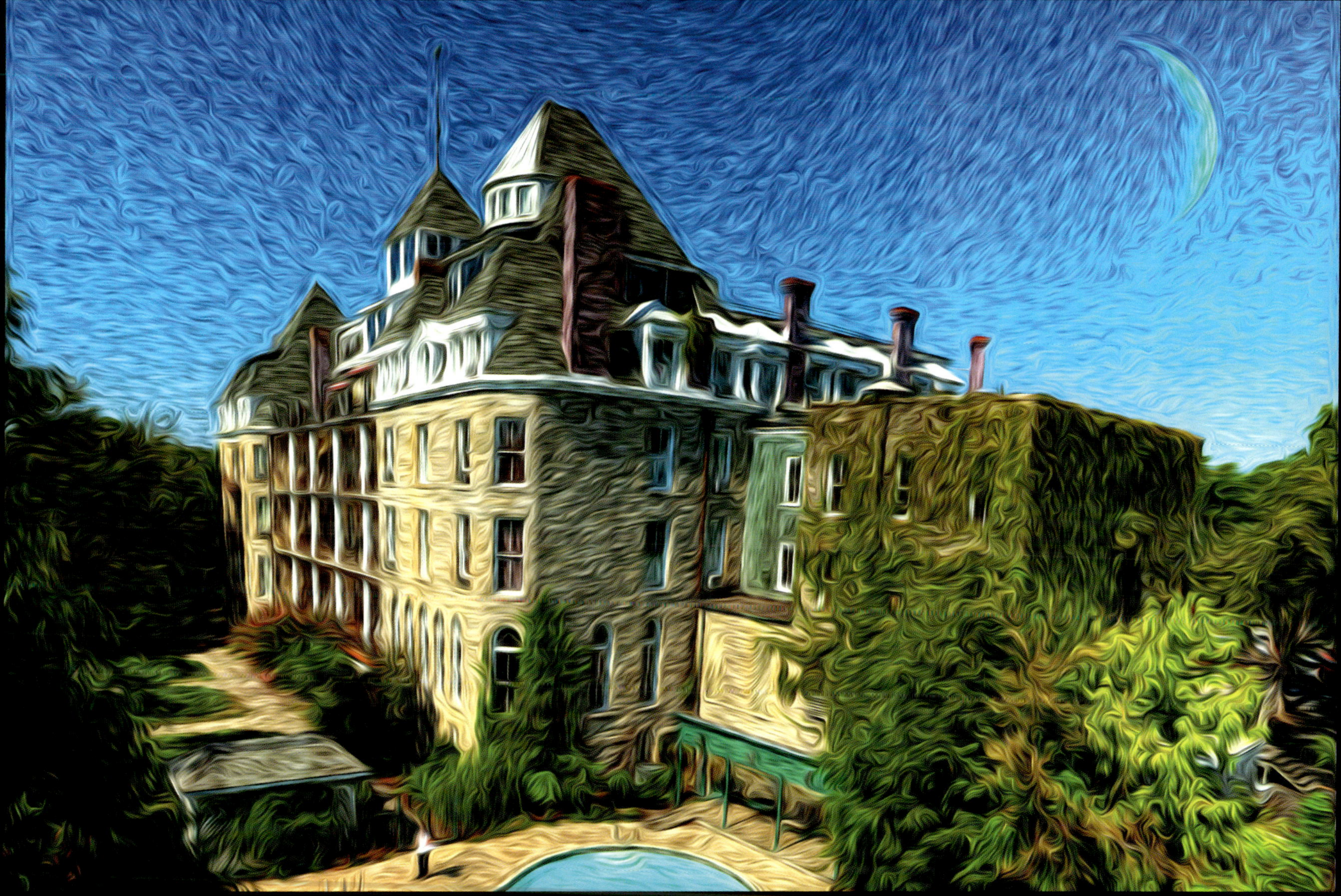

The Crescent Hotel many referred to as the "castle in the wilderness" officially opened on May 21, 1886. Architect Isaac S. Taylor rendered the drawing in American gothic style for Powell Clayton and the Eureka Springs Improvement Company. The Frisco Railroad took it over in 1902 with a five-year lease and brought in architect Guy Crandall Morimer for a $50,000 in remodeling improvements. In 1908, Frisco did not renew the lease, and the hotel passed on to the Crescent College, who operated it until 1932. In 1937, the infamous Dr. Norman Baker obtained the hotel, turning the lustrous Victorian interior into one of America's oddest hospitals, adding even more subject matter to the ghost tales about the nationally-recognized haunted hotel. Baker painted the walls a vivid purple, dressed himself in purple, and reportedly drove a purple-toned automobile. In 1940, his illegal acts caught up with him and Baker lost his showcase in Northwest Arkansas.

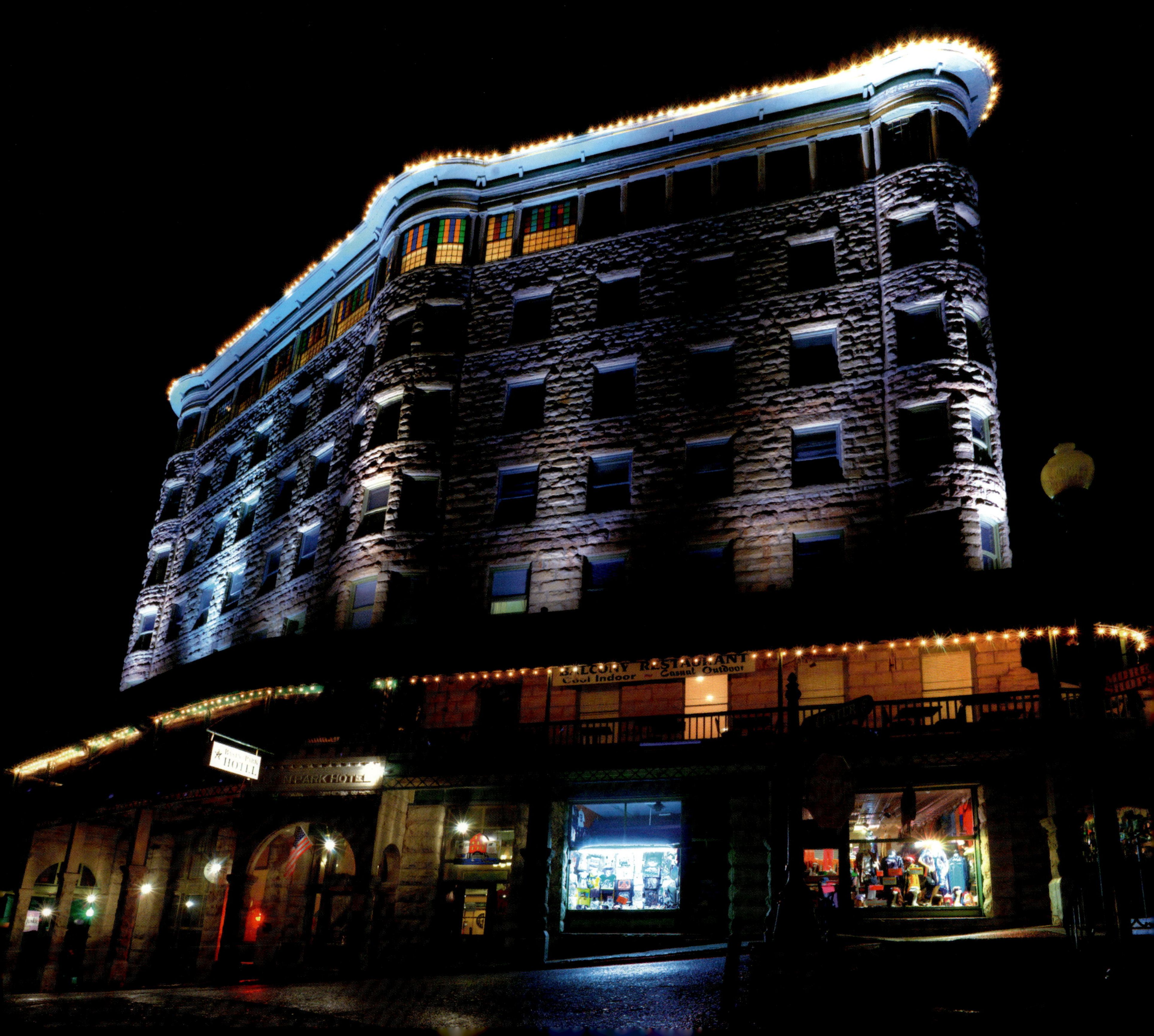
BALCONY RESTAURANT
Cool Indoor ~ Casual Outdoor
HOTEL

uly 1, 1905, marked the grand opening of the Basin Park Hotel. Built against a iillside, the hotel stands adjacent to the heart of Eureka Springs, Basin Spring Park. The eight story stone structure stands as the tallest in the downtown corridor. In 908, the hotel left the hands of W. M. Duncan and was leased to the managers of the Crescent Hotel. The 8-story building changed hands many times before C.A. Fuller, who was in his second term as mayor of Eureka Springs, took ownership in 1926. Fuller also owned the Crescent Hotel around that same time. Roy Parkhill purchased the hotel in 1944, and soon after operated illegal gambling and drinking within. The hotel was shut down and Parkhill was shipped to jail in 1955. Historic preservationists and philanthropists, Marty and Elise Roenigk, purchased the Basin Park and Crescent hotels in 1997, and both hotels underwent extensive renovations before becoming the beacons they are today.

N 36°24.117'
W 093°44.242'
Elevation 1221'

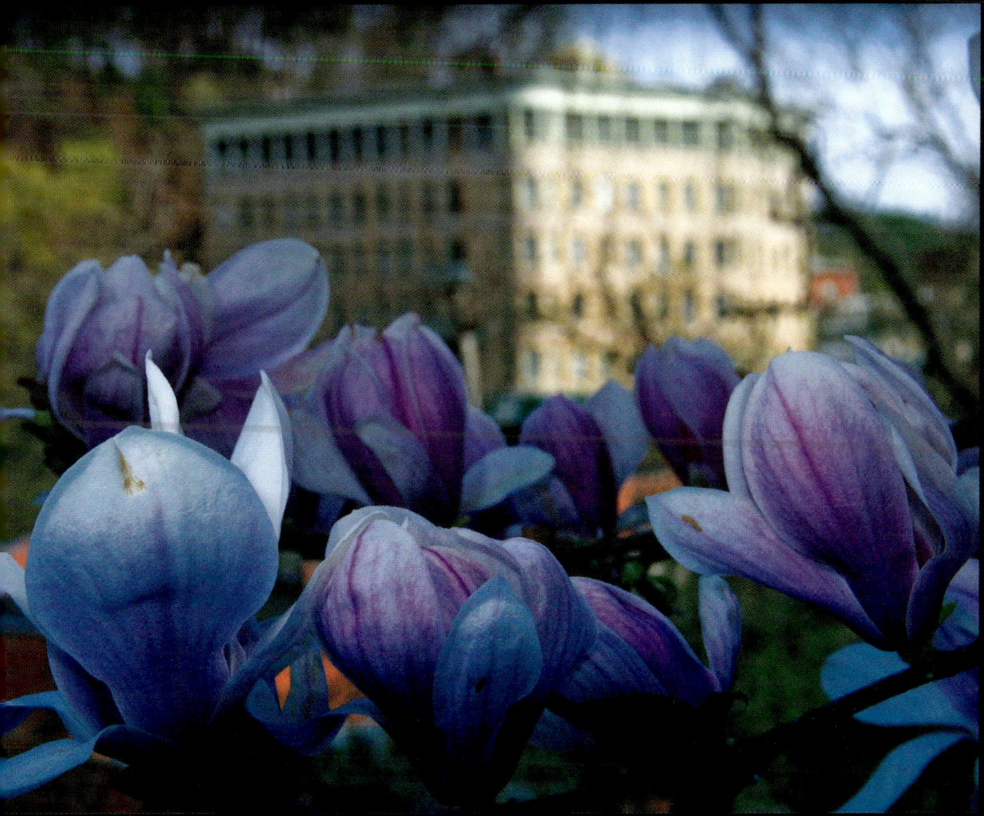

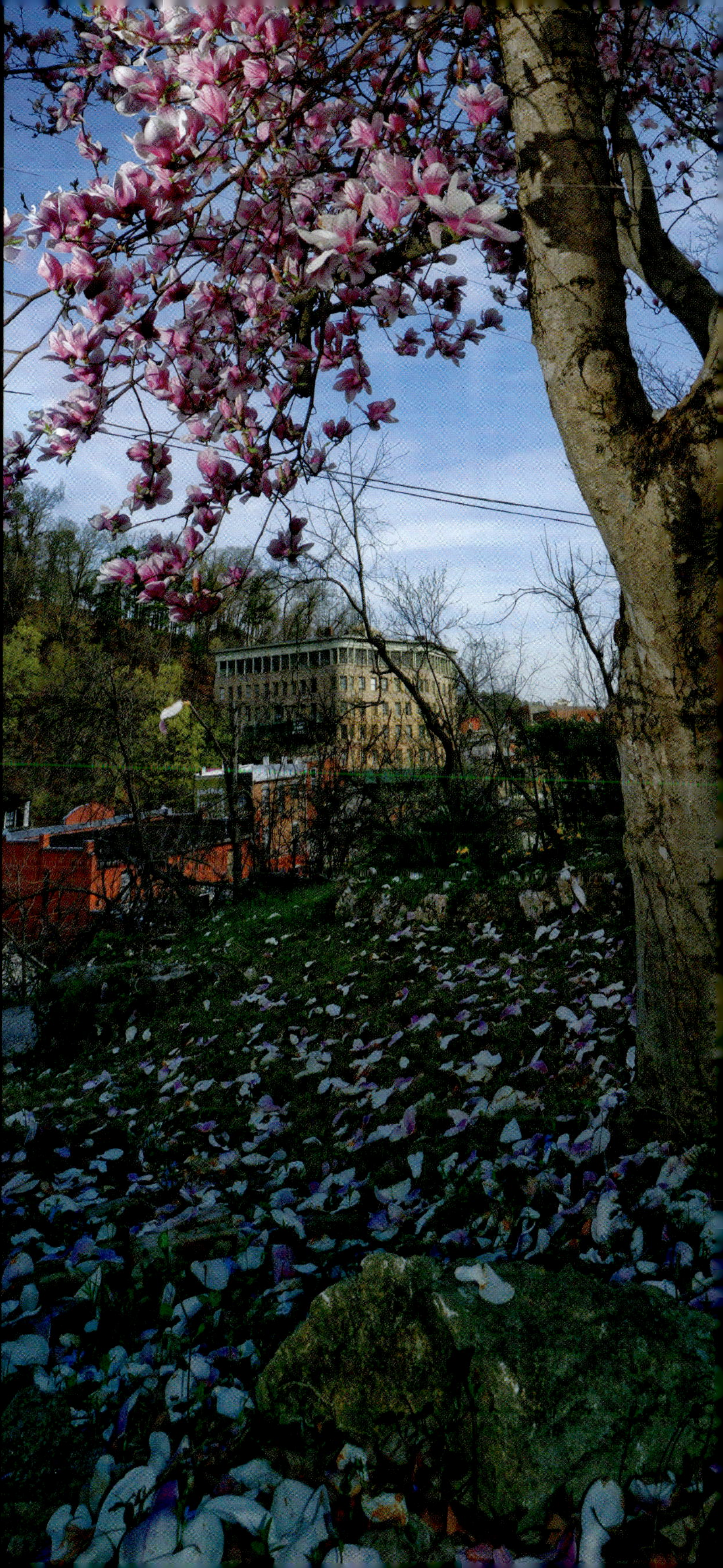

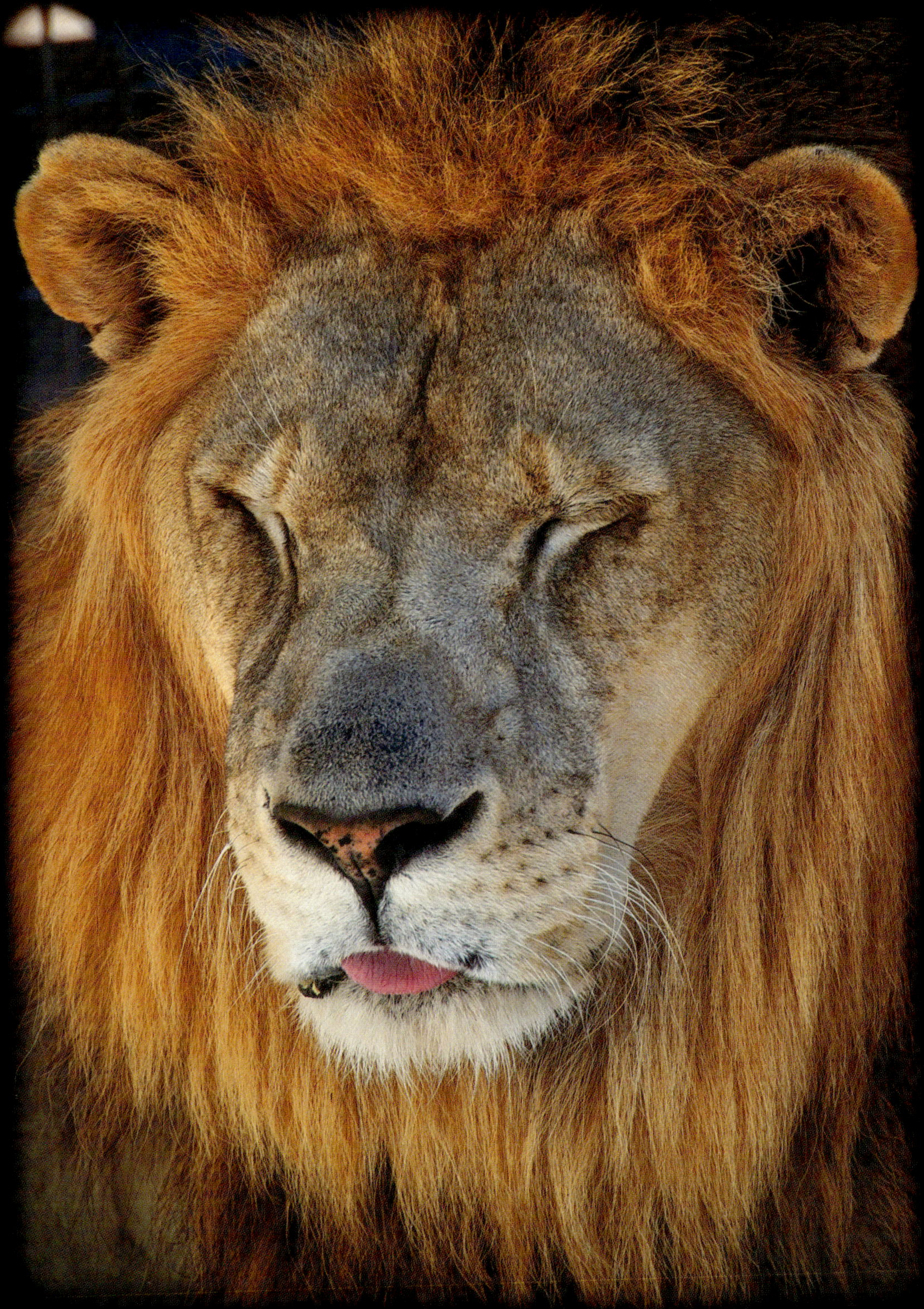

Seven miles from Eureka Springs sits Turpentine Creek Wildlife Refuge. The Jackson family; Don, Hilda, Tanya, and Robert, officially organized the refuge in 1992 with a desire to rescue big cats, which actually started in 1978 at the family homestead in Texas with one lone cat named Bum. Today the refuge houses not only lions, tigers, and cougars, but also has room for bears, monkeys, and birds within a vast compound, including several natural habitat enclosures. The refuge spans around 500 acres and offers tours of the animal enclosures with an opportunity to get up close (safely) to a big cat. They also offer personalized tours and photo tours for those on the more adventurous side.

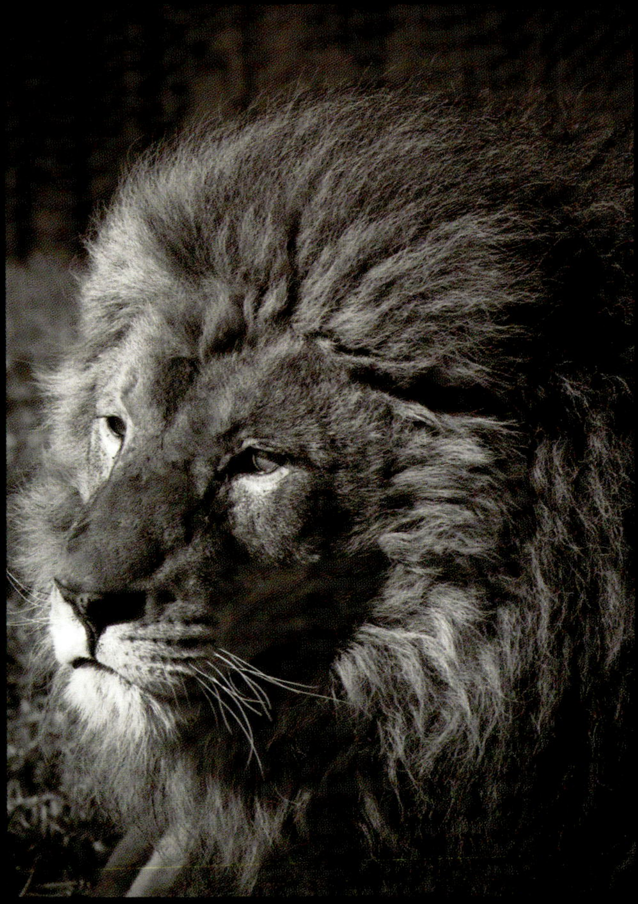

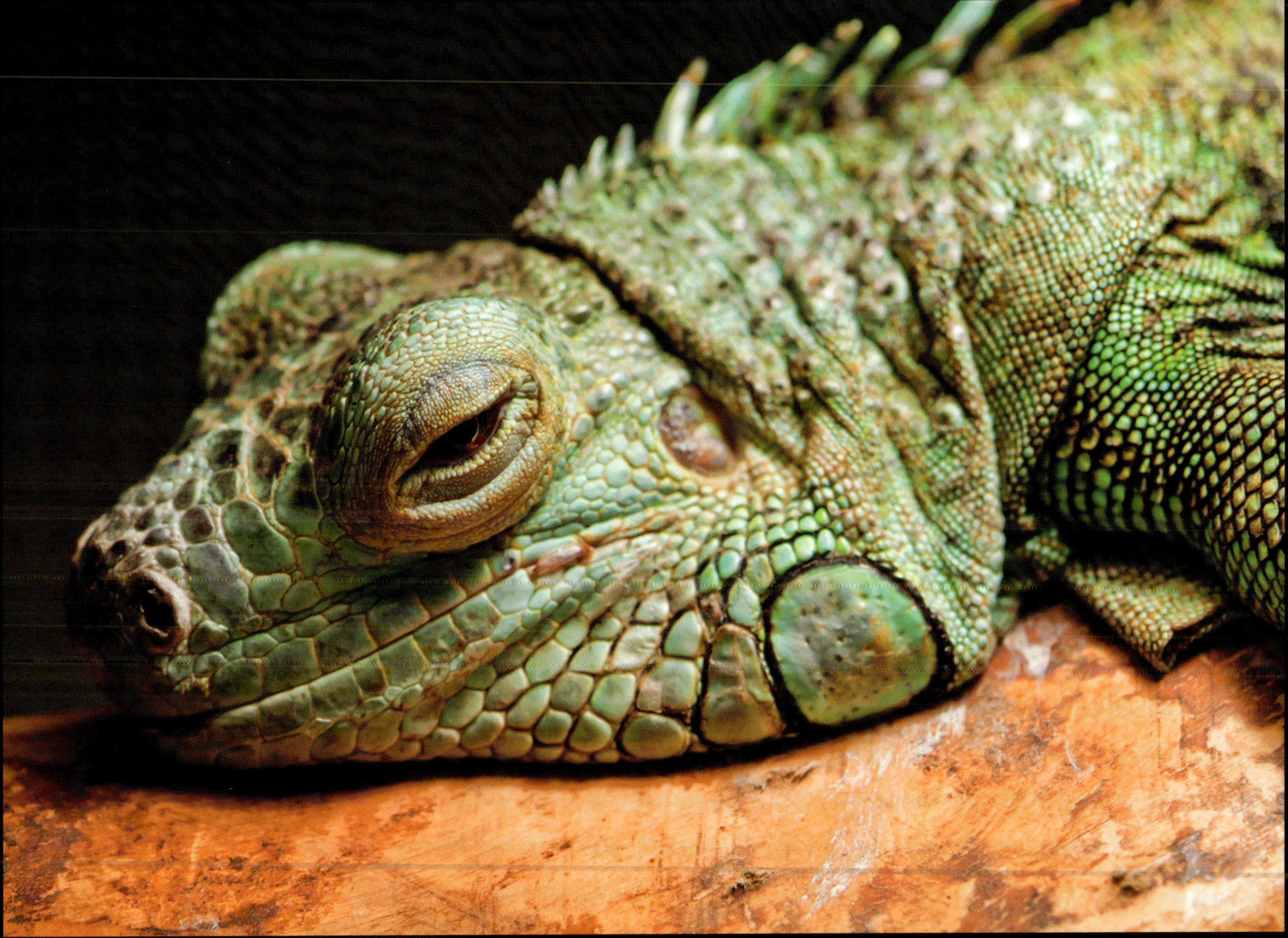

This rescued green iguana is housed along with another 600 animals representing 56 species at Promised Land Zoo. Jeff and Diane Sanders opened the doors in 1992. The zoo cares for animals gathered from every continent except Antarctica. What started as a desire to operate a small farm has expanded to include a rare-and-endangered animal breeding facility, along with a rescue facility for large reptiles and exotic birds.

N 36°31.717'
W 093°42.833'
Elevation 1090'

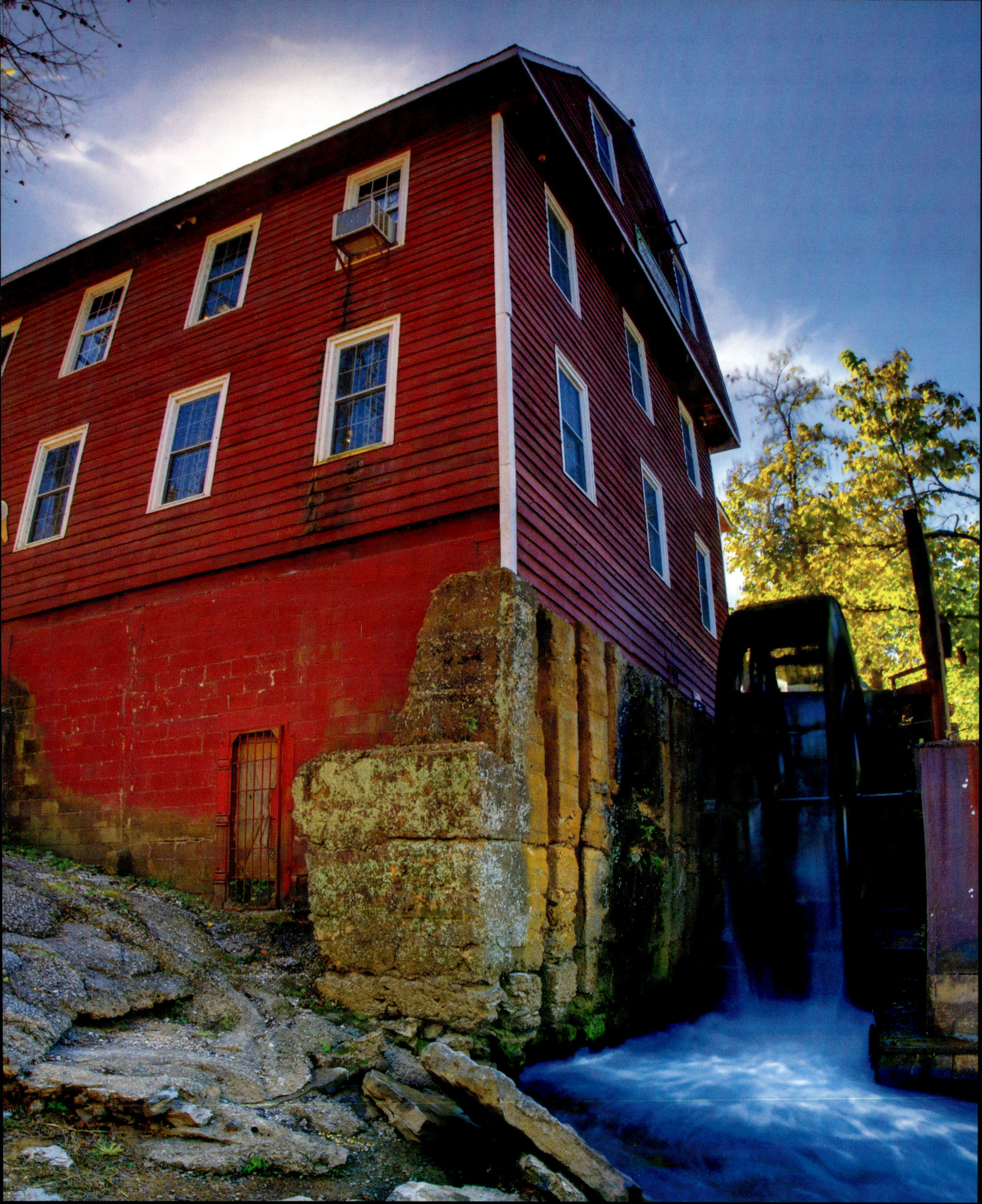

Sylvanus and Catherine Blackburn homesteaded the area and constructed the first mill around 1832. War Eagle Mill, nestled in aptly-named War Eagle Valley uses the waters of War Eagle Creek to run the mill. The War Eagle Hiking Trail and War Eagle Cavern begin at the mill. The area had a lumber mill in the past, in addition to the grain mill which is still in operation. Floods and fires destroyed the mill over the past century, and what stands today is the fourth rebuild. Originally built in 1907, the restoration of the 182 ft. bridge that stretches over the creek was completed October 1, 2010. The War Eagle Mill Fall Crafts Fair draws thousands to the mill as hundreds of artists showcase and sell their handcrafted wares. The mill offers a smorgasbord of in-house ground grains for sale alongside cereals, flours, jams, jellies, salsa, and a host of other products.

N 36°16.047'
W 093°56.587'
Elevation 1085'

N 36°25.919’
W 093°44.975’
Elevation 1355’

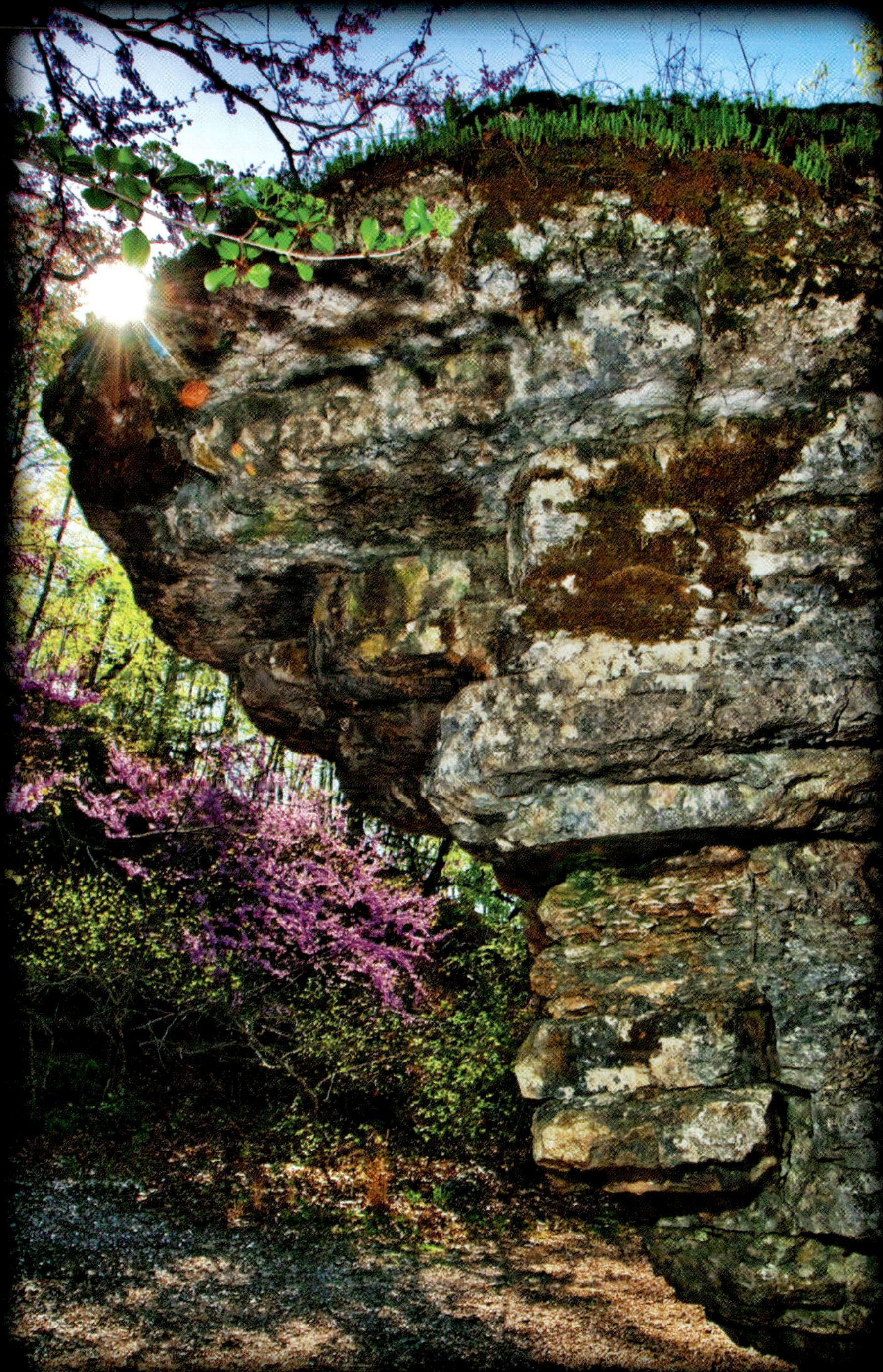

Locals believe the area around Pivot Rock hosted hideouts for bandits, including the likes of the James-Younger Gang, though no concrete evidence suggests their exact hideout location. The “pivot” rock stands 15 ft. tall and 30 ft. wide and is balanced on a base of only 16 inches. Ripley’s Believe It or Not featured the formation for its perplexing balancing act. Pivot Rock Park also has a trail system that spans some 600 square feet and boast another rock formation, the Natural Bridge.

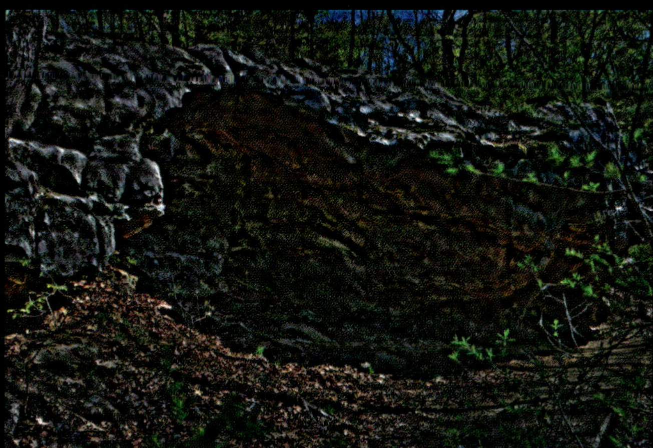

N 36°24.895’
W 093°44.895’
Elevation 1293’

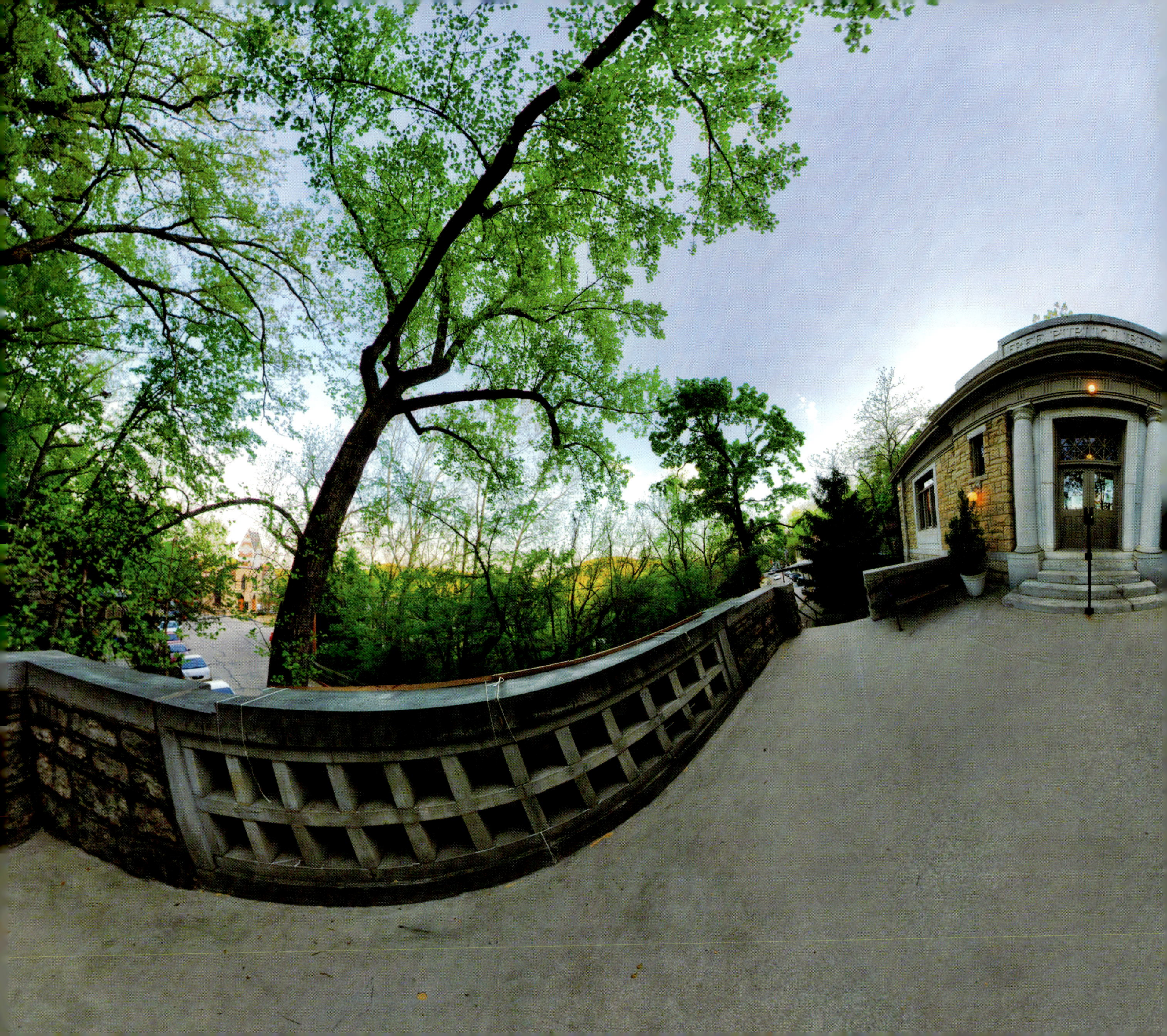

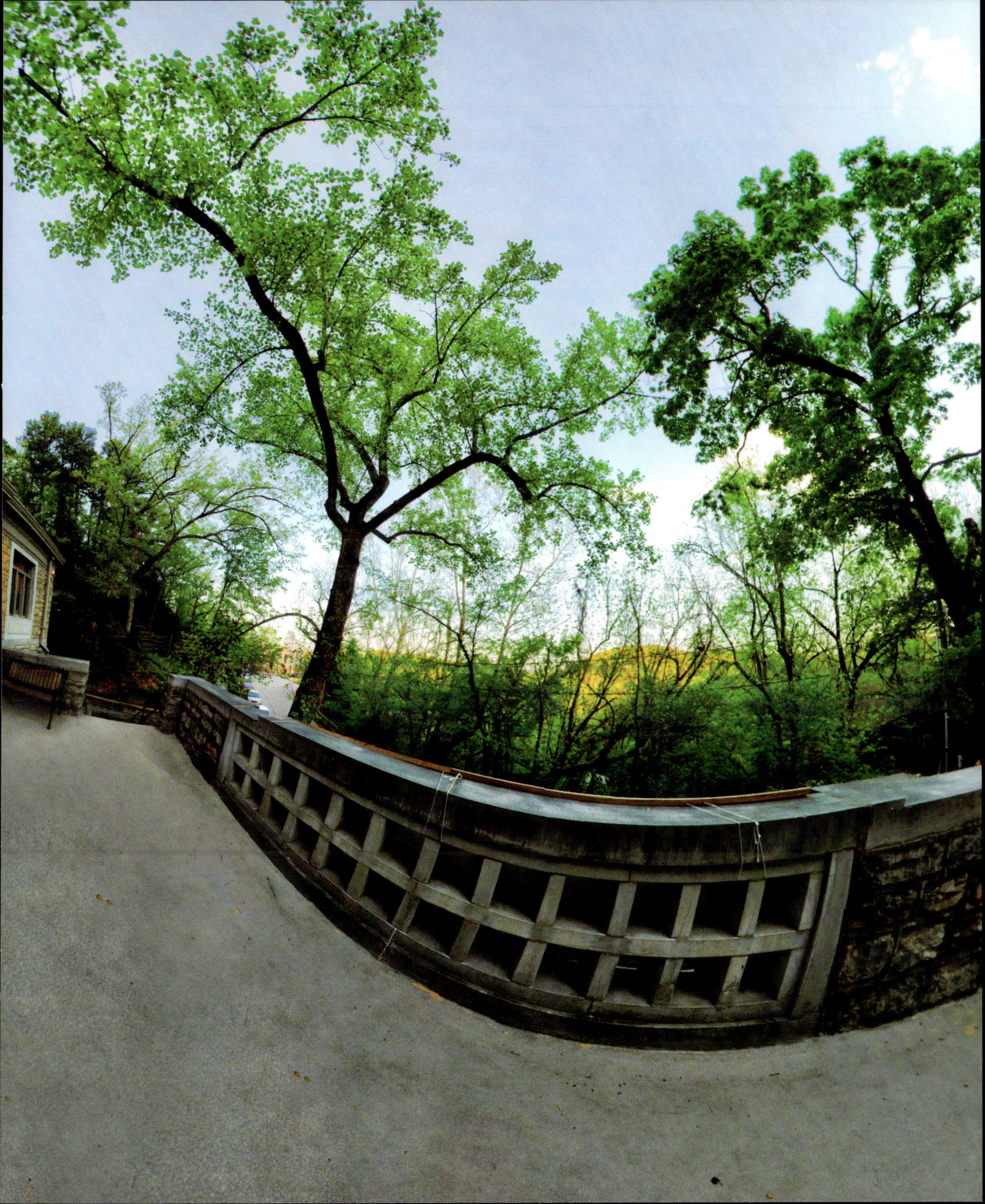

Andrew Carnegie donated $12,000 to Eureka Springs in 1910 for a public library, and the Eureka Springs Improvement Company donated the land for it in the area then known as West Mountain. The only stipulation Carnegie had was that the city provide the land and always operate it as a free public library. The building was completed in 1912. Carnegie went on to construct four libraries in Arkansas. Unfortunately, the doors were closed between 1916 and 1921 due to a lack of funding. In 1970, the structure was listed on the National Register of Historic Places, and in 1956 the library become incorporated into the Carroll County Library System.

N 36°24.451'
W 093°44.186'

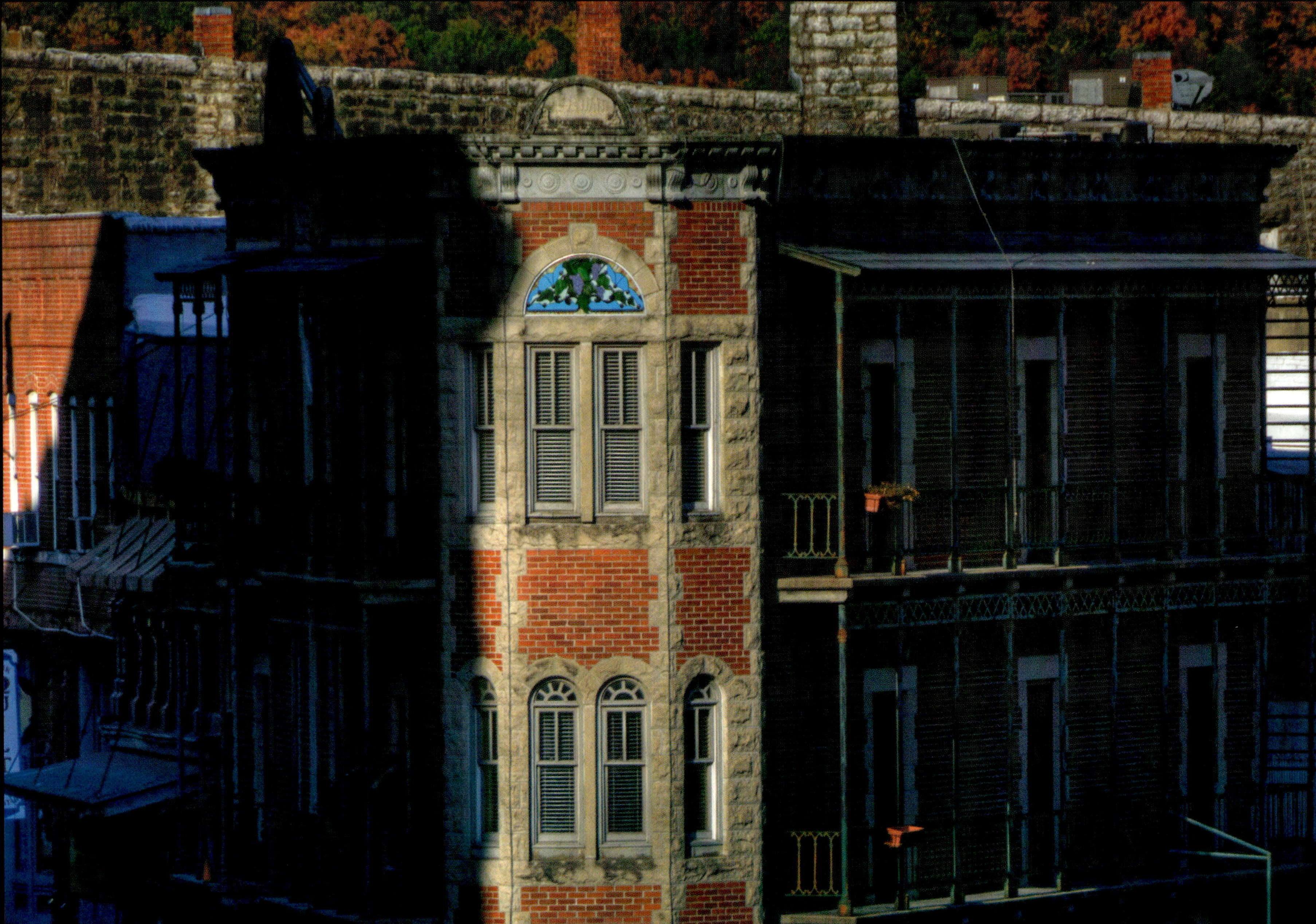

The Flatiron building in Eureka Springs was originally constructed in 1880 in an all-brick wedge design. The building housed the town's first banking establishment until succumbing to fire in 1890. Another Flatiron was built soon after and housed a saloon, a lodge, and offices; which succumbed to yet another fire in 1925. In 1989, after years of the site being void of any structure, a third Flatiron was constructed and is now a fixture of Eureka Springs.

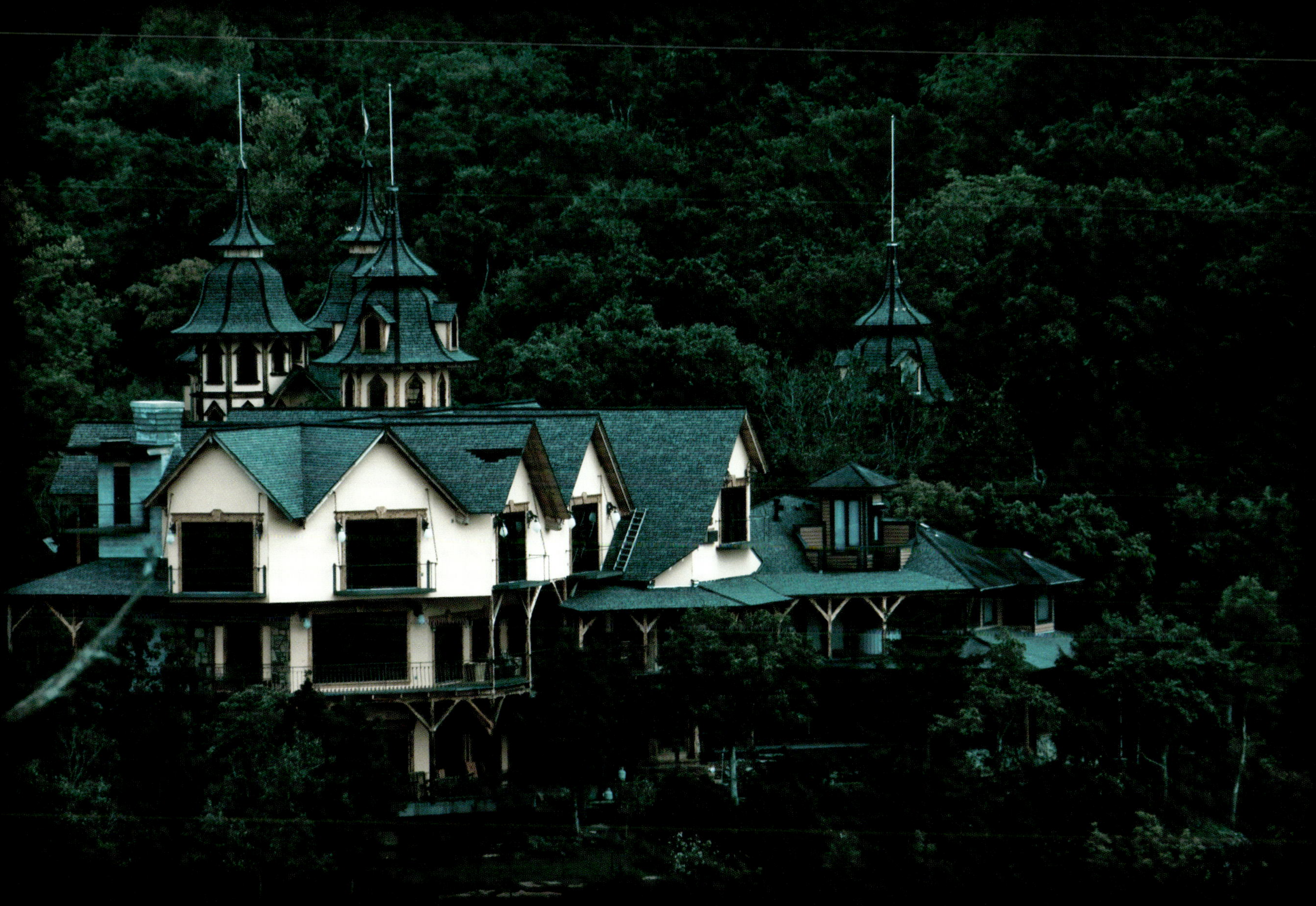

Perched atop the bluffline along the White River in Beaver is Castle Rogue's Manor. The medieval fantasy castle was constructed over the course of six years, blending red cedar, Douglas fir, redwood, and black walnut in what was constructed to honor Robert Treuer, Nancy Nelson, the Mia & Fritz Treuer Trust, and the Erliss & Lyman Nelson Trust.

N 36°28.671'
W 093°45.935'
Elevation 1078'

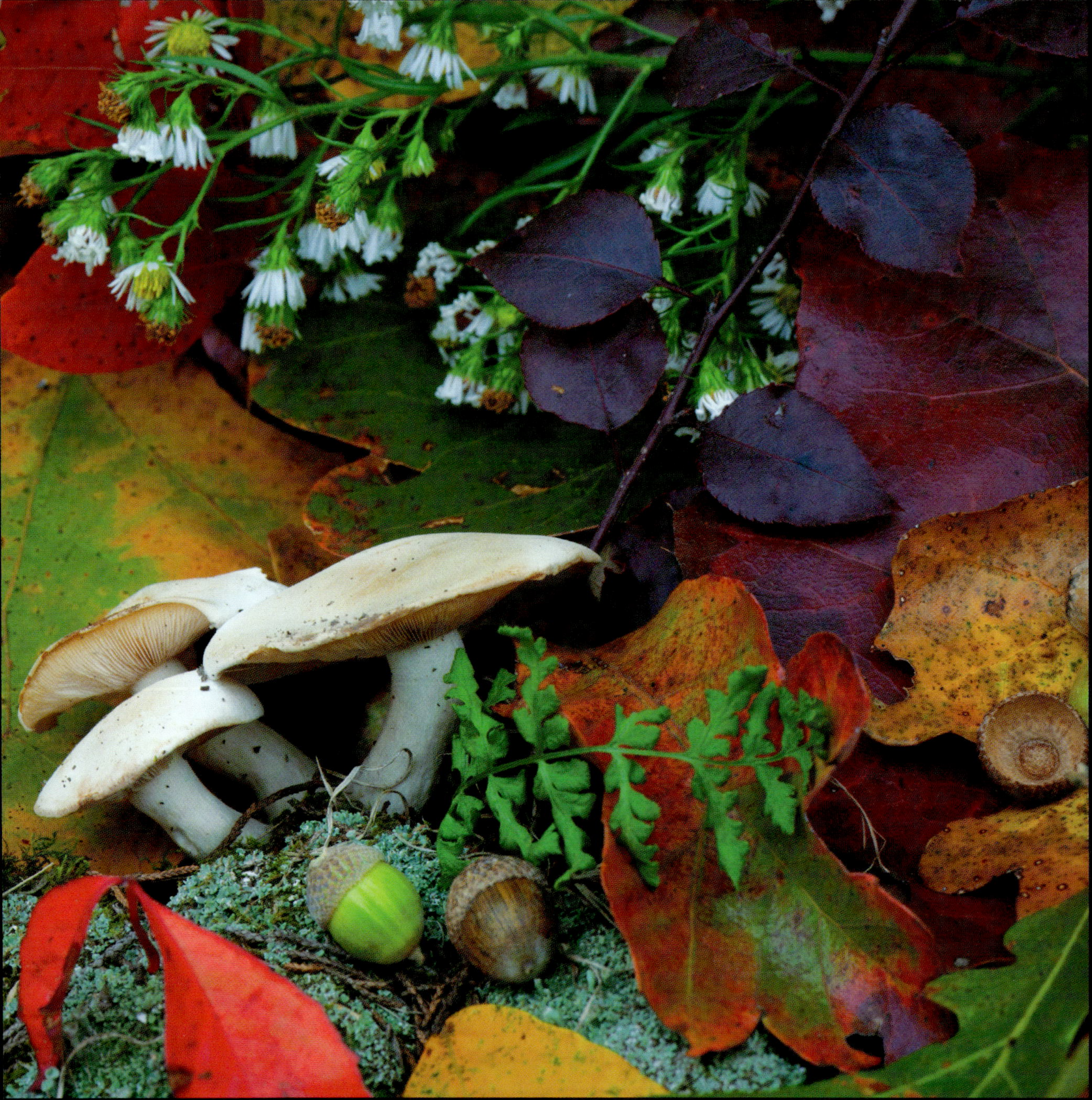

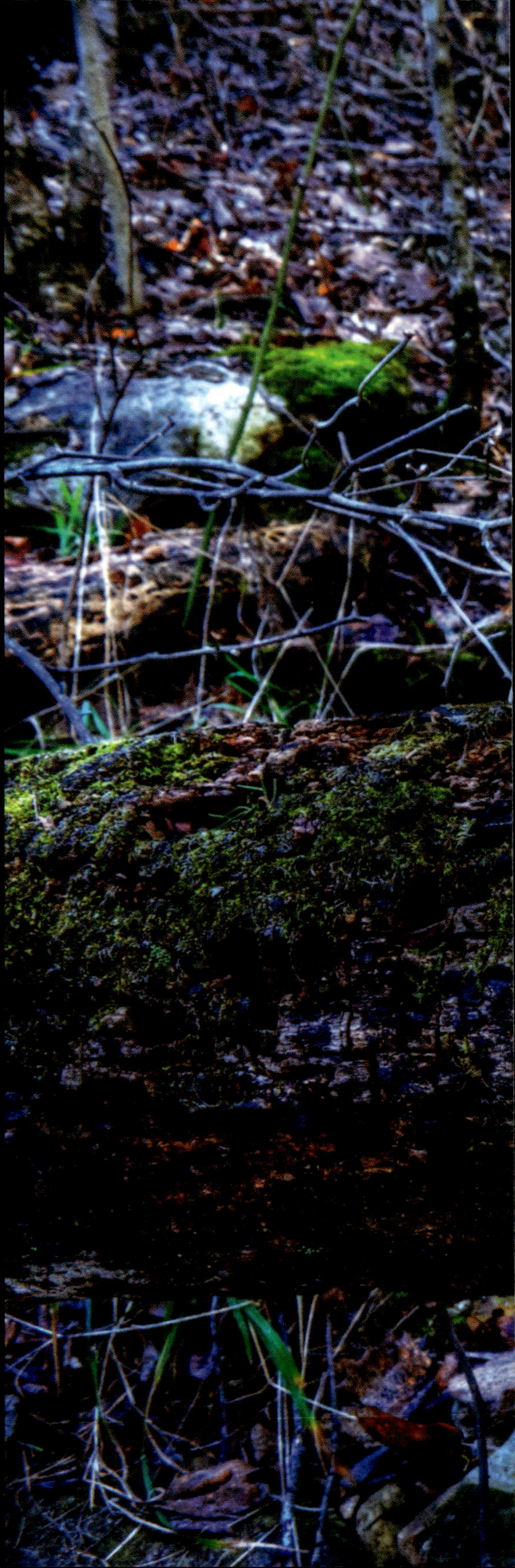

There are thousands of places to camp out under the stars beside a campfire in the wooded Ozarks and thousands of miles of trails within the surrounding countryside.

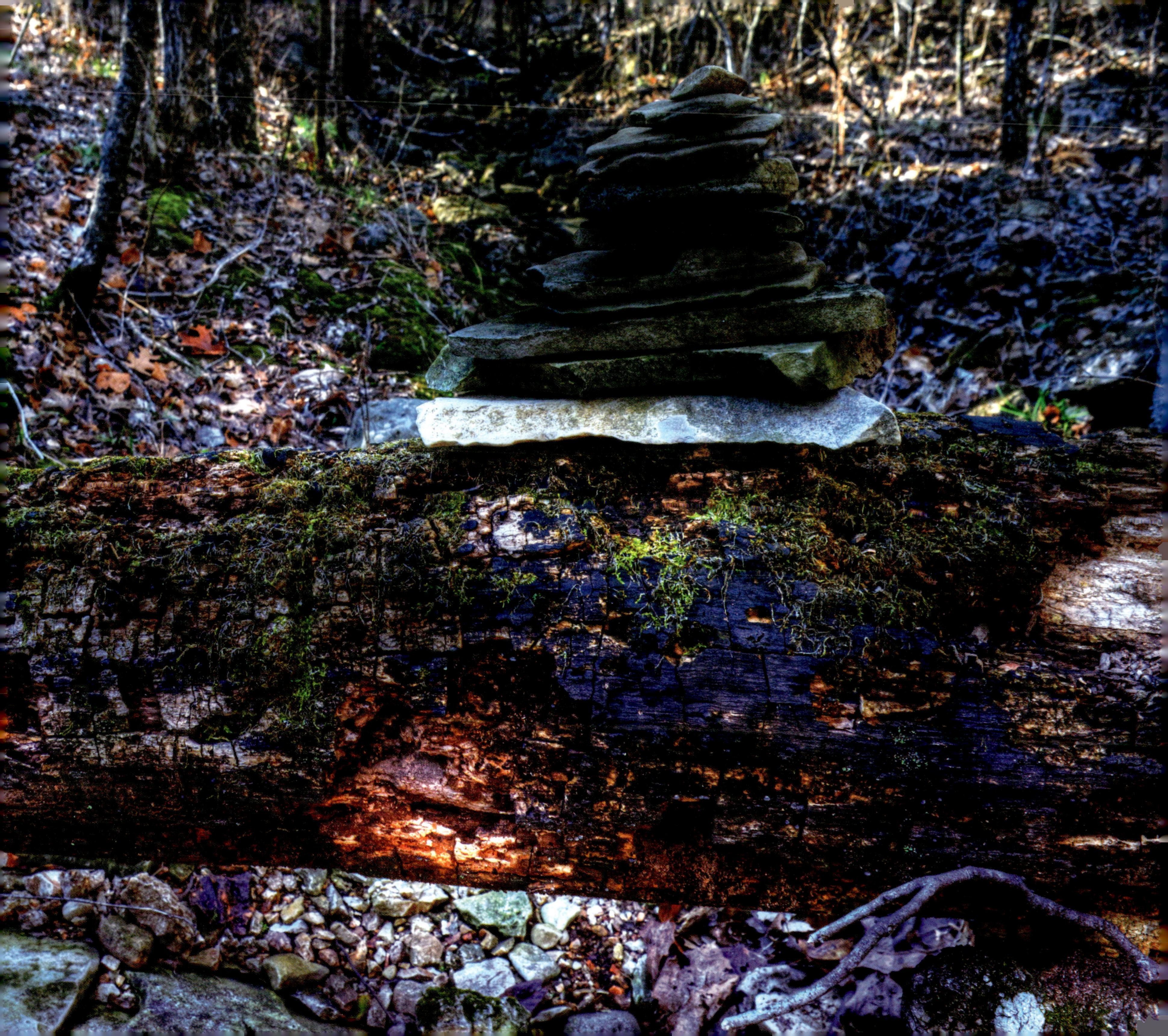

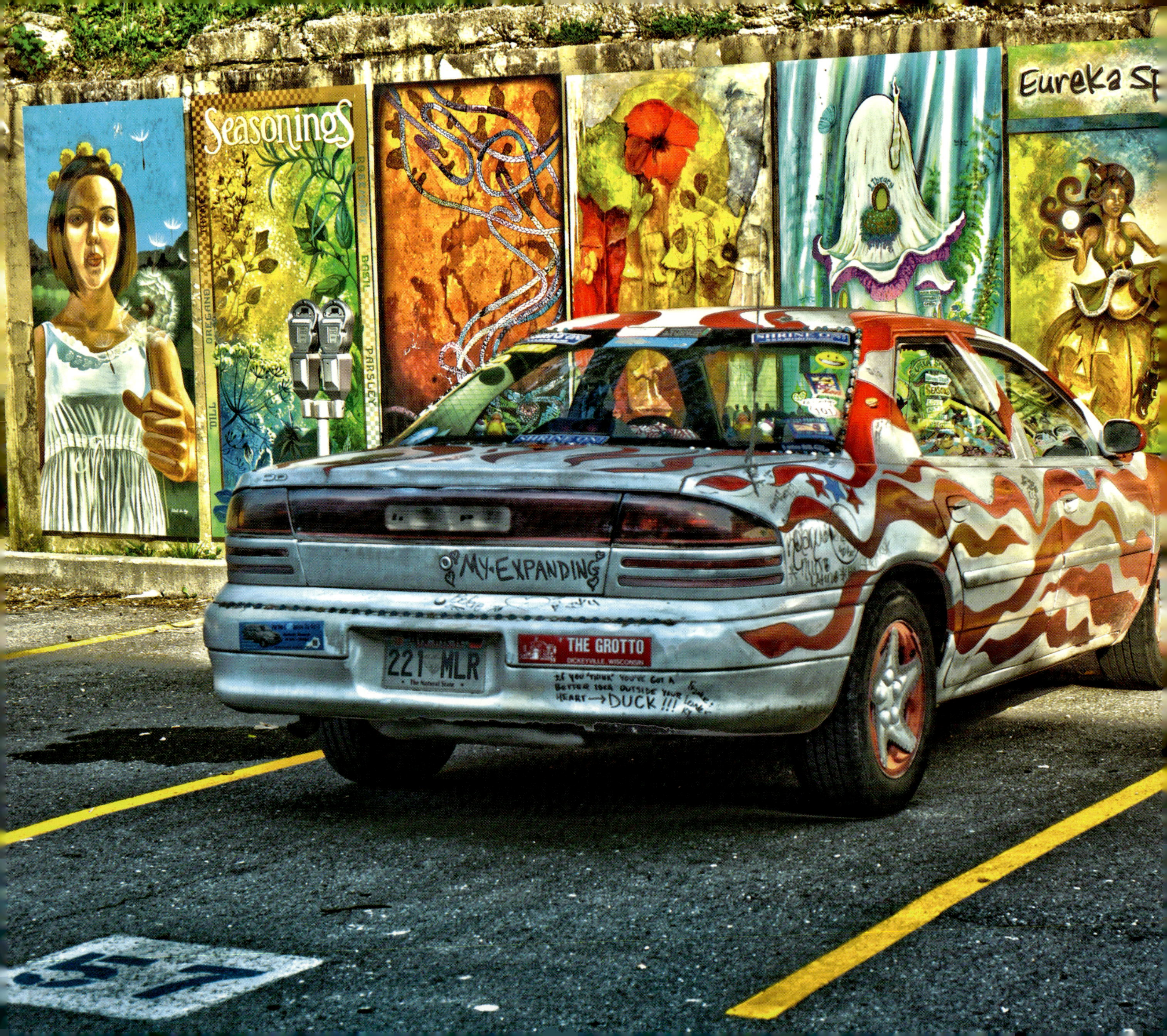
Seasonings
DILL
OREGANO
BASIL
PARSLEY
MY EXPANDING
THE GROTTO
DICKEYVILLE, WISCONSIN
221 MLR
DUCK!!!
57

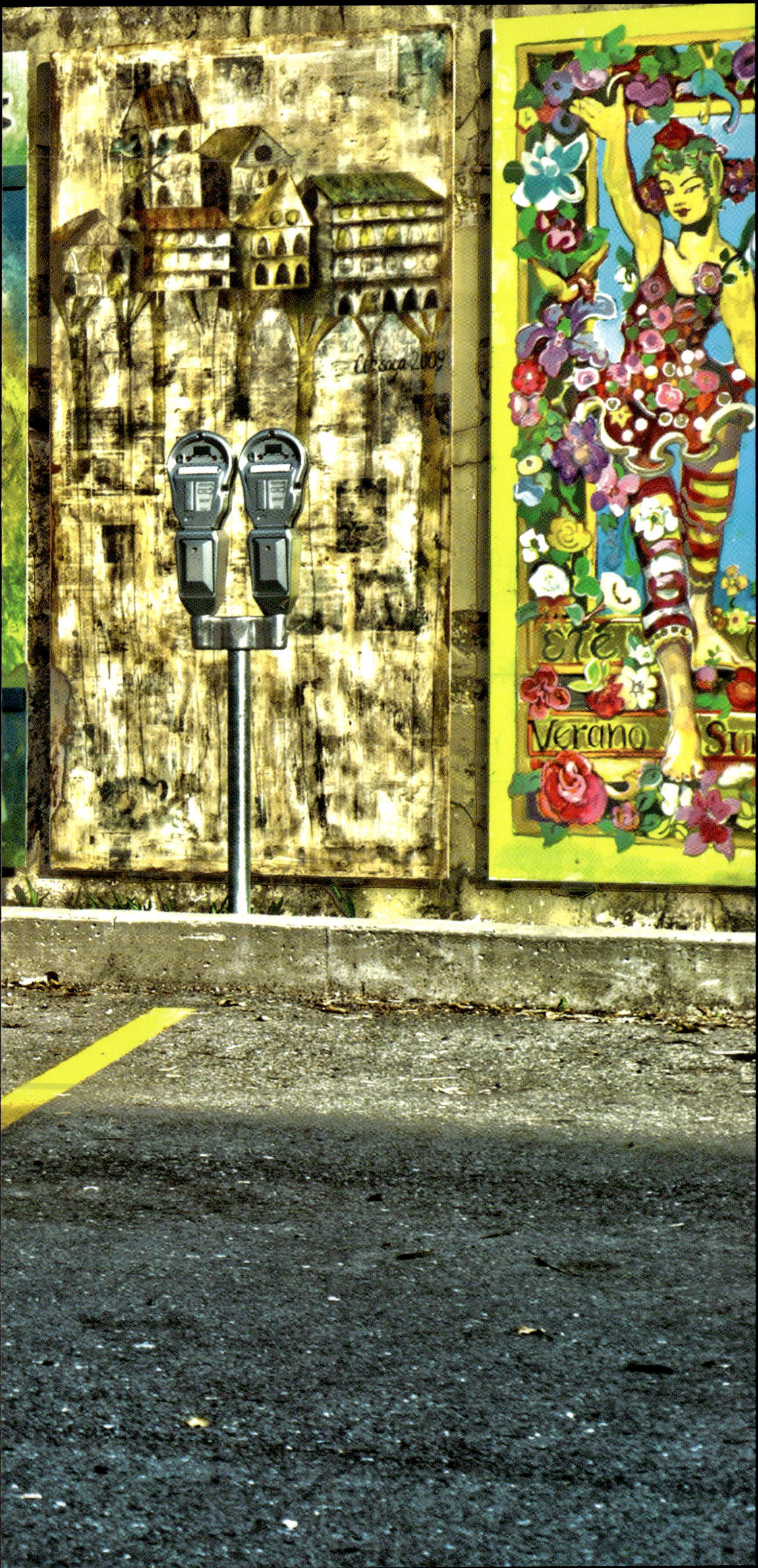


# Art

Creative people have always sought the beauty and serenity that the Ozarks bring. The arts culture is persistently leaving its mark on the surrounding area. Art galleries, mural-painted buildings, hanging art panels in parking lots, and even glass design work on sidewalks show ho artistic flair abounds throughout the city. An estimated 400 working artists from every perceivable medium call this area home. The city hos a month-long annual celebration, the May Festival of the Arts; and the area boasts dance schools, an opera, a writer's colony, and an art school. Crystal Bridges Museum of American Art, which houses American art from the Colonial era to present day, is admission free and located in neighboring Bentonville.

N 36°24.089'
W 093°44.230'
Elevation 1205'

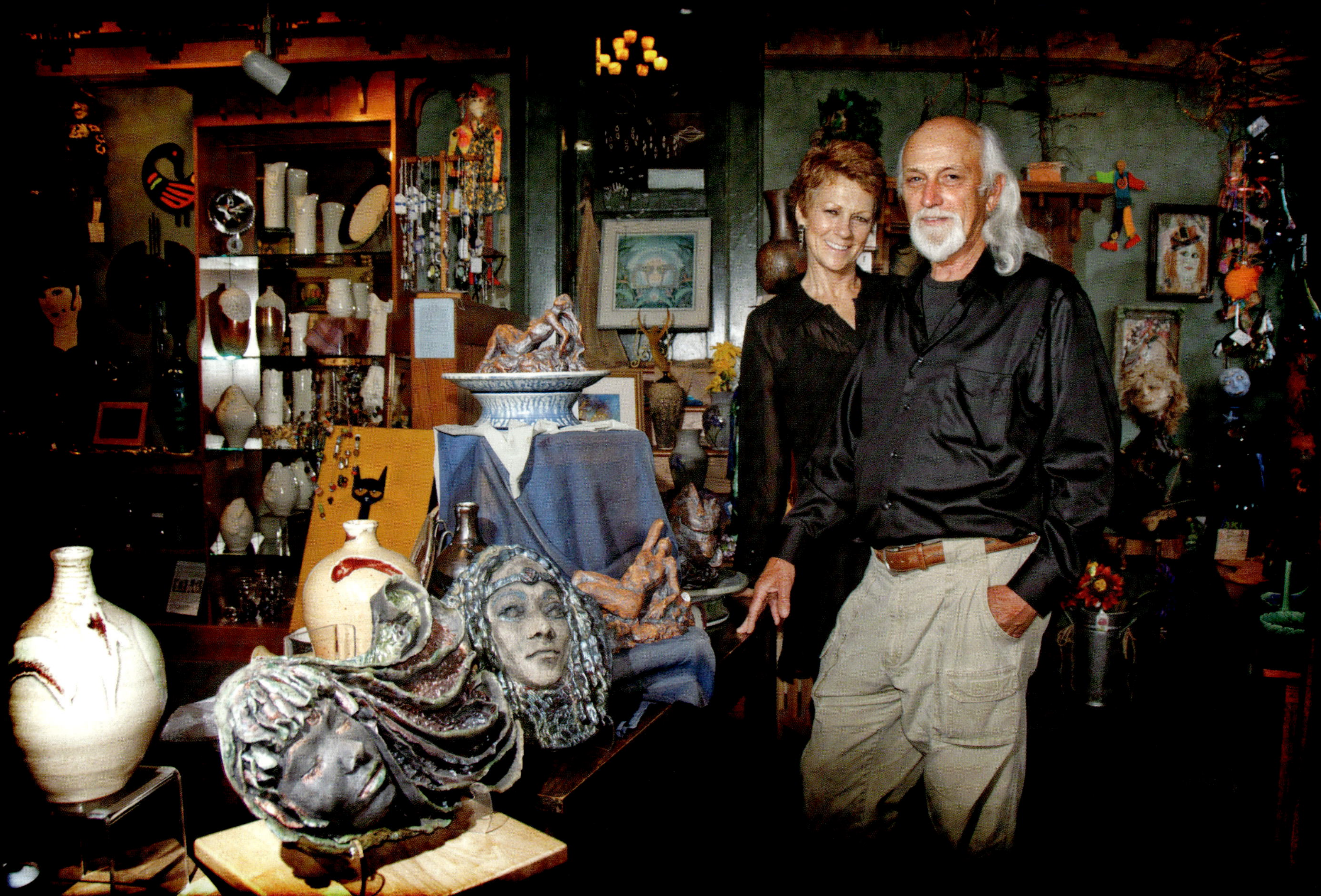

Sara and Terry Russel posed inside Iris at the Basin art gallery during one of a 2nd Saturday Gallery Stroll held in Eureka Springs during the tourist season. The duo have worked in the Eureka Springs and Berryville Public School systems for a combined 50 years. They also operate the local Ozark Blue Moon Studios where they craft acrylic, stoneware, oil, crystalline, and raku pieces of art. The couple meet as actors in the Great Passion Play in 1985 and have shared their love of art with every child passing through our public school systems. Terry retired in 2008 and his daughter, Jessica, is how the art director at the Eureka Springs High School – carrying on the family tradition of sharing the arts with our youth.

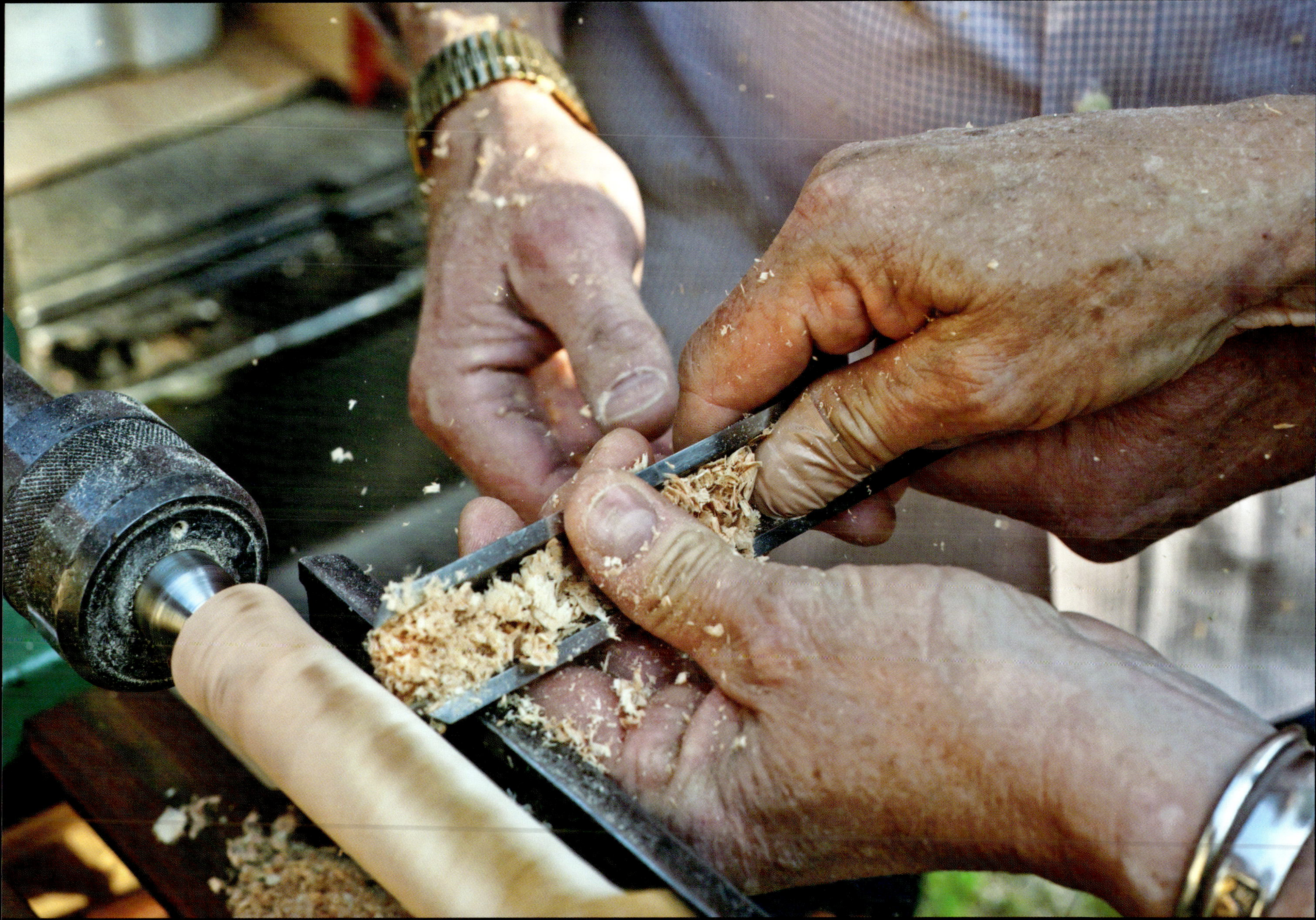

The Eureka Springs Art Guild reformed into non-profit status and became the Eureka Springs School of the Arts in 2003. During its beginning the school offered workshop classes at the studios of some of the founding members over a span of two weeks. The school relocated to its present location in 2004 and offers around 34 sessions and 80 workshops that span 8 months of arts and crafts culture. Classes involving drawing, painting (of all types), book making, weaving, wood furniture (turning), glass work (hot and cold), sculpture, basket making, fiber arts, clayworks, lampworking, metalsmithing, and fine jewelry are offered.

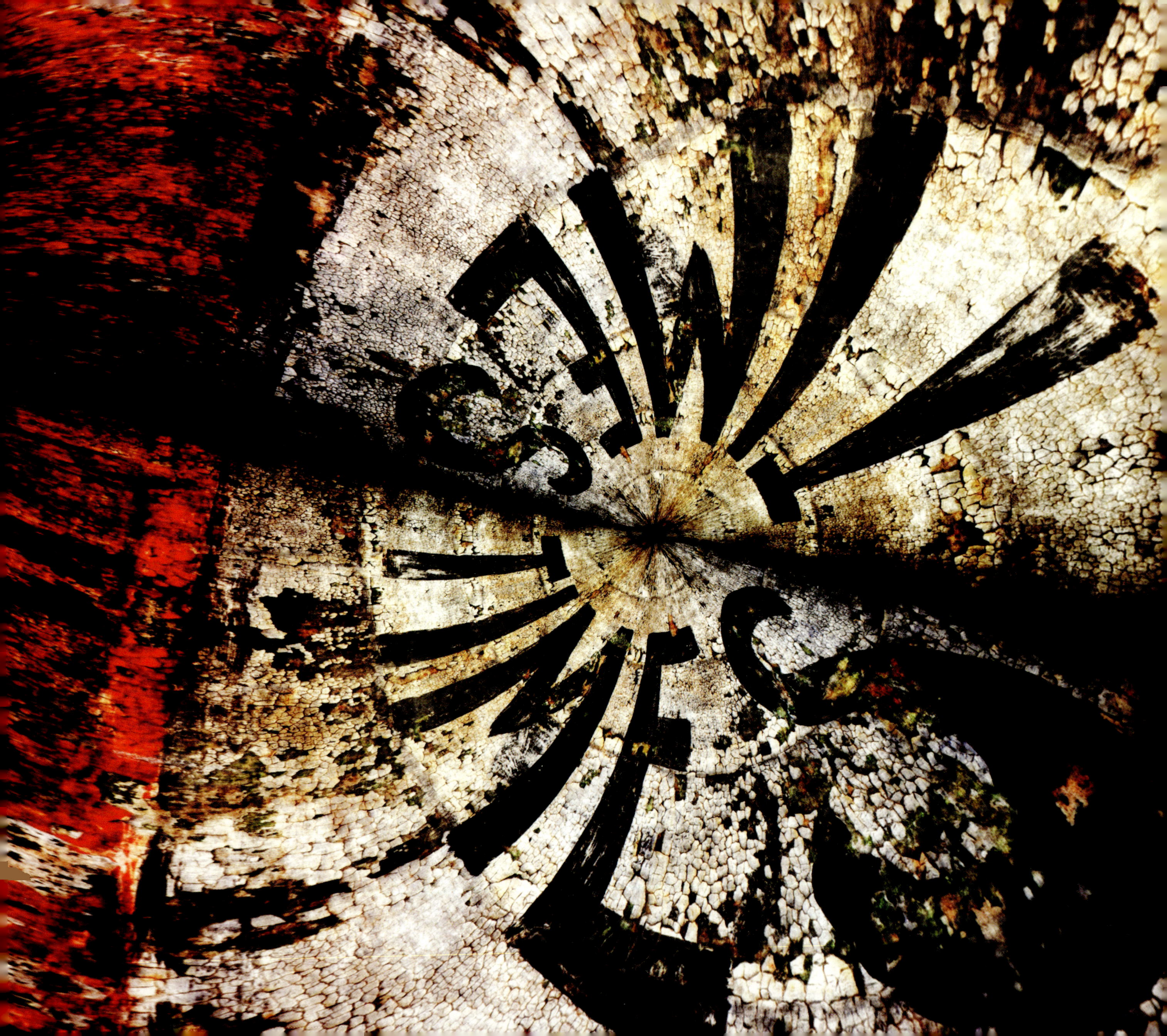

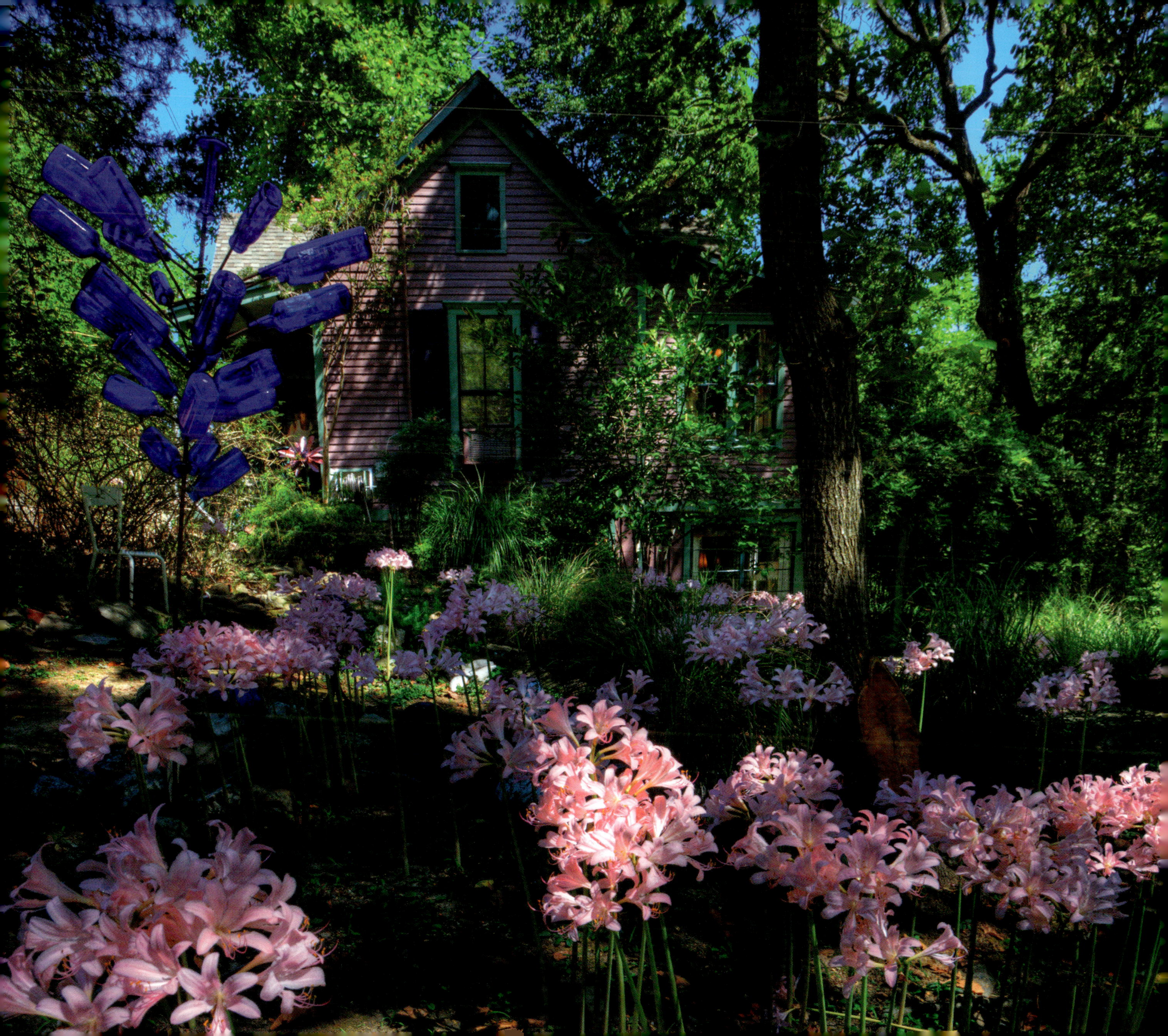

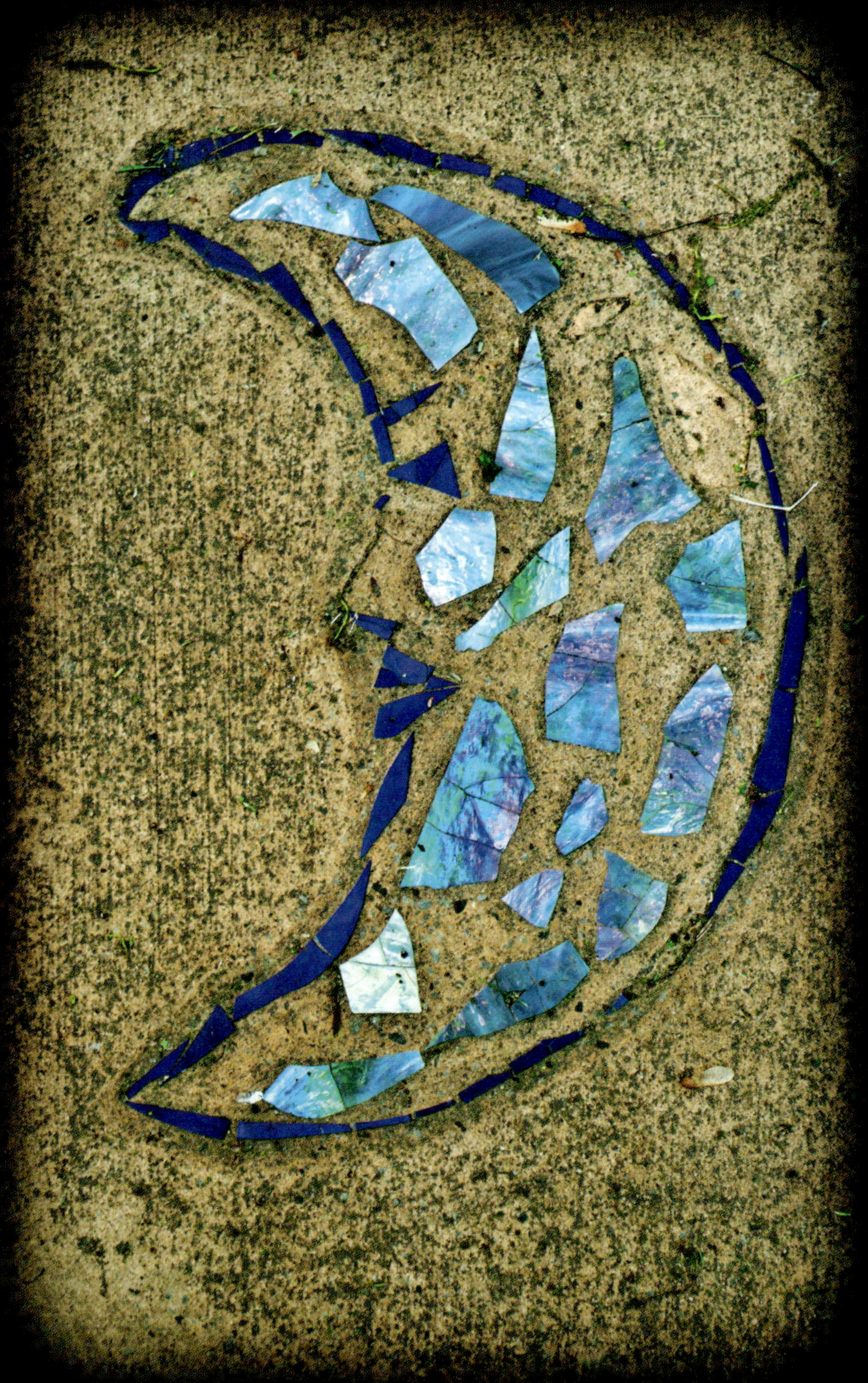

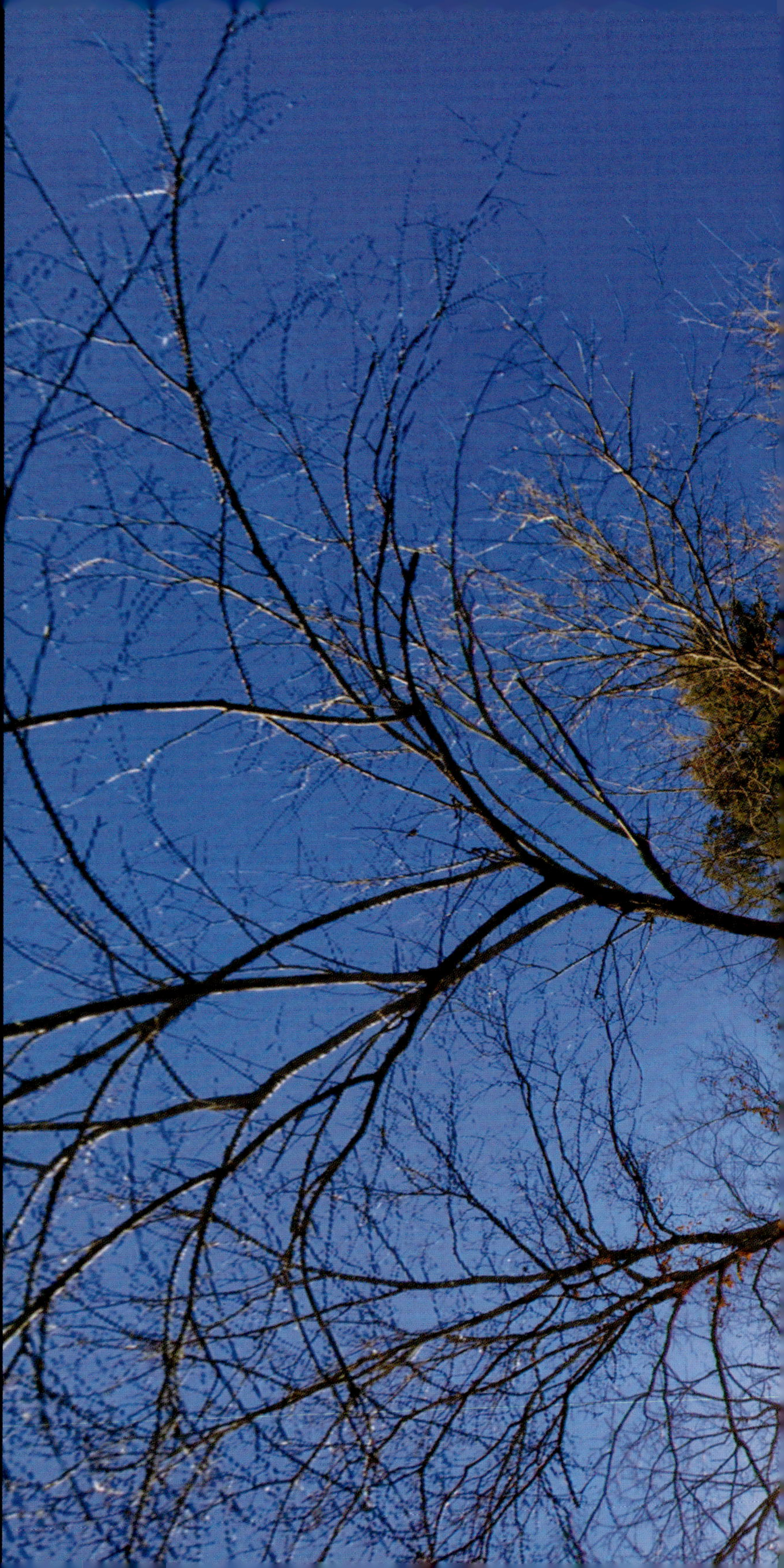

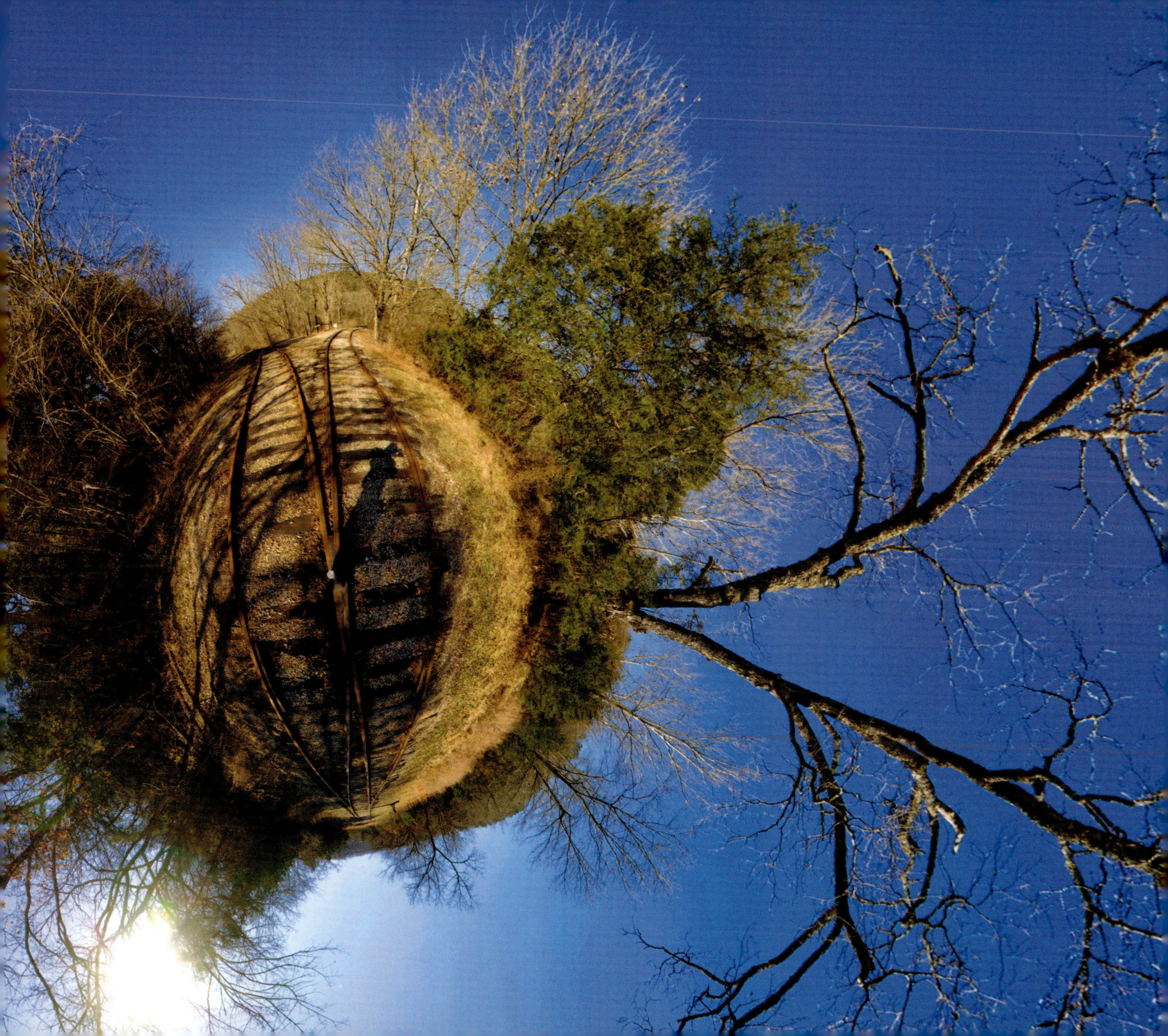

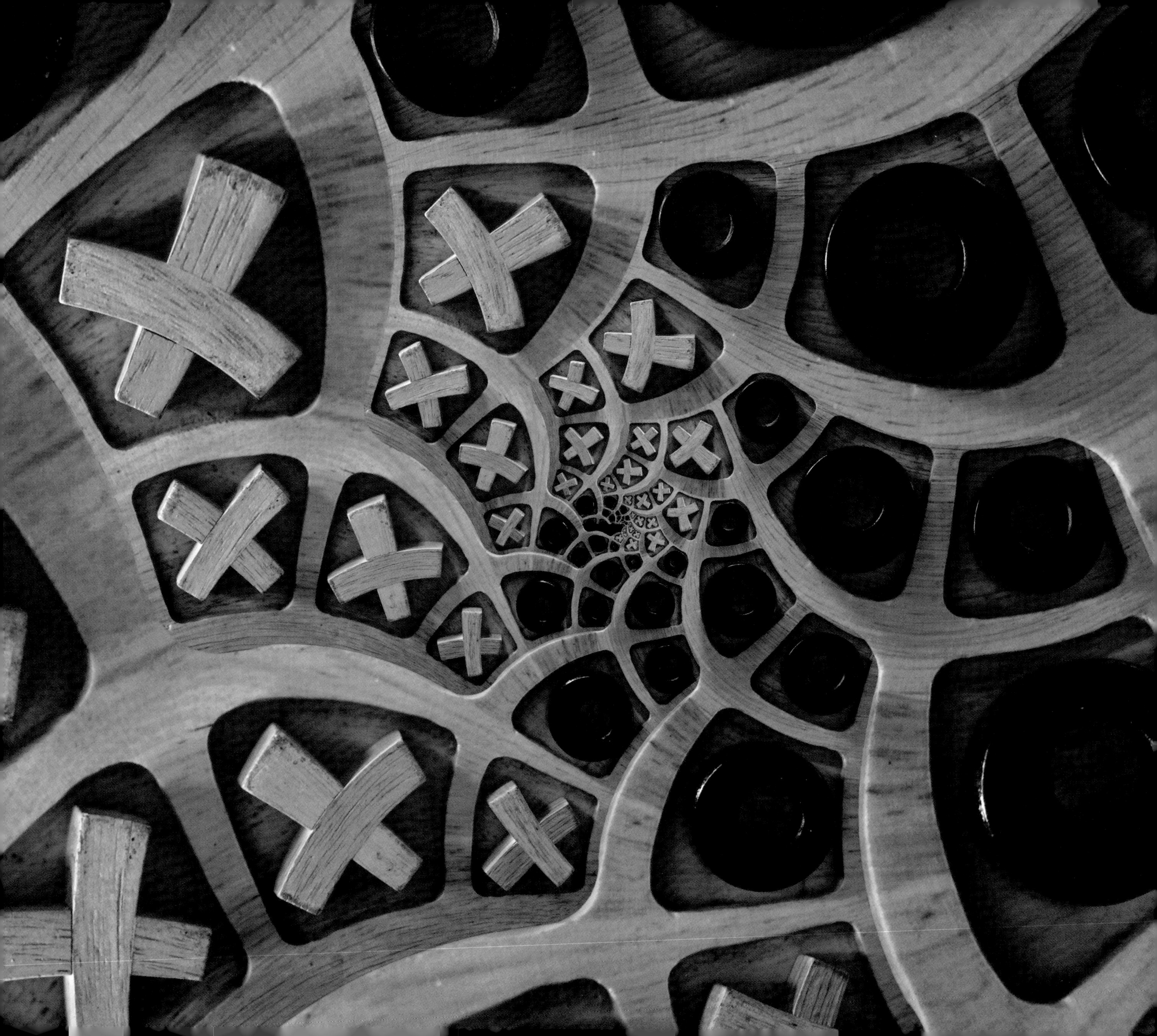

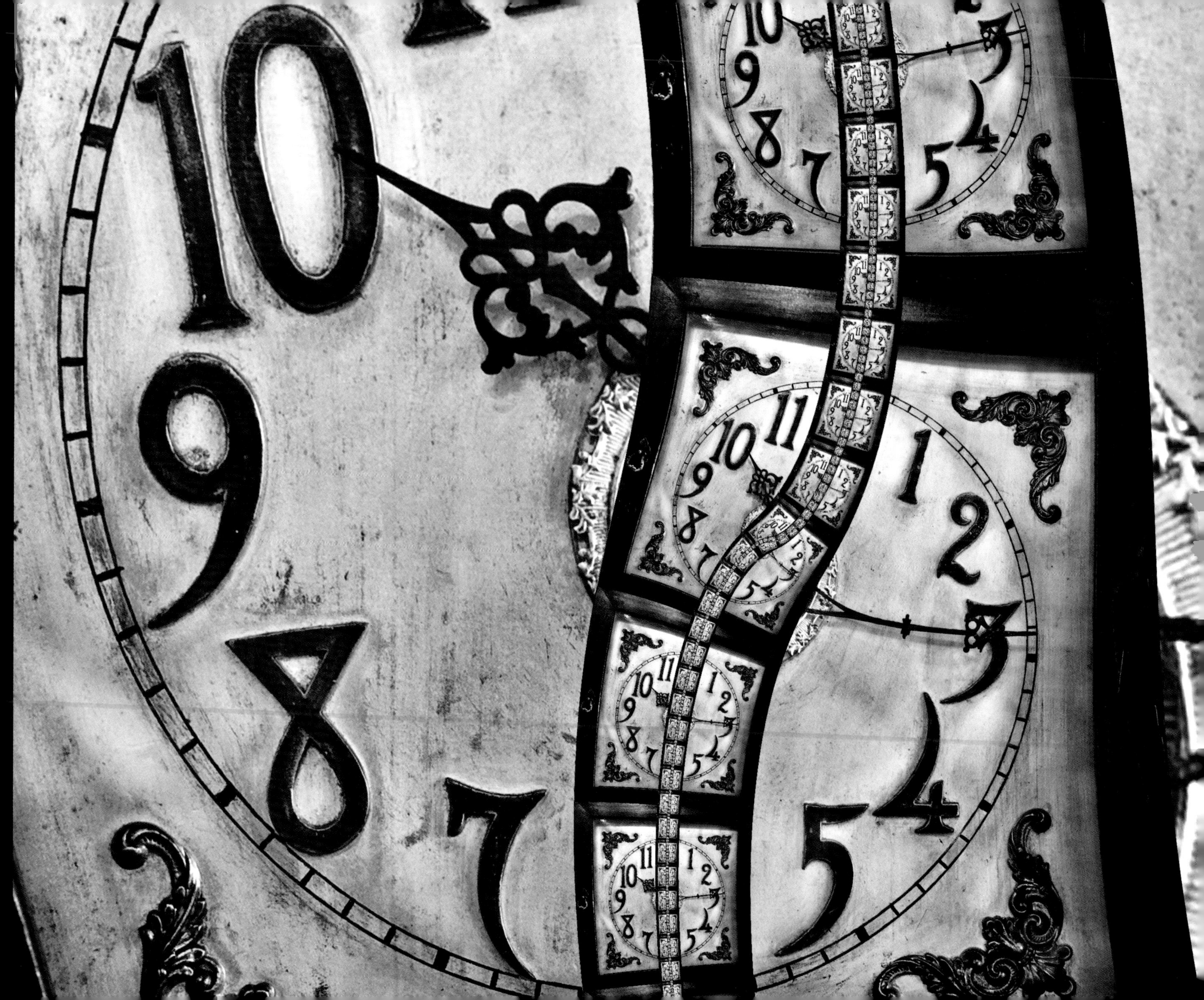

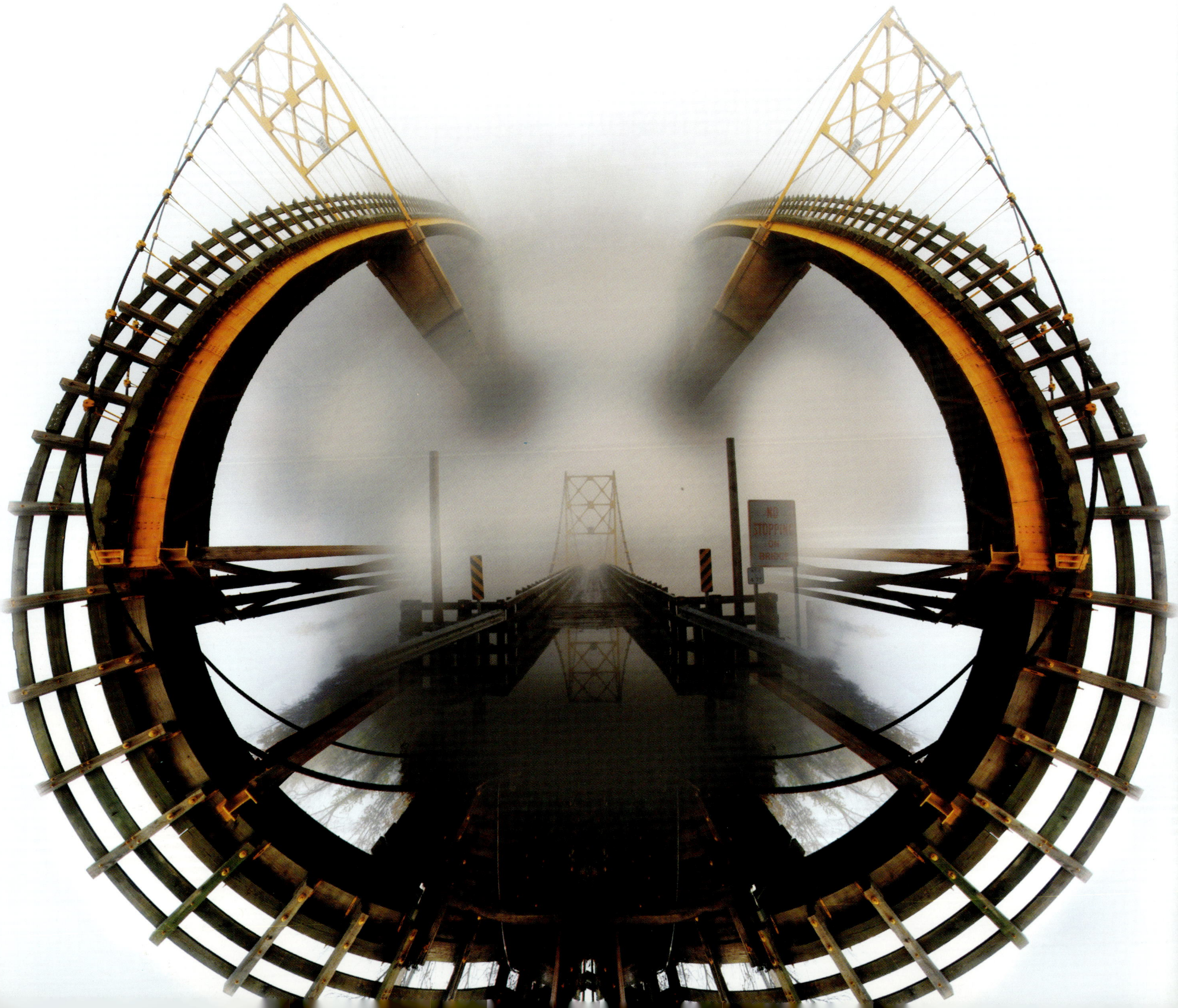

Thank you from Rylee, Rachel and Chip Ford for your acquisition of *Eureka Springs, Arkansas and the Surrounding Countryside, Volume 1.*

Please send questions, comments or requests to charleshenryfordii@gmail.com.

To purchase fine prints of the images within this book travel to www.EurekaSpringsBook.com

Follow Chip on Facebook www.facebook.com/charleshenryfordii

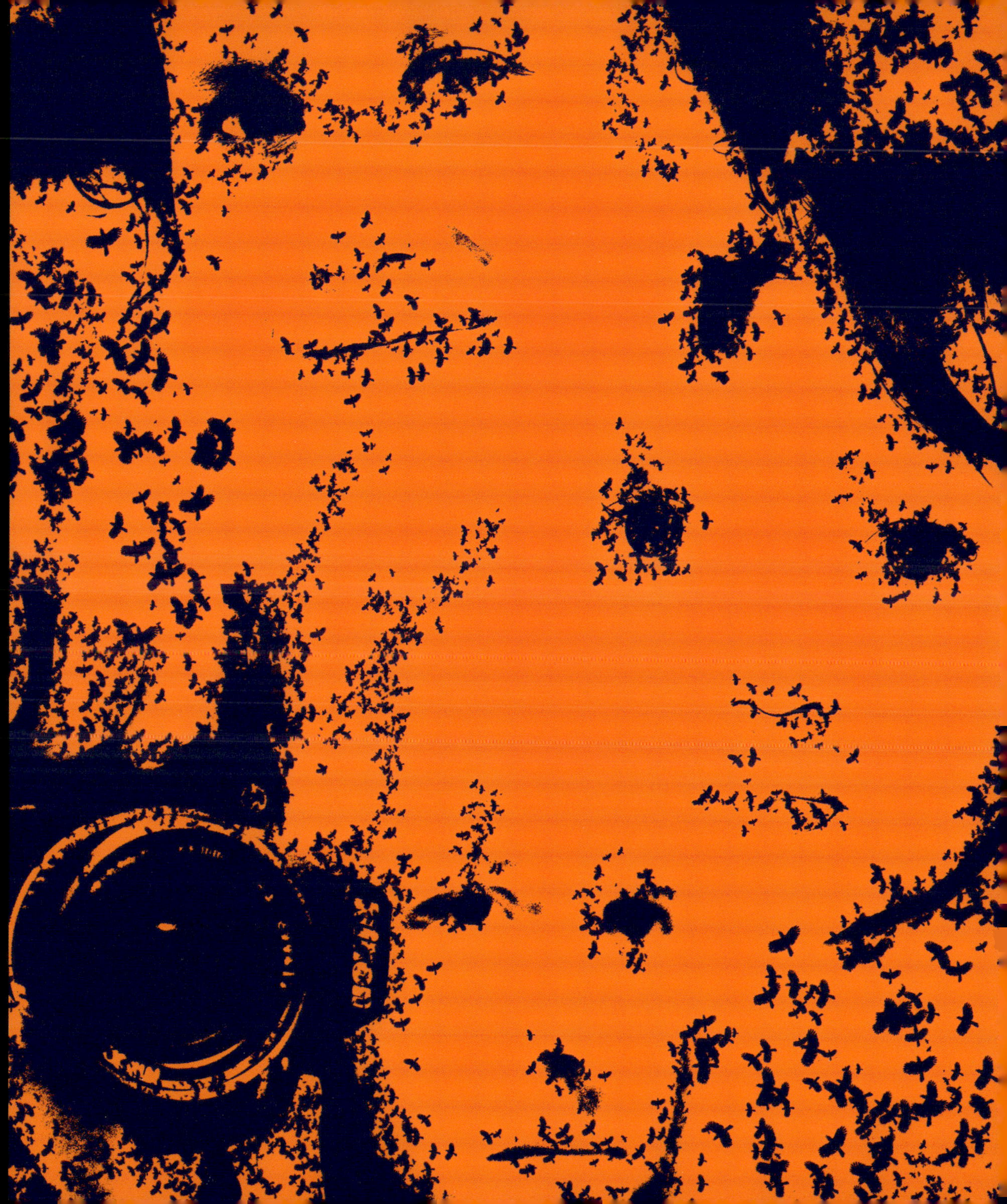

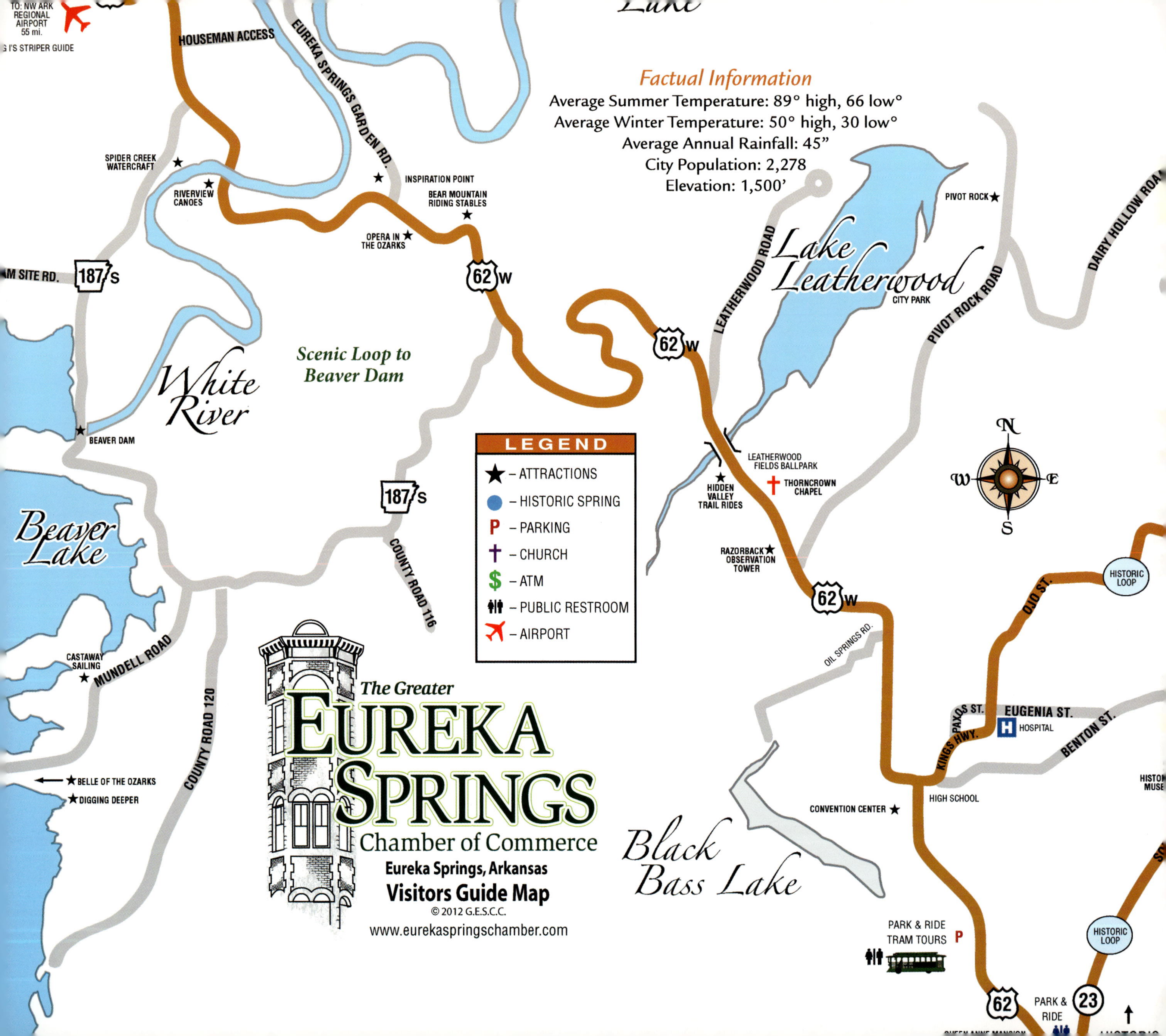

TO: NW ARK REGIONAL AIRPORT 55 mi.
HOUSEMAN ACCESS
EUREKA SPRINGS GARDEN RD.
Factual Information
Average Summer Temperature: 89° high, 66 low°
Average Winter Temperature: 50° high, 30 low°
Average Annual Rainfall: 45”
City Population: 2,278
Elevation: 1,500’
SPIDER CREEK WATERCRAFT
RIVERVIEW CANOES
INSPIRATION POINT
BEAR MOUNTAIN RIDING STABLES
OPERA IN THE OZARKS
PIVOT ROCK
DAIRY HOLLOW ROAD
LEATHERWOOD ROAD
Lake Leatherwood
CITY PARK
PIVOT ROCK ROAD
187 S
62 W
White River
Scenic Loop to Beaver Dam
BEAVER DAM
LEGEND
– ATTRACTIONS
– HISTORIC SPRING
– PARKING
– CHURCH
– ATM
– PUBLIC RESTROOM
– AIRPORT
LEATHERWOOD FIELDS BALLPARK
HIDDEN VALLEY TRAIL RIDES
THORNCROWN CHAPEL
N
W
E
S
Beaver Lake
COUNTY ROAD 116
RAZORBACK OBSERVATION TOWER
HISTORIC LOOP
OJO ST.
OIL SPRINGS RD.
CASTAWAY SAILING
MUNDELL ROAD
COUNTY ROAD 120
The Greater
EUREKA SPRINGS
Chamber of Commerce
Eureka Springs, Arkansas
Visitors Guide Map
© 2012 G.E.S.C.C.
www.eurekaspringschamber.com
PAXOS ST.
EUGENIA ST.
HOSPITAL
KINGS HWY.
BENTON ST.
BELLE OF THE OZARKS
DIGGING DEEPER
HIGH SCHOOL
CONVENTION CENTER
Black Bass Lake
PARK & RIDE TRAM TOURS
PARK & RIDE
62
23

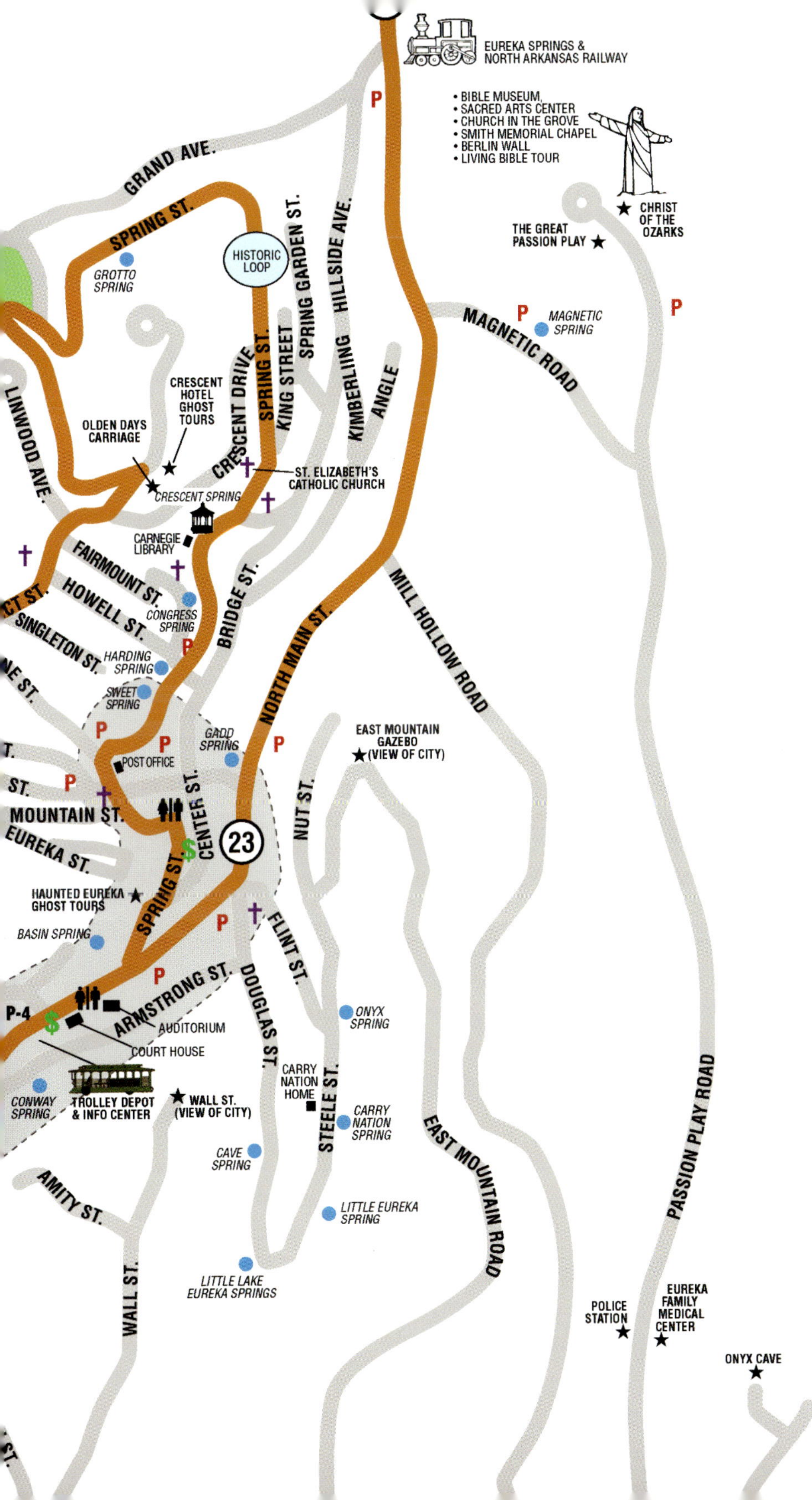
EUREKA SPRINGS & NORTH ARKANSAS RAILWAY
• BIBLE MUSEUM
• SACRED ARTS CENTER
• CHURCH IN THE GROVE
• SMITH MEMORIAL CHAPEL
• BERLIN WALL
• LIVING BIBLE TOUR
CHRIST OF THE OZARKS
THE GREAT PASSION PLAY
GRAND AVE.
SPRING ST.
HISTORIC LOOP
GROTTO SPRING
SPRING GARDEN ST.
HILLSIDE AVE.
MAGNETIC SPRING
MAGNETIC ROAD
CRESCENT HOTEL GHOST TOURS
OLDEN DAYS CARRIAGE
CRESCENT DRIVE
SPRING ST.
KING STREET
KIMBERLING
ANGLE
LINWOOD AVE.
ST. ELIZABETH'S CATHOLIC CHURCH
CRESCENT SPRING
CARNEGIE LIBRARY
FAIRMOUNT ST.
HOWELL ST.
CONGRESS SPRING
BRIDGE ST.
MILL HOLLOW ROAD
NORTH MAIN ST.
SINGLETON ST.
HARDING SPRING
SWEET SPRING
GADD SPRING
EAST MOUNTAIN GAZEBO (VIEW OF CITY)
POST OFFICE
MOUNTAIN ST.
EUREKA ST.
CENTER ST.
23
NUT ST.
HAUNTED EUREKA GHOST TOURS
BASIN SPRING
SPRING ST.
FLINT ST.
ARMSTRONG ST.
DOUGLAS ST.
AUDITORIUM
COURT HOUSE
ONYX SPRING
P-4
CONWAY SPRING
TROLLEY DEPOT & INFO CENTER
WALL ST. (VIEW OF CITY)
CARRY NATION HOME
STEELE ST.
CARRY NATION SPRING
EAST MOUNTAIN ROAD
PASSION PLAY ROAD
CAVE SPRING
AMITY ST.
LITTLE EUREKA SPRING
WALL ST.
LITTLE LAKE EUREKA SPRINGS
POLICE STATION
EUREKA FAMILY MEDICAL CENTER
ONYX CAVE

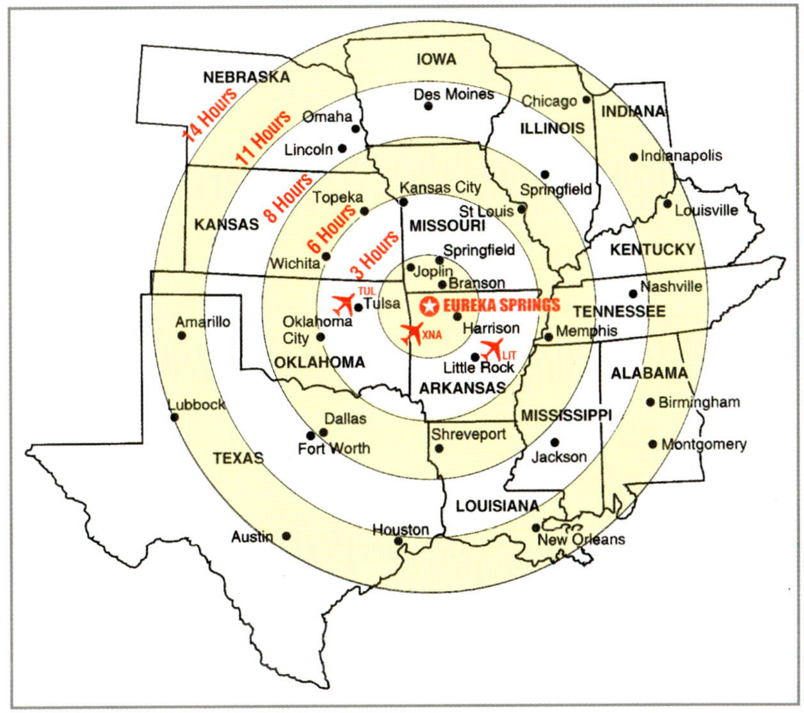
NEBRASKA
IOWA
Des Moines
Chicago
INDIANA
Omaha
ILLINOIS
Lincoln
Indianapolis
14 Hours
11 Hours
8 Hours
6 Hours
3 Hours
Topeka
Kansas City
Springfield
St Louis
Louisville
KANSAS
MISSOURI
KENTUCKY
Wichita
Springfield
Joplin
Branson
Nashville
TUL
Tulsa
EUREKA SPRINGS
TENNESSEE
Amarillo
Oklahoma City
XNA
Harrison
Memphis
LIT
Little Rock
OKLAHOMA
ARKANSAS
ALABAMA
Lubbock
Birmingham
Dallas
MISSISSIPPI
Shreveport
Fort Worth
Montgomery
TEXAS
Jackson
LOUISIANA
Austin
Houston
New Orleans

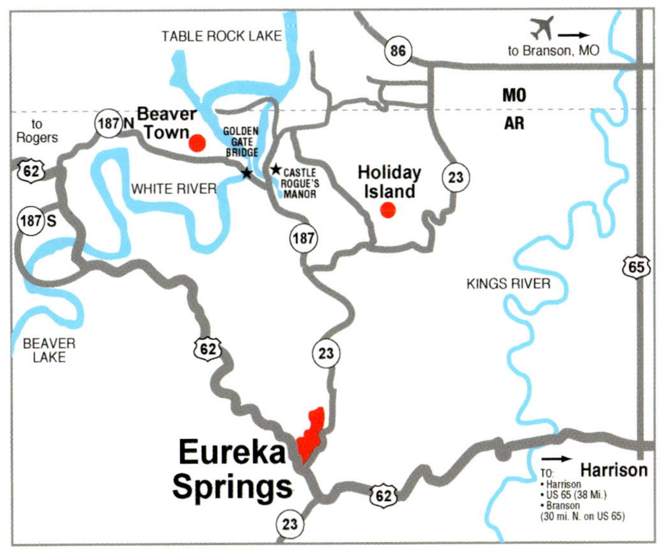
TABLE ROCK LAKE
86
to Branson, MO
MO
AR
to Rogers
187 N
Beaver Town
GOLDEN GATE BRIDGE
62
CASTLE ROGUE'S MANOR
Holiday Island
23
WHITE RIVER
187 S
187
KINGS RIVER
65
BEAVER LAKE
62
23
Eureka Springs
Harrison
TO:
• Harrison
• US 65 (38 Mi.)
• Branson (30 mi. N. on US 65)
62
23

# Location and Festival Index